Henri Van Laun

The French Revolutionary Epoch - Being a History of France, from the Beginning of the First French...

Vol. II

Henri Van Laun

The French Revolutionary Epoch - Being a History of France, from the Beginning of the First French...
Vol. II

ISBN/EAN: 9783337172404

Printed in Europe, USA, Canada, Australia, Japan

Cover: Foto ©ninafisch / pixelio.de

More available books at **www.hansebooks.com**

THE FRENCH REVOLUTIONARY EPOCH:

BEING

A HISTORY OF FRANCE

From the Beginning of the First French Revolution to the End of the Second Empire.

BY

HENRI VAN LAUN.

VOL. II.

NEW YORK:
D. APPLETON AND COMPANY,
549 AND 551 BROADWAY.
1879.

CONTENTS.

Book V.

THE EMPIRE.

CHAPTER I.

§ 1. — THE BEGINNING OF A NEW DYNASTY. — Napoleon proclaimed Emperor—He is acknowledged by nearly all the Crowned Heads of Europe—Their Simulated Friendship—Behaviour of Spain, Prussia, Austria, Russia, and Sweden—Conduct of England—Its Attack on Spain—Declaration of War of the latter Country—Preparations of France to invade England—Grand Naval Review at Boulogne—Voyage of the Emperor and Empress through Four of the Rhine Departments—Coronation of Napoleon by Pope Pius VII.—Its Influence on the People—Napoleon gathers around him some of the ancient Nobles and *Émigrés*—He desires Peace—He sends a Letter to George III.—A Coalition of England, Russia, Austria, and Sweden formed against him—Alteration of the Constitution of the Batavian Republic—Napoleon crowned King of Italy—Eugène Beauharnais appointed Viceroy—The Ligurian Republic incorporated with France—Piombino and Lucca erected into Principalities—Parma, Piacenza, and Guastalla also Incorporated—Preparations and Plan for an Invasion of England—Foresight of the English Admiralty—Villeneuve's Advance prevented by Sir Robert Calder—The French Fleet blockaded—Napoleon abandons his Attempt to Invade England—Engagements of England and Russia—Austria throws off the Mask—Treaty between France and Bavaria—The French Army marching into Germany—Defeat of the Austrians—Capitulation of Ulm—Prussia joins the Coalition—Defeat of the Russians—Battle of Dürrenstein—The French pass through Vienna—Artifice of the French to make themselves Masters of the Bridge over the Danube—The greater part of the Russian Army Escapes by means of a Pretended Armistice—The Archduke Charles leaves Italy and Crosses the Julian Alps—The Archduke John joins the Archduke Charles at Cilly—A War Contribution levied on Austria—Battle of Austerlitz—Armistice between the Austrian and French Emperors—Results of that Armistice—The King of Naples is dethroned—Napoleon's Brother, Joseph, appointed King of the Two Sicilies—Battle of Trafalgar 1

CHAPTER II.

§ 1.—THE PROGRESS OF IMPERIALISM. — Creation of a System of Federal States—Dissatisfaction of the French People and of the Despoiled Nations—The Law of Entail—Forest Property ceded to the *Émigrés*—Ancient Monopolies re-established—Increase of Taxation and of Arbitrary Measures—The Abbey of St. Denis becomes the Burial-place of the Napoleonic Dynasty—The Court is governed by a Code of Etiquette—Promulgation of many Beneficial Measures—Embellishment of Paris—Formation of the Confederation of the Rhine—Formation of a New Coalition against Napoleon—Invasion of Saxony by Prussian Troops—The Army of the Allies—The French Army—Death of Prince Louis of Prussia—The Battle of Jena—The Battle of Auerstadt—Entrance of the French into Berlin—Heavy War Contribution to be paid by Prussia—Surrender of Two Prussian Army Corps—Capitulation of the Fortresses on the Oder—General Blucher surrenders—Fall of Magdeburg—Publication of the Berlin Decree by Napoleon—Entrance of Russian Troops in Turkish Territory—The French enter Poland—Napoleon refuses to aid the Russian and the Gallician Poles—Conflict between the Russian and French Troops at Pultusk—The French go into Winter Quarters at Warsaw—Battle of Eylau—Surrender of several of the Fortresses in Silesia—Battle of Friedland—Interview between the Russian and French Emperors at Tilsit—Conclusion of the Treaty of Tilsit—Its Stipulations . . . 40

CHAPTER III.

§ 1.—THE DECAY OF IMPERIALISM.—Condition of the French Empire—Changes in the Constitution—Increase of Despotism in the Creations of that Period—Bombardment of Copenhagen and Seizure of the Danish Fleet by the English—Publication of the Decree of Milan—Refusal of the Russians to evacuate Moldavia and Wallachia—Entrance of the French Troops into Rome—Annexation of the Papal Provinces to the Kingdom of Italy—Resolution of the French Emperor to annex the Spanish Provinces—Junot marches into Portugal—The Spanish King, Charles IV., and his Son Ferdinand, ask Napoleon to Interfere in their Quarrels—French Troops sent into Spain—Abdication of Charles IV. and of his Son—Joseph Bonaparte becomes King of Spain—Revolt of the Spanish People—Defeat of the French at Baylen—Joseph Bonaparte leaves Madrid—Revolt of the Portuguese—Defeat of Junot—Signature of the Convention of Cintra—The Czar and the Emperor meet at Erfurth—The Two Emperors sign a Secret Convention—Napoleon and a large French Army enter Spain—Defeat of the Spaniards—Death of Sir John Moore at Corunna—Siege and Capitulation of Saragossa—The Austrian Coalition—Napoleon enters

Germany—Battle of Eckmühl—Entrance of the French into Vienna—
Battles of Aspern and Essling—Death of Marshal Lannes—Annexation
of the Roman States to the French Empire—Battle of Wagram—
Unfortunate Ending of the English Expedition to Walcheren—Retreat
of Soult—Battle of Talavera—Sir Arthur Wellesley created Viscount
Wellington—Peace Negotiations concluded at Vienna—Conditions of
the Treaty 56

§ 2.—THE LAST YEARS OF THE EMPIRE.—Arguments in favour of
Napoleon's desire for Peace—Social Condition of France—Divorce of
the French Emperor from Josephine—He marries again, Maria Louisa,
a Daughter of the Emperor of Austria—Birth of the King of Rome—
Attempt at Independence on the part of the Royal Creatures of
Napoleon—Annexation of Holland and the bulk of the Kingdom of
Westphalia to France—Refusal of Napoleon to accept Joseph's Ab-
dication—Movements of Soult and Joseph in Andalusia—Defeat of
Massena at Busaco—Wellington establishes himself in the Lines of
Torres Vedras—Retreat of Massena—His Defeat at Fuentes de Onoro—
Battle of Albuera—Taking of Ciudad Rodrigo and Badajoz by Welling-
ton—Success of Suchet in the East of Spain—Condition of England—
Dissension between the Czar and the French Emperor—Allies of France
and Russia—War between these two Countries—Napoleon's Reception
at Dresden—The French Army crosses the Niemen—Evacuation of
Wilna by the Russians—Offer of the Czar to treat for Terms—
Napoleon's Advance towards Moscow—Retreat of the Russians, and
Devastation of the Country—Attack and Capture of Smolensko by the
French—Sanguinary Battle of Borodino—Entry of the Grand Army
into Moscow—Conflagration of Moscow—Retreat of the French—
Horrors of that Retreat—Arrival of the French at Smolensko—Their
Further Retreat—Severe Losses of the French—Crossing of the
Beresina—Resolution of Napoleon to return alone to France—Murat
appointed Commander of the Forces—The Remains of the French Army
march to Wilna—Opinion of Michelet on Napoleon's Conduct—
Loss of nearly Half a Million of Frenchmen during the Russian Campaign—The Prussian Troops sign a Convention with Russia—Murat
hands over the Command of the Army to Eugène Beauharnais—The
Austrian Allies evacuate the Russian Territory—Valiant Conduct of
Prince Eugène—The French Legislative Assembly grants a Forced Sale
of Heritable Property—The Senate orders a Levy of Three Hundred
and Fifty Thousand Men—Failure of the Emperor's Attempt at Reconciliation with the Pope 76

§ 3.—THE FALL OF THE EMPIRE.—Coalition of Russia, England, Prussia,
and Sweden against France—Enthusiasm of the German People at the
intended Rupture—Dresden taken by the Prussians—Hamburg surrendered to the Russians—Battle of Lützen—Occupation of Dresden
by the French—Battle of Bautzen—Armistice of Pleswitz—Wellington
crosses the Douro—Battle of Vittoria—Interview between Metternich
and Napoleon—England negotiates with the Continental Powers—

Treaties of Reichenbach and Trachenberg—Congress at Prague—End of the Armistice—Austria openly joins the Coalition—Plan of the Campaign of the Allies and of Napoleon—Battle of Dresden—Defeat of Vandamme—Defeat of Macdonald—Defeat of Oudinot—Defeat of Ney—Battle of Leipzic—Retreat of Napoleon—Blowing up of the Bridge at Lindenau—Consequences of the Battle of Leipzic—Battle of Hanau—The French cross the Rhine—Capitulation of the Fortresses in Central Europe and the Rhenish Provinces—Holland and Denmark enter the Coalition—Napoleon's Return to Paris—Ordering of New Levies—The Representative Chamber protests against the New Levies—Dissolution of the Legislature—The Allies cross the Rhine—Blucher's Proclamation—Five Foreign Armies on the soil of France—Murat joins the Allies—Allies of the Foreign Monarchs within the Nation—Napoleon calls out the National Guard—Blucher falls back—Defeat of the Emperor at La Rothière—Severe Defeats of the Prussians—Defence of Antwerp by Carnot—Offer of Napoleon to treat with the Allies—Blucher in a Precarious Position—Capitulation of Soissons—Heavy Losses of Napoleon at Laon—Inactivity of Augereau at Lyons—Defeat of Soult by Wellington—Proclamation of Louis XVIII. at Bordeaux—Schwartzenberg and Blucher march upon Paris—Delay of the Advance of the Allied Armies—They renew the March upon the French Capital—Battle of Fère-Champenoise—Flight of the Empress, the King of Rome, and the Ministers from Paris—Proclamation of Joseph Bonaparte—Refusal to arm the Population of Paris—The Battle around the Capital—Message of Napoleon to inform his Brothers of his intended Return to Paris—Capitulation of Paris—Entrance of the Allied Sovereigns into that town—The Senate appoints a Provisional Government—The Senate decrees the dethroning of Napoleon—The Emperor offers to abdicate in favour of his Son—Marmont, Ney, and Berthier abandon him—Renunciation of Napoleon as Emperor—The Island of Elba appointed to him as his Residence—Death of the ex-Empress Josephine—Michelet's Description of Napoleon's Departure for Elba—Battle of Toulouse 106

Book VE.

THE RESTORATION.

CHAPTER I.

§ 1.—THE RETURN OF THE BOURBONS.—The Provisional Government decrees a Constitution, and summons the Bourbons to the Throne—Behaviour of Montesquieu—Entrance of the Count d'Artois into the Capital—Reception of the Senate and Legislative Body by the Count

d'Artois—Collection of Extraordinary Imposts—Substitution of the
White Flag for the Tricolour—Signing of a Preliminary Agreement,
removing the Limits of France—Departure of Louis XVIII. from
England—His Entry into Paris—Declaration of Saint-Ouen—The
King resuscitates the Titles and Sinecures of the *Ancien Régime*—The
First Ministry of the Restoration—Ratification of the Treaty of Peace
—The King grants a Constitutional Charter—Dissatisfaction of the
Émigrés—Restrictions on the Liberty of Worship, and on the Freedom
of the Press—Other Causes of Discontent—Proposal of a Bill for the
Restitution of Portions of Estates confiscated under the Republic—
The Congress of Vienna—Difficulties among the Plenipotentiaries—
France reduced to the Limits of 1792 145

§ 2.—THE RETURN OF NAPOLEON—THE HUNDRED DAYS.—Project of
Napoleon for the Recovery of all that he had Lost—Behaviour of the
Royalists—Return of the ex-Emperor—Address of Louis XVIII. to
the Chambers—His Journey to Ghent—Reception of Napoleon by the
French People—He recalls nearly the whole of his Last Ministry—He
expresses a hope for the continuation of Peace—Behaviour and
Declaration of the Sovereigns at the Congress of Vienna—Their
Decision to form a Large Army—Napoleon raises the Effective
Strength of the Army—The Nation expresses its will that he must
reign in future as a Constitutional Monarch—A Committee appointed
to consider the Amended Constitution—The Emperor's Objections to
an Hereditary Peerage—He insists upon retaining the Punishment of
Confiscation—The Supplementary Act published on his sole Authority
—The Act submitted to the Popular Vote—Celebration of the Acceptance of that Act—Discontent of the French Nation—Departure
of Napoleon for the Army—His Plan of the Campaign—Want of
Adequate Preparations of the Emperor—M. Quinet's attempt to
re-establish the Reputation of Ney—Order of Wellington to concen-
trate his Forces—Wellington and Blucher meet and arrange their
Plans—Battle of Ligny—Marshal Blucher is nearly taken Prisoner
—Severe Defeat of the Prussians—Their Retreat towards Wavre—
Battle of Quatre-Bras—Mistake of General d'Erlon—Behaviour
of the Belgians, according to M. Quinet—Death of the Duke of
Brunswick—Retreat of the French—Irresolution of the Emperor—
Grouchy receives Orders to pursue the Prussians—The English retire
upon Waterloo—The Battle of Waterloo—Attack and Defence of
La Haie Sainte—Arrival of the Prussians—Defeat of the French—
Retreat of Napoleon—His Arrival in Paris—His Abdication—Paris in
the Hands of the Allies—The French Army withdrawn behind the
Loire—Return of Louis XVIII.—Napoleon goes to England on the
Bellerophon—His Letter to the Prince Regent—He is sent to St.
Helena 158

§ 3.—THE SECOND RESTORATION.—The Allies are not so careful to hurt
the Susceptibilities of the French as they were in 1814—Requisitions of
the Allies in Pictures, Valuables, and Money—The Government issues a

CONTENTS.

Decree, ordering the Arrest of the Traitors against Louis XVIII.—It banishes Forty Persons from Paris—Davoust resigns his Command of the Army—Macdonald succeeds him—Trials of Labédoyère, Lavalette, and Ney—Massacres in the South of France—The New Chambers are elected—Resignation of Fouché and Talleyrand—The Duke de Richelieu forms a New Cabinet—Reactionary Measures of the Government—Quarrels between the Troops of Occupation and the Inhabitants—Treaties concluded at Paris between the Allies and the Government—Exorbitant Demands of the Austrians and Prussians—The Duke of Wellington and Count Nesselrode oppose them—Louis XVIII.'s Address to the Czar and Wellington—Reduction of the Boundaries of France—The Indemnity and the Period of Occupation are fixed—Separate Treaty of the Four Allied Powers—The Treaty of the Holy Alliance—Excitement of the People—Introduction and Adoption by the Chambers of a Bill of Amnesty—Prosecution of many Generals and Officials—Suppression of several Conspiracies—Death of Murat—Comparative Liberal Feelings of the King—Dissolution of the Chambers—Increase of Members of Moderate Views in the New Chamber—Extension of Electoral Franchise—Laws passed for arresting Suspected Persons, and for the Publication of Newspapers—Reduction of the Army of Occupation—Famine in France—Bloody Assizes at Lyons—Accession of Liberal Members in the Chamber newly elected—Activity of the Clerical Party and the Congregationists—Reorganisation of the Army—Withdrawal of the Allied Troops from French Territory—Dissatisfaction of the Extreme Royalists—Increase of the Liberals in the Elections of 1818—The Duke de Richelieu promises to limit the Franchise—His Resignation—He establishes a Charitable Institution at Bordeaux with a Donation granted to him by the Chambers—The Royalist Peers press the King to restrict the Franchise—Creation of Sixty New Peers—Public Opinion protests against any Alteration in the Electoral Law—Adoption of more Stringent Laws on the Press—Election of Thirty more Liberal Deputies—The Ministry proposes to elect a Chamber for a certain period—Unpopularity of the Proposal—Assassination of the Duke de Berry—Passing of Two Exceptional Laws restricting the Liberty of the Press and of the Individual—The Minister Decazes is insulted by the Royalists—His Resignation—Open Antagonism of the King and his Ministry to the Liberals—Adoption of a New Electoral Law—Popular Outbreaks—Discovery of a Military Conspiracy and many other Plots—The New Chamber chiefly composed of Royalists—An Austrian Army enters Naples—Increase of Confidence of the Extreme Royalists—End of the Sessions—Death of Napoleon Bonaparte—Coalition in the Chamber between the Royalists and Liberals—Resignation of the Duke de Richelieu—Prosecution of the Press—A New Press Law passed by the Chambers—Plots and Conspiracies agitate the Country—Supremacy of the Clerical Party in Education—Suppression of the Lectures of several Professors—The Allied Powers contemplate Intervention in Spain—Speech of the

French King at the Opening of the Sessions—Refusal of the British Government to interfere in Spain—Opposition to the War with Spain in the Chambers—The Deputy Manuel is expelled from the Chamber by Force—The Duke d'Angoulême and the French Army enter Madrid —Dissolution of the Chamber—Large Majority of Ministerial Deputies in the New Chamber—A Bill passed for a Septennial Chamber—Withdrawal of the Bills on Annuities and Sacrilege—Death of Louis XVIII. . 203

CHAPTER II.

§ 1.—AN EFFETE MONARCH.—Declaration of the New King—He abolishes Strict Censorship, and grants a Partial Amnesty—Charles X. shows himself a Believer in the Divine Rights of Kings—A New Law on Sacrilege—An Indemnity of One Thousand Million Francs granted—Great Indignation in the Country—Behaviour of the Clerical Party—Ovations of Casimir Périer, Generals Foy and Lafayette in the Provinces—Funeral of General Foy—Demonstration on the Acquittal of Two Newspapers—Death of the Emperor of Russia—Murder of Paul Louis Courier—The King replies harshly to the New Year's Congratulations of the Court of Justice—Difficulties of M. de Villèle—M. de Polignac and his Ideas about the Law of Primogeniture—Discussions on the Laws for ameliorating the Position of the Clergy, and on Indemnifying the Planters of St. Domingo—Reproof of the King to the Chamber of Deputies—Sentence on the *Journal du Commerce*—Opposition against the Law on Primogeniture—The Law is virtually thrown out—Rejoicings of the Parisians—The Peers censure the French Officers assisting the Turks—Encroachments of the Clerical Party—Religious Processions—The King encourages the Priests—The Liberals attack the Clericals—Effects of the Fall of Missolonghi on Civilised Europe—Cessation of Diplomatic Relations between Spain and France—Remarks of Canning on the Conduct of France—Opposition against the newly-proposed Press Law—Passing of Two Bills on Jury Laws—Discussion on the Press Law—Withdrawal of the Law—Great Joy at this Withdrawal—The Disbanding of the National Guard —The Re-establishment of the Censorship—The Three Great Powers signify to Turkey the necessity of ceasing hostilities against Greece—Death of Manuel—Journeys of the King and various Members of the Royal Family—Battle of Navarino—Election of many of the Opposition Candidates for the New Chamber—Disturbances in Paris—Resignation of the Ministry—Blockade of Algiers—The Martignac Ministry—The Opening of Letters discussed in the Chamber—A New Press Bill is passed—Agitation about the Jesuit Colleges—Expedition to the Morea—The *Letter to the Duke of Orleans*—Withdrawal of the Bills to change the Administration of the Departments and Communes —Rupture of the Negotiations between the Government and the Left— The Polignac Ministry appointed—Outburst of Indignation through

France—Attacks of the Newspapers—Ovation of General Lafayette in the Provinces—Acquittal of Two Newspapers indicted by the Government—Polignac attempts to introduce various Commercial Improvements—The New Year's Receptions—The Voting of the Budget discussed by the Newspapers—Programme of Polignac—The King displays his Authority in the Chambers—Their Prorogation—Reports of the Prefects—Dissolution of the Chambers—Election of a Large Majority of Opposition Deputies—Successful Termination of the Expedition to Algiers—Fresh Dissolution of the newly-elected Legislative—The Censorship re-established—A New Electoral Law promulgated—Protest of Newspaper Editors—Doings of the Police—Delusive Security of the Authorities and the King—Beginning of the Insurrection—Conduct of the People and the Troops—Behaviour of the Deputies—The Editors of the *National* propose the Duke of Orleans as the Future King—The Duke of Orleans accepts the Lieutenant-Generalship—Charles X. leaves France—End of the Restoration 237

Book VII.

THE REIGN OF LOUIS PHILIPPE.

CHAPTER I.

§ 1.—THE BEGINNING OF THE ORLEANS DYNASTY.—Convocation of the Chambers—Modification of the Charter—The Duke of Orleans takes the Oath to the Charter—He accepts the Title of King of the French—He appoints his First Cabinet—Lafayette becomes Commander of all the National Guards—Destitution in Paris—Arrest and Detention of Four Ministers of Charles X.—Bill for the Abolition of Capital Punishment—Measures passed by the Chamber of Deputies—Suicide of the Duke de Bourbon—Recognition of the New French King by nearly all the European Governments—The Peaceful Disposition of the King displeases the Majority—Rise of Bellicose Feelings—Prevention of the Attempts of the Spanish Liberals—Permission to all Political Exiles to enter France, save the Bonapartes—A Public Meeting demands the Abolition of Capital Punishment—The various Elements of the Opposition—The Revolt of Belgium against Holland—The Separation of these Two Kingdoms decided by the London Conference—Dissensions among the Ministry—Discussions on the Bill for abolishing Capital Punishment—Disturbances in Paris—Resignation of the Ministry—Death of Benjamin Constant—Trial of the Ministers of Charles X.—Their Condemnation—Excitement of Popular Feeling—Behaviour of the

National Guard and of the Students—The Chamber proposes to divide the Command of the National Guards—Resignation of Lafayette—General Clausel replaces Marshal de Bourmont in Algeria—Prince Leopold of Saxe-Coburg refuses the Crown of Greece—Impulse of Europe towards more Liberal Institutions—Revolution in Poland—The Duke de Nemours refuses the Throne of Belgium—Intrigues of the Legitimist and Clerical Parties—Devastation of a Church and of the Palace of the Archbishop by the Mob—Resignation of the Ministry—Casimir Périer forms a New Ministry—His Character—Reception of the King during his Journey in the Provinces—Dissolution of the Chambers—Opening of the Session for 1831—Invasion of Belgium by the Dutch—Prosecution of the Count de Montalembert—Abolition of the Hereditary Right of Peers—Proscription of the Members of the Elder Bourbon Branch—Insurrection at Lyons—Appearance of the Cholera—Its Victims—Attempted Insurrection in the Vendée—Arrest of the Duchess de Berry—Funeral of General Lamarque—Disturbances at that Funeral—Death of Napoleon II.—Entrance of French Troops into Belgium—Capitulation of the Citadel of Antwerp—Discussions about the Fate of the Duchess de Berry—She is conducted to Palermo—Imprisonment of Journalists—The Law on Primary Education—Abd-el-Kader emerges from Obscurity—A new Spirit of Progress appears—Repressive Measures of the Government—The Bill regarding Public Associations—Renewal of Disturbances at Lyons—Disturbances in Paris and in the Provinces—The Peers appointed to judge the Insurgents—Death of General Lafayette—The Legitimist Candidates for the Chamber—Changes in the Cabinet—Prosecution of the *National*—Appointment of a Governor-General of Algeria—The Chamber condemns the Political Conduct of the King—Discussions on the Indemnity to be paid to America—The Trial of the Insurgents and of their Defenders—Attempt on the Life of the King—Mutual Accusations of the Republicans and Legitimists—Promulgation of the Laws against the Press—Trial of Fieschi, the would-be Murderer of Louis Philippe, and of his Accomplices—Opening of the Session for 1836—Formation of a New Ministry—Another Attempt to assassinate the King—Death of Armand Carrel—The King does not hold the Annual Review of the National Guards 287

§ 2.—THE END OF THE ORLEANS DYNASTY.—Appointment of a New Ministry—Demands to expel Political Refugees from Switzerland—Liberation of the Ministers of Charles X.—Attempt of Louis Napoleon at Strasburg—He is arrested and sent to America—Proposed Laws for judging Conspirators, for Deportation, and for concealing Conspiracies—Rejection of the First Law—Formation of a Cabinet of Conciliation—Allowances voted for the Eldest Son and Daughter of the King—Promulgation of a General Amnesty—Marriage of the Duke of Orleans—Marriage of Princess Marie—Coalition against the Ministry—The French Government insists upon the Expulsion of Louis Napoleon from Switzerland—Birth of the Count de Paris—Recall of the French Troops from Ancona—Blockade of several Ports of Mexico and of

CONTENTS.

the Argentine Republic—Death of Princess Marie—Attempt at an Insurrection in Paris—A new Ministry formed—Breaking out of Hostilities between the Sultan of Turkey and the Pacha of Egypt—Demand for Internal Reforms—Refusal of an Allowance for the Duke de Nemours—M. Thiers appointed Chief of a New Cabinet—Marriage of the Duke de Nemours—Signature of the Treaty of London by the Four Great Powers—Another Attempt of Louis Napoleon at Boulogne—He is taken Prisoner and confined in the Castle of Ham—Louis Philippe is again shot at—A new Cabinet formed with M. Guizot as Prime Minister—France wishes to engage in a War for Egypt—Resistance of Louis Philippe and his Ministry—A Fresh Treaty signed in London—Return of the Remains of Napoleon I.—Discussions about the proposed Fortifications of Paris—Death of Garnier-Pagès—Disturbances in the Provinces—Treaty for the Right of searching Ships—Dissatisfaction about some of its Clauses—Majority of the Conservative Party in the New Elections—Death of the Duke of Orleans—Appointment of the Duke de Nemours as Regent—The Clericals demand Freedom for Secondary Instruction—A Vote of Censure passed on the Legitimist Deputies—Difficulties between France and England about Otaheite and Mr. Pritchard—The French attack the Emperor of Morocco—He is compelled to submit—Mr. Pritchard accepts a Pecuniary Compensation—Animadversions on the Ministry by the Peers and the Chamber of Deputies—M. Guizot tenders his Resignation, which is refused—Various other Bills passed—Interpellation of M. Thiers about the Jesuits—Alterations in the Right of Search—Disputes between Masters and Men—A Barren Session in 1846—Escape of Louis Napoleon from Ham—Increase of the Public Demand for Electoral Reform—Failure of Two Successive Harvests—Want of Energy in the Government—Disastrous Effects of M. Guizot's Foreign Policy—The Political Banquets—The King speaks of "Blind and Hostile Passions" in his Opening Speech for 1848—Indifference of the Majority—M. Guizot accused of Dishonesty—A Great Reform Banquet to be held—Disturbances between the People and the Crowd—Resignation of the Ministry—The Troops fire on the Crowd—M. Thiers, the New Prime Minister, issues a Proclamation—Counter Proclamation of the Insurgent Committee—Abdication of Louis Philippe in favour of the Count de Paris—The King and his Family embark for England—Appointment of a Provisional Government 330

Book VIII.

THE SECOND REPUBLIC.

CHAPTER I.

§ 1.—A FRESH ATTEMPT AT A REPUBLIC.—The Capital the Arbiter of France—Fitness of the Members of the Provisional Government for their Task—Proclamation of the Republic—Dissolution of the Chamber of Deputies—The Peers are prohibited to assemble—The Tricolour adopted as the National Standard—Opening of the National Workshops—The Pillage and Destruction of Noblemen's Seats and Public Establishments—Abolition of Capital Punishment for Political Offences—Many Functionaries and other Officials adhere to the Republic—Refusal of the Government to admit Louis Napoleon into France—Official Proclamation of the Republic—Assurance of the Pacific Intentions of France—Frustration of a Plot against the Government—A Republican Majority in the newly-elected National Assembly—Different Laws passed by the Provisional Government—Dissensions in the Assembly—Invasion of the Assembly on the 15th of May—Expulsion from France of the Members of the Family of Louis Philippe—Louis Napoleon is elected a Member of the Assembly—His Resignation—Decrees about the National Workshops—Insurrection of June—General Cavaignac appointed Chief of the Executive—His Character—Re-election of Louis Napoleon as Deputy—Resolution of the Assembly to have a President of the Republic chosen by Universal Suffrage—Election of Louis Napoleon as President—He takes the Oath to the Republic and the Constitution—His Aim—The Assembly is dissolved—Victory of the Extreme Democrats and the Reactionary Party in the Elections—Proposed Indictment of the President and his Ministers—Paris placed in a State of Siege—The Pope brought back to Rome—A New Ministry appointed—Growing Ascendency of the Clerical Party—Commencement of a Moral Reign of Terror—Mutilation of Universal Suffrage—Journey of the President through the Provinces—Tampering with the Army—Resignation of the Ministry—A Crisis at hand—The *Coup d'État* of the 2nd of December—Terrible Massacre in Paris—The Nation votes for Louis Napoleon remaining President for Ten Years—He crushes all Opposition—The New Constitution promulgated—The Omnipotence of the President—Another Journey of the President through the Provinces—The Nation desires an Empire—A Large Majority declares for the President assuming the Imperial Dignity—The President ascends the Throne as Napoleon III. . . 363

Book IX.

THE SECOND EMPIRE.

CHAPTER I.

§ 1.—THE REVIVAL OF IMPERIALISM.—The New Civil List—The New Court—Marriage of the Emperor—The Luxury of the Court imitated by all Classes War between England, France, Turkey, and Russia—Siege of Sebastopol—The Battle of the Alma—The Battle of

Balaklava—The Battle of Inkermann—Attack on the Malakhoff and the Redans—The Allies enter Sebastopol—Visit of the Emperor and Empress to England—Visit of Queen Victoria and Prince Albert to France—Laws passed for Substitutes in the Army and for rewarding Old Soldiers—The Universal Exhibition of 1855—Peace declared between Russia and the Allied Powers—A Son born to Napoleon III. —Zenith of the Emperor's Prosperity—Lowering of the Intellectual Standard—Attempt on the Life of Napoleon III. and the Empress—Demand of the French Cabinet to England to alter the Laws about Political Exiles—The Empress appointed Regent 387

§ 2.—PROGRESS OF THE SECOND EMPIRE.—Rumours about a Rupture between France and Austria—Marriage of Prince Napoleon to a Daughter of Victor Emmanuel—The French Emperor promises to aid Sardinia in case of Austria's Aggression—Ultimatum of Austria to Sardinia—Hostilities begun by Austria—War declared between France and Austria—The French Emperor Chief Commander of the Franco-Sardinian Armies—Battle of Montebello—Battle of Palestro—Austrian Defeat at Turbigo—Entrance of the French and Sardinians into Milan—Battle of Malegnano—Battle of Solferino—Abdication of the Dukes of Tuscany and Modena and the Duchess of Parma—Meeting of the French and Austrian Emperors at Villafranca—Results of that Interview—Treaty of Zurich—Allocution of the Pope—Prolonged Military Occupation of Rome—New Treaty of Commerce between England and France—Opening of the Sessions for 1860—Annexation of the Duchies and of the Legations to Sardinia—Annexation of Savoy and Nice to France—Quarrel between Italy and the Pope—Battle of Castel-Fidardo—Sanguinary Quarrels between the Christians and Turks in Syria—The French Expedition to Syria—Anglo-French War with China—Expedition to Mexico—The French invade that Country—Opening of the Sessions for 1862 and 1863—Attitude of the Government towards Poland—Moral Success of the Opposition—A New Ministry—Success of the French in Mexico—The Austrian Archduke Maximilian becomes Emperor—Opening of the Sessions for 1864—Speech of Napoleon III.—A Congress of Sovereigns proposed and refused—Increase of the Opposition—Convention between the French Emperor and the King of Italy 397

§ 3.—THE DOWNWARD COURSE OF IMPERIALISM.—Speech from the Throne at the Opening of the Sessions—The 2nd of December is called a Crime in the Legislature—Speech of Prince Napoleon at Ajaccio—Speech of the Emperor at Auxerre—His Letter to the Minister for Foreign Affairs—War between Prussia, Italy, and Austria—Battle of Sadowa—Treaties of Prague and Vienna—Venetia and the Four Italian Fortresses ceded to Italy—The North German Confederation formed—Changes in the Constitution—Interpellations in the Legislative—The King of Holland remains Grand Duke of Luxemburg—Discussions on the Budget—Opening of the Paris Exhibition of Arts and Industry—Death of the Emperor Maximilian—Declaration of M. Rouher in the

CONTENTS. xvii

PAGE

Legislative about Rome—Proposal of a New Press Bill—Discussions on
the Budget—Prosecution of several Newspapers—Speeches of the
Barristers—The Emperor promises more Liberal Reforms—Election of
Opposition Candidates in all the large Centres—A Senatus Consultus
proclaims several Liberal Measures—M. Emile Ollivier appointed Head
of the new Liberal Ministry—Murder of Victor Noir—The new Constitutional Programme laid before the Senate—Objections raised against
it—The Nation approves of it by a large numerical Majority—Discussions on Prince Hohenzollern accepting the proffered Crown of Spain
—Declaration of War between France and Prussia—Warlike Excitement in France—Napoleon III. takes the Chief Command of the Army
—France without an Ally—The Treaty proposed by Napoleon III. to
Prussia after the War of 1866—Great Disorder in the Organisation and
Discipline of the French Army—The State of the Prussian Army—Engagement at Saarbruck—Battle of Weissenburg—Battle between
Wörth and Fröschwiller—Battle at Forbach—State of Paris—Meeting
of the Legislative—Proposal of M. Jules Favre—Appointment of
Bazaine as Commander-in-Chief—Measures taken by the Legislative—
The Army at the Camp at Châlons—Battles of Borny, Gravelotte, and
Saint-Privat—The Army under Macmahon endeavours to join the one
under Bazaine at Metz—Battle of Beaumont—Battle of Sedan—
Capitulation of the French Emperor and his Army—Declaration of the
Minister of War—Great Excitement in Paris—Different Proposals in
the Assembly—The People invade the Legislative—Deposition of the
Imperial Dynasty, and Proclamation of the Republic—Appointment of
a Government of National Defence 413

THE FRENCH REVOLUTIONARY EPOCH.

Book V.

THE EMPIRE.

CHAPTER I.

§ I.—THE BEGINNING OF A NEW DYNASTY.

(*From the* 18*th of May,* 1804, *to the* 26*th of December,* 1805.)

THE news of the elevation of France into an Empire, and the proclaiming of Napoleon as its Emperor, was received by the sovereigns of Europe with an amount of complacency plainly indicating that such an event had been foreseen, if not altogether expected. Despite the protest of the Count de Lille, the chief of the Bourbons, staying at Warsaw, and who issued a most impolitical document to all the crowned heads, calculated to alienate the sympathies of France rather than to enlist them, these monarchs, with the exception of three, acknowledged the new member of their family so strangely thrust upon them. Not out of good-will to Napoleon himself, as may be supposed, for they could be no more indifferent to a change in the form of government of so great a nation as France than the nation herself. Not unmindful of this feeling either in his subjects or in the foreign Powers, Napoleon gave the former reasons for assuming his new dignity, which silenced and disarmed, if they did not destroy all opposition. He also made a pretence of sacrificing the Republic in order to allay the alarm of the absolute monarchs. If he imagined that they believed in this attempt at homogeneity, he was mistaken. They might hold out their hands in simulated friendship, but from the bottom of their hearts they knew that he was but a military *parvenu*, whom it was their interest to conciliate—nay, even to support—in his usurpation, rather than risk the prolonging of a state of revolution which could be but a bad example to their own peoples. In this way the European Courts silently watched each other as to which should take the initiative in congratulating the new Emperor. The King of Spain was the first, and curiously enough, the Cardinal de Bourbon, Archbishop of Toledo, added his officious congratulations to those of his sovereign. The King of Prussia followed suit, and sent a most flattering message to Napoleon. Austria, double-dealing as usual, and in secret intelligence with the British Cabinet, stood aloof for a little while. She approved of the transforming of the Republic into an hereditary monarchy, but raised an objection to the title of Emperor, though she assured the French Ambassador, who rather haughtily responded to these expostulations, that they arose neither from ill-will against his master, nor from any regard to the manifesto of the Count de Lille, of which she in common with other Courts had taken no notice. The difficulty was simply that the dignity of Emperor of Germany had been till now elective, and Francis II. feared that, if the title departed from him or his successors, they would no longer be on an equality of rank with the ruler of France, unless he himself adopted this title for his hereditary states. To this objection Napoleon made a very gracious answer, and Francis having proclaimed himself Emperor of Austria, hastened to acknowledge Napoleon as Emperor of the French.

Russia not only refused to acknowledge the new title of the house of Austria, pretending that it was a plot concocted between Francis II. and Napoleon, but by going in mourning for the Duke d'Enghien, and by various demurrers as to the violation of the Baden territory in connection with the late prince's murder and France's interference with the kingdoms of Naples and Sardinia, sought a pretext for war with Napoleon, and recalled her ambassador. Of this situation Francis, secretly inclining to Alexander I., and rendered somewhat bold by the conciliatory attitude of Napoleon in the late negotiations with regard to the Imperial dignity, sought to take advantage. Gustavus IV., of Sweden, the quixotic champion of the legitimacy of the Bourbons, imitated Russia's example, and declared himself the most stubborn enemy of France. This declaration Napoleon answered in the *Moniteur*, by saying that he looked upon the King of Sweden as a young fool, with whom he should be sorry to confound a brave and loyal nation. He assured them of the continued goodwill of France, promised that their merchant vessels should always be well received in her ports, and that Sweden's fleet might even revictual and repair there if it liked. This rendered Gustavus more enraged, and a note of the Swedish Minister, in which the Emperor was called *Monsieur* Napoleon Bonaparte, informed the French *chargé d'affaires* at Stockholm of the cessation of all relations between the two Governments. Already more than half influenced by England, Gustavus now signed a subsidiary and commercial treaty with the Cabinet of St. James's (7th September).

In England, the rupture of the Treaty of Amiens, an event scarcely expected so soon by Napoleon, had entailed the fall of the Addington Ministry, pledged to peace, as it were; and Pitt and his party resumed the direction of affairs, exciting the nation to hostilities by pretending to show that peace was a greater obstacle to her commercial prosperity than war. England's interests were supposed to be threatened by Napoleon's avowed intention to close the Continent to British trade; a reprisal, as the Emperor argued, for the arbitrary proceedings of England in connection with all maritime affairs. The whole war now took an aspect of unexampled ferocity, degenerating into personal calumny, as well as into the most unheard-of piracy, scarcely creditable to the admirals of civilised governments. English and French papers continued to vilify each other's rulers; and a pamphlet appeared in England, written by the Rev. Edward Hankin, which openly preached the destruction of France, whose existence was shown to be incompatible with the prosperity of England. Moreover, the English declared all French ports in a state of blockade, and prevented all neutrals, from Fécamp to Ostende, from entering, whilst their cruisers chased every ship they could see, and took even several members of the Emperor's family as prisoners to England.

No state was allowed to remain outside the strife. Spain, which, as we have seen, had redeemed by a sum of money her obligation to furnish a contingent to Napoleon, was importuned by the English Cabinet, after it had acknowledged the transaction, to come over to her side, and, unable to comply with the prescribed conditions, was openly attacked at sea, notwithstanding all absence of a declaration of war. Four Spanish frigates coming from Rio de la Plata, and containing more than a million pounds sterling, were summoned to surrender, and upon their refusal, an engagement took place, in which one of the Spanish vessels exploded, the other three being taken to Portsmouth. This unjustifiable act aroused the indignation of a large number of members of the English Parliament, but their protest notwithstanding, the spoliation continued in other places, the ambassadors remaining all the while at their respective courts, until Spain, feeble as she was, felt compelled to declare war against England, and signed a treaty with France, by which she placed thirty line-of-battle ships at the latter's disposal (12th December). Finding all his efforts to prevent an outbreak of hostilities fruitless, and knowing that England was trying to establish a Coalition between Russia, Austria, and Prussia— the last Power, however, still standing aloof,—Napoleon vigorously pushed his preparations for an invasion of the English coast. A hundred and twenty thousand men, distributed in seven camps along the French Channel, could be concentrated in thirty hours, and embark in more than two thousand gunboats and small vessels ready for the purpose. This project, though openly propagated, served mainly to hide a more important naval operation, for despite the opinion of many, that a landing might be attempted successfully with the troops of the flotilla, Napoleon did not deem it prudent to risk the flower of his army or to venture upon a naval engagement with two thousand "nutshells." He was determined not to endeavour to cross the Channel, save protected by a strong fleet, composed of ships now lying forgotten in the various French ports, but which were stealthily being put in commission with the utmost activity.

The great enterprise, to be accomplished with the co-operation of the Dutch and Spanish fleets, was to be entrusted to a brave and bold sailor, Latouche-Tréville, in whom Napoleon had great confidence, and who was to command the fleet of Toulon, in addition to being appointed Inspector-General of the Mediterranean coast. " Give us but the mastery of the Straits for six hours, and we will be masters of the world," he wrote to the latter.

Pending these preparations, and his own coronation, Napoleon made several journeys in the interior in order to consolidate his new power. He started from Paris on the 18th of July for Boulogne, where he passed in review the troops, stimulating them by his presence, and distributing several Crosses of the Legion of Honour, then recently instituted. He inspected most minutely every arsenal, depôt, and wharf, and was also an eye-witness of an engagement, which the English began, thinking to profit by a violent storm that overtook the French ships, and wherein the former were scarcely successful. From thence he visited all the camps and ports situated on that part of the coast, and returned to Paris to celebrate his birthday, on which occasion there were national *fêtes* throughout France.

Meanwhile, public institutions for the furthering of arts, sciences, and literature, in accordance with the Emperor's views, were founded under his protection. He visited, accompanied by the Empress, the four departments on the left bank of the Rhine, showing himself interested in the manufactures and industries, reorganising municipal and local affairs, planning high roads, canals, and various improvements favourable to commercial and sanitary welfare. By these means, while rendering his position more secure in the interior, he sought to inspire his foreign enemies with a dread of his importance in the exterior.

However secure Napoleon might pretend to be with regard to his new Imperial dignity, he wanted to render it more stable still by an appeal to the people. The nation sanctioned his title by an overwhelming majority. There was now but wanting one formality, prescribed by the Senatus Consultus, which had raised him to the throne : the oath to the constitution by the Emperor in presence of the great bodies of the State and the high dignitaries.

This ceremony Napoleon wished to convert into a coronation. The most ancient chronicles were ransacked to find examples for the pomp and splendour with which the Emperor wanted to invest it. He even wished it not to take place in Paris, ostensibly because the Parisians had not shown themselves sufficiently indignant at the late attempts upon his life, in reality because he feared their ridicule and discontent at the proposed splendour and consequent expenses. In remembrance of the feasts of the Federation, the Champ de Mars had been proposed; but the Emperor refused to be crowned there. Several members of the Council suggested that the ceremony should be celebrated in the church of the Invalides, as this fane would appeal more to the military enthusiasm, and be free from all the monarchical and religious traditions attached to Notre Dame, still somewhat repugnant to the scarcely slumbering spirit of the Revolution. But though Napoleon first selected the Invalides, in concession to the anti-religious tendencies of the people, he finally chose the latter for the very reason of its sacred associations in relation to the coronation of kings. This religious impression, for which he himself could have cared but little, was necessary, he imagined, to impose upon the peoples and Kings. He wanted to be consecrated by the Pope, and consequently overtures were made, almost before the Senatus Consultus had proclaimed him Emperor, to induce Pius VII. to come to Paris to perform the ceremony.

At first the Pope refused for various reasons, principally because he would not consecrate the usurper of a throne to which there was a legitimate pretender. Yet the Pontiff's reluctance may be more justly ascribed to the wish of enhancing the price of this favour, and by these means to obtain once more possession of the Legations, Bologna and Avignon, of which Napoleon, even before his accession, had deprived him. Nor is there any doubt that Napoleon lulled him with this hope, though, while doing so, he had already secretly resolved to transform these same states into a Kingdom of Italy, and assume himself the iron crown of the Lombardian Kings.[1]

However, by dint of promises and threats, Pius was prevailed upon to come, while Josephine, enjoying but a doubtful reputation, and only civilly married to Napoleon, went through the religious part of the marriage ceremony, which was secretly performed by the Cardinal Fesch, the Emperor's uncle.

[1] Michelet, *Histoire du XIX. siècle*, vol. iii., bk. ii., ch. 6.

About the middle of November the Pope reached the end of his journey, and was met by Napoleon, dressed as if he were out hunting, a few miles from Fontainebleau, whence they entered a carriage and arrived at the castle, being welcomed by thunders of artillery and the military presenting arms. A few days later, the whole Court removed to the Tuileries, where the Pontiff was installed in the Pavilion of Flora, and received the congratulations of the high dignitaries, and notably of the Senate, in his private apartments.

All this while the Pope had never doubted but that he would place the crown on Napoleon's head, and that the latter would publicly partake of the Holy Communion. The Emperor flatly rejected both proposals, Pius being secretly rejoiced at the refusal of one, knowing full well that its acceptance would have been tantamount to sacrilege.

Still fostering the greatest hopes as to the result of his journey, the Holy Father showed himself anxious to please in every respect, going even as far as to propose the canonisation of a certain Bonaventura Bonaparte, a distant relative of the Emperor, and who died many years ago obscurely in a cloister. "Holy Father," answered Napoleon, "spare me this ridicule. As you are in my power, people would not fail to say that I had compelled you to provide a saint in my family."

The preparations for the coronation being completed, each performer's part in the ceremony having been carefully rehearsed,[1] the coronation took place on the 4th of December, with a pomp and splendour unsurpassed, and scarcely equalled, by anything in modern history.

This magnificence notwithstanding, the people, attracted by the novelty of the spectacle, remained cold and indifferent, only condescending once to depart from their stolidity at the sight of a priest on a broken-down hack, in the suite of the Pope, the two appearing like a comic interlude in a vastly serious play.

"I, who was on the Boulevard (I was six years old)," says M. Michelet, "I noticed nothing on that ice-cold day, save a gloomy and dispiriting silence."[2]

Nor did any of the subsequent festivities make the people relax in their cool and silent indifference to the new state of things. Without openly expressing their discontent, save in the isolated case of one individual,[3] the sight of all this theatrical show, so foreign to their recent Republican institutions, made them feel that this was not the wished-for culmination

---

[1] These rehearsals took place, some openly in the gallery of Diana, and others secretly in the private drawing-room of the Emperor, on a large table, by means of a model of Notre Dame and of wooden puppets, made by the painter Isabey, and representing in full costume all the personages, even the Emperor and the Pope.

[2] Michelet, *Histoire du XIX. siècle*, vol. iii., bk. ii. ch. 6.

[3] A young medical student, Faure, two days after the coronation, made a fruitless attempt to reach the Emperor whilst he was distributing the Orders of the Legion of Honour, in order to assassinate him. The attempt was regarded as that of a madman, and he was merely sent back to his parents.

to fifteen years of constant sacrifice of wealth and life. They had hoped to find in Napoleon the worthy military chief of a Republic, who would in no way remind them of the senseless etiquette of the *ancien régime*, so distasteful to the masses; now they saw, more "in sorrow than in anger," that he, like the kings of old, would be separated from the people by a crowd of dignitaries and courtiers. They regretted that nearly five million francs should have been spent in aping the ceremonies of courts, against which they had of late so energetically protested, the more so as the transition of a Republic into an Empire had been signalised by several fiscal and monetary changes, entirely to the disadvantage of the poorer classes.

It is a question whether Napoleon, in reality anxious for the welfare of the nation, in trying to impose upon others, did not in the end impose upon himself. His desire for peace led him to imagine that, by imitating the trappings of legitimate sovereignty, he might invest the new order of things with an aspect which should prove it to be in no way hostile to ancient Europe, and show at the same time an indestructible stability of its own. Thus he thought to pave the way for an amicable settlement of all differences between his enemies and himself. With the same intentions, perhaps, he gathered around him many of the former nobles and *émigrés*. It need hardly be said that personally he cared little for their pretensions, but between them and the rest of the European aristocracy there existed a bond which might tend to alloy the bitterness felt against a usurper, and bring about a more friendly feeling, which undoubtedly was wished for by Napoleon. Besides, if there was to be a court, it should be as graceful and refined as possible, and with his surroundings of *parvenus* and swash-bucklers, this was well-nigh impossible without the assistance of the ancient nobles, trained to obsequious court-service, and who did not disdain those offices which his generals and their wives would have haughtily refused. The reason of this was not far to seek; it lay in the difference of morals and manners. "The old noblesse," said the Emperor, "showed much more grace and zeal in their attendance. A lady of the Montmorency family would have rushed to tie the strings of the Empress' shoes; the wife of Marshal Lannes would have shrunk from doing this, for fear of being mistaken for a lady's-maid; a Montmorency had no such fear."[1]

The hopes of Napoleon to induce his enemies to preserve peace were doomed to disappointment; and it is probable that he has been unjustly accused of wishing to wage war just then, for it was his interest not to do so; though we do not pretend to say that he may not have desired it later on. Even M. Michelet, who persistently and conscientiously attacks him, is reluctantly obliged to admit that the hatred of Pitt caused the war, rather than the vain, but, perhaps, provoking preparations for the invasion of England. It is certain that, despite the rebuff which he had already once

[1] Las Cases, *Mémoires*, vol. ii., p. 332.

received, when First Consul, from George III., he wrote to him a second time to put an end to the hostilities already begun. It was a rather manly letter,[1] from which the moderate party in England conceived the strongest expectations of a lasting peace. But the forms of a representative government did not allow the King to answer, and a reply was sent (Jan. 14th) by the Secretary for Foreign Affairs, in which England asked for time to consult the Continental Powers. This was followed, three days later, by a confidential communication of the English Prime Minister to the Russian Ambassador in London, and of which the contents presupposed long anterior negotiations. This memorandum aimed at nothing less than to make France return almost to her ancient territorial limits, and to share between the contracting Powers her conquests; a proposal which was to be the basis of the Coalition-treaty, signed on the 11th of April of the same year, between England, Russia, and, later, by Austria, despite that State's most amicable relations with the French Empire, and her recent congratulations to Napoleon. Nor were the angry and indignant remonstrances of Fox of any avail. Napoleon could doubt no longer the enmity of England and of Russia—of Austria he had his suspicions, but no certainty—while an attempt was made to inveigle Prussia into the alliance by the promise of Belgium, failing to comply with which demand Alexander, secretly supported by the Queen of Prussia, threatened

[1] Letter to the King of England, 2nd January, 1805, in the Napoleon Correspondence.

to occupy Pomerania, in case the King of Sweden should be attacked. Nevertheless, the Prussian Cabinet resisted.

Napoleon had now no other choice left but to baffle and defeat the Coalition by fresh battles, and by the subjugation of the Continent. Driven, as it were, to acts of usurpation against the neighbouring States, in order to secure his own position, he began by altering the Constitution of the Batavian Republic according to a less democratic model, though probably he considered this but a provisional state of things, previous to annexing Holland to France, so as to be more fully protected against hostile attempts from that side. For this reason the supreme government of Holland was entrusted to a Legislative of twenty members, and the executive to a Grand Pensionary, elected for life. Schimmelpenninck, who was chosen for this office, was entirely devoted to the interests of France (May 30th).

In Italy, things were dealt with more summarily. This country had borne the name of a Republic for three years, during which time her Constitution had worked smoothly; and though Napoleon, as President, disposed of an almost absolute power, he did not much abuse it, thanks to the sensible influence of the cool-headed Vice-President Melzi. To defy England and terrify Austria, Napoleon now prepared to have himself crowned King of Italy, stipulating at the same time, in deference to the national susceptibilities of the Italians, that after his death none of his successors should wear the crown of Italy united to that of France. The

Emperor had offered the Italian crown to his brother Joseph; but the latter, for various private and political reasons, saw fit to refuse. The coronation of Napoleon took place at Milan with great splendour (26th May). The Pope, who had been invited to be present, declined, scarcely satisfied with the results of his journey to Paris, of which he had entertained great expectations, which were not realised. The vice-royalty of Italy was entrusted to Eugène Beauharnais, Napoleon's stepson, whom he intended to be his successor, an article in the new Constitution giving the King of Italy such a right of selection from among his male issue, legitimate, illegitimate, or adopted.

The State of Genoa, lately known by the name of the Ligurian Republic, had sent a deputation, headed by the Doge, to the coronation of the King of Italy. It was received with all honours as the embassy of an independent people, but no one imagined that Napoleon had the intention of incorporating Genoa with the newly-erected kingdom, the more so as he had always stipulated for and respected its independence. Lately, however, there had been signs that a secret influence was at work to induce the Genoese themselves to propose this incorporation, under the pretext that as an independent Republic they were not sufficiently powerful to protect their coasts against English aggression; and although the Austrian Ambassador, who saw through the scheme, disliked it, and protested, the deputation who had come to Milan beseeched Napoleon to unite to his empire this "Liguria, the first theatre of his victories, the first step of the throne on which he was now seated, and to grant them the happiness of becoming his subjects" (4th June).

In an answer which accorded with their expressed inability to protect themselves, the Emperor accepted, and the Ligurian Republic was divided into three departments, and provided with a reconstructed Constitution, based as usual on the French model. About the same time, he erected Piombino, ceded to France in 1801, into a principality for his sister Eliza, while the Republic of Lucca, re-enacting the fable of the frogs, asked the Emperor for a ruler belonging to his family and for a new Constitution, both of which were granted, Prince Baciochi, the husband of Princess Eliza, being selected for their ruler. Parma, Piacenza, and Guastalla, hitherto under their own particular laws, were now also provided with new Constitutions, and incorporated to France, according to the new Imperial system.

During his triumphal and pacific journey through Italy, on which the eyes of all Europe were now turned, Napoleon had not lost sight of his chief aim, the war with England. He was aware of the doubtful attitude of the other powers, of Austria, arming under many specious pretexts, and of the threatening symptoms of a new Coalition. While it was believed in France and even in England that all these great preparations for invasion were but so many scarecrows, Napoleon, amidst the various occupations, necessitated by the great reforms he was accomplishing in the interior, found time to be in daily communication with the

Minister of Marine, Decrès, who alone possessed his confidence, since the death of Latouche-Tréville at the end of 1804. Far from abandoning his idea of invading England, he had conceived a new strategic plan. The admirals of the Toulon, Rochefort, and Brest fleets, Villeneuve, Missiessy, and Gantheaume, were each to set sail for the West Indies, land reinforcements, and then return together suddenly to Europe, while the English would despatch their ships to succour their threatened colonial possessions.. Then, when the French admirals should have come back safe, they would be masters of the Channel, and might prove the truth of the words Napoleon never ceased repeating, ". Give us but the Channel without the English fleet for six hours, and England shall have ceased to exist."

In fact, though the scheme did not succeed, it at least caused one of the English admirals, Nelson, to be seeking for Villeneuve in Egyptian waters, whilst the latter eluded his vigilance, and arrived safely at his destination. Having received information on his arrival that Missiessy had already been there and returned, and that Gantheaume could not appear because he was blockaded in Brest by Admiral Cornwallis, he was instructed to set sail for Martinique and afterwards for Corunna, to meet there fifteen Franco-Spanish ships of the line, and with these to start for Rochefort, join Missiessy's squadron, relieve Gantheaume still locked in, and then to enter the Channel with the combined fleets. Villeneuve was to take the supreme command, and to steer for Boulogne, where Napoleon himself would await him. If they could be but masters of the Channel, wrote the Emperor, there would be no difficulty in landing a hundred and sixty thousand troops on the English coast. Everything had been prepared, every adverse chance foreseen and guarded against. If Villeneuve found it impossible to raise the blockade of Brest without giving battle, he was to begin an engagement as near as possible to that port, in order that Gantheaume might take part in it; if insuperable obstacles prevented him from entering the Channel, the fleet was to repair to Cadiz, to occupy the Straits of Gibraltar, to ravage its roadstead, and to revictual.

Such were the last instructions to Villeneuve, and from them may be seen that Napoleon had almost provided against and for everything to assure his descent on the English coast.

Unfortunately, Villeneuve was not the man to enter fully into the spirit of such a vast enterprise, nor had he the genius to execute it. Of this Napoleon became fully aware a few days after Villeneuve had started, when he received a dispatch from the admiral, in which the most puerile events were magnified. He there and then resolved to appoint Gantheaume, still lying at Brest, and wrote to dismiss Villeneuve from his command, and to let the fleet, under Gantheaume, sail to her appointed destination.

While Villeneuve was slowly making for Ferrol, wasting time in capturing unimportant merchant vessels, Nelson had followed him to the West Indies, where he only arrived to learn the departure of the foe of which he was in search. Penetrating the design of Napoleon, he cautioned the Admiralty, who commanded the concentration of the different fleets, the very thing which Napoleon had wanted Villeneuve to do. It is worthy of notice, that in the letters to his Minister of the Navy, Napoleon, commenting on the news received from London, foretold, as it were, the decisions which the situation would inspire in the lords of the English Admiralty. Be this as it may, Nelson was ordered, as Napoleon had foreseen,[1] to reinforce the squadron before Brest; and the fleet cruising before Rochefort, under Admiral Stirling, was to join that at Ferrol, commanded by Sir Robert Calder.

The French flotilla and the army which it had to transport being in readiness, and the Dutch fleet, fighting along the whole of her route, having also arrived at Ambleteuse, near Boulogne, Napoleon himself returned from Milan. Nothing was wanting now but the naval forces, whose appearance upon the scene was hourly expected. Beginning to grow uneasy about the fleet of Villeneuve, of whom he had no tidings, and strongly preoccupied by the turn affairs were now taking on the Continent, he started for Boulogne, resolved to await there the arrival of the fleet, without whose assistance he dared not cross the

[1] There is a letter to this effect in Napoleon's Correspondence, dated 20 Prairial, Milan, addressed to his Minister of the Navy, Decrès.

Channel. He hoped that the report of his meditated invasion would be sufficient to keep the Continent in respect,—for Austria was massing her troops on the Inn and the Adige,—and that the reverses of England would prevent all further Coalition. In case his enemies, profiting by his absence, should begin hostilities on the Rhine, he calculated to have his expedition terminated before then, and to be back in France to oppose an invasion of the Empire. He sent word to Gantheaume to hold himself prepared, because Villeneuve could not fail to appear shortly. In fact, he thought that the missing admiral, informed of Nelson's pursuit, might have steered for Cadiz instead of for Ferrol, in which case every precaution was already taken to assist him.

After waiting for three days, during which he reviewed the army in sight of the English cruisers, he received the news that Villeneuve, with a very superior force, had fought an engagement with the united fleets of Admirals Stirling and Calder, about sixty miles to the westward of Cape Finisterre (July 22nd); that both parties claimed the victory, but that two Spanish line-of-battle ships had fallen into the enemy's hands. Instead of following his orders, and trying to join the squadron of Rochefort, Villeneuve wasted another two days, and then entered Ferrol, and with thirty ships of the line allowed himself to be blockaded by twenty vessels. Napoleon was indignant that one man should have upset all his plans. In the midst of his anger, his thoughts immediately reverted to the Continent, where he thought to strike England in her Allies, and he sketched out a campaign, which subsequent events proved to have been one of the masterpieces of military strategy.

Nevertheless, he still hoped that Villeneuve would manage to break the blockade, and sent him orders to do so. He was to make for Brest, where Gantheaume would attempt an engagement and join him. The Emperor was, indeed, loth to abandon a plan which, notwithstanding its difficulties, was likely to be successful, for while awaiting for further news he tried the forces of his flotilla by a bolder movement than had hitherto been attempted. This movement answered all his expectations, and made the more bitter his regret at being so inefficiently supported by his admirals.

According to his orders, Gantheaume left Brest harbour to offer battle to the enemy, expecting Villeneuve to come to his succour. The latter had, indeed, left Ferrol, but instead of steering for the north, he remained in the Ferrol roads, afraid of the responsibility, and then finished by running into Cadiz, where he was blockaded by the united fleets of Calder and Collingwood, of which Nelson had taken the command.

When the news of Villeneuve being unable to appear reached Napoleon, he knew that his great projects against England had vanished. In less than four-and-twenty hours the whole army was directed on Germany, to punish Austria, which was going to pay for England. As may be seen, Napoleon's plan of an invasion of England was far from being intended as the mere scarecrow which some historians have so persistently maintained it to be.

In order to understand the subsequent events, we must retrace our steps for a few months to the time when Napoleon left for Italy to be crowned at Milan.

On the very day of Napoleon's departure (11th April), a treaty, the result of long negotiations, had been signed between England and Russia, aiming principally at, and ostensibly compelling France to restore the European equilibrium, to despoil her of the advantages which she had obtained by fifteen years of incessant war and bloody sacrifices, and to isolate her from the rest of Europe, with which, since the Revolution, and especially now, she had nothing in common.

England engaged to support these demands by co-operating with Russia, by furnishing her naval and military forces, by subsidising every other Power which should league itself with her to the annual amount of £15,000 for every ten thousand men supplied in return for which subsidies she was to be considered the chief of this third Coalition, and to have the right of establishing commercial depôts in the States of her Allies. At the same time all her pretensions on the sea were recognised.

Another article accorded similar monetary advantages to the King of Sweden, who had openly joined the Coalition. As for Austria, Alexander sent his aide-de-camp to Vienna to discuss the plan of the campaign, and despite the assurances of the French Ambassador that the camp of Alessandria was dispersed, that the one of Brescia would share a similar fate within a fortnight, Francis continued to mass his troops upon the Italian frontiers, though he was too double-dealing to declare war at once, thinking that the time had not yet arrived.

To give the Coalition leisure to complete its preparations, and to assemble its forces, the farce of a pretended negotiation was attempted in which Alexander should play the part of mediator. Prussia was also invited to enter the Coalition. Its King was in a critical position. Scarcely confident of being able to maintain his neutrality, he had hoped all along that actual hostilities should be prevented. Suddenly, undeceived by the appeal of the Russian Ambassador in favour of his master, he fell into his former irresolution, aggravated on one side by his ambition, on the other by some political motives, which made him loth to refuse the bait held out to him by France in return for his alliance, namely, the cession of Hanover; while at the same time he dreaded the aggression of Russia, in case he should by accepting this offer appear to lean to Napoleon's side. In this emergency he pursued a double-faced policy, by declaring his wish to remain neutral, merely consenting to take Hanover as a depôt, free, as he thought, to side afterwards with the Power who should prove the stronger.

Meanwhile the preparations for war on the part of the Coalition continued with redoubled energy, especially on the part of Austria, who on the reiterated demands of Napoleon, threw off the mask at last, and clearly showed that the drift of her supposed mediation was to gain time in order to complete her plans. She declared that the violation by Napoleon of the Treaty of Lunéville, one of whose articles stipulated and guaranteed the independence of the Italian as well as of the Helvetian and Batavian republics, had led her to enter the Coalition.[1] She still professed herself willing to re-open negotiations, but this also was done in order to gain time and to obtain the alliance of the Electors, who of late had become important princes, and on whose attitude much depended in the coming campaign. In this instance Napoleon, however, had been too quick, and forestalled her, especially with the Electors of Bavaria and Baden, who could not possibly remain neutral in the struggle, though, above all, the first desired to do so. This Elector expressed this wish to the Emperor Francis, but saw it daily disregarded by the invasion of his territory by Austrian troops, eager to reach the Rhine before Napoleon had broken up his camp near Boulogne. Napoleon had foreseen this, and extracted a promise that in case such an event should happen, the Bavarian army would seek refuge elsewhere, and effect its junction with his army. The Austrians having passed the Inn on the 9th of

[1] According to some French anthors this was a mere pretext, sufficiently proved by the fact that Austria had entered the Coalition before the changes in the existence of the Italian Republics had happened.

September, the Elector gave the order for his troops to enter Franconia, and abandoned his capital to transfer his Government and himself to Wurtzburg, where a treaty with France was definitely arranged on the 23rd of November, much to the disgust of Austria.

The troops of the Boulogne camp crossed France by forced marches, and in three columns, making for the Rhine by parallel roads. Germany was to be the theatre of the war, the French Emperor having resolved to act merely on the defensive in Italy. The army in Italy, only fifty thousand strong, was entrusted to Masséna, supported by the troops which were evacuating the Naples territory, after the King had signed a treaty of neutrality, and promised to prevent the landing of foreign troops. Napoleon himself having taken various measures for the due government of the interior, and for the levy of conscripts, joined his troops, who had already passed the Rhine (24th September).

Bernadotte, commanding the first corps, had evacuated Hanover, merely leaving there a garrison, and joined the electoral troops at Wurtzburg; the second corps, under Marmont, left Holland, and was moving on Mayence; four corps under Davoust, Soult, Lannes, Ney, and a reserve of cavalry under Murat, starting from Boulogne, were stationed along the Rhine from Mannheim to Strasburg. Another corps, under Augereau, moved from Brest upon Huningen, as reserve. There were a hundred and sixty thousand troops in all, exclusive of the Bavarians. Murat and Lannes crossed the Rhine at Kehl, threatened the issues of the Black Forest, and masked the movements of Ney, Soult, and Davoust (25th September). The following day Ney crossed near Lauterburg, Soult near Spires, and Davoust near Mannheim, the three marching on the Necker, to intimidate the Electors of Baden and Wurtemberg, whom they induced to sign treaties, whereby they secured sixteen thousand electoral troops to guard their communications. Marmont crossed at Mayence, and joined Bernadotte and the Bavarians at Wurtzburg, so that in two days a hundred and eighty thousand men were stationed in *échelon*, on the right flank of the Austrians, facing Lannes and Murat, in the Black Forest, whose lines extended towards Stuttgard, where they joined those of Ney. Mack, the Austrian general, in reality directed and browbeaten by the Austrian princes, who treated him with contempt on account of his inferior birth,[1] understood nothing of all these complicated movements. Counting upon the Russians, who were expected hourly, he lost his head at the enemy's rapid marching and countermarching, and mistaking their intentions, he found himself outmanœuvred, his supports beaten on all sides, and compelled to enter Ulm. Being summoned to capitulate, he ultimately agreed to surrender if he was not relieved within eight days. In the meantime the news spread that a division of Austrian troops who still kept the field before Mack had entered Ulm, had surrendered at Trochtelfingen, with the exception of two thousand horsemen under the Archduke

[1] Michelet, *Histoire du XIX. siècle*, vol. iii., bk. iii., ch. 4.

Ferdinand, who had made good their escape. A part of the French army had marched a hundred and thirty-five English miles in five days, had killed or made prisoners twenty-two thousand Austrians, taken a hundred and thirty guns, and a large number of caissons and waggons. The French Emperor sent this news to Mack, who immediately surrendered with thirty-three thousand prisoners, sixty cannon, and forty standards (20th October). Well might the world stand astonished at the spectacle of an army of eighty-five thousand men destroyed, as it were, without one great battle having been fought. Well might the French soldiers say, "The Emperor has beaten the enemy with our legs, and not with our bayonets." They were proud of their general, and not without reason. For two days the rain had fallen in torrents, the troops were drenched to the skin, they had received no rations, they were up to their knees in mud, but their sufferings and privations were shared by Napoleon, as if he had been the meanest private.

As he was standing in their midst, a batch of Austrian prisoners passed, and a colonel expressed his surprise that the Emperor of the French should be covered with mud and exhausted with fatigue like the humblest drummer in the army. One of his aides-de-camp having explained what the Austrian said, Napoleon sent him back the following answer, "Your master has reminded me that I was once a soldier; I trust that he will acknowledge this time that the purple has not made me forget my previous occupation."

One would have thought that after the crushing lesson inflicted upon Austria, Prussia would not have courted the risk of a similar defeat, and, if departing at all from her professed neutrality, would have sided with France. She did the very opposite. In their rapid march from Wurtzburg to the Danube, Marmont and Bernadotte had entered the Prussian State of Anspach. The King of Prussia showed himself very indignant at this, and declared that henceforth he was free from any engagement with France. This was probably a pretext, as the same thing had happened before without the least notice being taken; but Alexander took advantage of this. He proposed an interview to Frederick William, and arrived unexpectedly at Berlin on the 25th of October, five days after the capitulation of Ulm, when the full extent of the disaster was not known. He was received with the greatest warmth, the two monarchs embracing each other amidst the loud applause of the people. At Potsdam, where the illustrious guest was entertained, there was nothing but festivities, exchange of presents, and of congratulations. From that moment France was utterly disregarded. The French Ambassador, already recalled by Napoleon, took leave of the King of Prussia on the 1st of November, and on the 3rd an offensive and defensive treaty was signed, by which the King entered the Coalition, though he still reserved the right of withdrawal, in case Napoleon should consent to the evacuation of Holland and Switzerland, grant an indemnity to the King of Sardinia, and separate the crowns of Italy and France. An ambassador was despatched with this ultimatum, who took care not to arrive at the French head-quarters until a month after the signing of the treaty at Potsdam.

The key to the above-mentioned reservation is to be found in the tidings of the disaster at Ulm, communicated by the Austrian Archduke Anthony, two days before the signing of the treaty, and which tempered the warlike ardour of the Prussian Court and Cabinet. Nevertheless, the alliance was cemented in a somewhat theatrical performance arranged by the Queen. The two monarchs went at night to the tomb of Frederick the Great, where Alexander swore to die for the honour and defence of Prussia.[1]

Despite Napoleon's willingness to explain the passing through Anspach, the Prussian army was mobilised, Hanover invaded in the name of the Elector-King, and every preparation made to enter upon a campaign.

Meanwhile Napoleon, resolved to strike terror into the hearts of his enemies, was rapidly invading the Austrian provinces, scarcely meeting with any resistance either from the Austrians or from the Russians, who had now arrived, and were retreating upon Vienna to protect the capital, and to give the armies of the Tyrol and Italy the opportunity of joining them. The French troops under Ney and Augereau, who were left behind, were ordered to invade the Tyrol, to drive out the Archduke John, and to cover at the same time the right flank of the army of Germany as well as the left of the Italian army. The Inn, totally undefended, was passed

[1] Hardenberg, *Mémoires*, vol. ix., pp. 14, 55, quoted by Michelet.

by all the French corps; Braunau, one of the great victualling depôts of the Austrian Empire, taken without a blow; whilst Lannes and Murat, forming the vanguard, drove the enemy successively from their various positions. Kutusoff, the Russian general, finding it impossible to effect a junction with the armies of the Tyrol and Italy, abandoned the plan of defending Vienna, and retreated into Moravia, where he hoped to meet the second Russian army. Scarcely had he reached the other side of the Danube before he was attacked by Marshal Mortier, sent thither to watch Bohemia, and who had but a small contingent under his command, the remainder of his division being a march behind. Nevertheless, the French took the offensive, ignorant of the exact numbers of the enemy until too late, when they found out the superiority of the Russians by being completely surrounded at nightfall and their retreat cut off. From assailants they became defenders until the remainder of their division came up, when the Russians, taken between two fires, were compelled to fall back on Krems. This engagement is better known under the name of Dürrenstein, the village near which it was fought (11th November).

The Emperor Francis and the Court had left Vienna and taken refuge at Brunn, in Moravia. From there they started for Olmütz, where the Emperor of Russia, with his second army, was stationed. The Austrian capital was a prey to the greatest confusion. One day the most confidential reports as to the ultimate success of the war were circulated, the whole population being

called under arms to ensure this success; the next
the treasures, the archives, and valuables were hastily
packed up, and an embargo laid upon every boat to
remove them into Hungary. Meanwhile an envoy
was sent to Napoleon to propose an armistice; a
proposal which the latter declined, saying, that at the
head of two hundred thousand victorious troops, he
could not very well grant an armistice to a beaten
army. The French continued their way to Vienna,
which city they merely passed through, and marched
straight to the great bridge over the Danube, which
led across that river to the northern provinces of the
Empire. That bridge was mined and watched from
the other side by fourteen thousand Austrians under
Count Auersberg, who had orders to blow it up on
the least attempt at violence. On the Vienna side
of the river there was only an outpost. In this
emergency Lannes and Murat bethought themselves
of a stratagem. They tried to persuade the Austrians
that the armistice of which there had been rumours
afloat for the last few days was actually signed. Two
French generals were the first to arrive on the bridge
at the head of the 10th Hussars; they demanded
to speak to the German commander, and were
allowed to pass, but alone. Some French soldiers
followed and halted, whilst Lannes and Murat dismounted, and with a small detachment passed on
to the bridge. General Belliard, as if taking
a stroll, advanced also, his hands behind his back;
Lannes joined him; they were gaining ground

notwithstanding the objections of the captain on duty. These were seemingly unnoticed, and two or three French officers engaged him in conversation and talked about the armistice. He, however, was losing patience, and when he saw the detachment advancing still farther, he began to rally his men; but Lannes and Belliard took hold of him and shouted louder than he. The dispute was waxing hot, the moment critical, when the French troops quickened their pace, crossed the remaining distance, reached the other side, and made themselves masters of those who were to fire the train. Auersberg had been duped, and was summoned before a council of war, deprived of his rank and dignity, and condemned to a year's confinement in a fortress.

The Suchet division and the grenadiers of Oudinot crossed also; the light cavalry immediately continued their advance, in order to impede the march of the Russian general, Kutusoff, the same who had been defeated by Mortier, at Dürrenstein; Soult followed; Bernadotte had passed the Danube at Mautern, while Davoust occupied Vienna. Kutusoff, knowing that Bernadotte was in his rear, is said to have sent a flag of truce to Murat in the name of the Czar, and to have escaped by means of a pretended armistice with the French general. When Murat, aware of the deception, and severely reprimanded by the Emperor, resumed his march, he found that the whole of the Russian army had defiled rapidly in his rear, and that only a corps of ten thousand troops had remained stationary. A sanguinary engagement ensued, but the

Russians offered a stout resistance, which gave their general time to reach Brünn (18th November).

The Allies, aware that the war was assuming a new aspect, ordered the Archduke Ferdinand to raise an insurrection in Bohemia, while his army should cover the left flank of the Russian troops and the remainder of the Austrians, who had effected their junction at Brünn. The Archduke Charles re-crossed the Alps, entered Hungary, and was thus enabled to protect the Austro-Russian contingent on the right.

This Archduke had been scarcely more fortunate in Italy than his fellow-generals in Germany. When Austria first resolved to join the Coalition, she intended to carry the war into Italy, while merely remaining on the defensive in Germany. In furtherance of this plan, approved of by her Allies, she had despatched thither a numerous army under the Archduke, who had instructions to invade the newly-created kingdom the moment the Russians should appear on the Inn. We have seen how this intention was frustrated by the rapid advance of the French on the Rhine, but Napoleon, who intended to remain on the defensive in Italy, and had taken his measures accordingly, emboldened by his first successes on the Rhine, also changed his tactics, and ordered Masséna to take the offensive, mainly to prevent the reinforcements which Charles might send into Germany. Acting upon this, Masséna attacked Verona, and the *tête du pont* at Legnago, carried them both after a violent engagement (17th October), crossed the Adige, and followed the Archduke, who had entrenched himself at Caldiero. Another engagement took place, in which the Austrians maintained their positions for three days, though with a loss of four thousand killed, whilst the French lost as many (30th October). When the news of the defeat of Ulm arrived, the Austrians precipitately retreated towards the Alps. Masséna, still at their heels, failed for some days in bringing them to a standstill to offer battle. The Archduke, harassed and fatigued, wishing to give his troops some rest, threw four battalions of grenadiers and some field artillery into Vicenza. After a fruitless summons to surrender, Masséna resolved to take that town, and being unsuccessful, contemplated to resume the attack the next day; but the Austrians evacuated the place during the night, having accomplished their aim, namely, to give time for the artillery and the wings of the army to join the centre. Masséna pursued them, without being able to force them to give battle, until he arrived at the right bank of the Tagliamento, where the Archduke, after throwing a garrison into Venice, made a stand in order to cover the march of his baggage-waggons on Palma-Nova. A serious engagement took place, a repetition of which was again avoided by the Archduke, who crossed the Julian Alps, concentrated his troops at Laybach, and there awaited the junction with the army of the Tyrol in order to march to the assistance of Vienna. Masséna was not in a position to follow him, as troubles had broken out afresh in the Kingdom of Naples, where the Queen, disregarding the treaty entered into by her husband, had invoked the aid of the Anglo-Russians, and placed an army of twenty-five thousand troops at their disposal, with which the Roman territory was to be invaded. Without communication with the grand army, unaware of the taking of Vienna, of the operations of Ney and Augereau on his left, of the position of the Archduke John, uneasy at the reported arrival of the Anglo-Russians in Dalmatia and in Naples, Masséna deemed it wiser not to venture too far, and contented himself by sending out strong reconnoitring parties, and by making himself master of Trieste. The corps which on the conclusion of the treaty with Naples had left that kingdom was employed to invest Venice.

The troops under the Archduke John, after remaining for some time idle in the Tyrol, held in check by Ney, and harassed in their retreat by a detached brigade of Masséna, had managed to join the Archduke Charles at Cilly, whence both endeavoured to get to Vienna by way of Hungary and the Danube, in this way to harass the flank or rear of the French, and join the Russians in Moravia. But Marmont going to their encounter, compelled them to make for the Raab, while Davoust, possessing himself of Presburg, and forcing the Hungarian Diet to remain neutral, opposed a formidable barrier in front; Masséna, having passed the Alps, harassed their rear.

Meanwhile Napoleon had moved his head-quarters into Moravia, as far as Brunn, the Russians having retreated to Olmütz. At the moment when another great battle was to be fought, a war contribution of forty millions of francs was levied on Austria, Moravia, and the remainder of the conquered provinces, whilst one of the same amount had already been paid before. The stores of the Austrian arsenals which could not be used were sold, and their proceeds distributed among the French army in the shape of three months' extra pay to every general, officer, and soldier who had been wounded in the present war.

After several days passed in pretended negotiations, tacitly encouraged by Napoleon, who wished to gain time in order to discover the blunders of his enemy, the Allies took the offensive on the 27th of November by driving the French outposts from Wischau, and executing a movement towards Austerlitz, which betrayed their intentions of cutting off the French from Vienna, whither, however, the latter had no thought of retiring. The military movements of Murat, Lannes, and Soult were mistaken for retreats, and the Russians continued their tactics to cut off the French communications with the Danube.

Napoleon left them in their error to attract them to the spot chosen by himself, which was the plateau of Austerlitz. He succeeded in this; for the Russians, fearing that the French army should escape them, slowly left their positions, and executed a flank march in column, by which they attempted to turn the right flank of the enemy. From that moment Napoleon was certain of the victory. "To-morrow, before nightfall, that army will be mine," he said.

On the 2nd of December the battle began. The

Allies commenced the attack by carrying the village of Sokolnitz; but the French troops, under Soult, stormed the heights of Pratzen, and after a desperate conflict of two hours' duration, the allied army was pierced through the centre, and its left wing entirely separated. The Russian right was also completely defeated, by Bernadotte, Murat, and Lannes, with the loss of nearly half their number. At last, after a tremendous cavalry encounter between the Russian Imperial Guard and the French Cavalry of the Guard, the Russians gave way and retreated. The loss of the Allies was immense. Thirty thousand men were killed, wounded, or made prisoners; a hundred and eighty pieces of cannon, four hundred caissons, and forty-five standards fell in the hands of the conquerors. Napoleon might well say to his brave troops, "I am satisfied with you; you have covered your eagles with immortal glory."

The consequences of this victory were very great. Two days after a personal interview between the Austrian and French Emperors (December 4th), an armistice was concluded, which was ratified three weeks later at Presburg, and by which it was stipulated that the French were to occupy all those portions of Upper and Lower Austria, the Tyrol, Styria, Carinthia, Carniola, and Moravia, at present in their possession; that the Russians should return to their own country; that all insurrectionary movements in Hungary and Bohemia were to be stopped, and no armed force of any other Power should be permitted to enter Austrian territory. The Russian

Emperor was allowed to retire with his troops by slow marches, but renewed the war later on, so that Napoleon said of Alexander, that "he was as false as a Greek of the Lower Empire." The King of Prussia sent an envoy to compliment Napoleon on his victory, and signed a treaty with the latter by which he ceded to France the Margravate of Anspach and the principalities of Neufchâtel and Cleves, for which he received in return the Electorate of Hanover. The King of Naples, who had assisted the Coalition by placing his army on a war-footing, under the direction of a Russian general, was to be dethroned, and Joseph, Napoleon's brother, was some time afterwards appointed King of the Two Sicilies (March 30th, 1806).

But whilst the French were triumphant on land, the English gained a naval Austerlitz. The French admiral, Villeneuve, wishing to retrieve his reputation, and being in command of thirty-three line-of-battle ships and five frigates, attacked the English fleet, composed of seven-and-twenty ships of the line and four frigates, under Nelson and Collingwood, a few leagues to the north-west of Cape Trafalgar (October 21st). The result was that nineteen large French or Spanish vessels were taken, of which five afterwards escaped to Cadiz, sixteen were either wrecked, burnt, or sunk, and only four arrived safe at Gibraltar, as well as three French admirals and seven thousand prisoners. By this victory England remained mistress of the sea, and had no longer any maritime rivalry to dread. It was, however, dearly bought, by the death of the great English admiral, Nelson.

CHAPTER II.

§ I.—THE PROGRESS OF IMPERIALISM.

(From the 27th of December, 1805, to the 7th of July, 1807.)

IMMEDIATELY after having gained the battle of Austerlitz, it seems that Napoleon intended to form three compact nations of fifteen million Italians, thirty million Germans, and fifteen million Spaniards, and to create a system of federal States to the French Empire. We have already seen that Joseph Bonaparte had been appointed to fill the Neapolitan throne; another of the Emperor's brothers, Louis, was named King of Holland; Massa and Carrara were given to his sister Eliza; and Guastalla to another sister, Pauline; Murat became Grand Duke of Berg, Berthier Prince of Neufchâtel, Talleyrand Prince of Benevento, Bernadotte Prince of Pontecorvo, Cambacérès and Lebrun Dukes of Parma and Piacenza; whilst he created the Venetian provinces Dalmatia, Istria, Treviso, Conegliano, Belluno, Feltre, Friuli, Bassano, Vicenza, Cadore, Rovigo, and Padua into duchies, which were bestowed as fiefs on the principal officers of his army.

The creation of these Imperial fiefs caused great dissatisfaction, not alone amongst the nations who were despoiled and partitioned without being consulted, but even amongst the French people, who had shed their blood for what they thought liberty, and found they had only done so in order to create a new dynasty and a military aristocracy. Since the victory of Austerlitz Napoleon became more despotic, and cared more for the aggrandisement of his family and partisans than to benefit France. He also made a law by which persons ennobled were entitled to entail a certain income, under the name of *majorat*, in favour of their direct descendants, and thus could continue an hereditary title. Through similar means he endeavoured to prove to Europe that he was an enemy to anarchy and the restorer of society.

All the arts of government seemed to bear the same aristocratic impress. Forest property was arbitrarily ceded to *émigrés* who had possessed it before the Revolution; for it was the opinion of the Emperor that it was impossible to govern without the ancient families receiving back their large fortunes. Many monopolies of former times were re-established; the taxes on salt, sugar, and the town-duties were increased, the prefects became more tyrannical, arbitrary imprisonments were multiplied, letters were broken open; at the Abbey of St. Denis, where until now only Kings had been buried, tombs were prepared for the Napoleonic dynasty, the Republican calendar was abolished, the 15th of August was declared to be the feast of the patron saint of the Emperor, and, finally, the Imperial Court was governed by a code of etiquette, consisting of eight hundred and nineteen clauses. But it must also be stated that the Bank of France was reorganised on a better footing, that a corps of engineers, *des ponts et chaussées*, was created, that schools for daughters of members of the Legion of Honour were erected, that councils to arrange the quarrels between masters and men were instituted, and that prizes were founded for improvements in arts and sciences. Moreover, the roads of Mont Cenis and of the Simplon were completed, a vast network of canals was spread over France, and, finally, Paris became greatly embellished, for it was the Emperor's wish "that that illustrious city, which had become the first in the universe, should befit by its splendour so glorious a destiny."

Yet the governments of Europe did not credit Napoleon's pacific intentions. How could they, when at his instigation the Confederation of the Rhine was formed (July 12th), by which the Kings of Bavaria and Wurtemberg, the Archbishop of Ratisbon, the Elector of Baden, the Grand Duke of Berg, the Landgrave of Hesse-Darmstadt, and ten other petty German princes, severed themselves for ever from the German Empire, and placed themselves under the protection of the Emperor of the French? A new Coalition was formed against France, of which England, Russia, and Prussia were the chief members. War was declared, and Saxony was invaded by Prussian troops (15th September). The army of the Allies, under the command of the Duke of Brunswick, numbered about a hundred and thirty-five thousand men, whilst the French had about a hundred and ninety thousand troops, of which the bulk was concentrated round Coburg and Bamberg. The Duke of Brunswick arrayed his army on both sides of the

Thuringian Forest, with the design of pushing on to Eisenach, pierce the centre of the valley of the Maine, the base of the operations of the French, and cut them off from their communications. Napoleon formed his army in three columns, of which the right was commanded by Soult and Ney, the centre by Bernadotte and Davoust, with Murat at the head of the cavalry, and the left by Lannes and Augereau. The latter column met the enemy near Saalfeld, and defeated him (October 10th) with a loss of twelve hundred killed, amongst whom was their general, Prince Louis of Prussia. On the news of this defeat, the Duke of Brunswick hastened to evacuate the Thuringian Forest and to retreat towards Weimar, in order, if possible, to save the stores at Naumburg, and to give time for the reserve to come up. But Napoleon, with the army under his command, prevented this; so that the Prussians had to march to Freyburg to gain the Elbe, whilst the left wing, under Prince Hohenlohe, kept the pass of Jena, and was to be supported by the right wing still at Weimar.

At the approach of the French troops, Hohenlohe evacuated the heights of Jena, intending to join the army under the Duke. The French Emperor was not slow in perceiving this, and thinking that he had the whole Prussian army before him, he ordered Murat to hasten from Dornburg to Jena; while Davoust and Bernadotte were directed to advance from Naumburg, the first upon Apolda, in order to threaten the enemy's rear, the second upon Dornburg, to cut off his retreat to Prussia. " Soldiers," said the Emperor, " the Prussian army is turned, as the Austrian was a year ago at Ulm; it now only combats to secure the means of retreat. The corps which should permit itself to be broken would be dishonoured." And during the night he made of the Landgrafenberg, the steepest hill of the mountain-ridge near Jena, a kind of fortified camp, whence, on the 14th of October, the French, under Lannes, Augereau, Soult, and Ney, rushed down. After a battle which raged furiously for several hours, the Prussians were defeated, whole regiments were destroyed, whilst a German corps of twenty thousand men, which came too late on the field, was almost totally annihilated. The cavalry, under Murat, completed the victory and bore down with loud cheers on the retiring lines. Soon the rout became general; infantry and cavalry were blended together, and fled pell-mell to Weimar.

In the meanwhile the army under the Duke of Brunswick and the King of Prussia had arrived at the village of Auerstadt, and a division was ordered to seize the defile of Koessen. But that defile had been already occupied by Davoust, who was marching upon Apolda, and who had only twenty-six thousand men of whom four thousand were cavalry, to oppose against fifty thousand infantry and ten thousand cavalry. One of the French divisions, commanded by General Gudin, had in the beginning to bear the whole brunt of the attack of the enemy, because the other two divisions had not yet crossed the Saal. These brave troops formed themselves into squares, and supported by a terrible artillery fire, resisted all the charges of the Prussians with indomitable resolution, though they lost nearly half their number. At last the two other divisions of Davoust's army appeared, and the conflict became more equal. In vain did the Prussians repeatedly try to break the French squares; they were always received by an uninterrupted fire and by the hedge of bayonets of the kneeling front ranks. At last the French became masters of the heights of the Sonnenberg, from whence their guns could command the field of battle and open a tremendous fire of grape and canister upon the enemy's columns. Then Davoust resolved to strike a decisive blow, and though the Prussian reserve troops were fifteen thousand strong, posted on an eminence and protected by the fire of a powerful battery, they were driven from their positions with the loss of twenty pieces of cannon. They retreated and met the fugitives from the former army of Hohenlohe, who had been defeated at Jena. Now the retreat became a complete rout: infantry, cavalry, and artillery fled in the greatest confusion, leaving their guns, horses, and ammunition-waggons behind them; there were no longer any generals, there was no longer any order. Even the King of Prussia himself narrowly escaped being made a prisoner. The loss of the Prussians was enormous. Nearly twenty-five thousand were killed in these two battles, and more than that number made prisoners; of their four principal generals, General Schmettau was killed, whilst the

Duke of Brunswick, Marshal Moellendorf, and General Ruchel were severely wounded. Besides this three hundred pieces of cannon and sixty standards fell into the hands of the French. Erfurth surrendered the day after the battle, and the King fled first to Sommerda and then to Magdeburg; the remaining Prussian troops, under Kalkreuth, were defeated by Soult, at Nordhausen, and, after losing three thousand men and twenty pieces of cannon, completely disbanded.

The French Emperor left his enemy no rest, but ordered his troops to advance. Bernadotte defeated the Prince of Wurtemberg, who lost many men and guns; Davoust took Leipsic and Wittenberg, and his corps was the first to enter Berlin (October 25th). Napoleon made his triumphal entry two days later, and stopped first at Potsdam, from whence he sent the sword of Frederick the Great to Paris. He also levied an extraordinary war contribution of one hundred million francs on the Prussian States to the west of the Vistula, one of twenty-four million francs on the smaller States in the Prussian Confederacy, and one of twenty-five million francs on the Elector of Saxony. Moreover, the civil authorities were compelled to take an oath of fidelity to the French Emperor; and later on the conquered territory was divided into four departments. Then he addressed a proclamation to the army, in which he said: "Soldiers! you are worthy defenders of my crown, and of the great people. . . . One of the first Powers in Europe, which recently had the audacity to propose to us a shameful capitulation, is annihilated. . . .

All the Prussian provinces, from the Elbe to the Oder, are in our hands. Soldiers! the Russians boast that they are advancing to meet us. . . . We will spare them the half of their journey; they will find an Austerlitz in the heart of Prussia."

Prince Hohenlohe, after various adventures, was obliged to lay down his arms near Prentzlow, with sixteen thousand men; Lannes and Murat captured there sixty cannons and forty-five standards. Another Prussian column, six thousand men strong, surrendered also at Passewalck. The fortresses on the Oder soon capitulated. Stettin was the first, Custrin followed, though both might have held out, as they had enough guns and were well garrisoned. The only corps of the Prussian army still remaining in the field was composed of eighteen thousand infantry and six thousand cavalry, under General Blucher. He was compelled to throw himself into Lubeck, which he defended until that town was carried by assault. He finally was driven with his troops to the very edge of Danish territory, and obliged to surrender, having only four thousand foot-soldiers and three thousand seven hundred cavalry left. That same day (8th November), Magdeburg, with twenty thousand men, eight hundred pieces of cannon, and immense magazines, well stored, fell into the hands of the French. The King of Prussia had fled to Königsberg with fifteen thousand men, the only remnant of his once powerful army, and refused to ratify the armistice proposed to him by the French Emperor, by which he was to give up to him all the provinces between the Rhine and the Elbe.

The conquest of Prussia was now ended, but a hundred thousand Russians were arriving on the Vistula, and the war was becoming more complicated than ever. In the meanwhile Napoleon, on the 20th of November, published his Berlin decree, which declared:—"1. The British Islands are placed in a state of blockade. 2. Every species of commerce and communication with them is prohibited; all letters or packets addressed in English, or in English characters, shall be seized at the post-office, and their circulation interdicted. 3. Every British subject, of what rank or condition whatever, who shall be found in the countries occupied by our troops or those of our allies, shall be made prisoner of war. 4. Every warehouse, merchandise, or property of any sort, belonging to a subject of Great Britain, or coming from its manufactories or colonies, is declared good prize. 5. Commerce of every kind in English goods is prohibited; and every species of merchandise belonging to England, or emanating from its workshops or colonies, is declared good prize. 6. The half of the confiscated value shall be devoted to indemnifying those merchants whose vessels have been seized by the English cruisers, for the losses which they have sustained. 7. No vessel coming directly from England, or any of its colonies, or having touched there since the publication of the present decree, shall be received into any harbour. 8. Every vessel which, by means of a false declaration, shall have effected such entry, shall be liable to seizure, and the ship and cargo shall be confiscated as if they had also belonged to England." It further provided two prize-courts, one at Paris and one at Milan, and stated that this decree should be communicated to all Kings and Princes allies of the French Emperor. It was ordered to be acted upon with the utmost severity. The consequences were that smuggling went on on a large scale; that all colonial produce and warm clothing tripled in price; "that women with their half-naked children knelt around the piles where English goods were burned, shouting, 'For Heaven's sake, give them rather to us!'"

The dismissal of the Hospodars or governors of Wallachia and Moldavia by the Turkish Sultan, without the consent of Russia, and which was against the stipulations of the treaty concluded between these two Powers in 1802, led to hostilities. The Russian troops entered the Turkish territory under General Michelson, and advanced as far as Bucharest. Servia revolted against the Porte, and Turkey sent an army on the Danube, whilst it concluded a close alliance with France.

In the meanwhile the French troops advanced still farther into Prussian Poland, and the Poles rose up in rebellion both against Prussia and Russia. When Napoleon arrived at Posen he was received with great applause by the people, who entreated him to assist in the restoration of their country. He hesitated. he armed the Prussian Poles, and gave them a Provisional Government; but he refused to enter upon any engagements with the Russian Poles, and even reassured Austria about Galicia. In a bulletin addressed to the Poles, he said: " Is the throne of Poland about to be restored, and is the nation destined to resume its existence and independence? From the depth of the tomb is it destined to start into life? God alone, who holds in His hands the combination of great events, is the Arbiter of that grand political problem; but certainly never was an event more memorable or worthy of interest." The Russians had not been idle, and, accompanied by fifteen thousand Prussians, occupied Warsaw; but on the approach of the French, they evacuated that town, and took up a position towards Pultusk on the Narew. There a serious conflict took place, in which the latter were victorious, as well as at some other places; so that, finally, the Russian general, Kamenskoi, in full retreat, ordered the artillery, which impeded his march, to be sacrificed. But General Benningsen disobeyed him; he resolved to delay the French army at Pultusk, in order to give time to the artillery and equipages to come up (December 26th). The mud was ankle-deep, a heavy fall of snow blinded French and Russians, who both lost a large number of men, but the object of the latter was attained; the advance of the French troops was delayed. The frightful state of the roads and the severity of the season also contributed to this, and finally the French Emperor issued orders for the troops to go into winter quarters whilst he returned with the Guards to Warsaw.

The Russians did not leave the French at rest. Benningsen, who commanded them, crossed over into East Prussia, but met a check at Mohrungen (January 24th). Napoleon ordered Bernadotte to retreat towards Thorn, so as to draw on the enemy, whilst he himself would attack their rear. His dispatches were intercepted; and finally the Russians made a stand at Eylau, resolved to give battle in order to free Königsberg. The French troops under Soult drove them out of Eylau, and Napoleon believed them in full retreat, when the next day (February 7th), the Russians again attacked this town. The battle raged amidst a heavy fall of snow, the loss on both sides was immense, but the victory was undecided, though Benningsen retreated in good order towards Königsberg. There never was a more hideous field of battle fought in the depth of winter, amidst ice and snow. Even Ney shrugged his shoulders and said, "All this for nothing!" And Napoleon himself, perceiving his own troops to be very gloomy, shared in their emotion, and said, "What a curse is war . . ." "It might be said that no one was able to fight any more through cold, horror, and inability to stir. . . . Therefore the French declared themselves victorious, and remained masters of a field of dead bodies. On the evening after the battle, Napoleon invited the officers of the artillery, who had saved the army, to take supper with him. In order to arrive at the Emperor's quarters they had to pass between two heaps of bodies, limbs torn asunder, arms, heads—alas! those of their friends. It can easily be believed that no one had any appetite. But what was still more disgusting and sickened everybody was to find a bank-note in each of the table-napkins. Such was the delicacy of the Emperor. He paid ready cash for the death of their friends."[1]

Several of the fortresses in Silesia had already been taken by the French general, Vandamme, and Dantzic finally surrendered on the 27th of May.

Napoleon again prepared to take the offensive. The Russians had been foiled several times in their attacks on Soult and Bernadotte, and as the French troops had crossed the river Passarge, the former were obliged to fall back on the entrenched camp at Heilsberg, which was attacked by the French on the 10th of June. They had to withdraw amidst frightful loss on both sides, but Napoleon moved on the enemy's flanks and threatened his magazines, which compelled the Russians to evacuate their camp, and to establish themselves in front of Bartenstein. The superior military tactics of the French Emperor, however, forced the enemy to retreat by forced marches to Friedland, a town situated on the left bank of the river Alle, which there flows in a northern direction towards the Baltic. Benningsen crossed the river and attacked Lannes at Posthenen, a village about three miles from Friedland (June 14th); a fresh French corps, under Mortier, arrived to support the latter, and in spite of the vigour of the onset, the French held their ground.

[1] Michelet, *Histoire du XIX. siècle*, vol. iii., bk. iii., ch. 12.

Napoleon, who soon afterwards came on the field with the whole of his army, exclaimed, "This is the anniversary of Marengo; the battle could not be fought on a more propitious day." The order was given to advance, and amidst prodigious carnage Friedland was taken, and the Russians driven to retreat. A few days later Königsberg fell also into the hands of the French, but without magazines or stores of any importance.

As soon as the Russian Emperor Alexander saw the French on the Niemen, and threatening the Polish provinces of Russia, he resolved to ask for peace. A personal interview between the two Emperors, which lasted two hours, took place on a raft moored in the centre of the river Niemen, near Tilsit. Finally Alexander and Napoleon, as well as the King and Queen of Prussia, went to reside in Tilsit, and after a fortnight's conference the treaties, named after that town, were formally signed, the first treaty between France and Russia on the 7th, the second between France and Prussia on the 9th of July. By the first, the Emperor Napoleon, as a mark of his regard for the Emperor of Russia, agreed to restore to the King of Prussia Silesia and nearly all his German dominions on the right bank of the Elbe, with the fortresses on the Oder and in Pomerania. The Polish provinces of Prussia were erected into a Grand Duchy of Warsaw, and bestowed on the King of Saxony, with the exception of the province of Bialystock, containing two hundred thousand souls, which was ceded to Russia; Dantzic was declared a free and independent city; the Dukes of Oldenburg and Mecklenburg were reinstated in their dominions, but their harbours were occupied by French troops to prevent the introduction of English merchandise; the Prussian provinces on the left bank of the Elbe, with Hesse, Brunswick, and a part of Hanover, were erected, in favour of Jérôme Bonaparte, the Emperor's brother, into a kingdom of Westphalia, whilst Napoleon was accepted as mediator between Russia and Turkey. By the second treaty, the King of Prussia acceded to the stipulations of the first, closed his harbours to the ships and commerce of Great Britain, and consented to leave the fortresses in Silesia or on the Oder in the hands of France, as a security for the payment of the war-contributions, which amounted to over twenty-four million pounds sterling. A secret convention was also concluded between the French Emperor and the Russian Autocrat, by which it was agreed that France should unite with Russia to wrest from Turkey all its provinces in Europe, except Roumelia and Constantinople; and that Russia should make common cause with France against England if peace was not concluded by the 1st of November, on terms stipulating that the flags of every nation should enjoy a perfect and entire equality on every sea, whilst all the conquests made of French possessions since 1805 were to be restored. The Courts of Copenhagen, Stockholm, and Lisbon should also be summoned to close their harbours against English vessels. It is said that the two

Emperors entered upon a still more secret convention by which Moldavia, Wallachia, Bulgaria, and Servia were to be allotted to Russia, whilst Greece, Macedonia, Dalmatia, and all the sea-coasts of the Adriatic were to be given to France; princes of the family of Napoleon were to be placed on the Spanish and Portuguese thrones; and Russia was also to take Finland.

Thus Napoleon abandoned the principles of French politics; he considered the Turks and the Poles but as auxiliaries, and after having entered upon an engagement not to restore Poland, he even promised to aid in the dismembering of Turkey. All the glory and splendour belonged to the French Emperor, but all the profit of the interview accrued to Alexander, for the acquisition of Finland, the final consecration of the partition of Poland, and the ruin of the Turkish Empire, were of immense advantage to him, whilst the problematical thrones of Spain and Portugal not only did not give Napoleon any direct benefit, but were the first causes of his ruin. He had hoped to gain over and to dazzle Alexander, to bring him at any price to consent to the realisation of his grand dream, the destruction of England, and he had only nominally succeeded. The Czar promised everything, but left it to the future to decide if he should keep his promises.

CHAPTER III.

§ I.—THE DECAY OF IMPERIALISM.

(*From the 7th of July,* 1807, *to the* 14*th of October,* 1809.)

THE Revolution had been in existence only twenty years, and already the whole of Europe was overturned. The French Empire had a population of forty millions, and the Federal States, which were grouped around it, were peopled by an equal number. The Emperor seemed to be firmly established on his throne, the public confidence was unshaken; the Princes and monarchs of Europe who appeared in succession at his court, dazzled the eyes of the multitude; the halo of his military glory prevented the view of internal misery; the grandeur and supremacy of the French nation compensated for the absence of liberty; and the despotic head of the State governed nations, as well as potentates, with a rod of iron. Napoleon's activity did not slacken; he directed all the affairs of the State, whilst giving grand entertainments; he held councils, travelled far and near, and had the most magnificent court in Europe, whilst he restored palaces, planned monuments, and protected letters, arts, and above all sciences. New industries sprung up under his reign; beet-root sugar replaced cane-sugar; madder became extensively cultivated; spinning and weaving machines were invented, and large sums were spent on public works. But all this grandeur was erected without sufficient foundation, and, therefore, could not last. France had not a single ally, whilst in the north and in the south, Russia and Spain were her enemies, though disguising their feelings of hatred under the mask of alliances. The conscription was exhausting the population, the finances did no longer work regularly, the army became gradually more despotic, and, in short, the whole fabric of the State rested only on the life of one man.

After the battles of Jena and Friedland, Napoleon suppressed the Tribunate (September 18th, 1807), which was replaced by three Committees of the Legislative Body, each composed of seven members; a new nobility with high-sounding titles was organised (March 1st, 1808); the grand dignitaries of the Empire received the title of Princes; the ministers, the senators, the councillors of State, the President of the Legislative Body, and the archbishops became Counts; the presidents of the different courts, the bishops, and the mayors of thirty-seven large towns, Barons; and the members of the Legion of Honour, Knights. Those titles could be transmitted upon certain conditions, whilst the Emperor reserved to himself the right of admitting into the new nobility those men who, in his opinion, had deserved it. Now he began to distribute dignities, titles, money, and estates, not only to his victorious generals, but even to former Jacobins. He thought, by acting thus, to reconcile ancient to modern France, to favour the fusion of the former nobility with the nation; but he was mistaken. The aristocratic *émigrés* ridiculed the bearing and behaviour of the Imperial nobles, who strutted about, flaunting the rags of the *ancien régime*, which did not even become them. Moreover, foreign nations mocked the crowned adventurer, who thought to create a nobility with fortunate soldiers and renegade and apostate partisans of the Revolution.

All the creations of that period, though excellent in themselves, bore a despotic impress. The censure of the press was made more stringent; by the final organisation of the University (March 17th, 1808), the freedom of instruction became entirely destroyed, and education was based on "fidelity to the Imperial monarchy, the depository of the happiness of the people, and to the dynasty of Napoleon, the preserver of the unity of France, and of all the Liberal ideas proclaimed by the Constitution." The Penal Code and the institution of the jury became entirely changed, so that there were less guarantees for personal liberty. A court was established to verify the income and expenses of the State, and to audit the public accounts; but from this auditing was excepted the private domain of the Emperor, which had then already risen to four hundred millions of francs. However, the splendour of the Peace of Tilsit dazzled every one, and France, which had formerly worshipped on the altar of liberty, now prostrated itself before the altar of glory.

The English Government, having become aware that the French Emperor was going to seize the Danish fleet, resolved to forestall him. It sent a formidable armament and a large fleet to the harbour of

Copenhagen, and demanded every ship belonging to the Danish navy, promising that at the conclusion of the general peace it should be restored to Denmark. This demand was refused, whereupon the British troops disembarked without meeting with any resistance, and the town was invested. The artillery was landed, a summons to deliver up the fleet was made anew, and this being again rejected, the bombardment began, and was continued for nearly three days and nights. Part of the city was set on fire, and the Danes had no alternative left but to sign a capitulation (September 7th, 1807). Early in October the British fleet and army returned to England, bringing with them eighteen Danish ships of the line, fifteen frigates, six brigs, and twenty-five gunboats. The Danish Government had immediately all English subjects living on its territory arrested, confiscated their property, and concluded an alliance with France, which was broken only on the downfall of Napoleon. Russia declared that the seizure of the Danish fleet was "an act of violence of which history, so fertile in wickedness, does not afford a parallel example." It broke off all diplomatic relations with England until satisfaction should have been given to Denmark. Prussia and even Austria were obliged to act in the same manner, and finally Napoleon, by a decree dated from Milan, December 17th, 1807, declared that "every vessel, of whatever nation, which shall have submitted to be searched by British cruisers, or paid any impost levied by the British Government, shall be considered as having lost the privileges of a neutral flag, and be regarded and dealt with as an English vessel !"

The Turkish Sultan Selim, having been replaced by his nephew, Mustapha IV. (May 29th, 1807), the new Sultan signed an armistice with the Russians, who continued to occupy Moldavia and Wallachia, and even refused to evacuate it on the solicitation of Napoleon; whilst at the same time they invaded Finland, which, later on, was ceded to Russia (September 17th, 1809). The harmony between the Pope and the French Emperor was also not of long duration, and at last the French troops entered Rome (February 2nd, 1808). Two months afterwards an Imperial decree annexed several of the Papal provinces to the Kingdom of Italy, on the ground "that the actual sovereign of Rome had constantly declined to declare war against the English, and to coalesce with the Kings of Italy and Naples for the defence of the Italian peninsula." The Papal troops were incorporated with the French army, the cardinals were sent to their respective dioceses, and the authority of the Pope was confined within certain narrow bounds. Public opinion declared itself generally in favour of Pius VII., who showed great resignation, whilst Napoleon alternated between violence and moderation.

Spain, since the reign of Louis XIV. the ally of France, had remained faithful to that alliance, even after the Bourbons had descended from the French throne. But when Napoleon was waging war with Prussia, the Prime Minister, Manuel Godoy, the Prince of Peace, the favourite of the old King Charles IV., and, above all, of his wife, had been informed of the intended spoliation of Spain, and had published two proclamations (October, 1806), "in which he invited all Spaniards to unite themselves under the national standards .... to enable the nation to enter with glory in the lists which were preparing." After the battle of Jena the Prime Minister offered some excuses, and only obtained his pardon by sending a contingent of fourteen thousand Spanish troops to the shores of the Baltic to join Bernadotte. But by this time Napoleon had clearly perceived that he could no longer reckon on a Spanish alliance, and that the Spaniards would attack him in his rear whilst he should be engaged in a war with Germany. He, therefore, resolved to make the Peninsular monarchies French, either by reforming them, by giving them monarchs of his own choice, or by annexing the Spanish provinces north of the Ebro; and to give Portugal as a compensation to Spain. After the Convention of Tilsit, the French Emperor summoned the Court of Lisbon to shut her ports against England. The British Cabinet advised compliance with this demand; but Napoleon perceived that he was being temporised with. He sent Junot, at the head of twenty-five thousand men, to reduce the Portuguese to submission, and the approach of the French to the capital had the desired effect. The Portugeuse Prince Regent declared war against England; but it seems probable that this step also was taken with the connivance of the latter country. Before Junot could make his way across the mountains, the royal family of Portugal, accompanied by fifteen thousand Portuguese nobles and wealthy gentlemen, had quitted Lisbon for Brazil, and the English had taken possession of the fleet.

Napoleon pushed his designs against Spain with great vigour, and found a ready instrument for his intrigues in Ferdinand, the son of the King, and Prince of the Asturias, who actually asked the French Emperor to assist him in his ambitious schemes. The latter could have wished for no better pretext of interference, and he forthwith sent Dupont with twenty-eight thousand men across the frontier. These were soon followed by an equal force under Moncey, by ten thousand under Duhesme, and by further contingents at brief intervals, whilst a new levy of eighty thousand men was ordered in France. Charles IV. and Godoy could do little or nothing against this display of force. The French, placed under the command of Murat, seized all the strong positions south of the Pyrenees, and on the northeastern coast; and on the 1st of March, Napoleon plainly declared his intention to annex the provinces between the mountains and the Ebro, for which he offered Portugal as a compensation. Godoy seemed disposed to accept this bargain; but on second thoughts he advised the King and Queen to flee before the impending storm. Preparations were actually being made for a migration to America, when the popular indignation was roused by the news. At Aranjuez,

where the Court was then assembled, the party of
Ferdinand took advantage of the feeling to provoke
an outbreak. The royal residence was besieged,
Godoy's house was attacked, and Charles IV. was
compelled to abandon his project, and to dismiss
his Minister. Ferdinand pressed his advantage, and,
in the end, the King abdicated in favour of his
son.

The accession of Ferdinand VII. was hailed by the
Spanish people with enthusiastic applause, and in the
meanwhile Murat marched upon Madrid. The populace
received him with open arms (March 23rd), and
Charles and Ferdinand both appealed to him to take
them under his protection. At last the aged King
retracted his abdication, and wrote to Napoleon accusing
his son of treachery. The Emperor advised his Marshal
to temporise, and betook himself to Bayonne, probably intending to continue his journey to the Spanish
capital. If that had been in his mind, it was rendered
unnecessary by the abject conduct of the two claimants
to the throne. First the son, and then the father, came
personally to sue for the Emperor's recognition. Napoleon, without any idea of permitting the restoration of
the father, demanded that the son should renounce his
claims to the throne. This Ferdinand at first refused;
and whilst Napoleon was meditating upon his next
step, a sanguinary revolt broke out in Madrid. It
was not suppressed without much bloodshed; and the
effect of the news at Bayonne was to make the
Emperor yet more sternly demand the abdication of

Ferdinand, who was finally obliged to comply. As a matter of form, Napoleon offered to replace Charles IV. upon the throne; but the King was disenchanted by all that had happened. He also signed his final abdication (May 5th), which was acquiesced in by his two sons. Under the inspiration of Murat, the Spanish Government at Madrid offered the throne to Joseph Bonaparte, who was already King of Naples and Sicily, a crown which was, later on, given to Murat.

It is worthy of remark that Napoleon subsequently, in his exile at St. Helena, attributed the beginning of his disasters to the intrigues by which he drove the Bourbons from Spain.

The revolt of the Spaniards spread. The whole people rose in indignation against the treachery of their rulers, and the presumption of the invaders. This insurrection was hailed with acclamation in England, which had long been waiting for a new opportunity to strike a blow at Napoleon. An alliance was forthwith concluded between Great Britain and the Spanish juntas, and in the course of the year 1808 the former country provided the Spaniards with three millions sterling, and two hundred thousand muskets.

In the meantime the Spanish patriots themselves were not idle. Murat delayed his assumption of the purple in Naples in order to direct the movement of the French forces. After a few minor successes obtained by the French, the Spaniards were beaten in Castile; and they made no better stand in Galicia and Valencia. But at Baylen the French under Dupont suffered a notable defeat. Fifteen thousand regulars and twice as many irregulars, commanded by Castaños, who had received his orders from the supreme junta of Seville, managed to surround Dupont, who had only twelve thousand men. The French general was obliged to capitulate, including in his surrender ten thousand troops under General Vedel, whom Murat had sent to his assistance (July 20th). The consequence of this disaster was that the scattered French forces fell back upon Madrid, Duhesme was besieged in Barcelona, Joseph Bonaparte fled from the capital, whilst even Junot found his position in Portugal untenable.

It was now the turn of the Portuguese to rise against the invader; and England at once came to the aid of the insurgents. Sir Arthur Wellesley, who had landed at Oporto on the 26th of July, went with the expedition to Mondego Bay, where he arrived four days later, and advanced, with fifteen thousand men, upon Lisbon. Junot attacked the English forces, now sixteen thousand strong, at Vimiera (August 21st), with such ill-success as to compel him to retire upon the defiles of Torres Vedras. The defeat at Baylen had shut off his retreat into Spain, and he therefore proposed to evacuate Portugal, on condition that his army should be sent back to France by sea, with all the arms, baggage, and artillery, threatening to lay the capital in ruins if his terms were not complied with. The English thought fit to agree to this, and the Convention of Cintra, erroneously so called, was signed (August 30th), and carried out, greatly to the dissatisfaction of public opinion in England, which bitterly reproached Sir Hew Dalrymple for concluding such a compact.

Napoleon would doubtless have come to the rescue of his armies in the Peninsula if it had not been for the disquieting news of the armaments of Austria, which was busily stirring up the whole of Central Europe against her enemy. Under these circumstances it became necessary for the French Emperor to cultivate good relations with Russia, and to this end he arranged a meeting with the Czar Alexander at Erfurth (September 27th). The Czar had set his heart upon gaining possession of Constantinople; but Napoleon was not prepared to pay so high a price for the Russian alliance. He agreed, however, to a scheme whereby the Czar was to appropriate Finland, Moldavia, and Wallachia, in return for which Alexander was to guarantee an army of one hundred and fifty thousand men, in the event of an Austro-French war. Simultaneously with the signature of this Convention, the Czar secretly assured England of his continued attachment to the cause of European independence. From Erfurth the two Emperors offered a termination of hostilities to the Government of Great Britain; but the latter power refused to negotiate on any other basis than the restitution of Naples and Spain to the Bourbon dynasties.

The fear of an immediate attack from Austria was removed by this meeting of the Emperors; and

Napoleon carried his grand army from Germany across the Pyrenees. On this occasion he induced the Senate to grant him one hundred and sixty thousand men, of the old and new levies. His brother Joseph had taken up his residence at Vittoria, where a French army of a hundred thousand men was assembled. Hither came Napoleon with his veterans and his new conscripts; and within a few weeks the Spaniards were beaten and cut to pieces at Burgos, at Espinosa, at Tudela, at Madrid. An English force of about twenty thousand men, under Sir John Moore, was on its way to aid in the defence of the Spanish capital, when an intercepted despatch made the English general acquainted with the fall of that town. It became, therefore, necessary to save the army by a rapid retreat, and Moore at once fell back towards Corunna, being hard pressed by Soult, and by Napoleon himself. It was a desperate march for the English. They lost most of their artillery, and much of their baggage. Many thousand men died of fatigue, disease, and the severity of the winter; but the remainder escaped from their pursuers. Napoleon, once more alarmed by the news from Austria, resigned the direction of the pursuit to Soult, and departed from Spain. The Marshal succeeded in forcing a battle on the English at the moment when they came in sight of Corunna (January 16th, 1809). Sir John Moore died in action; but his retreat had been so far a triumph that it enabled the survivors to take ship and embark with all the sick, wounded, artillery, stores, and even prisoners, three days before the fall of the town.

Meanwhile Saragossa was being besieged by Lannes, directing the corps of Mortier and Moncey. Palafox, at the head of a garrison of irregular troops and undisciplined volunteers, heroically defended the city for fifty days in open trenches, and for six weeks in desperate conflicts, during which first the walls, then the streets and houses, were successively contested. It capitulated on the 21st of February, and as many as sixty thousand human beings are said to have fallen on both sides in the course of this sanguinary siege.

The success of the French was now complete. They had regained the whole country, re-entered Madrid, driven the English contingents from Spanish soil, and bade fair to re-establish Joseph Bonaparte more firmly than ever. But in the meantime affairs had grown to a head in Central Europe. Austria's efforts were bearing fruit, and Napoleon's enemies were assuming more and more boldness in his absence. England, too, had sent a hundred million francs to provide sinews of war for the new Coalition. Prussia, and even Russia, in spite of the Erfurth meeting, made contingent promises of assistance.

Leaving his brother Joseph in charge of the army in Spain, with Marshal Jourdan as his major-general, Napoleon returned to France and prepared to meet the Austrian Coalition. He ordered Davoust from the north of Germany, with forty-five thousand men, to advance upon Bamberg, whilst Masséna, with fifty thousand, marched from Ulm to Augsburg. Berthier was provisionally appointed to the chief command, and Marmont, Poniatowski, Prince Eugène Beauharnais, and Bernadotte approached with auxiliary forces from various directions. There were in all two hundred thousand men at the immediate disposal of Berthier, whilst about a hundred thousand more were ready to cross the frontiers. The levy of the Austrians, *en masse*, had raised the strength of their army to three hundred and ten thousand men, of whom a hundred and seventy-five thousand were in Germany, under the Archduke Charles; twenty-five thousand in the Tyrol, under Jellachich; fifty thousand in Italy, under the Archduke John; twenty thousand in Dalmatia, under Giulay; and forty thousand in Galicia, under the Archduke Ferdinand.

The French Emperor had ordered Berthier, in case of attack, to concentrate his forces on the right bank of the Danube, between Augsburg and Donauwörth; but he either misunderstood or neglected this order, and left his divisions scattered over a great extent and on both sides of the river. Davoust was virtually surrounded at Ratisbon, and if the Archduke Charles had displayed greater genius or vigour, the French would probably have suffered a severe defeat. The Emperor saw the danger, and hastened to place himself at the head of his troops. He at once made a fresh distribution of the various corps, and concentrated one hundred and twenty thousand men upon Abensberg, where, after several days' fighting with the Austrian general, Hiller, who was driven back upon Landshut, he cut off the left wing from Charles's army. Masséna, advancing on the right bank of the river, compelled Hiller to fall back still farther, with a loss of ten thousand prisoners and almost as many killed. Meanwhile Archduke Charles, having taken Ratisbon, slowly advanced, in the expectation of being joined by Hiller. But encountering Davoust near Eckmühl, he offered battle, and Napoleon, taking him suddenly in the rear, defeated him with a loss of five thousand dead, and fifteen thousand prisoners. The Archduke retired to Ratisbon, whither the French Emperor immediately followed him. The town was attacked and taken; but Charles, cutting the bridge over the river, escaped into Bohemia with the bulk of his army. In the five days' fighting between the 17th and the 22nd of April, the French took many thousand prisoners, a hundred guns, forty standards, and three thousand caissons.

Napoleon now had a march of sixty leagues before him to the Austrian capital. Hiller made a desperate stand at Ebersberg, in order to give the Archduke time to cross to the right bank of the Danube, and after a terrible massacre, in which he lost one-fourth of his army of thirty thousand men, and the French about the same number, he joined Charles with the remains of his force at Zwettel. Meanwhile Napoleon pushed on to Vienna, which he reached, with Masséna and Lannes, in the second week of May. After a bombardment of a few hours, the capital surrendered on the 13th of May, and Bernadotte simultaneously defeated a detachment of the Archduke's army at Lintz.

The great bridge at Vienna had been burnt, and it became necessary for Napoleon to cross the Danube in the face of a hundred thousand men. He himself had only sixty thousand; though Davoust was coming up with his corps, whilst Bernadotte and Vandamme held the banks of the river as far as Passau. The Emperor selected for his point of crossing a spot some few leagues from the capital, where the Danube, of considerable width, is divided into four branches. A bridge of boats having been constructed, forty thousand Frenchmen crossed the stream, and took up their position in the villages of Aspern and Essling, on the plain of the Marchfeld. Here they were suddenly attacked by the Austrians, who outnumbered them by more than two to one, and who concentrated upon them the fire of two hundred cannon. The Danube was heavily swollen by the rains, and at the commencement of the fight the bridge was broken. Lannes and Masséna defended the villages throughout the day, and retained possession of them at night. By the next morning Napoleon had repaired the disaster, and sent over three divisions, whilst Davoust was ready to follow with the artillery. The Emperor himself assumed the offensive with sixty thousand men, and the Austrian centre had already given way before the impetuous attack, when the bridge was once more swept away. The ammunition of the French was all but exhausted, and Napoleon was obliged to order a retreat upon Essling. Six times in the course of that day the two villages were taken and retaken, the

French being almost restricted to the use of the bayonet. After a sanguinary struggle, during which Lannes was killed, the night again found the French troops in possession of Aspern and Essling; but it was impossible to maintain the ground under such conditions. The army was taken back across the Danube (May 22nd), Masséna holding the Archduke in check; and Lobau, the largest of the islands in the river, was retained until an opportunity should occur for a fresh attempt.

The news of this partial victory of the Austrians inspired the Coalition with fresh courage. Prussia ordered a levy of a hundred thousand troops; England engaged to land forty thousand men in Northern Germany. Meanwhile Napoleon took a rest of six weeks. On the 17th of May, from the Palace of Schönbrunn, he issued a decree annexing the Roman States to the Empire, for which he was excommunicated by Pius VII. on the 20th of June. By Murat's orders the Pope was taken prisoner, and confined in Grenoble, from whence Napoleon had him transferred to Savona.

In the meanwhile the French had fortified the island of Lobau, which they had connected by four bridges with the right bank of the river; and three other bridges were ready to be thrown across to the northern bank, so as to take the Austrian defences in the rear. Davoust, Eugène Beauharnais, and Marmont had joined the Emperor, whose army was thus brought up to a strength of a hundred and fifty thousand men. The Austrians were reinforced to the number of a hundred and seventy-five thousand, and rested upon the villages of Aspern, Essling, and Enzersdorf, protected by redoubts mounting a hundred and fifty guns. Napoleon made a show of his intention to cross again at the same point as before, and actually threw two bridges on the bank in front of Aspern; but on the night of the 5th of July, amidst a violent artillery fire against Enzersdorf, the whole army crossed from the extreme east of the long island of Lobau. Napoleon thus took the Austrians on the flank, turning the defensive works which they had constructed with so much labour; and the Archduke was compelled to fall back with his troops, behind the Russbach, on Wagram. The French followed them, and at nightfall the two armies faced each other.

On the next day, July 6th, Napoleon began the attack, with Beauharnais, Oudinot, and Marmont in the centre, Masséna and Bernadotte on the left, and Davoust on the right. The Archduke's right drove back Bernadotte, and took Essling from Masséna, thus threatening the bridges; but Davoust succeeded in crossing the Russbach. As soon as Napoleon saw these troops appear, he exclaimed, "The battle is gained!" and immediately sent forward to the attack twenty-one battalions and a hundred guns, supported by two divisions of cavalry and the Guard. Not without great loss, this column pushed back the centre of the Austrians; and the Archduke, who personally commanded the right, was obliged to fall back from Essling. Meanwhile Davoust advanced on Wagram; and the enemy, his line being completely broken, retreated in good order, leaving twenty-five thousand men upon the field. The loss of the French was scarcely inferior. Napoleon pursued the Austrians, and overtook them at Znaym, where, instead of risking another battle, the Archduke proposed an armistice. So ended the fifth Coalition against the Emperor.

The remainder of the year 1809 was distinguished by the unfortunate expedition of forty thousand English troops to Walcheren, of which the object was to destroy the French armaments at Antwerp, and by desultory fighting, without great results, in the Peninsula. Sir Arthur Wellesley, who had been busy reorganising his army at Lisbon, compelled Soult, whom Napoleon had charged with driving the English out of Spain and Portugal, to fall back, in a retreat no less disastrous, and no less glorious, than that of Sir John Moore. Soult managed to join Ney at Lugo (May 29th), but, unable to agree with his brother marshal, he soon left him again; and the latter was obliged to fall back. The jealousy displayed towards Soult by the other French generals produced more than one unfortunate result in the Peninsular campaigns. Sir Arthur Wellesley, after shaking off Soult in Portugal, determined to advance into Spain, and to threaten the capital; and, whilst Beresford and Del Parque, with a strong force of Spaniards, kept the French occupied on the Douro, he made his way as far as Talavera. Joseph Bonaparte set out from Madrid, and, with the army of Victor and Sébastiani, went to meet Wellesley, whilst Soult was ordered to join the divisions of Ney and Mortier, and to fall upon the flank and rear of the English. But the two last-named generals were slow to carry out this arrangement, and the consequence was that Joseph attacked the English without their assistance, and was badly beaten, with a loss of ten thousand men (July 27th and 28th). For this victory Sir Arthur Wellesley was created Baron Douro of Wellesley and Viscount Wellington of Talavera.

The Spanish King retired, leaving Victor, with the bulk of his forces, behind; and the English commander, hearing of the advance of Soult with a very large force, thought it prudent to recross the Tagus, and make for Portugal. French military authors pretend that there was a moment during this retreat when the French might have had the Allies at their mercy; but Soult's advice was not followed to march with ninety thousand men at once on Coria and Lisbon, and during the whole of the campaign such an opportunity never again occurred. These authors also believe, that if Napoleon had been in Spain, he might, perhaps, have subjected for a while the whole Peninsula, and have driven the English temporarily out of the country. He was otherwise engaged, and his marshals were unequal to the task in his absence.

It was not until the 14th of October that the peace

negotiations were concluded at Vienna. By this treaty Austria ceded Istria, Croatia, and Carniola to France, Saltzburg and the surrounding districts to Bavaria, Western Galicia to the Duke of Warsaw, and a part of Eastern Galicia to Russia. The Emperor Francis recognised Joseph as King of Spain, agreed to limit his army to one hundred and fifty thousand men, and to pay £3,400,000 as a war indemnity. The defences of Vienna were levelled to the ground, and the resistance of Central Europe was crushed for more than five years to come.

§ II.—THE LAST YEARS OF THE EMPIRE.

(From the 15th of October, 1809, till the 9th of March, 1813.)

BONAPARTE was wont to declare in the most solemn manner that his great aim was to live at peace with his neighbours, and to consolidate the Empire to which he had attained. It has, indeed, been plausibly argued by some of those who incline to the most favourable view of his character, that many of the great wars in which he was engaged were the results of hostile Coalitions against him, rather than of new aggressive schemes on his own part. For instance, he did not court the war against Austria, last recorded; and excuses have even been found for his conduct in the Spanish dynastic quarrels. It has been said that he frequently expressed a wish that he could devote himself to the arts of peace, to the encouragement of the national industries, and the development of social life in France. And, in fact, the arts of peace did flourish, strange as the paradox may seem, in the midst of the Emperor's warlike enterprises. The French Court was splendid and magnificent, its example of display set a fashion throughout the country, and did much to extend the refinement and polish, hitherto confined amongst the wealthier classes, to all grades of Frenchmen. Vast sums of money were spent on public monuments, and on artistic achievements of every kind. In 1810, there was appropriated to public works a sum of a hundred and thirty-eight million francs; and in the following year this large amount was increased by sixteen millions.

In order to strengthen his dynasty, as well as to add brilliance to his court, the Emperor determined to separate from his childless wife Josephine, and to marry into one of the reigning families of Europe. Though the Empress was extremely popular with the French people, he was divorced, first by a decree of the Senate, and next by the municipal authorities of Paris. On the 2nd of April, 1810, he took to wife Maria Louisa, a daughter of the Emperor Francis of Austria, who was received in France with effusive demonstrations of enthusiasm. This act was, in one sense, the acme of Napoleon's triumph. The Continent was virtually at peace, in spite of the continued disturbances in Spain. The authority of the Emperor was acknowledged from the Baltic to the Mediterranean. Rome, Naples, Amsterdam, and Madrid had fallen into his hands. England, to all appearance, was being gradually ruined by her exclusion from Continental trade; and Russia, though less subservient than her western neighbours, was yet afraid of uttering a hostile word against the mighty despot. France was enabled to recover from her more open and conspicuous wounds. In 1810 the expenditure of so vast an Empire fell as low as seven hundred and forty million francs; and there were even calm and sensible men in. every country of Europe who perceived in the home government and social condition of the Empire a wise and beneficent rule. To crown the glory and the hopes of Napoleon, a child was born to him on the 20th of March, 1811, on whom its father, in his overweening pride, bestowed the title of the King of Rome.

Meanwhile the royal creatures of the Emperor, his brothers and his marshals—Louis, King of Holland; Jérôme, King of Westphalia; Joseph, King of Spain; Murat, King of Naples; Bernadotte, Crown Prince and subsequently King of Sweden—had all more or less begun to identify themselves with the spirit of their peoples, and to play an independent part which caused Napoleon no little embarrassment. Especially was this the case with Louis and Jérôme, and with the Swedish Crown Prince. The King of Holland shared even the animosity of the Dutch against the French, or permitted its display at his court; and he counteracted the anti-English policy of his brother by not suppressing the contraband trade between Holland and England, whereby the former country became a kind of warehouse for English goods. Napoleon called him severely to task for this conduct, and finally demanded that he should come to Paris. After heaping reproaches upon him, he exacted his signature to a treaty, by which Holland engaged to break off all intercourse with England. The whole Dutch territories on the left bank of the Rhine, including the isles of Walcheren, South Beveland, and Cadsand, were ceded to France, and eighteen thousand French troops were despatched to guard the coast. A few months later (July 9th), on the abdication of Louis, Holland was formally annexed as well as the bulk of the Kingdom of Westphalia, including the towns of Hamburg, Bremen, and Lubeck. "A new order of things," said Napoleon himself, "dominates the universe. Fresh guarantees having become necessary for me, the union of the mouths of the Scheldt, Meuse, Rhine, Ems, Weser, and Elbe with the Empire appeared to me to be the first and most important of these." Davoust was selected to preside over these new departments, the appropriation of which excited the greatest indignation in Europe generally, whilst it was a severe blow struck against England in particular.

Joseph himself, recently as he had been lifted to the throne of Spain, was already meditating an alliance with England; and he entered into negotiations with the insurgent Spanish leaders. The Emperor replied to this ingratitude, as he naturally considered it, by placing many of the Spanish provinces under the control of his generals, with the express intention of preparing them for union with France. Joseph tendered his abdication; but his brother preferred to keep him in Spain, rather than increase the difficulties of the situation. Soult, Ney, and Kellermann continued to gain isolated and barren successes over the insurgents, whilst Wellington for a long time held aloof in Portugal; and Napoleon, retained in France by his marriage, and by the many cares of his Empire, began to see that a more united and determined effort would be necessary before the English could be expelled from the Peninsula.

The beginning of 1810 found Masséna at the head of sixty thousand men marching upon the western kingdom by way of Ciudad Rodrigo; whilst about sixty-five thousand troops under Joseph and Soult were directed to converge with the same purpose by way of Badajoz. These latter took upon themselves to neglect the Emperor's advice, and marched southwards into Andalusia, where they defeated the insurgents on several occasions, but did not succeed in reaching Cadiz and Gibraltar. Wellington remained unmoved on the frontier, fortifying the approaches to the capital, and training his Portuguese allies. Meanwhile Masséna, deprived of the assistance of Soult, occupied his three divisions, under Junot, Reynier, and Ney, against Astorga, the province of Estremadura, and Ciudad Rodrigo, the French being successful in each case. Uniting his forces, the Marshal advanced upon Almeida, captured it, and threatened the English army, which fell back upon the summit of the ridge of the mountain-range of Busaco, commanding the Coimbra road. The

French attacked this position, and were repulsed with a loss of five thousand men killed and wounded (September 27th), upon which they turned the British left, and reached Coimbra. Wellington at the same time established himself in the lines of Torres Vedras, devastating the country behind him, and ordering the inhabitants to seek refuge in the capital. It was now that the English commander reaped the benefit of his long preparations. The lines of Torres Vedras, in Portuguese Estremadura, nearly thirty miles north of Lisbon, stretched between the Tagus and the sea. The outer line ran from Alhandra, on the Tagus, to the sea-coast; the second was about eight miles in the rear of the first, and the inner one was merely intended to allow the army to embark on board the fleet in the Tagus, if this were necessary. These lines consisted of three distinct ranges of defence, protected by a hundred and fifty redoubts, with six hundred guns, and held by one hundred and thirty thousand men, of whom thirty thousand were English troops.

In the middle of October Masséna arrived in sight of these lines, remained before them for nearly a month, and on the 14th of November retired to Santarem, which he fortified. Wellington first took up a position in front of him. For nearly four months the armies faced each other. Wellington drew abundant supplies from Lisbon, and from the English fleet, whilst Masséna had the greatest difficulty in providing his troops with food, which they were obliged to seek from a hostile country, within a circuit of fifty miles, and perpetually harassed by the Portuguese. Drouet, with twelve thousand men, swelled the French army to something like seventy thousand; and meanwhile Soult was doing his best to reach the position from the south, along the left bank of the Tagus. The capture of Olivenza and Badajoz detained him till the 10th of March, 1811; and then a sortie on a grand scale from Gibraltar and Cadiz compelled him to return to Andalusia.

Masséna found himself at the end of his resources, and on the 4th of March he was obliged to commence his retreat towards Spain. Wellington dashed after him without a moment's delay, and drove him to Coimbra, and thence to Almeida. The disaffection of Masséna's troops rendered it impossilbe for him to hold the latter town, and he fell back upon Ciudad Rodrigo. Here he found reinforcements, and turning round upon Wellington, attacked him on the plain of Fuentes de Onoro, where he was beaten (May 5th). Seeing this, the Governor of Almeida blew up his fortifications in the night, and cut his way through the English lines to join the force of Masséna.

At the same time Beresford and the Portuguese army assumed the offensive, re-took Olivenza and laid siege to Badajoz. Soult came to the assistance of the latter town with twenty thousand men, but, after a doubtful battle at Albuera, was obliged to retire, whilst Wellington joined his colleague and threw fresh life into the investment. Marmont, replacing the unfortunate Masséna, now joined the forces of Soult, and

Drouet coming up at the same moment, the English were obliged to raise the siege of Badajoz, and retire once more across the frontier (June 18th).

Soult now returned to Andalusia, where the garrison of Gibraltar had caused another diversion, and Marmont, left alone, forced Wellington to raise the siege of Ciudad Rodrigo, and then went into winter-quarters at Salamanca. The English general thereupon suddenly attacked Ciudad Rodrigo (January 19th), and Badajoz (April 6th), both which towns were taken by assault. Some little time before these victories of the English on the Portuguese frontier, Suchet, in the east of Spain, had reaped important successes over the Allies, especially in the capture of the fortress of Saguntum, or Murviedro, and in the taking of Valentia, where Blake and twenty thousand men were made prisoners (December 26th, 1811).

During the whole of this time Napoleon's policy of closing the Continent to England had thrown this country into the gravest embarrassment. English trade was brought to the verge of ruin, her debt had increased enormously, and her government was surrounded by vast difficulties and dangers. In spite of Wellington's successes, and his preparations for carrying the war into the heart of the Peninsula, it appeared to Napoleon, and not unnaturally, that his good fortune was at its very zenith, when a new and fatal disaster was prepared for him at the eastern extremity of the Continent. "The English aristocracy," as M. Lavallée somewhat vaguely puts it, "aroused amidst the frozen ice-plains of the north the great enemy of France, the enemy most opposed to her in every idea, principle, interest, the enemy whose hatred and antagonism Napoleon had so blindly conceived that he had disarmed by the greatest sacrifices. Russia was on the point of taking up arms, never to lay them down again until after the defeat of Napoleon, of France, of the Revolution."[1]

Russia had never forgiven Napoleon for the aggrandisement of the Duchy of Warsaw, which the Czar described as thenceforth destined to become the Kingdom of Poland. This aggrandisement, in fact, though it may have been prompted by nothing more than a desire to humiliate and weaken Austria, was one of the most beneficial acts of the French Emperor in the plenitude of his power and authority, and no doubt Napoleon would have completed the restoration of the divided kingdom, if he had succeeded in reducing Russia to submission. Already at the beginning of the year 1810, as the result of certain negotiations entered into between the two monarchs, with a view to removing the irritation existing between them, Napoleon consented to renounce all idea of friendship for Poland. It was proposed to sign a convention for this purpose, and the Czar suggested for the first clause the following laconic words: "The Kingdom of Poland shall never be restored." Napoleon substituted for this: "The Emperor of the French binds himself not to favour any enterprise calculated to re-establish the Kingdom of Poland,

[1] *Histoire des Français*, vol. iv., ch. iv., § 6.

not to give any assistance to any Power having this end in view, nor any support, direct or indirect, to any insurrection of the provinces constituting that kingdom." The Czar refused to accept this alteration, and continued the correspondence in a bitter tone.[1] Eventually he suffered it to drop; but on the annexation of Holland and the Duchies he threw off the mask. On the last day of 1810 he abandoned the "Continental system" directed in the main against England, and prohibited the import of French goods. Napoleon had warned him that friendship for England meant war with France, and the Czar had no other idea in his mind. He assembled large forces on the western frontiers of his Empire, and waited the result.

Napoleon was enraged, but did not at once declare war. He even offered Erfurth to the Czar as a solatium for the Duchy of Oldenburg, the Duke of the last-named state being Alexander's brother-in-law. The Czar declined. He was constantly urged to take up the cause of Europe against Napoleon by England and by his own nobles, and nothing would have availed to restore the good understanding of the two Emperors.

Up to the spring of 1812 the time was occupied by preparations for war, and by the effort to secure alliances on both sides. Russia was openly promised

---

[1] The bitterness was aggravated by Napoleon's marriage with Maria Louisa. He had previously proposed for a sister of Alexander's, but the negotiations were broken off because the Empress Dowager pretended that the princess was too young.

assistance by the English Cabinet, and secretly by other governments. The King of Prussia, choosing what he held to be the lesser of two evils, hastened to offer an army of twenty thousand men to Napoleon, and the latter accepted this alliance for what it was worth, sending Victor with thirty thousand men to insure a safe passage for his troops through Berlin. Austria also engaged to provide a contingent of thirty thousand men. Napoleon was less successful with Sweden and Turkey, which, from their position in regard to Russia, would have been immensely serviceable to him. In the former country the Crown Prince, Bernadotte, had shown a disposition to rebel against the blockade of the Continent, and did not suppress the contraband trade of his merchants. As soon as he understood that his aid would be valuable to France, he tried to strike a bargain, and asked for the annexation of Norway. Napoleon refused, and occupied Pomerania with a small force on the 27th of January. Upon this, Bernadotte immediately accepted the Anglo-Russian alliance. With Turkey the negotiations proceeded more slowly. The Porte had been at war with Russia for some time past; but English influence and English money secured its neutrality.

At that time, during the reign of the first Napoleon, every Power of Europe had to be considered and negotiated with previous to an outbreak of hostilities. There was scarcely any such thing as a conflict between two nations in the earlier years of the present century; and hence every war was European. No one country could take up arms without anticipating that Coalitions on either side might set ablaze the whole Continent. When alliances were not avowed, they were entered upon in secret; when assistance was not given in the shape of men, it was given in money—especially in the case of England. And it happened in many instances, as in those of Prussia and Austria at the period now in question, that open promises were made to one belligerent, and secret promises to another.

Diplomacy having performed its work, Napoleon felt himself in a position to enter upon a campaign against Russia; and as soon as he deemed that the hour had come to strike a blow, he demanded from the Czar an explanation of his armaments (February 25th). He bade Lauriston, the French Ambassador at the Russian Court, express the hope that the four hundred and fifty thousand men whom he had set in motion would inspire the Cabinet of St. Petersburg with serious reflections, would induce it to return to the system established at Tilsit, and would "reduce Russia to the subordinate condition in which she then stood." The last sting drew a decisive reply from the Government of the Czar. It sent Napoleon an ultimatum, comprising a demand for the evacuation of Prussia and Pomerania, an equivalent for Oldenburg, and freedom of commerce for neutrals. The Czar at the same time ordered his Ambassador to demand his passports, and himself proceeded to the head-quarters of his army at Wilna.

Napoleon perceived that he could accept this in no

other light than as a declaration of war; and early in May he joined his army in Saxony. But it seems evident that he entered upon this contest with Russia in a less confident, and less enthusiastic mood than he had been accustomed to exhibit in similar circumstances. After his repudiation of Josephine, and his marriage with Maria Louisa, he would perhaps gladly have inaugurated a second epoch of his reign—an epoch of peace—during which he might consolidate the Empire which he had won by his sword, and firmly establish the system which he had imposed upon Europe. The birth of his son inspired him with new prospects and a new hope. He saw in the infant King of Rome the second Emperor of the French, who might continue the dynasty which he had founded. If he could have foreseen the days of the second Empire he might at all events have felt that his dream was destined to some sort of realisation; but he scarcely could be so infatuated, even in his most sanguine moments, as to expect that Europe would long submit to the yoke of his conquests. A misgiving of this kind must have crossed his mind as he set out for his campaign; but his reception at Dresden, where he found the Emperor of Austria, the King of Prussia, the Princes and Archdukes of the German Confederation of the Rhine, eager to salute him, had an exhilarating effect.

The old heroic spirit returned to him forthwith. He ordered the army to advance and cross the Niemen, which it accomplished at three different points on the 22nd of June, and following days. Nothing could withstand the first onset of the French and their allies, who believed, with their leader, that this war against Russia was the natural completion of all that had previously been effected by the hero of the Revolution, who was to vindicate the rights of civilisation and progress against the representatives of oppression and barbarism, and by which, as Napoleon himself said," the European system will be confirmed, the cause of the century will be won, and the Revolution accomplished."

The French line, before crossing the Niemen, stretched from Tilsit on the left to Grodno and Galicia on the right. Macdonald, Davoust, Oudinot, Ney, Murat, Lefebvre, Mortier, Bessières, Eugène Beauharnais, Jérôme held the posts of honour; Victor and Augereau stood a little in the rear, with reserves of eighty thousand men. Between the Vistula and the Niemen were close upon half a million men; and facing these, with Wilna as a centre, the three Russian armies, in three successive lines, were hardly inferior to their enemy in point of number.

The passage of the Niemen, and the advance upon Wilna, practically cut in two the first line of the Russian forces; and the early days of July witnessed hte evacuation of that town by the Russian general Barclay de Tolly, who burned his stores before abandoning it. Retiring upon the entrenched camp at Drissa, he was pressed hard by Murat and Ney, whilst his right was driven back by Oudinot, and his left by Eugène and Jérôme. By these movements Bagrathion, who had been stationed with fifty thousand Russians between the Niemen and the Bug, and who, on the evacuation of Wilna, had begun to fall back on Minsk, was in imminent danger of being cut off. Davoust, who with Napoleon commanded the centre of the French army, anticipated Bagrathion at Minsk, and the latter thereupon retreated, narrowly escaping Jérôme on the road,[1] by way of Mohilow towards Witepsk, where he hoped to join Barclay de Tolly.

The Czar made a last effort to restore peace (June 25th), and signified to Napoleon his willingness to treat for terms; he offered, if the French army were withdrawn, "to regard all which had taken place as though it had not happened." He was justified in taking this tone; for he had made terms with Sweden and Turkey, and he had reason to feel tolerably confident, notwithstanding his first misfortunes. He probably knew that the French had already to struggle with vast difficulties in their supply and commissariat; that affairs at Wilna, and in the various camps, were in extreme disorder; that the country around them was a virtual waste, from which little in the way of sustenance could be obtained for the troops. At any rate, he was aware that Napoleon had not been able to take immediate advantage of his first success in the field, and that although he had sent a haughty

---

[1] Jérôme had received the Emperor's orders to occupy Nesvige, on the route of Bagrathion, but by the slowness of his advance he had suffered the Russian general to escape him. His command of the Westphalians was instantly transferred to Junot.

refusal to the Czar's offer to treat, he continued to reside at Wilna, where for upwards of a fortnight he was engaged in superintending the work of contractors and of the commissariat. The great difference between fighting at home and fighting abroad, between drawing supplies and reinforcements from the distance of a few miles and having to seek them across a practically hostile continent, was realised by both Emperors; and the realisation was calculated to sustain the hopes of Alexander and his generals.

Barclay de Tolly had expected that the invader would turn northwards, along the St. Petersburg road, and it was with the object of opposing such a march that he had established himself in the entrenched camp of Drissa. But Napoleon determined to advance in the direction of the ancient capital of Russia; and on the 15th of July he set out on the Witepsk and Smolensko road, in the direction of Moscow, thereby threatening to turn the position of the Russian commander. Barclay, perceiving this, left Wittgenstein to guard the camp at Drissa, and made the best of his way to Witepsk, which Bagrathion also was attempting to reach, having eluded Jérôme. But Napoleon had despatched Davoust to cut off the retreat of Bagrathion at Mohilow. This movement was so far successful that the latter was compelled to make for Smolensko instead of Witepsk; and Barclay himself, hard pressed, and hearing that the French troops were already at Mohilow, fell farther back on the Moscow road, and joined his fellow-commander at Smolensko.

Meanwhile Oudinot, Saint Cyr, and Macdonald gained successes at Polotsk, and northwards as far as Riga. Everywhere the Russians fell back; but their retreat was almost as disastrous to their enemy as would have been their victory in a succession of pitched battles. The Russian Government had ordered the generals to offer the most obstinate resistance in their power; and at the same time the stern decree was issued that not the army alone, but the whole nation should roll back before the invader. The edict was obeyed with marvellous completeness. Wherever the French advanced they found only devastated plains or smoking ruins. Houses, inhabitants, crops, and herds disappeared, and the victorious army marched through a desert. The effect of this strategy upon an army already half-starved, and destitute of its necessary supplies, may be imagined. The Grand Army was not many miles beyond the frontier when it was discouraged, disheartened, full of gloomy apprehensions for the future.

Barclay de Tolly and Bagrathion, having united their forces at Smolensko, thought the moment opportune for assuming an offensive attitude. They turned round upon Witepsk, and expected that their challenge would be immediately accepted by the French; but Napoleon, diverging by his right, and crossing the Dnieper, ordered Murat, Ney, Eugène, and the Guard to join him, who all obeyed the order with surprising alacrity. There can be little doubt that Napoleon would have entirely succeeded in the stroke of genius which he had contemplated, and caught the Russian armies in a trap, if it had not been for the splendid resistance offered by a force of ten thousand Russians, who had been detached by Barclay in order to observe the movements of Davoust. This division covered the Smolensko road for many hours, sustaining charge after charge of cavalry, and losing one-half of its numbers; and its obstinate courage gave time to the Russian commanders to send it assistance, and to draw it back upon Smolensko. Thus Napoleon was obliged to attack his enemy at the latter place; and after he had unsuccessfully attempted to take it by surprise, the French army was drawn up in front of the town, to the number of one hundred and forty thousand men.

The Russian Generalissimo perceived that a retreat upon Moscow was inevitable. He sent Bagrathion in advance, with a third of the forces at his disposal, and remained with eighty thousand men in the sole hope of securing a favourable retreat, and affording time for the usual conflagration and wholesale devastation. In this he succeeded admirably. On the 18th of August he defended the suburbs, the public buildings, the bridges, the gates, the walls of the town, in slow' succession, and contrived to hold out, though with a loss of twelve thousand men, until nightfall. Next morning the French, who had themselves suffered a loss of fifteen thousand, entered a wilderness of burning ruins, but found that the enemy had escaped them.

Barclay saw fit to retire by the St. Petersburg road, and thence across the country to the route taken by Bagrathion. It is quite possible that the French might have destroyed, or at least divided, the two Russian armies within the next few days, if they had followed up the retreat with sufficient rapidity and determination. Ney did, indeed, attack the rear of the army on the Moscow road; but he encountered a resistance so desperate, that he was obliged to ask for reinforcements. Napoleon did not recognise the actual significance of the situation, and sent only a single division; but he subsequently ordered Junot to cross the river, and attack the Russians in the rear. By some misunderstanding the Marshal failed to execute this movement, which might easily have been fatal to the enemy, and thus the forces of Barclay and Bagrathion were once more united, though with a further loss of eight thousand men.

The Russians fell gradually back upon the ancient capital of their country, contesting every step, and still burning remorselessly all that they left behind them. Meanwhile, Barclay de Tolly was relieved of the supreme command by the veteran Marshal Kutusoff, then nearly seventy years old, and who had conducted the recent war in Turkey. Kutusoff took up a strong position at Borodino, in front of the river Moskwa, which he strengthened by redoubts and entrenchments. His left, under Bagrathion, held the village of Semenowskoi; his right, under Barclay, held a bastioned redoubt commanding the river Kolotza and the Moscow road. A hundred and thirty thousand Russians awaited the onslaught of a somewhat superior force of French troops, and on the 7th of September the battle of Borodino, one of the most sanguinary of all Napoleon's victories, was fought. Davoust and Ney, after a desperate engagement, obtained possession of Semenowskoi, and in the effort to retake the position, Bagrathion was mortally wounded. The village of Borodino was captured by Eugène, and recaptured by the Russian Marshal, who was preparing to attack the French lines when Napoleon ordered an assault upon the great redoubt. A frightful struggle at this point ended in the defeat of the Russians, who withdrew behind the ravine of Semenowskoi, leaving no less than fifty thousand men upon the field of battle, whilst the total loss of the French was even larger.

Napoleon, unwilling to risk too much by an immediate advance, suffered the enemy to retire upon Moscow, where he expected that he would have to fight another battle. But Kutusoff had received orders to evacuate the city. He did so, being accompanied in his retreat by one-half of the inhabitants, whom he assured that the abandonment of the capital would prove "a snare wherein the ruin of the enemy is certain."

On the 15th of September, the Grand Army entered Moscow, chanting the *Marseillaise*, and Napoleon took up his residence in the famous Kremlin, the palace of a hundred Czars. His triumph was but a brief one. That same night a thousand fires broke out in the wooden streets of the city, and for five days afterwards Moscow was the scene of a vast conflagration. Acting on secret orders from the Government, the governor, Rostopchin, had liberated the convicts from the prisons, and given them the ghastly commission of setting fire to the town, which they had only too faithfully carried out.

Napoleon was exasperated by this act of barbarism, as he naturally called it. "This is how the Russians make war!" he exclaimed. "The civilisation of St. Petersburg has deceived us. These men are still Scythians." His generals advised him to stay at the Kremlin, and make terms with Alexander, instead of marching northwards and joining Oudinot and Macdonald, as he had been first inclined to do. He took their advice, and remained amidst the ruins, sheltering his army as well as circumstances allowed. Whilst there he heard of the disasters suffered by the army in Spain, where Wellington had taken Salamanca, defeated Marmont (July 22nd), and entered Madrid. Soult compelled the English to retire again; but the general results of the campaign were decidedly adverse to the French cause.

The reason which finally determined Napoleon to leave Moscow was the extreme danger with which he was menaced by the designs of the Russian commanders. The Czar had refused to treat with his enemy, and blamed Kutusoff for so much as entering into preliminary negotiations. The latter, before the middle of October, had a re-organised army of one hundred and seventy thousand men at his disposal, and he now resolved to resume the offensive against the French, whilst Tchichagoff and Wittgenstein, whose forces amounted in the aggregate to a hundred thousand, were to aim at Smolensko, in order to cut off the retreat of Napoleon. Murat, who displayed less than his usual ability during the Russian campaign, was surprised and beaten by Kutusoff at Winkowo, on the 18th of October. The French Emperor had already commenced his retreat on the 14th of the same month, and during five days above eighty thousand soldiers, with as many as fifty thousand non-combatants, were sent towards the frontier. Large stores had been provided at Smolensko, Witepsk, Minsk, and Wilna; and Napoleon hoped to reach the first-named town by the road to Kalouga, before the winter set in. But the snow began to fall at the moment when the army commenced its retrograde movement; and the winter, even before the close of the year, was destined to be one of the severest on record.

The horrors of this long and bitter retreat of the Grand Army have often been related, but it is questionable whether any of the accounts can give an adequate idea of the terrible disaster. The whole route was blocked and surrounded by an overwhelming number of Russians, whose Cossack cavalry inflicted the gravest loss upon the French troops, and upon the miserable crowd of fugitives who accompanied them. Kutusoff pressed them hard along the Kalouga road, and Eugène, to whom the vanguard had been entrusted, had to take the town of Malo-Jaroslawitz seven times in succession before the Russian general gave way. Napoleon, perceiving that the enemy held the route from Kalouga to Smolensko in great force, determined, against the advice of Eugène and the other members of his staff, to diverge to the right, through Mojaisk —the same district by which they had advanced six weeks before, and which was consequently devastated. It may have been that by striking another blow at Kutusoff, the opposition to the retreat would have been virtually suppressed; and it has been maintained that this decision of Napoleon's was one of the principal causes of the subsequent disaster. At all events Kutusoff had expected to be attacked, and fell back in haste to Tarutino, only to recover himself immediately, and fix upon the flanks of the retreating army.

The French marched in four divisions, led respectively by Napoleon, Ney, Eugène, and Davoust—Ney subsequently relieving Davoust with the rearguard. There was but little stability in any of these divisions. The cold, the Cossacks, the perpetual fighting, carried off combatants and non-combatants by thousands in a day. Ill clad, almost without food, the men fell by the roadside, or died by the bivouac fires; and the host was already grievously weakened and reduced when it reached Smolensko on the 12th of November. Even here there was no rest for them. The divisions which had previously sojourned in or passed through the town had all but exhausted the provisions which had been stored there; and the famished army consumed the remainder in a single day. Worse than that, the Russians held the homeward route by Witepsk and Minsk, which two places were taken by Wittgenstein and Tchichagoff, who prepared to oppose the passage of the Beresina, whilst Kutusoff was on the road to Roslawl and Mitislav. It would clearly have been impossible for the French to remain in Smolensko; and there was nothing for it but to continue the disastrous retreat. The fortifications were levelled to the ground, and then, on the 14th of November, amidst ever-increasing difficulties, and exposed to the bitterness of a winter which was the most formidable of all their enemies, the devoted host set out across the trackless snows. Now the soldiers went mad by hundreds and thousands at a time. They blew out their brains, ran themselves through the body, or cast themselves upon the bloodthirsty bands of Cossacks, who kept vigilant watch for their prey. "More than thirty thousand horses died within a few days," says one bulletin. The cavalry marched on foot; the artillery had to be abandoned continually; and at every indication of the growing calamities of the Grand Army, the pursuing columns took fresh courage.

On the 16th of November Napoleon, finding himself almost surrounded by Kutusoff at Krasnoi, in the neighbourhood of Orcha, halted in order to give the three divisions which followed him time to come up; but the Russian troops had already occupied the road in his rear. Eugène, after a desperate attack against Kutusoff, succeeded in escaping with his best troops during the darkness of the night, and joined the Emperor; and then Napoleon, leading his guard, rescued Davoust from the sixty thousand Russians who stood between them. He was compelled to leave Ney to his fate; but the gallant Marshal, at the head of his rearguard of some six thousand men, cut his way, step by step, through the dense masses of the enemy. Three times he had shaken them off, and three times they closed in upon him. He reached Orcha at last, with barely fifteen hundred men; and then the whole army, now reduced to twenty-four thousand, pushed on to the Beresina. Thirty-six thousand men were lost in that terrible retreat between Smolensko and Krasnoi. Witepsk, Minsk, Borissow, every town of importance, every depôt where Napoleon had collected his stores for the relief of the army, was in the hands of the enemy.

At the Beresina, Napoleon, joined by the remains of Oudinot's and Victor's corps, and yet numbering barely forty thousand men in all, received a new check from the cruel winter. The ice had broken up, and there were no means of crossing the swollen stream. The Russians, driven from Borissow by Oudinot, had burnt the bridge over the Beresina; and it was necessary for the French to improvise others at all hazards. This was accomplished by the most heroic efforts, and at an immense loss, in the face of an ever-active enemy. On the 25th and 26th of November, the army crossed the river, nearly opposite to Studienka, on rafts and rough pontoon-bridges, which were perpetually broken by the ice, or by the confusion and strain of the fugitive multitudes. Tchichagoff and Wittgenstein attacked the French simultaneously, in the midst of the crossing, on both sides of the river. The first was driven back to Borissow; and Wittgenstein, on the left bank of the Beresino, only succeeded after a combat lasting a day and a night in defeating Victor, who was covering the retreat with ten thousand men, reduced in the conflict by one-half. The Russians soon established a battery of twelve pieces, which commanded the narrow bridge, choked by a struggling mass of camp-followers, women, wounded, and sick, who pushed each other into the river, or fell beneath the murderous fire of the Russians. Through the midst of this seething crowd Victor had to force his way, burning the bridge behind him. The picture is one of the most ghastly which the history of war has ever presented.

On the 5th of December, Napoleon, having reached Smorgoni, on the way to Wilna, came to the resolution of returning alone to Paris, where many affairs of the greatest importance required his presence. He resigned the command of the forces, which had been recruited by numerous detachments, into the hands of Murat, and secretly departed; and then the last misfortunes of the Grand Army fell upon it. Murat was unequal to the task imposed upon him; and, indeed, it may be doubted whether any ability, however great, could have rescued the devoted host from its miserable condition. On the road to Wilna all discipline was lost. The men cast down their arms, and crawled painfully along; others rushed about madly until they dropped; and it is estimated that within three days as many as twenty thousand died of cold and hunger. On the 8th, many thousand starving men descended upon the town, and seized whatever they could lay their hands on to stay the pangs of famine. The Russian generals meanwhile lost no time in pursuing their advantage. They approached Wilna from three directions; and the French hastily fled to Kowno, across the Niemen, and along the Königsberg road. Once more the heroic Ney came to the rescue of his compatriots. Putting himself at the head of four thousand men, he covered the retreat of the fugitives; and at length the pursuit was stopped.

The conduct of Napoleon in thus hastily leaving the army, before it had been rescued from danger, has been variously estimated by his contemporaries and by historians. Michelet, always severe on him, is especially so in connection with this circumstance, and with the Emperor's callous behaviour on his return to Wilna. "This vast shipwreck," he says,[1] "of three hundred thousand men destroyed, buried beneath the snow, was a very different thing from the loss of a single army. It was the loss of a world, of the remains of a levy and conscription of twenty years; it was, in other words, the ruin of heroic France, which had conquered the world, and, drawn by its blind faith, had come there to die and be buried. All that remained of our Republican armies, of those of Italy, Egypt, Germany, had been brought together for this common catastrophe. And for this cataclysm, this shipwreck of a world, not a single tear and not a single regret! Add to this picture the whole of France,

[1] *Histoire du XIX. Siècle*, vol. iii. bk. vi. ch. 5.

which will have to lament the army of Moscow for so many years.' . . . Thirty years later there still lived in the asylums old women who continued to expect their sons, and to mutter, 'They will return!' The Russians themselves were moved by these fatal scenes, this immeasurable disaster. They remembered that they were men, and thought themselves too well avenged. One man there was, one alone in the whole human race, of such savage pride, that in order to escape the scorn so well deserved by his madness, he was found only laughing, or uttering an abominable irony."

Of the half a million men who had crossed the Niemen on the 22nd of June, more than four hundred and fifty thousand found a grave or a prison in Russia; whilst on the side of the Russians themselves the total loss in men alone must have been very large. Even those who were left could not be looked upon as an army. No sooner had Napoleon departed for Paris than the disaffected Allies began to desert his standard. The Prussian general York, attached to the command of Macdonald, signed a convention with the Russians, leaving the French commander with about nine thousand troops out of a force of eighteen thousand; whilst Murat, discouraged, and unable to restore the shattered army to order and discipline, made some excuses about the critical condition of affairs in his kingdom of Naples, and handed over his command to Eugène (January 16th, 1813). Meanwhile the situation of the French was rendered still more grave by the attitude of the Prussians. The King of Prussia had expressed great indignation about the convention of General York and his ten thousand men, and had engaged to supply the contingent at once by a fresh levy. He immediately called out the whole male population of the kingdom; but the most discerning men perceived that this measure was directed, not against Russia, but against France. The corps sent to take the place of the troops who had left lost no time in following the example of its predecessor; and the Austrian general Schwartzenberg, who had behaved very bravely with the rear of the Grand Army, finally evacuated the Russian territory on the 7th of January. Eugène had done his best to restore the tone of the army, and had drawn it back in good order from the Vistula, where Murat left it, to the Oder and the Elbe. Starting with seventeen thousand Frenchmen, whom he took in hand on the 18th of January, he raised the army to a solid force of forty thousand on the 9th of March, by which day he had assumed a strong position, stretching from Magdeburg to Dresden. At Leipzic, in the centre of his line, he awaited reinforcements, which Napoleon was exerting himself to procure and send to the front.

France had been horrorstruck at the disasters suffered by the Emperor and the Grand Army in the retreat from Moscow, but she assented, with almost as much enthusiasm as ever, to new sacrifices, new levies, new imposts, and burdens. The Legislative Assembly was convoked, and supplied pecuniary means, by the forced sale of all the heritable property belonging to the municipalities, public hospitals, and Communes, whilst the Senate ordered a levy of three hundred and fifty thousand men. It is true that Napoleon's conduct during the retreat, and especially his sudden departure from the army at Smorgoni, had been much criticised in France; but it was confidently believed that he would be able to restore everything in a new campaign. His popularity was almost as great as it had ever been, and Europe saw that the Russian armies, and the unparalleled severities of the winter of 1812, had done nothing to tame the spirit of Bonaparte.

The Emperor made a special effort to come to terms with the Pope before setting out on a new campaign. Pius VII. had been brought to Fontainebleau, where he was a veritable prisoner, unable to hold a Court, or even a Council. Here Napoleon visited him, and induced him to sign a Concordat, by which his Holiness was to reside at Avignon, with the Sacred College, and was to enjoy complete liberty and authority in all things—the question of the States of the Church alone being reserved. Pius had signed this convention on the persuasion of the Emperor; but subsequent reflections, and especially the protests which he encountered from the majority of the Cardinals, led him to write to Napoleon repudiating the compromise, "signed without consideration, and in a moment of human weakness." However, the Concordat was published, the Pope remained a prisoner at Fontainebleau; and thus the Emperor's attempt to conciliate the Church, and to gain the goodwill of the French clergy, was unsuccessful.

§ III.—THE FALL OF THE EMPIRE.

(From the 9th of March, 1813, to the 11th of April, 1814.)

THROUGHOUT the spring of 1813 the French Government was continually sending reinforcements towards the Elbe. A hundred battalions, four regiments of the Guards, and two of cavalry were transferred from Spain. Six hundred cannon and six regiments of artillery were provided within three months, in addition to a large force of gunners, and all the necessary ammunitions of a great army. In all two hundred thousand men were despatched to the front, destined for various points on the new French positions, whilst another hundred thousand were prepared in all haste to follow them. These were independent of the German contingents, and of the force which Austria, who was believed to be still faithful to the alliance with France, had undertaken to supply.

Meanwhile Russia, England, Prussia, and Sweden were busy cementing their Coalition, and preparing for the impending attack. The King of Prussia, after offering to mediate between Napoleon and Alexander— an offer instantly rejected by the former—had entered into a secret compact with the Czar, in order to restore the independence of Europe, and to re-establish Prussia as it had been in 1806; whilst at the same time he continued to carry on friendly relations with Paris.

It was not until the 17th of March that he suddenly declared war against the French; and two days after this he concluded an open Convention with Alexander at Breslau, and called upon the minor German princes to rise in defence of the Fatherland, under pain of deposition; the Confederation of the Rhine was declared to be dissolved; the *landwehr* and *landsturm*[1] were called out. This rupture between Prussia and France was welcomed with enthusiasm by the whole German people, or rather it was the direct outcome of an enthusiasm which had long been growing up, which had been fostered and spread by German poets and orators, and which finds its reflection in the pages of Schiller and his contemporaries. The German rulers knew how to avail themselves of a force which, though it assumed the form of a struggle for freedom against the creature of the French Revolution, was yet in reality itself the offspring of 1789.

The conduct of Austria was marked by still greater duplicity than that of the Prussian Government previous to the Convention of Breslau. The Emperor Francis renewed the most solemn promises to Napoleon, whilst secretly assenting to the pact between Russia and Prussia. He had listened to the representations of the English emissaries, and to the despatches of the British Government, which held out a hope of Austrian aggrandisement in Italy; and, whilst solemnly

[1] The *landwehr* is a kind of militia, composed of men from the age of seventeen until the age of forty-five, who in time of war are called out in Germany on permanent duty; the *landsturm* is a levy of the male population from the age of forty-five till the age of sixty.

affirming that he would for ever maintain the system established in Europe by Napoleon, he privately counselled Denmark, Bavaria, and even Naples, to abstain from "useless armaments, which would render the Emperor less capable of being brought to reason."

Hostilities broke out immediately after the Prussian declaration, and before Napoleon had had time to bring the main army to the front of the French positions, Eugène was attacked by a hundred and fifty thousand men, Dresden was taken by the Russian troops (March 26th), and Hamburg surrendered to the Russians, owing to an insurrection of the citizens (March 12th). Beauharnais, however, occupied the enemy in a masterly manner for about a month, and fell back with the utmost deliberation until he could effect his junction with the vanguard of Napoleon's army. The Emperor had with him a hundred and fifteen thousand men, under Oudinot, Ney, Bertrand, and Marmont, whilst Soult, Mortier, and Bessières commanded the guard; Davoust was sent against the Cossacks in Westphalia; and, in addition to these forces, the cavalry, scarcely yet prepared to take the field, was daily expected from France.

Napoleon ordered a general advance towards Dresden, and Ney with the vanguard gained a preliminary advantage over Wittgenstein at Weissenfels, on the last day of April, and at Rippach on the 1st of May. On the following day, near Lützen, the two armies contested a long and obstinate battle, in which the Prussian general, Blucher, distinguished himself by several times taking and retaking from Ney the villages of Kaia and Klein Görschen, forming the centre and key of the position. The fighting was of a most sanguinary character, and the casualties amongst the officers, even amongst the Marshals and generals, were especially high. Napoleon urged forward his young troops in the midst of the battle, whilst Alexander and Frederick William watched the varying fortunes of the day from a neighbouring height. The opportune arrival of Eugène and Bertrand towards the evening, followed by the gallant recapture of Kaia by sixteen battalions of the Young Guard, decided the struggle; and thus Napoleon was able to congratulate himself on a victory which restored to his army all its ancient prestige. He praised his newly levied troops in enthusiastic terms, declaring that he had never seen more courage and devotion.

The Allies retired and crossed the Elbe, whilst Napoleon, pressing them close, occupied Dresden, and restored to the throne the King of Saxony, from whom he received a contingent of fifteen thousand men. Wittgenstein and Blucher turned towards Silesia, in order not to be too far from Bohemia, and in the hope of receiving decisive assistance from Austria, whom they knew to be playing fast and loose with France. At this moment the Emperor Francis proposed a Congress to Napoleon, in which he assured him that "he himself as an umpire would be his sincere friend." The French Emperor did not refuse it, but he none the less pressed forward against the enemy, whom he attacked on the

20th of May in a strong position at Bautzen. The Russians and Prussians had formed an entrenched camp behind the town, which they had fortified with great care. The town itself was taken by the French, after hard fighting, and the Allies withdrew to their camp, Blucher alone maintaining his first positions on the heights of Kreckwitz. On the next day Wittgenstein held his own, chiefly through a want of judgment on the part of Ney, but Blucher was almost surrounded, and had to save himself by a timely retreat. His colleague, of course, followed him, and the Allies withdrew by way of Hochkirch, Lobau, and Weissenberg, leaving eighteen thousand dead and wounded on the field, whilst the French loss was at least twenty thousand.

During a long pursuit, in which the French almost invariably had the best of the encounters, though at a great sacrifice of men, the Allies continued to hold close to the borders of Bohemia, with the same object in view of securing Austrian assistance. Early in June Napoleon seemed to have the enemy at his mercy, and to be in a position to enforce his own terms. Another sanguinary and perhaps decisive battle might probably have been fought near the Oder; but at this juncture the Emperor Francis proposed an immediate armistice, which his son-in-law did not refuse. A Convention was signed at Pleswitz on the 4th of June, and the armistice was to last until the 28th of July. Napoleon himself saw how much he might possibly lose by this cessation of hostilities at such a critical moment. "If the Allies do not keep faith," he said at the time, "this armistice will be simply fatal to us." He must have implicitly believed in the sincerity and honour of the Emperor of Austria, or he would never have placed himself in a position of such extreme danger. It had always been his custom to strike first in every quarrel; and, as he was wont to observe, his attacks were often essentially defensive. Here he was leaving two open enemies, whom he might have crushed, at liberty to enter into a league with others whom ordinary prudence should have prevented him from regarding as friends to be depended on.

Meanwhile Suchet had maintained the honour of the French arms in Spain. It was not until the 22nd of May, that Wellington re-entered the country from Portugal, at the head of fifty thousand English and about seventy thousand Spaniards. This army crossed the Douro, above Zamora and at Toro, whilst King Joseph, with whom were generals Foy and Clausel, evacuated Madrid and Valladolid (June 4th), and subsequently Burgos, and retired to Vittoria, at the junction of the roads to Bilbao and Madrid. Wellington attacked the French on the 21st of June, and drove them back upon Pampeluna, capturing during the retreat a hundred and fifty-one guns, and large quantities of stores. The French never stopped until they had crossed the Pyrenees; and thus the Anglo-Spanish army stood upon the frontier of France, ready to carry war into the country which had enjoyed so long an immunity from invasion. Soult was immediately sent to take the command of Joseph's troops, but before he could act events of great significance were passing elsewhere.

It was the end of June before the treachery of Austria began to bear fruit. Francis had occupied the time in negotiations, and in military preparations. The English Government had refused to have anything to do with the Congress, but Russia and Prussia had assented, and had formulated the terms which they desired to secure. On the 28th of the month the Austrian Prime Minister Metternich had an interview with Napoleon at Dresden, and, after a good deal of hesitation, named the price which Austria set upon her friendship. The demands were so high, including for Austria herself Illyria and the half of Italy, and stipulating for the return of the Pope to Rome, the abandonment of Holland, of the Confederation of the Rhine, of Switzerland, and Spain, that Napoleon rejected them with indignation. He insulted Metternich by asking him how much he had received from England for making war upon France; and from that moment forward there was no more deception on either side. The armistice, however, was extended to the 10th of August, and preparations for the holding of the Congress actually went on.

Meanwhile England was persistently negotiating and intriguing with all the Continental Powers, most of whom she assisted with large subventions. By the treaty of Reichenbach, signed on the 14th of June, she agreed to give two hundred thousand pounds sterling every month, during the continuation of the war, to Russia and Prussia. At Trachenberg on the 27th of July, when Austria formally entered the Coalition—occupying all the time the position of a mediator between France and her enemies—the English Government engaged to send to Vienna a subsidy of half a million sterling, and military stores and equipments for a like sum. The plan of a new campaign was carefully drawn up; arrangements were made for establishing relations with the malcontents in France; intrigues were set on foot in every country where the French had secured a hold; and then the Congress was opened. The hypocrisy of Europe may have been necessary, but it was none the less hypocrisy. The negotiators met at Prague on the 29th of July; and Austria, still assuming the part of mediator, used all her arts to delay the proceedings until the 10th of August. Napoleon insisted on hearing from Metternich the terms which were demanded by Europe; and at length the Austrian minister enunciated them. The Allies required the final partition of Poland, the re-establishment of Prussia, the dissolution of the Confederation of the Rhine, with a number of other points more or less humiliating to the French Emperor. Great as the effort was, Napoleon assented; but his answer did not reach Metternich until the 11th of August, and the plenipotentiaries had taken care to disperse on the 10th. The armistice was at an end, and Napoleon saw that his concessions had come too late. Austria now for the first time avowed her entrance into the Coalition; and Napoleon naturally enraged at her perfidy, accused her of desecrating "all that is most sacred amongst men—mediation, a congress, and the name of peace."

The armies of the Allies now amounted to an aggregate of more than seven hundred thousand men, while about five hundred thousand were at Napoleon's disposal. The plan of the Allies was to despatch two hundred thousand men—Russians, Prussians, and Austrians, under the command of Barclay de Tolly, from Bohemia to Dresden, whilst Blucher and Bernadotte were to command two other armies, persistently avoiding a conflict with Napoleon, and challenging his Marshals. The French Emperor, on the other hand, divining the intentions of his enemies, resolved to prevent the junction of Barclay's force with the Austrians, whilst at the same time he purposed to send Oudinot and Davoust from Wittenberg and Hamburg against Berlin. He lost as little time as possible, and marched at once into Bohemia; but this time the Allies had been more prompt than Napoleon. Even before the Congress separated they had effected their junction, and were already on the road to Dresden.

After some unimportant movements against Blucher, Napoleon left Macdonald to confront the Prussian general, and hastened to the relief of Dresden, which Saint-Cyr held against a vastly superior force of the Allies. The Emperor reached the town just in time to repel a desperate attack from Schwartzenberg, on the 26th of August; and on the next day he sallied forth and took the offensive. Murat distinguished himself in this battle by driving in the enemy's left, and capturing ten thousand prisoners, whilst Ney and Mortier successfully engaged the right. Napoleon himself threw his force upon the centre, and inflicted great loss, so that at length the Allies, learning that Vandamme was approaching with twenty-five thousand fresh troops, resolved to retreat, leaving behind them twenty-five thousand men, two hundred cannon, and a hundred and thirty caissons. They withdrew across the mountains in great disorder, and might have been almost annihilated; but Napoleon's panegyrists say, that whilst directing the pursuit, he was overcome by a sudden indisposition, the effect of his long-sustained efforts and anxieties, that he returned to Dresden, and left the conduct of affairs to his Marshals. If this were the case, then this temporary illness was an omen of something infinitely worse. The battle of Dresden was fated to be the last great victory of Bonaparte.

Meanwhile Vandamme had marched from Königstein to Pirna, and had occupied a strong position at Peterswalde. On the 28th of August he pushed on to Culm, and thence towards Töplitz, in his attack on which town he made sure of being assisted by Napoleon. But the Emperor was at Dresden, and his Marshals do not appear to have given Vandamme a thought. The latter encountered an obstinate resistance at Töplitz from the Russian guards who held the place; and finding himself left unprotected, he fell back upon Culm. Here he was in turn attacked by sixty thousand of the Allies; and, attempting to resume his position at Peterswalde, he was taken between two forces, a large body of Prussians having in the meantime occupied the heights. About half of his force cut its way through, and escaped, but the remainder, with Vandamme amongst them, were obliged to surrender. This was on the 30th of August; and four days previously Macdonald had suffered a severe defeat at the hands of Blucher, on the Katzbach, losing ten thousand men, and fifteen thousand prisoners, and being driven back upon Goldberg.

These disasters did not happen alone. Oudinot, marching upon Berlin, was attacked at Gross Beeren by Bernadotte, and beaten. Davoust was compelled to abandon Schwerin and Wismar, which he had just occupied; and Ney, after replacing Oudinot, attacked the Prince of Sweden at Dennewitz, and being unsupported, owing to the defeat of Macdonald, suffered a loss of seventeen thousand men, of whom one-half were prisoners, and thus left Saxony and Westphalia at the mercy of Bernadotte. Napoleon himself began to feel discouraged. He recognised that his only hope lay in a great victory which should paralyse his enemies, as Jena, Austerlitz, and Wagram had done; and he was unable to create the chance. During the greater part of September Napoleon hesitated between attacking Schwartzenberg in Saxony and Blucher in Bohemia, fearing to engage either, lest the other should take advantage of his absence.

Whilst the Emperor hesitated, the Allies were

manœuvring so as to cut him off from the frontier of France, and they succeeded in forming a semi-circle from Wittenberg, through Bautzen, to Töplitz. Their object was almost accomplished, and Napoleon, perceiving the critical nature of his position, resolved to carry the war back into Prussia, selecting for the field of his operations the plains between the Elbe and the Oder. But now a new danger assailed him; Bavaria, Baden, and Wurtemberg threatened to increase the forces of the Allies, and the former country actually sent a contingent of sixty thousand men into the field. Napoleon instantly altered his plan, and massed all the forces which he could bring together—that is to say, barely a hundred and seventy-five thousand—at Leipzic, the centre of the enemy's line, held at the moment by Schwartzenberg alone. Bernadotte and Blucher were hastening to Schwartzenberg's assistance, and Napoleon sent Ney forward with forty-five thousand men to hold them in check. Bertrand, with fifteen thousand troops, was detached to open up the Lützen road, and Napoleon himself, with the remaining one hundred thousand, prepared to fall upon Schwartzenberg with his one hundred and thirty thousand.

The latter, however, did not wait for this. He attacked Napoleon on the 16th of October, and engaged in a desperate conflict, which lasted the whole day, and of which the result was doubtful; but he had given time to Bernadotte and Blucher to beat Ney, and to make their appearance, together with Benningsen, on the 18th. On that day the Allies, to the number of three hundred thousand, attacked less than half that number of Frenchmen, who had determined to risk another battle, and had drawn themselves up in front of Leipzic.

A sanguinary struggle ensued, as many as sixty thousand men falling on the first day of this "battle of nations," as it was afterwards called by the Germans. The French fought with the utmost valour and determination, but they were hopelessly outnumbered. The treachery of the Saxons, who, to the number of twelve thousand, went over to the enemy in the midst of the fight, and turned their guns upon the comrades whose side they had just left, contributed to the disaster. In the night Napoleon determined upon a retreat. Fortunately Bertrand had been able to open the Lützen road; but Napoleon's orders for the construction of temporary bridges over the Elster had been disobeyed. There was only one passage over the river Elster, namely, the great bridge at Lindenau; and this the French had mined, with the intention of blowing it up as soon as their rear-guard should have crossed.

A terrible conflict took place in the town and its suburbs on the 19th of October; every street, almost every house, was attacked and defended. Napoleon and the Guard, Victor, Ney, Marmont had quitted Leipzic, and were already at Lindenau, on the Lützen road. In an evil moment the French sappers, deceived by appearances, blew up the bridge, and thus thirty thousand men, with a hundred and fifty guns, were left at the mercy of the Allies. A few threw themselves into the river and escaped; others swam their horses across and reached safely the opposite shore (Macdonald was one of these); but many, like Poniatowski, were killed whilst attempting the same thing. The rest were either slaughtered or taken prisoners, and the loss in the three days' battle, in killed and wounded alone, is computed at one hundred and ten thousand on both sides.

This defeat was in effect the death-blow of Napoleon's power in Europe. Not only were the French armies demoralised and dispirited; not only did some of the Marshals lose confidence in their chief, and begin to negotiate with his enemies; not only was France left virtually alone from this moment—the example of treachery set by Austria and Saxony being followed by other allies of the Empire;—but Napoleon himself realised that the old enthusiasm and dash of the soldiers of the Revolution had passed away, and that he could no longer count upon France for an unlimited supply of recruits.

The retreat was conducted in good order, so far as it was possible for Napoleon and his generals to inspire order in their defeated and decimated ranks. They were pursued closely by Blucher and Schwartzenberg, and were threatened by Giulay on the Weissenfels road; but avoiding a battle, and picking up the force of Bertrand on their way, they pushed rapidly on to Erfurth, with the intention of crossing the Rhine. In order to reach Hanau, it was necessary to pass through a densely-wooded defile. Blucher and Schwartzenberg were converging upon it, and at Erfurth they learned that Hanau was already occupied by fifty thousand Bavarians, under the command of Marshal Wrede. The retreating army was obliged to fight its way through the defile. The rearguard, under Bertrand and Mortier, was delayed by an attack of the pursuers' vanguard, whilst the Emperor, with Macdonald, Sébastiani, and Victor in the front, Marmont, Ney, and Augereau in the centre, inflicted on the Bavarians a loss of ten thousand men. Wrede, subsequently returning to his positions, attacked the French rear, but he was again defeated. On the 2nd of November the French army, by this time reduced to a total of sixty thousand men, crossed the Rhine, and before the year was out one-half of this number had been carried off by typhus, by the effects of their wounds, or some other legacy of that disastrous campaign.

The Allies did not immediately pursue Napoleon across the Rhine; but the interval was industriously employed in reducing the fortified places which remained in the hands of French garrisons, in Central Europe and the Rhenish provinces. Dresden, Stettin, Zamosc, Torgau, Dantzic, Wittenberg capitulated before the middle of the following January. Holland finally cast off her allegiance; and Denmark, the last ally of France, shortly afterwards entered the Coalition. By these capitulations an immense number of prisoners —above thirty thousand from Dresden alone—were sent into captivity.

Meanwhile Napoleon had reached Saint-Cloud on the 9th of November, and five days later he met the Senate at Paris, to whom he communicated the results of the campaign. The Emperor spoke the truth when he reminded them that the whole of Europe, so lately on their side, was now marching against them. Strenuous efforts were made to prepare for the campaign of 1814. The levies ordered for 1814 and 1815 were drawn upon to the number of three hundred and eighty thousand men; whilst, before the year was at an end, the new troops ordered to be raised were even more numerous.

But France herself was becoming heartily weary of perpetual war; and the misfortunes of the past two years inspired the Representatives with sufficient courage to protest against the new levies. They sent to Napoleon a plainly-worded address in which the sufferings and exhaustion of the country were set forth. "A barbarous and aimless war," they declared, "periodically swallows up a rising generation, snatched from education, from agriculture, from commerce and the arts. Are the hearts of mothers, then, and the sweat of the people, the patrimony of kings?"

It was the language of the Revolution, employed against one who, himself the product and the idol of that Revolution, had acquired, by the usual influences of unchecked power and ambition, the worst vices of absolute monarchs. Napoleon was enraged by this address, which he refused to receive after it had been read to him. On the last day of the year 1813 he dissolved the Legislative Body, determined to enforce his will without its assistance.

On the 21st of December Schwartzenberg had crossed the Rhine; and on the 31st Blucher followed him. Both issued proclamations to the French people, in which they declared that their quarrel was with Napoleon alone, and that their troops would be animated by no sentiment of revenge. Blucher's proclamation was in the following terms :—

"I have ordered the army of Silesia to cross the Rhine in order to restore the liberty and independence of the nations, and to secure peace. The Emperor Napoleon has united Holland, a part of Germany, and Italy, to the French Empire, and has declared that he would not give up a single village of his conquests, even if the enemy should occupy the heights commanding Paris.

"It is in opposition to this declaration and these principles that the armies of all the European Powers are marching.

"Every inhabitant of the towns and country districts must remain quietly at home, each official at his post, and continue to discharge his functions.

"From the moment of the entry of the Allied troops, all communication with the French Empire must cease. All who do not conform to this order will be considered guilty of treason to the Allied Powers; they will be brought before a council of war, and punished with death."

Before the spring had set in there were five foreign armies on the soil of France. Schwartzenberg, with three hundred thousand Austrians and Russians, had marched through Switzerland, accompanied by the two Emperors. Blucher, with a hundred and eighty thousand Prussians, forming the centre, had come by way of Neuwied. Bernadotte had crossed the Rhine lower down, at the head of two hundred thousand Swedes, Russians, and Prussians; Wellington had crossed the Pyrenees with a force of English and Spaniards; whilst an Anglo-Dutch army under Graham advanced by way of the Scheldt. In addition to these, Murat joined the Allies, in the selfish hope of retaining his crown, and threatened his old friend and leader with an army of thirty thousand Neapolitans, who had already invaded the Roman States. Thus nearly a million men stood upon the frontiers of France, and summoned the conqueror of Europe to answer for his conquests.

Napoleon, menaced by grave dangers, both from within and from without, faced them all with the same coolness which he had always shown in the great emergencies of his career. The Declaration of Frankfort, issued by the Powers (December 1st, 1813), in which they demanded that France should be restricted to its natural limits between the Rhine, the Alps, and the Pyrenees, and stated that they did not wage war against France, but against Napoleon, contained the same assurances, and appealed to the same sentiments as the manifestoes of Schwartzenberg and

Blucher; and a large portion of France had answered the appeal. Napoleon saw how closely he was pressed by his enemies, and how shrewdly the Coalition had availed itself of the discontent which had arisen in France. The foreign monarchs had, in fact, two powerful allies within the boundaries of the nation—the bulk of the people itself, satiated with military glory, and anxious to save the popular liberties before they were completely extinct; and the partisans of the legitimate monarchy, who hoped for a restoration which should place Louis XVIII. on the throne. The first of these two influences, and of course the most powerful, had been stimulated by the Emperor's injudicious acts in dismissing the Legislative Body, in promulgating the budget of 1814 by a personal decree, and in attempting to organise the national defences, without appealing to the nation for its sanction. Napoleon called out the National Guard in the capital and several of the great towns; but he hesitated to put arms in their hands, and naturally failed to evoke popular enthusiasm. He had armies of one hundred and fifty thousand men in Italy and Spain, which he refused to recall, in his overweening confidence that he should soon be able to resume the offensive. Thus the defence of the country against invasion was but artificial. The people rose here and there, and displayed a spirit which, as auxiliary to a powerful and well-disciplined army, might have been invaluable. As it was, Napoleon had nothing worthy of the name of a Grand Army.

On the 25th of January, Napoleon left Paris,

and proceeded to the head-quarters of the eastern army, which, under Marmont, Ney, and Victor, faced the Allied armies at Vitry. Of the seventy thousand men who had assembled here, Napoleon had detached a force under Macdonald to cover Châlons and the Marne, and another, commanded by Mortier, to protect Troyes and the Seine. He himself took the direction of the remaining forces into his own hands, and advanced to Saint-Dizier, where he met the van-guard of Blucher's army, attempting to form a junction with the troops of Schwartzenberg. Having driven back these troops, he pushed on through Vassy, and found Blucher concentrated at Brienne. The town[1] was taken, and the Prussian general fell back, but within a day or two he effected his junction with Schwartzenberg on the Bar-sur-Aube road. Instead of husbanding his resources and waiting for reinforcements, Napoleon continued to pursue Blucher; and at La Rothière, being almost surrounded by four times his numbers, lost six thousand men, and was driven back upon Troyes. Meanwhile Macdonald had been compelled by Blucher's rearguard to evacuate Châlons, and occupy Epernay in its place.

The Allied armies appear to have held Napoleon and his handful of men in very wholesome dread. They neither attacked him nor pushed straight forward on Paris, but separately followed the courses

---

[1] After a sanguinary conflict, in the course of which Napoleon found himself engaged in attacking the very military college in which he had been educated for the army.

of the Seine and Marne towards the capital. Blucher was strong enough to oblige Macdonald to quit the town of Epernay; but the latter defeated a force sent against him, blew up the bridge at Château-Thierry, and retired slowly upon Meaux. Napoleon, on his part, having received reinforcements, and learning that Blucher had again separated from Schwartzenberg, fell upon the former, with Marmont and Ney, on the Châlons road. After cutting to pieces a column of five thousand Russians at Champ-Aubert, he defeated the German general, Sacken, at Montmirail, and subsequently Sacken and York together, in front of Château-Thierry. The Russians burned the town and fled; and a vengeful pursuit was undertaken by Mortier and the armed bands of the district. Napoleon then rejoined Marmont, who had been obliged to fall back before Blucher; but now the latter, true to the admirable strategy adopted by the Allies, avoided an. encounter with the French Emperor. Napoleon, however, was not to be denied; he overtook the Prussian general at Vauchamp, and inflicted upon him a series of severe defeats, between the 14th and 16th of February, putting ten thousand men *hors de combat*. Meanwhile, part of the army of the Rhine, commanded by Winzingerode, had captured Avesnes, Laon, and Soissons, whilst reinforcements had been sent to Blucher to replace the men whom he had lost. A division under Bulow, with an English contingent, also attacked Antwerp, but was obliged to retreat without making any impression upon that city, which was defended by Carnot, a veteran of the Revolution, who, having always held aloof from Napoleon, had offered him his sword as soon as the soil of France had been invaded. Brussels, however, was evacuated by the French, under Maison, who, nevertheless, did good service in holding the Allies in check.

In the meantime General Caulaincourt had sought out the representatives of the Allies, assembled at a Congress at Châtillon (February 5th), at the instance of Napoleon, who had expressed himself anxious to save Paris from attack, and was prepared to accept the basis of the Declaration of Frankfort.

Caulaincourt asked on what conditions the Allies were prepared to treat. They demanded the abandonment even of the French conquests antecedent to the Empire, the liberty of arranging the frontiers of the other European countries without the interference of France, and the occupation of Belfort, Besançon, and Huningen. The Emperor repelled these offers with disdain. "They forget," he said, "that I am much nearer to Munich than they are to Paris."

However, the negotiations at Châtillon were continued, whilst Napoleon pursued his operations in the field; and every success against the forces of the Allies rendered the Emperor less inclined to listen to their demands.

Early in March most important operations were conducted to the north of the Marne, the result of which virtually decided the fate of the campaign. Blucher, who had suffered much at the hands of

Napoleon and his Marshals, was still marching upon Paris when he heard that the French Emperor was starting from Troyes, by way of Sézanne and La Ferté-Gaucher, and was advancing to attack him with twenty-five thousand men. The Prussian general at once crossed the Marne, and fell hurriedly back upon Soissons, a town at that time besieged by Winzingerode and Bulow. Pressed hard by Marmont, Mortier, and the Emperor, he found himself in a precarious position, and there seemed but small hope of his escaping, when, at this juncture, Soissons, most unfortunately for the French, capitulated (March 9th); and Blucher found a refuge open to him. If it had not been for this lucky coincidence, the army of Silesia might, according to some military authors, have fallen into the hands of the French.

Napoleon, enraged but not crushed by this disappointment, at once attacked the left of the Allies, and fought more than one desperate battle at Laon, losing within a few days a sixth of his small army of thirty thousand men. However, Blucher evacuated Soissons, which was occupied by Mortier. Napoleon then turned round upon Rheims, which had been surprised by a Russian force, and which town he captured, with a loss to the enemy of five thousand men.

Meanwhile Augereau at Lyons remained comparatively inactive, and made no effectual response to the urgent commands of Napoleon to advance upon the Rhine. He protested that his army was not ready for the field, and Napoleon sent him a sublime reply.

"I have at this moment," he said, "a division of four thousand National Guards, in round hats and vests, without pouches, armed with every kind of gun, of whom I think very highly; and I only wish I had thirty thousand of them." Augereau did attempt to retake Macon, and fought an unsuccessful battle near Lyons, which he was obliged to evacuate. Then he took up an inefficient position between Valence and Pont-Saint-Esprit, under the pretext of preventing the union of the Austrians with Wellington. But he too had entered into negotiations with the Allies, and was betraying the Emperor.

Wellington, with seventy thousand men, occupied the roads from Saint-Jean-de-Luz and Saint-Jean-Pied-de-Port to Bayonne, facing Soult, who stood with his right on the latter town, and whose army had been weakened in order to reinforce Napoleon. The British general attacked him, and drove him from Bayonne and the Adour to Orthez, and from thence to Aire. Meanwhile the Royalists, encouraged by the presence of the Duke d'Angoulême, whom the English had brought to Saint-Jean-de-Luz, invited Wellington to Bordeaux. A detachment of the Anglo-Spanish army entered the city, and there, on the 12th of March, Louis XVIII. was first proclaimed.

When Schwartzenberg heard of the capitulation of Soissons and of its subsequent evacuation by Blucher, he crossed the Seine, and drove Macdonald upon Nangis, hoping to co-operate with the Prussians; but the approach of Napoleon, who had taken a three days' rest at Rheims, caused him to fall back again, and to give the still redoubtable Emperor as wide a berth as possible. The boldness of the French, and the circumspection of the Allies, show how completely the terror of Napoleon's name had been established during the past twenty years, when even the disasters of 1812 and 1813 had not sufficed to extinguish it. But now a more courageous policy was adopted by the Allies, at the instance of the Czar Alexander. It was decided that Schwartzenberg and Blucher should do what they might safely have done six or eight weeks before—unite their whole forces and march upon Paris.

The Austrian general marched upon Arcis, in order to join Blucher at Vitry or Châlons, as occasion might offer. Napoleon instantly challenged him, and drove him back again; but as Schwartzenberg took up a strong position, with a hundred thousand men the Emperor was compelled to retire. He turned back upon Saint-Dizier, in the hope of entering Lorraine, of collecting there a large number of volunteers, and of cutting the communications of the invading armies. It was a last resource. Paris lay practically open to the Allies, for Marmont and Mortier, with their eighteen thousand men, had also been recalled from Rheims, in order to join the Emperor. The attempt of Napoleon was so far successful that it induced Schwartzenberg to return to Vitry, in order to watch his opponent's movements, whilst the bulk of the forces remained at Châlons.

Thus there was another delay, and another period

of hesitation. The French malcontents, and the Royalists in particular, who were eager to receive from the invading armies that power and those privileges which they could not obtain from the French people, began to grow tired of waiting. They urged the Allies to advance upon the capital, and assured them that they could do so with perfect safety. "You can do anything," wrote Talleyrand, a member of the Senate, hitherto subservient to Napoleon; "and you dare do nothing. Be daring for once!"

The Czar once more urged before a council of war the necessity of a resolute march on Paris. It was arranged that Winzingerode, with a strong force of cavalry and artillery, should occupy the attention of Napoleon, and if necessary fall back before him, whilst the two armies—that of Schwartzenberg by Vitry and Coulommiers, and that of Blucher by Châlons and Montmirail—should hastily advance upon the capital. At the same time the Allies issued another declaration from Vitry, in which they repeated their former protestations, and expressed their desire and resolve to "reconstruct the social edifice."

Meanwhile Marmont and Mortier, attempting to obey the directions of the Emperor, encountered the advancing columns of the enemy. They fell back fighting upon Fère-Champenoise, losing a large number of men, and took refuge in Sézanne. They were saved from further destruction by a force under General Pacthod, nearly wholly composed of National Guards, raised from the invaded districts, and which at this moment opposed an heroic resistance, in front of Fère-Champenoise, to an overwhelming number of the cavalry of both the Allied armies. Seventy cannon played upon these six thousand brave men for a period of twelve hours, who steadfastly refusing to surrender, were cut to pieces and mown down, until barely a thousand contrived to escape. This brilliant feat enabled Marmont and Mortier to withdraw with the remainder of their troops, and ultimately to reach Charenton, almost simultaneously with the arrival of the Allies in the environs of the capital.

The capital justified the predictions of Talleyrand and the Royalists; it offered no resistance worthy of the name. On the 29th of March, at the first news of the approach of the Allied armies, the Empress fled to Blois, accompanied by the infant King of Rome and a number of the ministers. The Parisians had, for the most part, believed in Napoleon to the last; and when the enemy's cannon saluted their ears on the 30th, and they heard that the Emperor was at Saint-Dizier, they began to think that he had really abandoned his cause. Some feeble efforts were now put forth to place the city in a state of defence. Joseph Bonaparte, who was in Paris, issued a proclamation, inciting the people to resistance. "Let us arm ourselves," he said, "to defend this city, her monuments, her wealth, your wives, your children, all that is dear to you. Let this vast city become for a season a camp, and let the enemy be defeated under the very walls which he expects to pass in triumph. The Emperor is marching to your aid. Second him by a brief resistance, and let us save the honour of France!"

All this might have been true, and a check to the enemy for a few weeks might have been equivalent to the raising of the siege by Napoleon, but Joseph and his advisers themselves took care that their proclamation should have no effect. They would not trust the people with arms; and though half Paris was ready to rise, and actually clamoured for them, none were given. Joseph was assisted by Clarke, Minister of War, and General Hullin; and, whether from indecision or from treachery, the triumvirate on whom the fate of Paris depended, and on whom Napoleon relied for his last chance of saving the capital, did nothing effectual. The Allies occupied gradually the heights round Paris, La Villette, La Chapelle, Pantin, Charonne, and Romainville; and at Noisy, at the foot of the hills which surround the capital, and in the wood of the same name, Blucher took up his quarters unopposed. A hundred and forty thousand Russians, Prussians, and Austrians surrounded the city; and the first show of opposition came from without, not from within its walls.

Marmont and Mortier had followed in the wake of the invaders, and on the 30th they made several furious and sanguinary attacks upon the overwhelming forces of the Allies. Around Romainville, Menilmontant, and Belleville the battle raged with the utmost ardour; and Schwartzenberg was at one time so hard pressed that he was obliged to call upon the Prussian Guards. The latter advanced against the heights of Belleville, which Marmont had already surmounted with his artillery, and which, served by the Marshal's troops, assisted by the pensioners, received them with a withering fire. The Prussians broke and retreated, but presently, reforming at Pantin, they charged in a similar manner against the hills (*buttes*) of Chaumont. Here the marines gave them an equally warm reception, whilst the National Guards, and the few citizens who had been able to obtain arms, fired upon them from every protected point. A second time the Prussians broke and withdrew; the French cavalry pursued and cut them down, recaptured Pantin, and held the seventy thousand men of Schwartzenberg's army at bay for seven hours until fatigue put an end to the struggle.

The resistance of Paris depended upon Marmont and Mortier alone, aided by a handful of veterans, and by the pensioners, marines, and military students of the capital. The few ministers and officials who had not fled with the Empress, and the two incompetent brothers of Napoleon, Joseph and Jérôme, had contributed nothing to the honour of the day. The Emperor, now on his way to Paris, sent General Dejean to Montmartre to inform his brothers of his return. The messenger came too late to find the representatives of the Imperial Government. A domestic placed in his hand the following letter of Joseph, which he had been charged to convey to the Marshals:—

"Paris, March 30th, 1814. If Marshal Mortier,

Duke of Treviso, and Marshal Marmont, Duke of Ragusa, cannot continue to hold their positions, they are authorised to enter into negotiations with Prince Schwartzenberg and the Emperor of Russia, who are opposed to them. They will afterwards withdraw upon the Loire."

And in fact, as soon as this letter was written, the two Bonapartes, with the minister Clarke in their company, precipitately fled to Versailles, having scarcely taken a single effectual step for the protection or assistance of the vast city which had been entrusted to their care.

Dejean instantly set spurs to his horse, and overtook the retreating brothers of the Emperor in the Bois de Boulogne. He entreated them to return, and assured them that Napoleon would reach the capital on the following day. Joseph told him that it was too late, and he would not listen to the arguments and entreaties of his brother's messenger.

The general, therefore, returned to Paris, where he found the two gallant Marshals still hotly contesting every foot of ground. But even Marmont and Mortier began to recognise that further resistance was hopeless. Toward nightfall they despatched an aide-de-camp to the head-quarters of the Allies at La Villette, who agreed upon an armistice for four hours, in order to arrange a capitulation, which was concluded at midnight, under the following conditions :—

"The French troops shall evacuate the capital of France on the 31st of March, at seven o'clock in the morning. All the arsenals, manufactories, military buildings and stores, shall remain in the condition in which they were before the capitulation."

It was afterwards discovered that the city contained thirty thousand new muskets, a hundred and twenty-five cannon, two hundred and fifty thousand hundred-weights of powder, five million cartridges, and a vast quantity of military stores of all kinds, which had been studiously withheld from a population anxious to defend themselves. As it was, the possession of the city had cost the Allies, on their own confession, eighteen thousand men. How would it have been if all Paris had been armed, and had held out until Napoleon had seconded its efforts with his army of forty thousand men? This, indeed, is what the Emperor had, at the last moment, attempted to do. As soon as he learned that Winzingerode was merely covering the forward march of the main armies of the Coalition, he hastened towards the capital, counting upon reaching it as soon as the enemy. At Troyes he received information which caused him to hurry on to Fontainebleau alone; and from thence he was continuing his journey when he met the troops of Marmont and Mortier.

On the 31st of March, the Allied sovereigns and their armies entered the French capital. They were received with enthusiasm by the partisans of the Bourbons, and cries of "Long live Louis XVIII." were alternated with "Long live Alexander!" The masses were subdued; they felt their helplessness, and were not consoled by the project of a monarchical restoration. The Czar and his allies paid apparently great respect to the national will, and compelled their troops to behave with the utmost moderation. Though the idea of interfering forcibly in the internal affairs of France was never entertained by the English Ministers, they privately inclined to the return of the Bourbons to power. Wellington had already tacitly allowed their conduct at Bordeaux, and the other Allies were sufficiently indifferent in the matter. It is true that Alexander emphatically declared, to the Royalists who assiduously paid him court, "The nation has only to manifest its will, and we shall maintain it;" but there was only one flaw in this professed deference to the popular wishes, and that was that the people were not consulted in the matter. Talleyrand assured the Allies that the "authorities" were in favour of the Bourbons; and, at length, the Czar, in the name of the Sovereigns, invited the Senate to appoint a Provisional Government, which should draw up a Constitution, and provide for the administration of affairs. But from beginning to end there was no thought of an appeal to the people.

On the 2nd of April the Senate named the following members of its body as a Provisional Government:— Talleyrand, Beurnonville, Jaucourt, Dalberg, and Montesquiou. On the next day they decreed the downfall of Napoleon and his dynasty.

"Considering"—so ran this decree—"that Napoleon Bonaparte has torn up the contract which bound him to the French people by raising taxes otherwise than in virtue of the law, by needlessly adjourning the Legislative Body, by illegally issuing sundry decrees involving the infliction of death, by suppressing ministerial responsibility, judicial independence, freedom of the press, &c.; considering that Napoleon has crowned the misfortunes of his country by misapplying all the men and money entrusted to him for the purpose of war, and by refusing to treat on conditions which the national welfare required to be accepted; considering that the manifest wishes of all Frenchmen call for a state of things whereof the first result should be the re-establishment of the general peace, and which should also be the epoch of a solemn reconciliation amongst all the States of the great European family—the Senate decrees: Napoleon Bonaparte is dethroned; hereditary right is abolished in his family; the French people and army are absolved from their oath of fidelity to him."

This decree caused a great sensation; though there were found many individuals ready to hail it with enthusiasm, and to treat the memory of the fallen Emperor with contempt. When Napoleon was informed of it, and found moreover that the spirit of his oldest and best generals had died or was dying out, and that the troops who yet remained with him revolted at the idea of engaging in a civil war, he determined to submit to his fate. On the 4th of April he abdicated in favour of his son, appointed the Empress Regent, and sent Caulaincourt, Ney, and Macdonald to treat with the Allied sovereigns. The latter received these envoys with respect; for Napoleon was still a redoubtable name, and he had still an army. But at this critical moment a new and remarkable desertion took place in the camp at Fontainebleau. Marmont, the hero of a hundred well-contested battlefields, signed a secret convention with the Allies, in accordance with which he suddenly withdrew with his men, arms, cannon, and baggage, to Normandy.

The Allies at once rejected the propositions of the Emperor. The latter, enraged and desperate, declared that he would march upon Paris; but the spirit of his remnant of an army was utterly broken. Even Ney and Berthier now abandoned him; and at length, one week after signing his first abdication, he signed another in these terms:—

"The Allied Powers having proclaimed that the Emperor Napoleon is the only obstacle to the reestablishment of peace in Europe, the Emperor Napoleon, faithful to his oaths, declares that he renounces, for himself and his heirs, the thrones of France and Italy, forasmuch as there is no personal sacrifice, not even that of life itself, which he is not willing to make in the interests of France."

Immediately afterwards a convention was signed between Napoleon and the Allies, whereby the former stipulated for the retention of his titles and rank, as well as for those of his mother, his son, his brothers, sisters, nephews, and nieces; for the island of Elba as a residence, to be considered a principality and his own property, with an income of £100,000; for the duchies of Parma, Piacenza, and Guastalla, for his wife and son; and for an income of £40,000 for the ex-Empress Josephine, who did not long survive the downfall of her divorced husband, but died at Malmaison, on the 29th of May.

On the 16th of April, 1814, the deposed Emperor bade farewell to his soldiers, and departed for Elba, with generals Bertrand, Drouot, and Cambronne, and four commissioners of the Allies, an Englishman, an Austrian, a Russian, and a Prussian.

Michelet is worth quoting here, in connection with the departure of the fallen monarch for his temporary exile, and the attitude of the French people in the provinces.

"Napoleon had himself requested, as a guarantee of his safety, that commissioners of the five great Powers should conduct him to Elba; so that what follows was seen by five witnesses. If the most hostile witness, the Prussian, made a point of recording these discreditable circumstances, they were also attested by the Russian, and by the Austrian who saw in Napoleon the son-in-law of his master. The Russian and the Austrian, indeed, were so humane and well-disposed that, in order to reassure him, they exposed themselves, consenting to disguises, to changes of garment, which, with a populace intoxicated by rage, might turn to their own injury, and cause them to be massacred themselves.

"Near Valence he (the Emperor) encountered Augereau, and for the first time saw how completely he had fallen. Augereau did not salute him, but, as he embraced him, spoke with coarse familiarity, and reproached him with the ambition which had brought him to such a pass. Napoleon received all this in good part, and returned his embrace. Augereau departed without saluting.[1]

"At Avignon a thousand invectives were uttered by the crowd. At Orgon they were terrified by the sinister exhibition of a gallows, from which hung a figure (the image of the Emperor) covered with blood. The Russian commissioner, who came last, endeavoured to pacify the crowd, speaking of the pity due to an unfortunate prisoner. Bonaparte, very pale, at the bottom of his carriage, at first tried to conceal himself behind his companion, General Bertrand. But he was not satisfied with that; fear induced him to don the white cockade and a courier's dress, and he began to ride in the front.

" The carriages came on at a slower pace, which was almost causing a tragedy. At Saint-Canat the people tried to open the carriage, in order to assassinate Bertrand, who occupied the place of the Emperor.

"He himself, having vainly tried to pass for an Englishman, proposed to retrace his steps as far as Lyons, in order to take another road. He wept,

---

[1] Savary, Duke de Rovigo, denies this in the seventh volume of his *Mémoires pour servir à l'Histoire de Napoléon*, and says that Augereau spoke to the fallen Emperor with the same respect he had always shown him.

and looked round like a child, to see if there was any escape by the window of the small inn where they stopped; but it was barred, and probably watched by a hostile crowd. The landlady, coming forward, declared that the people would undoubtedly assassinate or drown Bonaparte. The better to dissimulate, he himself declared that this was a very good idea.

"At times he fancied that the commissioners might poison him, and would touch nothing at their meals. In fine (a thing which bore witness to a brain giddy with terror), occasionally, in the midst of his tears, he spoke volubly, and assumed an amiable and genteel manner, so that a clown would have blushed to behave thus.

"At midnight they were going on, and a Russian, an aide-de-camp to Commissioner Schouvaloff, offered, in order to reassure him, to put on the garment in which he had played the part of a courier. Bonaparte converted himself into an Austrian general, by assuming the white uniform of the commissioner Koller, and above that the cloak of the Russian Schouvaloff. Koller took him in his carriage, and, in order to dispense with all notion of etiquette, whistled at his request, and told his coachman to smoke.

"In the end, they met two companies of Austrian hussars, who served as an escort, and brought his terrors to a conclusion.

"I have given this lamentable account on behalf of those who, like Montaigne, are amused to observe the variations of human nature, which are strong, but by no means capricious, and are capable of an excellent physical explanation."[1]

The campaign of 1814 did not end with the capitulation of Paris. On the 8th of April, Marshal Soult concentrated an army of about forty thousand men near Toulouse, the ancient capital of the southern provinces of France, and well known to him, as he had been born and bred in its immediate neighbourhood. The Garonne flows to the west of that city, with a deep curve, and on its left bank is situated the suburb of St. Ciprien, defended by a strong wall, massy towers and redoubts; so that to attack the town from that side would have been hazardous. Wellington, who had arrived at the head of nearly fifty-two thousand Englishmen and Spaniards, resolved, after various attempts made for about ten days, to cross the Garonne at Grenade, fifteen miles below Toulouse. But only fifteen thousand foot and three thousand horse could be carried over, for the river was so swollen and tempestuous that the grappling-irons and supports of the bridge were swept away, so that the rest of the troops could not cross. The French Marshal instead of attacking these isolated soldiers, neglected the opportunity, and seems to have been ignorant of the comparative small number opposed to him. But five days later the whole of the Anglo-Spanish army crossed, and then the English general, early in the morning, commenced the battle (June 10th) which was vigorously and bravely con-

[1] *Hist. du XIX. siècle*, vol. iii., bk. vi., ch. 5.

tested on both sides, but which resulted in the retreat of Soult with a loss of over three thousand killed. Wellington, who had lost nearly five thousand men occupied Toulouse on the 12th, and found in that town sixteen hundred wounded, amongst whom were three generals. He was received by the inhabitants with great demonstrations of joy, and soon afterwards they united with those of Paris in declaring in favour of Louis XVIII.; and the French Marshal, after a fortnight's hesitation, tendered his submission to the Duke d'Angoulême.

Book VI.

THE RESTORATION.

CHAPTER I.

§ I.—THE RETURN OF THE BOURBONS.

(From the 11th of April, 1814, till the 20th of March, 1815.)

THE reaction against the Imperial *régime*, and the consequent abdication of Napoleon, rendered it necessary for France to consider how she should fill the vacancy caused by the Emperor's withdrawal. The Provisional Government lost no time in decreeing a Constitution, and in summoning the Bourbons to the throne. But the Senate, which had pronounced the downfall of the Empire, seemed to concern itself chiefly with the maintenance of its temporary dignity and authority; unless, indeed, we accept the more charitable construction of its apparent lethargy, and ascribe it to the presence of the foreign armies on the soil of France.

There were, as we have seen, a considerable number of men who, perceiving that a decided course of action must be entered upon by the nation, had the courage to pronounce their opinion more or less openly.

Amongst these was Montesquiou, a Legitimist, and a member of the Provisional Government, who had persistently advocated the cause of the Bourbons. Montesquiou played in France much the same part that Monk and his friends had played in England, after the death of Cromwell had paved the way for the restoration of the Stuarts. He not only expected his colleagues to invite Louis XVIII. to Paris, but he also carried on an active correspondence with the Pretender, who resided then at Hartwell, in Buckinghamshire, and prepared the way for his return.

Louis XVI. had left two brothers—the Count of Provence, now Louis XVIII., and the Count d'Artois. The late King's son, a prisoner in the Temple at the time of that monarch's execution, was known as Louis XVII., or, at all events, the Legitimists had made it a point of honour to speak of him under that title; and on his death, a couple of years later, his uncle, Louis Stanislas Xavier, pretended to the throne of his late brother, as Louis XVIII. The youngest of the three brothers, the Count d'Artois, who had professed an ardent devotion to his sister-in-law, Marie Antoinette, but whose amours had gone much farther afield in other directions, had latterly renounced the pleasures of the world, and had sought consolation for the death of his last mistress in a life of religious asceticism. Recalled to mundane cares by the collapse of the Empire, the Count, with his two sons, the Dukes d'Angoulême and de Berry, now bestirred himself in the interests of his brother, and, favoured by the indirect assistance of the English, had made his way through Switzerland into France.

Louis XVIII. issued a manifesto to the French people from his English home; but he left his brother and his nephews to take the more active, more dangerous, and more effectual measures which the times rendered necessary. The Count began by promising the abolition of the conscription, and of the heavy imposts levied under Napoleon; and the country, worn out by enforced military service, and exhausted by taxation, soon welcomed the prospect of a monarchical restoration. The King's proclamation had been issued early in the year; and after some hesitation the Count d'Artois advanced, through Vesoul, Nancy, and Troyes, to the capital, which he entered amidst a display of enthusiastic welcome, on the 12th of April. The National Guard, the municipal authorities, a portion of the Senate, and six of Napoleon's Marshals—Ney, Oudinot, Kellermann, Moncey, Marmont, and Serurier—were amongst those who hastened to adhere to the Legitimist cause.

Meanwhile the Allies had refused to lend any direct countenance to the attempts of the Legitimists. They had thrown their ægis over the Senate, and guaranteed the observance of the Constitution framed and voted by the last-mentioned body, who finally agreed to recall Louis XVIII. on condition that he should accept the newly made Constitution. It was doubtless the more resolute in demanding this acceptance from a recollection of the manner in which Louis XVI. had observed the oath taken by him to the Constitution of 1789. On the 13th of April the Czar paid the Count d'Artois a visit, in the course of which he explained to him the nature of the guarantee given by the Allies to the Senate, and declared that they had no disposition to break their word. As soon as this interview was at an end, the Count expressed his willingness to receive the Senators, which he had hitherto declined to do. The latter saluted him as Lieutenant-General of the kingdom; and the Count thereupon declared that, though he had not been authorised by his brother to accept the Constitution, yet he knew his sentiments and principles, and believed he should not be disavowed if he affirmed, in the King's name, that he would admit its fundamental propositions. The Legislative Body, which followed the Senate, was less exacting, and, probably because it was satisfied with the Count's qualified adhesion to the Constitution, made no demand on its own account; whereupon the Lieutenant-General could not deny himself the pleasure of exclaiming that here, at last, he recognised the " genuine representatives of the French people."

The Count d'Artois now set himself to work to reorganise the public services, and to place the power in the hands of the staunch adherents of the old dynasty, who came pouring back into the country. This was by no means the only test of loyalty imposed upon France by the first representative of the restored dynasty. No sooner had the *ancien régime* began to re-establish itself upon the ruins of the Empire than its old unscrupulousness and folly revived. The first violation of the King's word was resorted to for the purpose of raising money. The coffers of the State were not yet empty; but so far from steps being taken to relieve the burden of taxation, the Count and his advisers demanded the collection of certain extraordinary imposts, decreed by Napoleon just before his abdication. Perhaps a still more fatal blunder was committed by the hasty substitution of the white flag for the tricolour, a measure which caused much unnecessary discontent in the army, and may have contributed not a little to the disasters of the Hundred Days.

The Allies lost no time in requiring the Count, in the name of his brother, to sign an agreement, without prejudice to the final terms of peace, removing the limits of France to those which had existed in the beginning of 1792, and directing the complete evacuation of all places beyond this boundary. Talleyrand, who conducted these negotiations, has never been forgiven by his fellow-countrymen for the apparent pliability with which he thus consented to abandon every advantage gained by two-and-twenty years of prodigious sacrifices, and unparalleled military prowess.

Louis XVIII. left England towards the end of April, after an ill-judged compliment addressed to the Prince Regent, in which he attributed his recall " to the counsels of the Prince, to this glorious land, and to the confidence of its inhabitants." The phrase was naturally looked upon as humiliating for France; and it was but the first of many similar displays of a spirit lamentably out of harmony with the most valuable results of the Revolution.

The work achieved by the French Revolution might be full of contrasted good and evil, and its sequel had undoubtedly assumed the form of a negation of popular liberties; but it had at least laid the foundation of freedom for France. The Restoration already threatened to cast away all that was really valuable in the legacy of 1789.

The King reached Compiègne on the 29th of April, and was immediately besieged by crowds of officials and courtiers, who wished to make the best possible terms with the new monarch. The Legislative Body more eager to welcome him than the Senate, hastened to lay the country at his feet. They demanded no guarantee, and asked for no assurance, beyond mildly requesting a general acceptance of the results of the past twenty years. The King's residence in England had, indeed, not been in vain. He was more liberal than many of his friends, and certainly more so than his brother; but he was still unprepared for Constitutional government, even as it had been conceived by the so-called Conservative Senate.

He entered Paris on the 3rd of May; and on the previous evening he signed the following manifesto, which was published and circulated throughout the country. The King attached his signature to this declaration in the village of Saint Ouen, whence it has taken its name:—

"Recalled by the affections of our people to the throne of France, instructed by the misfortunes of the nation which we are destined to govern, our first thought is to invoke that mutual reliance so necessary to our happiness, and to its welfare.

"After attentively reading the scheme of a Constitution proposed by the Senate, in its sitting of the 6th of April last, we acknowledge that its bases are good, but that a large number of articles, bearing the impress of the haste wherewith they were drawn up, cannot, as they stand, become fundamental laws of the State. Resolved to accept a liberal Constitution, desiring that it should be wisely put together, and unable to accept one which it is indispensable to correct, we will convoke the Senate and the Legislative Body, undertaking to bring under their notice the work which we shall have performed, with a Committee selected from amongst these two bodies, and to give as a basis for this Constitution the following guarantees: representative government in two bodies; taxation voted by the nation; public and individual liberty; freedom of the press; freedom of worship; the inviolability and sacredness of property; irrevocability of the judges, and independence of the judicial power; the guarantee of the public debt; the maintenance of the Legion of Honour; every Frenchman admissible to all employments; in fine, no interference with any individual for his opinions and his votes."

The King was a man of no forcible character, and his first care seems to have been to resuscitate from their quarter of a century of oblivion the empty titles and sinecures of the *ancien régime*. Amongst other instances of this, the Count d'Artois was named Colonel-General of the Swiss Guards and of the National Guards; the King's cousin, the Duke de Bourbon-Condé, was appointed Colonel-General of the Infantry, a rank he had held before the Revolution; the Duke d'Angoulême Colonel of Cuirassiers and Dragoons, and Marshal of France; the Duke de Berry Colonel-General of Chasseurs and Lancers, and the Duke d'Orléans Colonel-General of Hussars. At the same time Oudinot and Ney accepted the command-in-chief of the grenadiers and dragoons respectively.

The first ministry of the Restoration was not appointed until the 13th of May, when it was constituted as follows:—Chancellor and Keeper of the Seals, Dambray; Foreign Affairs, Talleyrand; Minister of the Interior, Montesquiou; of War, General Dupont; of Finances, the Abbé Louis; of Marine and the Colonies, Malouet; of the King's Household, De Blacas. One of the most able of these ministers was the Abbé Louis, who did much to ensure the financial prosperity of the country during the Restoration. The least popular appointment was that of General Dupont, who had been responsible for the capitulation of Baylen,[1] and whom Napoleon had at the time accused of treason.

Meanwhile the final treaty of peace was being

[1] See bk. v., ch. iii., § 1, p. 65.

prepared, and it was ratified at Paris on the 30th of May. After this there was no delay in the evacuation of the country by the Allied troops. France was not treated as a conquered nation in 1814; and the sovereigns, well satisfied to have their victory regarded as one over Napoleon alone, avoided as much as possible all interference with the action of the authorities, and readily acquiesced in the Bourbon Restoration. The Emperor of Russia left Paris on the 2nd of June, the King of Prussia one day later.

On the 4th of June the Chambers were opened, and the famous Constitutional Charter was signed and granted by the King.[1]

This document, containing seventy-six articles, destined to be very frequently cited and appealed to in subsequent years, with some notable exceptions, was a fairly liberal compromise between popular freedom and the privileges of a Legitimist monarch. It guaranteed equality before the law, individual liberty of person, action, religion, and speech. The election, powers, and privileges of the Chambers were conceived in a spirit which displayed a genuine desire on the part of those who framed the Charter to work out a scheme of constitutional monarchy. The concession was of course regarded as too great by the more ardent

[1] This Charter was drawn up in accordance with the declaration of Saint-Ouen, by a Committee appointed on the King's behalf, and consisting of three royal commissioners, Montesquiou, Ferrand, aud Beugnot; nine senators, including Barthélemy, Boissy-d'Anglas, Fontanes, Garnier, Marshal Serurier; and nine deputies, including Bois-Savary, Chabaud-Latour, Duhamel, Faucon, and Lainé.

members of the reactionary party who had spent five-and-twenty years in longing for a restoration of the *ancien régime;* but Louis and his friends recognised the necessity of accepting accomplished facts, and dared not attempt openly to undo the work of the Revolution. The Charter was welcomed by those who had lamented the check to political and social development caused by the Napoleonic wars. They saw in it an honest effort to give France similar institutions to those which had been adopted by the governments of England, of the United States, and of Switzerland; and they were fully justified in accepting this new form of Liberal progress for their country and generation.

Louis le Désiré—for so he was hailed by the Chambers on the promulgation of the Charter—soon found that he had to reckon with opponents as formidable on the side of reaction as on that of popular progress. The *émigrés* as a body were enraged with the compromise entered into between the brother of Louis XVI. and the men who had beheaded him. This extreme reactionary party found its most influential exponent in the Count d'Artois, who did his best to gratify his friends. It soon became manifest that the Government itself, without the need of any external pressure, would accompany the text of the Charter with commentaries of anything but a liberal tendency. Even before the year was out severe police regulations were issued for the stricter observance of Sunday, and other days appointed for public religious services. Further restrictions of a similar kind served to show that the re-vindication of religion was to be one of the first cares of the new order of things, and that the liberty of worship granted by the Charter was not to extend beyond the line which might be marked out by the Roman Catholic authorities.

The freedom of the press was interfered with as early as the months of August and September, 1814, when a law to check all abuses, and which was to last until the end of the session of 1816, was passed by both Chambers. By this enactment the liberty accorded by the Charter was confined to publications of "more than twenty sheets," that is to say, to books containing a minimum of 336 pages. It was withdrawn from journals and periodicals, which thenceforth required an authorisation; whilst printers and booksellers were subjected to a license. Public opinion received this measure, as well as the regulations about the religious services, with much dissatisfaction, and it began to be perceived that the popular liberties were likely to rest on no stronger basis than the caprices of a Government not responsible to the people.

There were many other causes of discontent, which, early in the year 1815, afforded some sort of pretext and encouragement for the desperate attempt of Napoleon to recover his lost Empire. The King had done much for the *émigrés*. He had restored their titles; he had made generals of many who had been lieutenants in 1789, and had filled the army and navy with officers on the same generous and dangerous principle. The Government, moreover, brought in a bill to provide for the restitution to the former proprietors of the unsold portions of estates confiscated under the Republic, whilst at the same time sanctioning the sales which had already taken place. The reactionary minister Ferrand would have annulled these sales, and restored the property in its entirety; but public opinion would never have tolerated this. It was sufficiently excited by the proposal actually made, which seemed to undo a work to which the minds of men had become accustomed, and of which the advantage had been reaped.

It had been decided that a Congress for the general settlement of the political condition of Europe should be held in the capital of Austria; and at the end of September the Emperor Alexander, the Kings of Prussia, Bavaria, Denmark, and Wurtemberg, and many lesser princes, with Lord Castlereagh, and afterwards the Duke of Wellington, on the part of England, met there. Its negotiations were not finally completed until the eve of the battle of Waterloo. Some difficulty arose amongst the plenipotentiaries, owing to the demands of Prussia and Russia. The first Power claimed for itself the Kingdom of Saxony; the latter the duchies of Posen and Warsaw. A rupture was at one time imminent, as England, Austria, and France objected to these aggrandisements; but an understanding was arrived at by the Czar pledging his word that he would reconstruct a kingdom of Poland as an autonomous state. It need hardly be added that this

engagement was destined to be superseded by the
" progress of events."

France was reduced by this Congress to the limits
of 1792, and the various European States were rewarded
and punished according to the attitude which they
had maintained during the past quarter of a century.
Denmark, which had clung to the fortunes of Napoleon,
was deprived of Norway, which was added to the
possessions of Sweden, as a recompense for the conduct of Bernadotte. Finland—the Bessarabia of the
north—was made over to Russia. Austria resumed
Lombardy, to which Venetia was added—thus planting
the seeds of the war of 1859, when the nephew of
Napoleon I. deprived Austria of her Italian provinces.
The Emperor Francis Joseph also secured the Bavarian
Tyrol, Istria, and Dalmatia. Central Europe was
formed into a German Confederation, of which Austria
and Prussia were the leading States; and in this
arrangement also it is possible to discern the seeds
of future war. Switzerland was enlarged by the
cantons of Geneva, Neufchâtel, and the Valais, and her
independence was guaranteed. The Pope recovered
his states; the duchies of Tuscany, Modena, Lucca,
and several others were restored to their former rulers;
and Maria Louisa became, as we have seen, Duchess of
Parma, Piacenza, and Guastalla. England retained the
French colonies which her navy had conquered, and added
to her Mediterranean possession of Gibraltar the island
of Malta and the Ionian Islands. By her request, also,
the kingdom of Holland and Belgium was established.

The representative of France at this Congress was the Foreign Minister, Talleyrand, who was able to resist the annexation of Saxony to Prussia, though his protest against the confirmation of Murat on the throne of Naples was unavailing.

§ II.—THE RETURN OF NAPOLEON.—THE HUNDRED DAYS.

(*From the 20th of March to the 8th of July*, 1815.)

NAPOLEON, in his island of Elba, must have witnessed this repartition of Europe with feelings of intense bitterness; and, little as the world may have suspected it, he was nursing, even before the results of the deliberations of the Congress of Vienna were known, a bold and unscrupulous project for the recovery of all that he had lost. His dream was encouraged by the rising discontent of the French Liberals, and by the ever-increasing self-assertion of the Chambers. Reports concerning the sentiment of the army continually reached him; and at last he entered into a definite conspiracy with the most influential of his friends still remaining in France. The folly of leaving such a man at liberty, close to the frontier of the country in which he had attained his immense popularity, now became conspicuous; and Europe was doomed to a terrible punishment for its lack of prudence and foresight.

The zeal of the Royalists was exhibited during the early part of 1815 in many petty acts of spite against the memory of the Revolution, and idle exultation over the establishment of a new order of things. A solemn expiation was appointed for the 21st of January, the day on which Louis XVI. had been executed. The "victims of Quiberon"[1]—the Royalists whom Hoche had crushed out on the Breton coast—were officially glorified, together with the leaders and soldiers of the Vendean revolt. The ashes of the late King and of Marie Antoinette—or what was alleged to be their ashes —were gathered up from the dust of the cemetery of the Madeleine, and carried with great pomp to the abbey of Saint-Denis; the Charter was continually violated, and the return to an Absolute Monarchy was openly advocated by men like de Bonald and Joseph de Maistre. All these things were natural enough, and they would have had their counterpart in any other country under similar circumstances, as they had had their counterpart in England after the Restoration of the Stuarts. But France was deeply excited by the danger with which the popular liberties seemed to be threatened, and Napoleon thought, not altogether unreasonably, that this would assist him in his desperate enterprise.

On the 5th of March, France was electrified by the news that the ex-Emperor had already disembarked in the Gulf of St. Juan, near Fréjus, and that he was on his way to Paris at the head of an army. The Government, hard to move, even then, from its sluggish incompetence, declared Napoleon a traitor and rebel, and set a price on his head. The Chambers were convoked; Soult, who had obtained the Ministry of War by a policy of judicious sycophancy, was made to give

[1] See vol. i., bk. ii., ch. ii., § i., pp. 347 and 348.

place to Clarke, now Duke de Feltre; and the latter was ordered to assemble an army.

The Chambers met on the 15th, and Louis went down the next day and pronounced an address. "I come into your midst," he said, "to draw closer the bonds which unite us together. . . . I have laboured for the good of my people: I have received the most touching marks of their love. . . . He who has brought the torch of civil war amongst us brings also the scourge of foreign warfare: he comes to place our country under a yoke of iron; he comes to destroy that Constitutional Charter which I have granted —that Charter which will constitute my best epitaph in the eyes of posterity." The King and his Council deliberated what was to be done. Some proposed to make an appeal to the foreign Powers, others again wished Louis XVIII. to shut himself up in a strong fortress, whilst a few trusty friends advised the monarch to remain and to await the course of events. This last counsel tempted him, and he even expressed a wish "to meet the man who pretended to fill the throne of France," whilst he addressed a proclamation to the army in which he reminded it that he was the sole legitimate occupant of that throne.

Meanwhile Napoleon drew nearer and nearer to the capital, absorbing into his army all the troops which were sent to oppose his progress. Ney was amongst the commanders who could not restrain his soldiers from donning the famous tricolour; and his forced adherence to his old master was destined to cost him dear. The Duke de Berry quitted Paris on the 17th, at the head of the garrison and a company of volunteers. But as soon as they were fairly on the road the regular troops cast away the white cockade, and raised a cheer for the Emperor, leaving the Duke and his volunteers to return and tell the ominous tale.

Louis XVIII., as we have seen, displayed, at first, great courage of speech and intention; but as the danger approached his nerves played him false, and on the 19th he retired to Lille, after closing the Chambers, and assuring his subjects that he meant to return. At Lille he found Marshal Mortier, who warned him that the garrison was not to be relied upon. He instantly pursued his journey to Ghent, across the Belgian frontier; and almost at the same moment Napoleon was entering Paris amidst the enthusiastic welcome of a small portion of the populace, including many of his former officers.

No doubt the return of Napoleon was, to a certain extent, an experiment in the first instance. He could not have been thoroughly certain that the army would rally to his standard, though he had every reason to flatter himself that such would be the case; but if his expectations had been deceived, he would have contrived to abandon his enterprise before reaching Paris. Once in the capital, however, which had been deserted by its natural protector, and once assured of the success of his military movement, confidence immediately took the place of hesitation. On touching the soil of France, Napoleon encountered a battalion of infantry. He ordered his own men to stand at ease, and, throwing open his cloak, advanced to the King's troops, and said, "If any of you wishes to kill his Emperor, he can do so now." The soldiers answered with a shout, and at once fraternised with the invaders. The same spirit had been encountered at every pause in the journey; the army received him with a hearty welcome; and though the bulk of the civilians displayed little or no enthusiasm, at all events, the supreme power and authority fell instantly into Napoleon's hands.

He recalled nearly all the members of his last Ministry, and gave to Carnot the portfolio of the Interior. The step was a most judicious one, and was accepted as a guarantee by the old Republican party that their aspirations would be more likely to receive encouragement from a second epoch of Imperial Government than from the reactionary *régime* of the Bourbons.[1] The ex-Emperor, now again Emperor *de facto*, expressed the hope that peace would not be broken by his return to Paris, and that he would be allowed to resume the direction of affairs with nothing more than a protest from the fugitive King, and perhaps also from the European courts. At all events, he sent dispatches to this effect, not only to the Empress, but to the Sovereigns. But his messengers did not bear these dispatches to their destination. Maria Louisa had already found a consola-

---

[1] On the 24th of March Napoleon proclaimed the complete liberty of the press, and engaged Benjamin Constant to draw up a Liberal Constitution.

tion for her political divorce from the man whom she had probably never regarded as a legitimate husband, and she now declared her intention of leaving her son under the charge of his imperial grandfather, and assuming her position as Duchess of Parma.

The Congress of Sovereigns, which still sat at Vienna, declared on the 13th of March that "Napoleon Bonaparte had placed himself outside the pale of civil and social relations," and that "as an enemy and disturber of the peace of the world, he had exposed himself to public vengeance;" that, moreover, "they would use their whole resources and combine all their efforts to guarantee Europe against any outrage which might threaten to plunge the nations once again into the disorders and disasters of revolutions." On the 25th a treaty was signed, pledging the Powers to maintain the Treaty of Paris, ratified on the previous 30th of May, as well as the decisions of the Congress. Each Power also undertook to put a hundred and fifty thousand men in the field. On the last day of the month a Convention was entered into, providing for the formation of three armies: the first, of three hundred and forty-four thousand, under Schwartzenberg; the second, of two hundred and fifty thousand, under Wellington and Blucher; the third, of two hundred thousand, under the Emperor Alexander.

Napoleon, at the Tuileries, was actively preparing against attack. He directed the construction of defensive works around Paris and Lyons, and paid every attention to raising the effective strength of the army, and completing its equipments. Meanwhile he had much to engage him at home, where he found a very different state of things from that which he had left behind him eleven months before. As soon as the first excitement of his return had passed away numerous deputations waited upon him, and gave him clearly to understand that he must reign for the future, if he was to reign at all, as a Constitutional Monarch. The word Constitution met him at every turn, and weighed upon him like an incubus. "I no longer recognise France," he said; "the Bourbons have spoiled it for me." He was inclined to act in his old high-handed manner. He signed a decree confiscating the property of thirteen prominent men, with the Ministers of Louis XVIII. amongst them; but he could get no one to countersign it. Even General Bertrand, who had been with him in Elba, saw that the old order of things had changed, and that 1814 must be accepted as an integral part of the situation, just as the Bourbons had had to accept the Revolution. The Council of State, after admitting that Napoleon was still Emperor by virtue of popular election, which the decree of the Senate was not competent to overrule, reminded him that he had undertaken to maintain all the Liberal principles established under the Republic; whilst the Municipal Council of Paris expressed its conviction that "a Constitution guaranteed by Napoleon could not be violated as soon as it had been promulgated."

Napoleon gave way before such evidences of determination, and a Committee was appointed to consider the amended Constitution, chiefly drawn up by Benjamin Constant. The Emperor himself took part in the discussion, and, though his arguments were for the most part in restriction of Liberal progress, they were not without considerable shrewdness. His objections to an hereditary peerage are especially worth repeating. "From whence," he asked, "would you have me take the aristocratic elements which the peerage requires? The old fortunes are overthrown; some of the new ones have been acquired by discreditable means; five or six historic names are not sufficient. Without traditions, without historic splendour, without great possessions, on what shall my peerage be founded? The peerage of England is quite another matter; it is above the people, but it has not been against the people. It was the nobles who gave liberty to England; the Great Charter comes from them; they have grown with the Constitution, and are one with it. But for thirty years to come my mushroom peers will be only soldiers, or chamberlains; the people will perceive in them but men of the camp or of the ante-chamber."

Napoleon yielded this point, but he successfully insisted upon retaining the punishment of confiscation in cases of high treason. The Committee laboured hard to give the "Supplementary Act (*Acte additionnel*) to the Constitutions of the Empire" an initial, and independent authority of its own; but nothing would satisfy Napoleon except that it should be based upon, and professedly spring from, the former imperial *régime*. Another struggle arose on the manner in which the Supplementary Act should be sanctioned. Several members of the Committee urged that it should be voted by the Chamber of Deputies. After much discussion, when the text was finally agreed upon, Napoleon promised to consider this suggestion; but on the 22nd of April, the document was published and promulgated on the sole authority of the Emperor. Nevertheless it was decided that the Act should be submitted to the popular vote, in the same manner as the election of Napoleon to the First Consulship and to the throne had been—that is to say, by open voting in the electoral colleges. The franchise was at that time possessed by five million Frenchmen, and out of these one million three hundred thousand accepted the Supplementary Act, whilst four thousand two hundred voted in the negative. Nearly three-quarters of those entitled to vote had declined to express their opinion.

The acceptance of this Act, and its virtual ratification by Napoleon, were celebrated with great pomp in the Champ de Mars on the 1st of June. The ceremony had been appointed for an earlier date, and the assembly had thus acquired the name of the Champ de Mai. Napoleon came to the scene amidst all the splendour and display of the palmiest days of the Empire, in a gilded coach, in a coat of crimson silk, relieved with gold, over which hung a cloak of violet velvet. Then, surrounded by his " mushroom " nobility and court, the Emperor solemnly declared his love and devotion to France, and swore, with his hand upon the Bible, "to observe and cause to be observed the Constitutions of the Empire." This was followed by a grand distribution of imperial eagles to the various regiments, and by the oath of allegiance to the Empire from the assembled ranks.

But amidst the shouts and the *Te Deums* of the Champ de Mai there arose the murmurs of thousands of discontented Frenchmen, who saw with ever-increasing bitterness that the popular liberties were about to be once more overwhelmed by these imperial displays, and who knew that the second invasion of the country was a simple question of time. In La Vendée the white flag was once more raised; and it was necessary to send thither a force of thirty thousand troops to hold the Royalists in check, whilst the Allies were already pouring into Belgium.

On the 12th of June Napoleon left Paris, early in the morning, having entrusted the government to his brothers Joseph and Lucien—to the same Joseph who, little more than a year ago, had precipitately fled from Montmartre.

Napoleon had carefully considered the situation in which he found himself, and resolved not to wait for his enemies, but to attack them without delay, as suddenly as possible, and before they had time to concentrate. Wellington was already in Belgium with an army of ninety thousand men, of whom about half were English, and one hundred and ninety-six cannon, whilst sixteen thousand Hanse troops and Danes arrived after the opening of the campaign. Blucher was hastening to meet him with an army of one hundred and twenty-four thousand men, and three hundred and fifty cannon. Against these Napoleon had one hundred and twenty-eight thousand troops, and three hundred and forty-six cannon; whilst fifty-five thousand men were extended along the eastern frontier, as far south as the borders of Italy.

Avesnes was reached on the 14th, and here Napoleon issued to his army a proclamation in which he reminded them of the victories of Marengo, of Austerlitz, of Jena and Wagram, and urged them to prove themselves worthy of their fame. On the same night he crossed the Sambre, and on the following day he entered Charleroi, attacked the Prussians, and drove their advanced posts back upon Fleurus. His plan was to prevent the junction of Wellington and Blucher, to interrupt their communications, and to crush them one after the other, by a succession of heavy blows. At Charleroi Napoleon lost one of his generals by desertion—Bourmont, who had already been a Vendean, an Imperialist, and a Royalist again, before he accepted his second commission from the Emperor. He passed over to the Prussian lines on the 15th, in the sight of his troops; and Frenchmen have shown a disposition to suspect him of having betrayed Napoleon's plans to the enemy.

Wellington's lines were drawn from Nivelles to Mons, and thence to Ath and Oudenarde, his headquarters being at Brussels, where the sudden approach of Napoleon had caused the greatest surprise, not to say consternation. The first attack of the French was delivered before the Belgian capital knew that the formidable foe was on the frontier. Blucher was between Charleroi and Liége, nearer to the French frontier than Napoleon; whilst Ney, with a corps amounting to about forty-six thousand men, was at Frasnes, a mile from Quatre-Bras, and prevented the English from coming to the relief of Blucher.

The result of the attack on the Prussians on the 15th of June did not entirely answer the expectations either of Napoleon himself or of his enemies; and historians have criticised the conduct of the Emperor and of his generals alike. It must be remembered that the majority of the latter were comparatively new and untried men for the important posts which they occupied, except Vandamme and Ney, two of Napoleon's famous Marshals of the former campaigns, and Soult, who was Major-General of the Army. Vandamme himself had done much to jeopardise the success of the movement against Fleurus, by his tardy crossing of the Sambre, not having reached Charleroi until six in the evening, at least four hours after Napoleon had confidently reckoned upon him.[1] Marshal Grouchy

---

[1] He was to have commenced the passage of the Sambre at half-past two in the morning; but it is said that the messenger who bore the order broke his leg by a fall from his horse, so that Vandamme did not learn Napoleon's plan in time to set out before half-past seven. On this and all points connected with the events of the next few days I am much indebted to a series of papers by M. Edgar Quinet on *La Campagne de 1815*, in the *Revue des Deux Mondes*, Aug. 15—Oct. 1, 1861.

charged Vandamme with refusing him the necessary co-operation in the attack on Fleurus; but the morning's delay is sufficient to account for the circumstances of the case.

It is difficult, on the whole, to avoid the conclusion that Napoleon's attack upon the Allies was premature, or at all events ill-prepared. No doubt he considered it his best policy to strike the first blow; but it was after all a fortuitous circumstance that he crossed the Belgian frontier at the precise moment when it was possible for him to cut the communications of Wellington and Blucher. One of the most striking evidences of the want of adequate preparation for the attack is to be found in the fact that, up to the 11th of June, Ney was waiting in uncertainty at his home at Coudraux, not knowing whether he was to receive a command. On that day Napoleon sent for him, and it was only on the 15th that he joined his chief. The corps of d'Erlon and Reille were united under his orders, with the light horse of Piré and the heavy cavalry of Kellermann; and it was not before ten o'clock at night that he succeeded in taking up his position in front of the brigade of Duke Bernard of Saxe-Weimar, which held Quatre-Bras.

M. Quinet has done much to re-establish the reputation of the unfortunate Ney, upon whom Napoleon subsequently, at St. Helena, attempted to lay the blame of his defeat at Waterloo. The accusation against him is, in brief, that he failed to obey Napoleon's orders to occupy Quatre-Bras on the

15th, or at least early in the morning of the 16th.
If he had done so, or could have done so, no doubt
the position of the English army would have been
rendered precarious in the extreme, and it might
have been worsted in detail, as we are given to understand that Napoleon had clearly foreseen. It is true
that Wellington had still, on the 15th, nearly forty
thousand of his reserve forces at Brussels, and that
his concentration upon Quatre-Bras was far from complete when Ney first attacked the position. But it
has been proved, and M. Quinet offers a full confirmation of the statement, that Ney never received
his orders to occupy Quatre-Bras until the 16th,
at half-past eleven o'clock in the forenoon, though
he had himself previously urged Napoleon to attack
the English on the Brussels road. Napoleon declared,
in his last record of the events of the campaign, that he
sent positive orders to Ney during the night of the
15th. But the Count de Flahaut, who wrote down the
order from Napoleon's dictation, and who himself bore
it to the Marshal, affirms that he left Charleroi between
eight and nine in the morning of the 16th, having to
cover twelve miles before he could reach Ney at Frasnes.
The inaccuracy of Napoleon's account must be held
to be clearly established, at any rate as regards the
disobedience of Ney. And it is to be observed that
Ney, if he did not actually occupy Quatre-Bras, yet
prevented Wellington from giving his support to
Blucher, and thus made it possible for his chief to
win the battle of Ligny.

Meanwhile, Wellington was still at Brussels on the 15th, together with Picton's division and the reserves. At four in the afternoon he received from Blucher the first intelligence of Napoleon's approach. At ten a second dispatch arrived, informing him that the French had crossed the Sambre; and it was only then that Wellington ordered his forces to concentrate, the left wing, under the Prince of Orange, consisting of Cooke's, Alten's, Perponcher's, and Chassé's divisions, between Mons and Nivelles, and the right wing extended from Ath to Oudenarde; the reserves were quartered in the neighbourhood of Brussels, under Hill, Clinton, and Colville. Every Englishman knows how the General-in-chief, cool to the last, and anxious to inspire coolness in his army, went to the Duchess of Richmond's ball as though no danger were at hand. It was only at midnight that he received information which led him to order an immediate concentration of the forces upon Quatre-Bras, and to betake himself to the probable scene of conflict. Wellington has been blamed for his deliberation, or for his ostentatious coolness; and it must be admitted that a little greater success on the part of Napoleon and his generals would have upset the calculations of the Allies. Did Bourmont really give Blucher such information as, being transmitted to Wellington, justified the latter in holding his enemy somewhat cheap?

It was eight o'clock on the morning of the 16th before the Duke left Brussels; and at ten o'clock Wellington and Blucher met on the heights, between

Brye and Sombref, near the old windmill of Bussy. It was agreed between them that the Prussian army should court a battle with the French at Ligny, whilst the English, breaking through the opposition of Ney, should subsequently come to their aid. " Perhaps," as M. Quinet observes, " an immoderate desire of glory, of reprisals; of vengeance, an impatience to measure himself alone against Napoleon, of being the first to curb him, and above all the hope of overthrowing the colossus without sharing the honour with any one, had their effect in the resolutions of Marshal Blucher."

The Prussian army was drawn up near Fleurus, with its right resting on the villages of Saint-Amand and Wagnelée, its centre at Ligny, its left at Sombref and Tongrenelle, commanding the road to Namur. The position was a bold one to take up, having about it few elements of the defensive, and affording to a general of Napoleon's experience and resources a splendid opportunity for an irresistible attack. As soon as the Emperor perceived the plan of Blucher, it became necessary for him to guard against the consequences which would threaten him in case of a reverse— such, for instance, as the danger of being cut off from his base on the Sambre. In view of this possibility he stationed Lobau's division at Fleurus, and then made his dispositions to challenge Blucher on his right and centre; this choice of the point of attack being determined by the fact that at this end of the line he would be descending upon the enemy in his assault, whereas at the other end he would have to ascend a slight eminence to Sombref. Moreover, as Wellington's force lay behind the latter town, a successful attack on Ligny and Saint Amand would tend to drive the Prussians farther away from their allies. At the same time Napoleon could perceive that the enemy intended to make his strongest attack from his right, on which side Blucher had assembled forty-eight squadrons of cavalry for the transparent purpose of surrounding the French left, and driving it upon the Sambre. Instead of opposing cavalry to cavalry, or even strength to strength, the French Emperor placed his own fifty-seven squadrons on his right, opposite to Sombref, and concealed his reserves altogether, thus deceiving the enemy as to his plan of attack. Blucher, thinking that Napoleon meant to select Sombref as his principal object of attack, placed there an entire army corps, under Thielmann; and the consequence of the Emperor's ruse was that this large force was comparatively useless for the greater part of the day.

Napoleon did not order the advance until half-past two in the afternoon, although he had been able to finish all his arrangements at ten in the morning.[1]

[1] M. Quinet, by way of explaining this unaccountable delay, which can hardly have served any useful purpose, quotes from Napoleon's *Mémorial de Sainte-Hélène* a confession of a remarkable character, wherein he seems to give the key to the Emperor's conduct in this and several other occasions of the brief campaign of 1815. "It is certain," said the prisoner at St. Helena, "that in these circumstances I no longer had within me a feeling of eventual success. There was no longer my original confidence . . . I felt that something was wanting in me." Presage or conviction, cause or effect, Napoleon would appear to have lost the old spirit which enabled him at once to foresee and to command a victory.

The first assault was made by two divisions of Vandamme's corps upon the village of Saint Amand. Their dash was irresistible; the Prussian division of Steinmetz lost more than two thousand men within the hour. General Girard, with another division, penetrated the village, and long held his ground against the many corps of Prussians, who were replaced as fast as they fell by a constant supply of fresh troops. The French commander was killed, and a third of his men were *hors de combat*; but the remainder held their ground amidst the ruins.

Napoleon had given orders to another general, Gérard, to attack the village of Ligny in the centre, as this place was the key of the whole position. It consisted of two long streets, with meadows between the two; the houses being built of granite, and their walls affording by their apertures an excellent means of defence. It was necessary for Gérard to attack these streets in full force, whilst from either end the Prussians poured upon him a steady artillery fire. The only entrance to the interior of the village was through the doors and windows of the houses, or through occasional openings between them; so that the assault was in the nature of an attack upon a strong line of stone fortifications.

The carnage was terrible. There was a desperate hand-to-hand struggle in every courtyard and in every house; whilst the scene was lighted up by a ghastly glare from burning thatched roofs, and from the old castle of Ligny, set on fire by the artillery. Gérard attacked one street three times, both in the centre and at the extremities of the long row of stone houses, and at last his men occupied the majority of the inclosures and rooms. A fresh Prussian division came up, and, by a vehement sally, the French were driven out again. The Prussians prepared to follow them, but at that moment they found themselves assaulted in their rear by troops who had gained the interior of the village. They retired upon the second street; and the French, taking possession of a cemetery in the intermediate space, instantly mounted their cannon there. Another Prussian regiment was brought up, and attempted, in six successive assaults, to retake the half of the village which had been lost; but the effort was in vain. The General in command, Krafft, was obliged to send word to Gneisenau, the chief of the staff, that he was being forced back from Ligny, and received in reply only an earnest entreaty to hold his ground for half an hour.

At Saint Amand also the Prussians had the greatest difficulty in maintaining themselves; and towards nightfall Napoleon was able to put in execution the plan which he had formed from the beginning. Feigning a retreat, he drew after him the bulk of the Prussian forces, and at the same moment brought up his reserves from Fleurus—twelve battalions of foot guards, eight regiments of cuirassiers, dragoons, and grenadiers, who dashed in full force upon Ligny. In a short time Milhaud, with the heavy cavalry, had turned the Prussian centre, and took their right in flank. With immense loss the Prussians were driven from the field.

It was growing dark when Blucher saw the full effects of Napoleon's deceptive strategy. He had already advanced with his reserves from the extreme right, and now led three cavalry regiments personally against the enemy, in the hope of checking their progress. It was no more than he had done many times before; for old "General Forwards," as his soldiers were wont to call him, had all the vigour and dash of a young and impetuous captain. But his forlorn hope was unable to withstand the onset of the heavy French horse. The ranks were broken, and all was in confusion, when a bullet killed Blucher's horse under him, bringing him to the ground in the very track of the enemy. "I am a lost man, Nostitz!" he said to his aide-de-camp, as he fell. Nostitz leaped from his horse, and stood by the general's side. The French swept on, so intent, in the darkness, to overtake the retreating Prussians, that they did not perceive the prize which was within their grasp. Presently the French cavalry fell back again before a renewed charge of Prussian lancers; and the old Marshal, narrowly escaping the weapons of his own men, was rescued and carried off the field of battle.

The defeat of the Prussians was a severe one. They had lost eighteen thousand men—eight thousand of these being dispersed, whilst the remainder were killed. Gneisenau, the chief of the staff, ordered a retreat in the direction of Wavre, for the purpose of ultimately joining the English army; and Napoleon, for one reason or another, did not take immediate steps to pursue his victory, but left the army to sleep off its fatigue.

Meanwhile Marshal Ney was engaged in his conflict with the English at Quatre-Bras. The hamlet of this name, situated at the cross-roads leading to Brussels, Namur, Charleroi, and Nivelles, consists of a few farms, with the small village of Pyraumont in the neighbourhood. The cross-roads meet on a slight elevation of the bare plain which they intersect; and towards this elevation, crowned by a white farmhouse, the English were concentrated.

As soon as Ney had received Napoleon's orders to attack Quatre-Bras, a little before noon, he ordered one of his two corps, comprising about seventeen thousand six hundred men, under General Reille, to attack the Prince of Orange, who had less than seven thousand Dutch and Belgians under his command, and less than half the strength of the enemy's artillery. At the same time he ordered d'Erlon, whom he had left in the rear, between Fleurus and Frasnes, to advance with the remaining corps, of about twenty thousand men. The French general, on receiving Ney's orders, had reached the latter town in advance of his troops, when he was overtaken by General Labédoyère, Napoleon's aide-de-camp, who showed him a pencilled note from the Emperor to Ney. It appears that this note contained directions to the effect that Ney, after repulsing the English at Quatre-Bras, should send his first corps to complete the expected discomfiture of the Prussians at Ligny. Such, at all events, seems to have been Napoleon's meaning; but both Labédoyère and d'Erlon misinterpreted the message, and the former took upon himself to dispatch the latter's corps to the Emperor's assistance. D'Erlon hastily followed his men, and this corps was actually perceived by Vandamme, in the course of his attack on Saint-Amand, causing him some alarm before he discovered that it was a friend, and not an enemy, who had thus suddenly appeared on his flank. Napoleon's attention was also drawn to that corps; and here another mystery presents itself in connection with the occurrences of this remarkable day. Whether the Emperor did or did not know who these troops were, or, in that case, whether he thought that Ney had already been successful at Quatre-Bras or not, it is certain that he sent no orders to d'Erlon, who thought it his duty to wait for instructions. But whilst he was waiting, a second and urgent command reached him from Ney, who had all this time been anxiously looking for his approach, and d'Erlon, therefore, leaving a small contingent behind him, forthwith hastened back to Frasnes.

Meanwhile Reille had advanced against the Prince of Orange's division, which gradually drew back. Ney had been deceived by appearances into thinking the small Dutch force greater than it was, and he had therefore attacked it with a certain amount of circumspection;

but he had decidedly the best of the battle up to about a quarter to three. At this time Picton was observed approaching with three brigades of infantry along the Brussels road; and shortly afterwards the Duke of Wellington arrived upon the scene, bringing with him a brigade of Belgian light horse. Next came the Duke of Brunswick; and before four o'clock the Allied forces were more numerous than the French.

"The Belgians," says M. Quinet, "sustained the first shock, and this is what eyewitnesses tell us of the affair. They say that the light cavalry, as soon as they opened out, fell into line for the attack. A French regiment, Piré's chasseurs, advanced slowly to meet them. The French were seen to approach from afar, not as if for an attack, but rather as though they had been on parade. With sabres lowered or hanging down, they held out their hands to the Belgians, and as soon as they were within speaking distance, they cried out to them to come into their ranks, declaring that they would be well received, that they were old friends, that they had served together in Spain, under the same generals and in the same corps, and they addressed by name those whom they recognised. The nearer they approached, the more their urgency increased. In this way they presently touched each other; but instead of yielding to these pressing invitations the Belgians began to use the sabre. Then the French, old friends as they were, became furious enemies. Each selected a foe, and, being by this time almost indiscriminately mixed together, they fought at close quarters. This first encounter was terrible, but it did not last long. Routed and cut to pieces, the Belgians fled in disorder from the field of battle."

Even after the English had been reinforced by Picton and Brunswick, Ney continued to have the best of the battle, especially on the right and left. The Duke of Brunswick, charging with his lancers against a strong body of French troops, and being driven back upon the Nivelles road, was shot through the body as he endeavoured to rally his men. Piré's light horse now succeeded in gaining a footing in Quatre-Bras; and these being supported by a fresh body of heavy cavalry under Kellermann, the English had recourse to their famous method of defence of forming squares, an arrangement which secured for them the honours of the day. On the approach of Kellermann's horse, Picton prepared to meet them with the Royals, the 28th, 42nd, 44th, and 92nd Regiments; and these were presently supported by the 32nd, 79th, and 95th Regiments. Judiciously arranged, and so placed as to concentrate their fire upon the enemy's horse—they themselves being partly concealed by the high-standing corn—the solid masses of the English troops sustained many a gallant and desperate charge of the French cavalry, which perpetually broke against the inflexible squares. Whatever may have been the case at other points of the line, the French attack could make no impression upon the centre, which resisted the utmost efforts of Ney. At five o'clock two more brigades of infantry, as well as the remainder of those of Kempt and Pack, reinforced the English; and at half-past six o'clock Ney was outnumbered by ten thousand men. Meanwhile continual and pressing orders reached him from Napoleon—who, for all the Marshal knew, was at the last extremity—and, to crown his anxiety, he learned that d'Erlon's column, the twenty thousand fresh troops which he had been expecting every minute to come to his assistance, had been wasting the day in a useless march to Saint-Amand.

We can easily understand the discouragement with which the French Marshal found himself so completely baffled. He turned to those who stood near him, and cried, "You see those bullets! I would they were every one of them in my body!" Nevertheless he ordered Kellermann to make a final attack upon the impassable squares of English infantry. "My dear general," he said, "we need a grand effort; we must drive in that mass of infantry. The safety of France is at stake!"

Kellermann needed no second invitation. He rode at the head of his cuirassiers, and charged under the fire of an English battery, which wofully thinned his ranks. He did, indeed, succeed in breaking the first lines by this heroic charge, which resembles nothing so much as Cardigan's charge of Light Horse at Balaclava. But nothing could withstand the withering fire of the English batteries and squares. The cuirassiers were mown down, Kellermann himself was unhorsed, and only escaped by clinging to the bits of two of his men's horses. The forlorn hope was beaten; and now it was Wellington's turn to assume the offensive.

Ney reluctantly and slowly retired, resuming the positions at Frasnes which he had held in the morning. As regards the result of the battle, it was undecided, though, if anything, to the advantage of the French. Both Wellington and Ney had been prevented from going to the succour of the combatants at Ligny; and, as Napoleon had beaten Blucher, it may be that the Allies would have profited most by being able to effect the junction.

Thus, in spite of all mistakes, Napoleon had opened the campaign as well as he had any reason to expect; and, except for the unfortunate blunder which led to the not using of d'Erlon's force, and for which the Emperor himself was in some measure responsible, it does not appear that Ney had much to answer for in the ultimate failure.

The amazing facility with which the Prussians were allowed to retire from the battle-field of Ligny, and to rally on the following day, lost to Napoleon almost the whole fruits of his victory. Incredible as it may seem, no attempt whatever was made to follow up the retreating army, or even to ascertain in which direction it had retired. When Marshal Grouchy went to Fleurus on the morning of the 17th, in order to ask the Emperor for directions, he found that Napoleon had come to no resolution whatever. From nine in the morning until midday the Emperor wandered about the scene of yesterday's conflict in apparent incertitude, actually entering at length into conversations with his generals as to the conduct of the authorities in Paris, and the discussions in the Assembly. It was not until noon that Grouchy received the order to pursue the Prussians with thirty-three thousand men; and it is said that the Marshal, perceiving the comparative hopelessness of the task, entreated the Emperor to confide this difficult commission to Ney; but Napoleon answered "No; I must have Ney with me." It was in vain that Grouchy pointed out the circumstances which seemed to render the pursuit useless from the beginning; Napoleon was obstinate in the resolution at which he had so tardily arrived, and even lost his temper over the Marshal's expostulation. The fact was that the French generals were fast losing their old confidence in their chief; and the unhappy procrastination of the past twelve or fifteen hours had done as much as anything to damp their ardour.

Grouchy, with the corps of Vandamme and Gérard, supported by Excelmans' cavalry and a hundred cannon, set out before three o'clock towards Gembloux, where Thielmann, finding himself free from pursuit, had bivouacked from seven in the morning until long after noon. It was dark night before the French arrived at Gembloux; and, as they found no traces of the Prussians here, they pushed on to Wavre.

It was not until the night of the 16th of June that Wellington learned what had happened at Ligny. On the receipt of a dispatch from Blucher, announcing his retreat and his present situation, the Duke thought it best, on the 17th, to fall slightly back upon Waterloo, both for the purpose of better covering the Belgian capital, and in order to afford time for his ally to join him. He wrote to the German Marshal to this effect, and expressing his intention to accept battle on the following day, the 18th.

It was about two in the afternoon of the 17th when the first columns of the French troops who had fought at Ligny came in sight of Frasnes; and the English had already begun to retire to Waterloo. The movement was slowly made, for a heavy fall of rain had reduced the country to the condition of a swamp. The French cavalry pressed the English hard; but every now and then the latter turned, and a sharp engagement took place. At Génappes in particular the rearguard, commanded by Lord Uxbridge, made a resolute stand. Uxbridge, immediately after passing through the long village-street, deployed his cavalry, under Ponsonby and Lord Edward Somerset, across the road; and thus the French, emerging from Génappes, found themselves confronted by a formidable body of the enemy, who attacked and defeated them with great slaughter. Frenchmen are fond of recording how, in that struggle, Colonel Sourd, who had had his right arm shattered, necessitating its amputation, mounted his horse within an hour of leaving the surgeon's hands, and resumed his position at the head of his column. Presently the English continued their retreat, and rejoined the main army.

At six o'clock in the evening the English army had reached the field which the following day was to render so famous, and on which Wellington had previously selected his positions. During the evening Blucher sent an answer to the English general, who had declared that he would accept battle on the 18th, and reckoned on the assistance of two Prussian corps. "I will come," Blucher wrote, "not with two corps only, but with my whole army; it being understood that if the French do not attack us on the 18th, we shall attack them on the 19th." This assurance was sufficient for Wellington. He slept at Waterloo, about a mile and a half behind the selected positions; the Prussians being at the same time at Wavre, a distance of about nine miles from Waterloo.

The English general had taken up his post of observation on Mont-Saint-Jean, in front of the wood of Soignies. Beneath him stretched the Charleroi road, along which the English army was drawn up, with its right resting on Hougoumont, its left on the hamlet of La Haie, and its centre upon the farm of La Haie-Sainte and the village of Mont-Saint-Jean. Napoleon occupied the height of Rossomme, on the other side of the plain, at the Maison-d'Ecosse, near La Belle Alliance, from which he commanded a good view of the English positions.

On the morning of the 18th of June, at half-past eleven, the battle began on the left of the French, and in the wood surrounding the château of Hougoumont.

The English replied vigorously to the fire, but after some time, General Reille drove a Nassau and Hanoverian battalion back into the grounds of the château, and down the walks on either side. Coming to a close thicket of young elm-trees, the French prepared to pass through it, but were received with a murderous volley from the apertures of a wall which the thicket had concealed, and which the English had loopholed. For some time the French were unable to make any impression upon the defenders of this strong position. A company of the Coldstream Guards had come up to reinforce the garrison, and when the gate was opened to admit them, many of the French troops entered also. But the gate closed upon the last of the Coldstreams, and all of the assailants who had penetrated to the inside were slain. Again and again did the French return to the assault of this position; they could make no impression upon it until Napoleon ordered Kellermann to bombard the building. This was done, and presently the place was on fire; but the battle still raged fiercely amidst the ruins, every point of vantage being obstinately contested. In the meantime, over the heads of the combatants was proceeding a vigorous artillery duel, between the batteries of Jérôme, Foy, and Piré on the one side, and those of Alten and Cooke on the other. The two first-named were wounded, and General Bauduin, with a third of his men, was killed.

On the French right Ney had opened the battle by directing four columns, partly composed of d'Erlon's corps, upon the farm of La Haie-Sainte, Mont-Saint-Jean, and the villages of La Haie, Papelotte, and Smohain, with the object of occupying the ground on the English left by which Blucher's advance-guard would have to approach. The columns were commanded by the Generals Donzelot, Marcognet, Durutte, and Quiot, and were supported by the fire of seventy-four cannon. They attacked with the utmost vigour, and seemed especially anxious to expiate their enforced idleness of the 16th. The villages were taken and retaken; and in the attack on La Haie-Sainte, a Belgian brigade fled at the first onset. But the temerity of the French in sending these four columns of infantry, first down a slope and then up heights, protected by British cannon and infantry, and by strong brigades of cavalry, all ready to receive them, and to pour their fire on their flanks, cost them very dear. The four columns recoiled in disorder, and were literally cut to pieces or ridden down. The remnant regained the height from which Ney had despatched them, disorganised, demoralised, and only rescued by Milhaud's cuirassiers and Jaquinot's lancers from annihilation.

It was the cavalry of Vandeleur and Ponsonby which completed the rout of the French, and which pursued them into the midst of d'Erlon's batteries. Here the English contrived to render some forty cannon useless; but they had scarcely done so when Milhaud and Jaquinot fell upon them with incredible fury; and partly owing to the surprise, and partly because the French horsemen had a great advantage in the length of their sabres, these latter took a terrible revenge upon the enemy. Ponsonby fell, pierced by seven thrusts, together with almost the whole of one of his regiments.

The French right had been greatly weakened by the destruction of d'Erlon's infantry, and it became necessary for Napoleon to modify his plan of battle. He now ordered Ney to take the farm of La Haie-Sainte; and at this point a desperate succession of conflicts ensued, in one of which Picton was killed by a bullet through the temple. As many of d'Erlon's troops as possible had been re-formed in the rear of La Belle Alliance, and they were now launched against the farm. It was another Hougoumont; but finally this position fell into Ney's hands, and was held by him until towards the close of the day. The advantage thus gained by the French was very considerable, and if they had been able to dispose of another ten thousand or twenty thousand infantry, the fortune of the day might have been very different. But it was precisely in infantry that their army was weakest. The corps under Reille was still engaged at Hougomont; the division of Lobau was watching for—or was by this time at work with—the first corps of the Prussians;

and the remnants of d'Erlon's troops were not strong and steady enough for an advance such as Napoleon now contemplated. For lack of infantry, the first line of the cavalry, over five thousand men strong, was sent into action, and Ney led them against the centre and a part of the right of the English—from the Charleroi road to the enclosures of Hougoumont.

The heavy cuirassiers and light squadrons of the French mounted the slope, their helmets, cuirasses, and lances glittering in the sun, whilst the fire of sixty English cannon was thinning their ranks as they advanced. On the other side of the plateau the Frenchmen found themselves suddenly confronted by dense masses of English infantry, ranged in squares, with fixed bayonets, their artillery by their side, and their cavalry ready to support them. The shock of that encounter was terrible. Time after time the English squares were broken; but each time they closed their ranks again. Wellington brought up the divisions of Clinton and Chassé from the right, and sent forward the Dutch and Hanoverian cavalry between the walls of the squares; but the French horsemen splendidly held their ground. Just then a whole regiment of Hanoverian hussars, a thousand strong, refused to charge, and fled precipitately upon Brussels, as the Belgians had fled in the morning. If at that moment the French could have brought up a corps or a division of infantry, it is possible, according to some French military historians, that the victory might have been theirs.

Ney sent to Napoleon entreating him thus to occupy the position which he had seized. "Infantry!" Napoleon answered to the aide-de-camp, "where would you have me get them? Do you want me to make them?"

Ney was unable to maintain his position without infantry, and had to order a retreat. His gallant men had already partly descended the slope; but every hollow, every square yard of the well-chosen field was commanded by English guns. He resolved to attack the English squares once more, assisted by fresh brigades of cavalry, under Kellermann, whom Napoleon had sent to his support. Even one thousand carabineers, who were held in reserve, were ordered to advance, in spite of the remonstrances of their commander. Seventy-seven squadrons of cavalry —ten thousand heroic and picked men—rushed once more upon the heights. But again the English formed their solid squares, and received the enemy with their concentric and terrible fire. The fighting grew now more desperate than before, and the loss was greater on both sides. Both armies were almost exhausted. Wellington had called up his last reserves, and his ranks were thinning fast, whilst Belgian fugitives were crowding the Brussels road. Six flags were captured, and taken to Napoleon in the midst of the battle; and he, accepting it as an omen of success, hoped every moment to witness the retreat of the enemy.

What then was it which caused the French, and

not the English, to retire from the heights, on the centre and right of the Allied positions? There can be little doubt that the battle of Waterloo, as a battle between French and English alone, was lost and won upon these heights, though its success was rendered complete by the arrival of the Prussians. It is therefore interesting to inquire how the victory was gained.

Perhaps the majority of foreigners are wont to maintain that the English were beaten by Napoleon, and rescued from utter defeat only by the opportune arrival of Blucher, by which the French army was overwhelmed. This, however, is a wrong opinion. Even if Napoleon, who was aware that the Prussians had arrived in the neighbourhood of Waterloo, had interfered with or recalled the cavalry under Ney's command, or had withheld any forces which he might otherwise have sent to Ney's assistance, the only argument which might be reasonably brought forward is, that the Prussians created a divergence in favour of the English defenders of the heights of Mont-Saint-Jean. But the cause of the withdrawal of Ney's gallant squadrons need not be looked for outside the circumstances of the desperate duel which had been waged from four to seven o'clock, and which must be regarded either as a drawn battle, or as a victory for the Allied troops.

"On the plateau," writes M. Quinet,[1] "the exhaus-

[1] *La Campagne de 1815. Revue des deux Mondes*, September 15, 1861.

tion of the French was equal to that of the English. Seven generals were seriously wounded—Lhéritier, Donop, Blancard, Picquet, Delort, Travers, Colbert. No one gave the order to retreat, no one sounded the recall. The diminished ranks, pierced by grape-shot, by musketry fire, and by the sabre, disorganised by three hours of unprecedented conflict, by the failing strength of the men, and yet more of the horses, necessity which sets a limit to everything—all these things occupied the place of orderly array."

If this was so, what is the conclusion, except that the French found it impossible to achieve what they had so gallantly attempted, whilst the tenacity of the English enabled them to remain glued to the ground when the enemy had disappeared ?

Meanwhile Blucher had done his best to keep his promise to Wellington. Early in the morning of the 18th his army had left Wavre in three columns —thirty thousand under Bulow, who had not fought at Ligny, seventeen thousand under Pirch, and thirteen thousand under Ziethen, the remaining eighteen thousand being left behind in the charge of Thielmann, in order to deceive Grouchy. The latter, although he heard the cannon of Waterloo, and had every reason to believe that the Prussians would attempt a junction with the English, persisted in going on to Wavre, according to the orders which he had received from Napoleon; and thus it happened that Blucher's columns were allowed to march unopposed to the aid of the English general.

The foremost column was that of Bulow, and by four o'clock in the afternoon it had reached the woods of Frichermont, on the right flank of the French army. By the time these troops had come upon the skirts of the field of battle, the desperate cavalry charge of Ney was proceeding on the plateau to the English right. Napoleon, perceiving the Prussians, ordered Lobau, with two divisions of infantry, comprising seven thousand five hundred men, to arrest their advance. Blucher, who accompanied Bulow, saw in an instant the importance of the crisis, and he lost no time in courting the attention of his Allies by firing his artillery, a sound which must have been as welcome to the English as it was ominous for the French. Yet it is in evidence that Napoleon himself knew of the approach of this second foe at least three hours before its arrival, but that he took no steps to prevent Blucher's intervention, or made any provision against a flank attack, unless it was by sending Lobau and his two divisions. In any case, there can be no doubt that the final success of the battle was, as we have already stated, rendered complete by the arrival of the Prussians, and by the consequent diversion made by a considerable body of fresh troops.

The conflict between the Prussians and the French in the plains of Planchenoit commenced by the former cannonading the cavalry of Subervie and Domon, who were compelled to fall back; but Lobau was able for some time to do more than hold his own against the foremost division of Bulow's corps.

Blucher, however, had his forces deployed on the Prussian left, so as to outflank his opponent; and this movement at the same time threatened the Charleroi road, by which it would be necessary for the French to retreat. Lobau, who had been resting upon Planchenoit, was supported, about six o'clock, by Duhesme, with eight battalions of the Young Guard; but the superior numbers of the Prussians enabled them to capture the village. Four battalions of the Old Guard were brought to the rescue by General Morand, and they drove the enemy back again at the point of the bayonet. It was now evening; the French were fully holding their own on the plain of Planchenoit; the attack on the English centre at La Haie-Sainte was still maintained, and Napoleon flattered himself with the hope that it might be possible to gain the victory.

At this crisis the division of Ziethen was coming up to the field of Waterloo through the woods of Frichermont and Ohain, without the slightest suspicion of their arrival having crossed the minds of the French. But before Ziethen appeared Napoleon judged that the hour had come to make a supreme effort, and to send against La Haie-Sainte five battalions of the reserves of the Guard, who had not yet taken part in the fight, and who were supported by all the remaining heavy and light cavalry. He addressed them in a few words, which roused them to a high pitch of enthusiasm, and amidst a general rally of the whole French line, they marched steadily forward, with bayonets fixed, against the hard-pressed ranks of the English. Wellington seems to have regarded the battle at this moment with the utmost anxiety, though he was perfectly collected. He strengthened the points of his line where the attack of the French Guards seemed likely to fall, brought up as many troops as he could venture to withdraw from other points, and told his officers that they must hold their position to the last man.

Two thousand nine hundred men of the Imperial Guard—of whom the second column was headed by Ney himself—pushed gallantly towards the plateau which had already been so hotly contested, amidst a dense shower of shot and shell. More than one French general was slain or wounded in this advance, and Ney lost his fifth horse in urging the men to the attack. The first battalion of the Guards was staggered by the English fire, and wavered. "Cowards!" cried Ney, "are you no longer able to die?" Again the assault was renewed, and the crest of the ridge surmounted. The Brunswick troops were driven in, and after them two of the Nassau battalions, overwhelmed by the severity of the fire, were pressed back upon the 10th Hussars; but, after a little time, they returned to the charge. When the Imperial Guard came up within a short distance of the English Foot-Guards, Wellington cried, "Up, Guards, and at them!" and the British troops, who had been lying down in a ditch three feet deep behind the summit of the ridge, answered the appeal, sprung up, and poured such a deadly volley upon the approaching foe, that the front ranks of the Old Guard were swept away. Ney ordered his men to extend their line and return the fire;. but the English artillery rained grape and cannister upon the flanks of the devoted battalions. In less than a quarter of an hour more than two thousand of the Old Guard were killed or disabled in this gallant but hopeless attack; and the rest turned and fled.

Napoleon formed the last remaining five battalions of reserve in more open order than their predecessors, and despatched them to the front. A column of French cuirassiers made a simultaneous dash upon the English batteries, but they were unable to reach them; and this last hope of the Emperor, the five battalions of his own Guard, advanced to the plateau unsupported, and under the same crushing fire as before. In front, to the right and to the left of them the English infantry and artillery poured their deadly volleys upon the advancing troops. Nothing could prevail against such a reception as this, and the heroic Frenchmen were all but annihilated.

Napoleon saw the disaster, and watched the remnant of his last reserves as they retreated. "*C'est fini!*— All is over!" he muttered. As the English horse pursued the Guards, he ordered his personal escort of four hundred men to the rescue, and added them to the holocaust. Then the victor in so many fights turned his horse's head, and galloped into the ranks of a regiment of grenadiers which was at that moment disengaged.

Meanwhile, Ziethen had arrived on the field of Waterloo; and his first exploit had been to hurl himself on the extreme left of the English, and to put the Nassau troops, mistaken for enemies, to flight. Discovering his error, he turned, and engaged the French right. The troops of Lobau and d'Erlon were overwhelmed by the numbers of the enemy, and at last a panic appears to have seized the whole French line; the Charleroi road was presently crowded with fugitives.

The tide of battle was turned. By half-past eight in the evening Wellington had assumed the offensive, and sent Vivian's hussars to drive in the few remaining battalions of the French troops who still held out. This they succeeded in doing, whilst Vandeleur on the right cleared the neighbourhood of Hougoumont, from which General Reille, who had been hotly engaged there throughout the day, withdrew towards the French centre, in ignorance of the disaster which had overtaken the army.

A few squares of the French Guard stood heroically amidst the rout of the defeated host, and against the still more formidable pressure of the English and Prussian columns. Other generals besides Napoleon himself had taken refuge in their ranks, and they held in addition a large number of French standards which had been entrusted to them by fugitives. One after another these squares were broken up. Halket's brigade swept down upon the last of them and surrounded it on three sides. The English

General called upon them to surrender; and it was then, according to the account which has been often denied and as often repeated, that Cambronne cried out, "The Guard dies, but does not surrender!"

The battle of Waterloo was ended, and the French were in full retreat. The moon rose upon the pursuit, which was kept up through the night; and before all was over the vanquished army had lost forty thousand men, or half of the number brought in the field, in killed, wounded, and prisoners. Wellington's army had not suffered so heavily, but its loss did not fall short of twenty-two thousand, or about a third of the troops who fought at Waterloo, whilst the Prussians, it is said, lost above thirty-three thousand men in the actions of the 16th and 18th.

As for Napoleon, he withdrew, escorted by a squadron of cavalry, through Quatre-Bras, to Philippeville, where he dictated the official record of the battle, and despatched orders to the generals commanding in the Vendée and on the eastern frontier to fall back upon Paris. His first idea had been to rally and re-form his own army at Laon, whither he had ordered Grouchy to meet him; but he was dissuaded from this course, and directed his steps to the capital. On the night of the 20th of June he reached Paris, and went, not to the Tuileries, but to the palace of the Elysée. He was taking a bath when Davoust came to him, and urged him at once to prorogue the Chambers. The Emperor hesitated. On the following morning, Carnot, Fouché, Lucien Bonaparte, and others tendered various counsels. Meanwhile the Chamber of Representatives had met, declared itself to be in permanent session, and menaced with the punishment of high treason any one who should attempt to dissolve it.

On the 21st of June the Chamber sent for the Ministers; and after two urgent summonses, Lucien Bonaparte and his colleagues made their appearance. The boldest of the members began to apostrophise the Emperor's brother. "The veil is torn away," said one. "I can see but a single man between peace and us." "Return to your brother," cried another, "and tell him that by abdicating he will save France. Tell him that his destiny urges him; that in a day, perhaps in an hour, it will be too late." Lucien returned to the Emperor and advised him to dissolve the Chambers. Napoleon hesitated for some time, and, it is said, contemplated an appeal to the nation, in the hope of recalling the enthusiasm of 1793. But in the end he consented to abdicate.

On the 22nd of June he wrote to the Chambers in these words:—"My political life is at an end, and I proclaim my son, under the title of Napoleon II., Emperor of the French. My interest in the welfare of my son leads me to invite the Chambers, without delay, to organise a Regency according to law."

Meanwhile, Grouchy, having repulsed the division of Thielmann at Wavre, on the morning of the 19th, was about to proceed to Waterloo when he received

Napoleon's dispatch. Falling back at once towards Dinant, he escaped his pursuers, and rejoined the troops collected by Reille, d'Erlon, and Vandamme. In this way an army of a hundred thousand men covered the capital before the end of the month.

Various minor engagements were fought around Paris between the French and the Allies; but it seemed to Davoust, who now commanded the army, and who had replaced Grouchy, that the best he could do under the circumstances was to yield without further delay. On the 3rd of July Davoust signed a convention, delivering Paris into the hands of the English and Prussians; and the Chambers ratified this act.

The French army, indignant at being withheld from the defence of the capital, was withdrawn behind the Loire; whilst the Allies, who had brought Louis XVIII. back from Belgium, established themselves at the Tuileries. On the 8th of July the King re-entered his capital; and on the 3rd of the same month Napoleon, who had quitted his house at Malmaison on the 29th of June, and had made quietly for the sea-coast, took refuge at Rochefort on a French frigate. But Fouché, Duke of Otranto, who had risen to honour under the Republic, and who was one of the first to work for the second Restoration of the Bourbons, warned Wellington of the projected flight of Napoleon. The consequence was that the ex-Emperor found his escape cut off at Rochefort by an English vessel, the *Bellerophon*, commanded by Captain Maitland. The latter offered to convey Napoleon to England; and the late Emperor, despairing of any better chance of safety, resolved to throw himself on the generosity of the English nation.

He went aboard the vessel, and addressed a letter to the Prince Regent. "I place myself," he wrote, "under the protection of the laws of England, which I claim from your Royal Highness as that of the most powerful, the most constant, the most generous of my enemies."

The *Bellerophon* sailed for Plymouth; but Napoleon was not allowed to land. His letter was forwarded to the Prince, and taken into consideration by the English Cabinet. The Allies had already decided that Napoleon, if he were taken prisoner, should be confided to the charge of England; but the Ministry hesitated as to whether they could regard him, under the circumstances, as a prisoner. They concluded to do so, and informed him that St. Helena, an island in the South Atlantic Ocean, had been appointed as his future place of residence. Napoleon protested against what he called a breach of faith and hospitality; and there were many, even in England, who agreed with him. But it is a question whether the ex-Emperor was justified in demanding a free residence in England. He gave himself up at Rochefort under virtual compulsion; he would probably have been taken prisoner if he had not done so; and his escape from Elba had made it impossible that he should again be set at large. The alternative to banishment to

St. Helena was, in the natural course of events, perpetual incarceration or death. It was, after all, not the least merciful fate which condemned him, after so long disturbing the peace of Europe, to his six years' captivity.

Napoleon was taken to St. Helena on board the *Northumberland*, in command of Admiral Cochrane, and landed there on the 17th of October. General Bertrand and his family, General Gourgaud, General Montholon and his family, Count de Las Cases and his son, accompanied him, and he remained there until his death.

§ III.—THE SECOND RESTORATION.

(*From the 8th of July*, 1815, *to the 16th of September*, 1824.)

THE Allied armies were by no means so careful not to wound the susceptibilities of the French in 1815 as they had been the year before. The English encamped in Paris in the Bois de Boulogne; the Prussians in the houses of the inhabitants. The museums were stripped of their pictures and other valuables which had been seized by Napoleon from various foreign towns during his twenty years' campaigns; and Blucher insisted on an indemnity of a hundred million francs, afterwards reduced to ten millions. One million two hundred thousand foreign troops occupied the soil of France up to the month of October. The whole country was overrun by the Allies, who demanded requisitions from the towns and the different departments. France was made to feel the bitterness of the humiliation which Napoleon's " Hundred Days " had brought upon her.

The Prussians were especially severe in their measures during this period.

On the 24th of July the Government, at the instigation of the Allied sovereigns, issued a decree, drawn up by Fouché himself, in which it ordered the arrest of "those generals and officers who had betrayed the King before the 23rd of March, or who had attacked France and the Government with arms in their hands," including Ney, Labédoyère, d'Erlon, Lefebvre, Grouchy, Cambronne, Rovigo, and several others. It also banished from Paris, until such time as the Chambers might decide upon their case, some forty more, amongst whom were Alix, Soult, Excelmans, Thibeaudeau, Carnot, Vandamme, Lobau, Piré, and Regnault.

The army of the Loire was greatly excited by these proscriptions, which affected many of its officers; and Davoust, after criticising them warmly, resigned his command. He was succeeded by Macdonald, who was directed by the Government to disband these troops, whilst another army was formed of young men raised in the provinces. Louis XVIII. and his Ministers began now to display their animosity against those who had assisted in the events of the Hundred Days. The first victim was General Labédoyère, who had been one of the earliest to join Napoleon. He was shot on the 19th of August, after a trial for high treason. Lavalette, who had been postmaster-general under the Empire and the Hundred Days, was condemned to death, but escaped from prison by a romantic plan formed by his wife.

The most striking of these acts of vengeance was the trial and execution of Marshal Ney, who was arrested on the 5th of August, and shot on the 7th of December. Horrible massacres took place in the south of France, and Bonapartists and Protestants were assassinated without any effectual interference of the authorities. Even Marshal Brune was murdered by an excited populace at Avignon (August 1st).

In the meantime the old Chambers had been dissolved, and new elections, with a larger representation, and a franchise extended in point of age, were ordered. On the 19th of August three hundred and ninety-nine representatives were elected, and commissioned to revise certain articles of the Charter. Twenty-nine peers who had continued to sit during the Hundred Days were replaced by ninety new ones, whose titles were declared hereditary. The new Chambers were found to be thoroughly inimical to both Talleyrand and Fouché; so that the King charged the Duke de Richelieu to form a new Cabinet. Richelieu, a returned *émigré*, a man of some ability, presided over foreign affairs; and amongst his colleagues were Clarke, Duke de Feltre, for War; Corvetto for Finance; Vaublanc for the Interior; and Decazes for Police. As for the two most prominent members of the previous Cabinet, Talleyrand lived a retired life until 1830, whilst Fouché, sent as ambassador to the Court of Saxony, died in 1820, in comparative oblivion, at Trieste.

In spite of the promised amendment of the Charter, and the new oaths taken to observe it by the King and his family, the Government showed no more liberality than had been the case before the return of Napoleon. Individual freedom was restricted, and the most reactionary measures were brought forward in the Chambers, which displayed little anxiety about the maintenance of the popular liberties.

The Allied sovereigns and armies can hardly be said to have found their sojourn in France particularly agreeable. Quarrels and insults were of daily occurrence, especially amongst the rank and file of the troops of occupation, whose very lives were not safe from the animosity of the inhabitants. This was naturally experienced in the capital still more than in the provinces; and the fact was doubtless an additional reason why the great Powers wished to complete the work of pacification without unnecessary delay.

The treaties between the Allies and the Government concluded at Paris on the 7th of October, and ratified on the 20th of November, were not dictated by the consideration for the French people which had marked the Treaty of Vienna in the preceding year; nor was it to be expected that they should be. The loss of men and money caused by the Hundred Days was immense, and at the same time peculiarly vexatious. Napoleon was regarded by the majority of foreign nations as an aggressive and dangerous disturber of the peace of Europe, whose ambition rendered him a pest to society, and whose freedom of action was absolutely incompatible with the welfare of his neighbours. It is true that Napoleon was now removed to a distance, and might be supposed to be in safe keeping for the remainder of his life. But it was impossible to overlook the fact that he had received a ready allegiance and active assistance on his return from Elba; and the French nation as a whole could no longer be treated as free from the responsibility involved in his acts.

Another reason for the more stringent character of the new treaties was the ill feeling of the Prussians towards their ancient enemies, and the covetousness of the courts of Berlin and Vienna. The latter went so far as to demand Flanders for Belgium, Savoy for Sardinia, Alsace, Lorraine, and part of Champagne for Prussia and the Eastern German States. In addition to this, the Prussians and Austrians claimed a war indemnity of six hundred millions of francs, and another two hundred million francs for the construction of fortifications on the frontier; and at the same time the cost of supporting an army of occupation, consisting of a hundred and fifty thousand men, for seven years. The Duke of Wellington opposed these demands as being too exorbitant, and his representations were supported by Count Nesselrode, the Russian Plenipotentiary. When Prussia and Austria refused to hear reason, Louis XVIII. in person sought an interview with the Czar and the Duke; and addressing the latter, said to him, " My lord, when I re-entered France I thought I should reign over the kingdom of my fathers. It seems that I had deceived myself; and yet I could only remain on this condition.

Do you think, my lord, that your Government would consent to receive me if I again seek a refuge from it?" The argument was a telling one, on various grounds, and the Czar was affected by it. "No, no, sire," he said, "your Majesty shall not lose these provinces; I will not allow it."

The demands of the German Plenipotentiaries would have been reduced even lower than they were if it had not been for an unfortunate alarm, supposed to have been created by Talleyrand from mistaken motives, and according to which France was on the eve of a general insurrection. Thanks to the panic caused by this rumour the Allies insisted on a partial confiscation of territory. It was for this reason that the Cabinet of Talleyrand was obliged to give way to that of the Duke de Richelieu.

France, which had been reduced in 1814 to the limits of 1793 (except as regards her colonies, which were further diminished by England's captures during the war) was now brought down to the boundaries of 1790, losing also Philippeville, Marienburg, Bouillon, Sarrelouis, Landau, Savoy, and a part of Gex, and undertaking to destroy the fortifications of Huningen. The indemnity was fixed at seven hundred million francs, and the period of occupation at five years— the foreign troops being assigned a line within the northern and eastern frontiers. An additional article stipulated for the union of the Allied powers to enforce the abolition of the slave-trade; for amongst the many crimes attributed in those days to the French Emperor, there seems to have been a vague sort of notion that he was answerable for the maintenance of slavery.

To the main treaty there were added two Conventions, by the first of which a Committee was appointed to arbitrate on the claims made by various foreign governments and subjects against France, whilst by the second the French Government undertook in a special manner to indemnify British subjects for their direct losses since 1793.

The four Allied Powers at the same time concluded a separate treaty amongst themselves, in which they solemnly re-affirmed the treaties of Vienna and Paris, and undertook to hold future meetings "devoted to important common interests, and to the examination of measures which shall be considered most salutary for the repose and prosperity of the people, and for the maintenance of European peace." Meetings were actually held under this stipulation—at Aix-la-Chapelle (14th February to 20th November, 1818), Troppau (20th October to 20th December, 1820), Laybach (17th December, 1820, to 6th May, 1821), and Verona (25th August to 15th December, 1822).

This sojourn in Paris was rendered famous in another and less practical sense by the Treaty of the Holy Alliance (September 26th), brought forward by the Czar Alexander, under the influence, as is generally alleged, of a certain German visionary lady, Madam Krudener. This treaty recorded, in the name of "the Most Holy and Indivisible Trinity," that their Majesties of Russia, Austria and Prussia, "convinced of the necessity of basing their progress on the sublime truths taught by the eternal religion of the Saviour," engage themselves before the whole world "to take for the sole rule of their conduct the precepts of His holy religion, to maintain a fraternal understanding, and to regard themselves in no other light than as delegated by Providence to govern three branches of one and the same family, thus confessing that the Christian nation of which they and their people form part has in reality no other Sovereign than Him to whom alone power justly belongs, because in Him alone are the treasures of love, knowledge, and infinite wisdom—that is to say, God, our Sovereign Saviour Jesus Christ, the Word of the Most High, the Word of Life." King Louis XVIII. acceded to this treaty with the utmost complaisance; but the English Government objected that it was not sufficiently practical, and declined to adhere to it.

Frenchmen felt bitterly the humiliation involved in the terms which Europe had forced upon them, and they were greatly disposed to resent their grievances on the Government. The execution of Labédoyère and Ney, the trial of Lavalette, and the establishment in every department of *cours prévôtales*, or courts, presided over by military men, to try all acts of rebellion or attempts at rebellion, had excited not a little indignation amongst a large section of the people. The general discontent was so loudly expressed that the Cabinet thought it wise to adopt a policy of professed clemency. Early in December the Duke de Richelieu introduced a bill of amnesty. The Count de la Bourdonnaye had previously proposed to extend the proscription, and had drawn up a number of categories of persons against whom he suggested that the terrors of the law should be directed. The Chamber appointed a Committee to consider this and other propositions of a like nature; and the proposal of the Government was referred to the same body. The Committee reported generally in favour of the Government's scheme, but it incorporated the categories of de la Bourdonnaye, which made amenable to the law all officials, military or civil, who had gone over to Bonaparte, or had caused his decrees to be executed. There was much opposition against this law in the Chamber and in the country; and when it came to be discussed, a majority of a hundred and eighty-four to a hundred and seventy-one in the Legislative Body rejected the suggestion of de la Bourdonnaye, thus declaring in favour of a mitigation, rather than an increase, of severity. An article proposing the confiscation of the income or property of all condemned persons was also rejected; and the law then passed (January 7th, 1816). Its result was to grant an amnesty to all who had taken part in the usurpation of Napoleon during the Hundred Days, with the exception of those who had been guilty of crimes against individuals, and of those mentioned in the proscription. It banished the family of Bonaparte for ever from France, and declared that they could never possess property, income, or pensions within the kingdom.

The debates on this law gave the measure of liberal feeling existing for the moment in France; and they showed also that the Government was already confronted by a strong opposition, which might easily become more troublesome still.

The law of amnesty turned out, as many had predicted, to be a virtual incitement to the prosecution of a great number of persons. One article of this law provided that those against whom proceedings had been commenced prior to its passing should be excepted from its operation; and the Duke de Feltre took care to authorise a large number of prosecutions against individuals designated by him, whilst the amnesty was still under discussion. In the course of this year many generals and officials of every rank were brought to trial, of whom several were condemned to death, though the capital sentence was in some instances commuted to imprisonment. D'Erlon, Lefebvre, the two Lallemands, and others of Napoleon's most distinguished generals, were condemned in their absence. Frenchmen have, not unnaturally, stigmatised this period as the *Terreur Blanche*, the White Terror.

The Government began to find its task more and more difficult. The Liberals on the one hand, and the reactionary party on the other, combined to make the work of compromise and pacification all but impossible for the Duke de Richelieu; and his embarrassments were increased by a succession of conspiracies, most of them framed with a view to putting an end to the persecutions of the Royalists. They were all easily suppressed, and had no other effect than to add to the number of the miserable victims of the White Terror. Napoleon's friends and servants, at that time, fully expiated their offences, at the hands of their fellow-countrymen as well as of the enemies of their country. Even in Italy, Murat felt the force of the Bourbons' vengeance. Having attempted a landing at Pizzo, on the coast of Calabria, he was taken and shot (October 13th, 1815), by order of Ferdinand, King of the Two Sicilies, whose grand-daughter had married, two months before, the Duke de Berry, nephew of Louis XVIII.

If the King was less liberal than the majority of the nation, he was more so than the men to whom the Reign of Terror of 1816 was due. Perhaps he saw, and if he did not, yet his ministers must have seen, that the vengeance of the reactionary party was not calculated to make the Restoration popular in France, whilst it raised up enemies for the Government, full of animosity and hatred, who would await their opportunity to compass its overthrow. Their prudence and that of the King was stimulated by the warning of more than one of the foreign courts, pointing out the dangers which must arise from the violence of the party of vengeance. The consequence was that a suggestion of one of the ministers, Decazes, to the effect that the Chamber should be dissolved and reconstituted, was somewhat reluctantly accepted by the Duke de Richelieu, and subsequently by the King. The latter was persuaded by the advice of the Czar and of the Duke of Wellington, both of whom he had good reason to respect, and who dwelt on the fact that the majority of the Chamber, "more Royalist than the King himself," were really attempting to usurp his authority.

The idea, once determined on, was carried out very adroitly. On the 5th of September, 1816, a royal decree was issued, in which Louis XVIII., re-affirming his intention of strictly observing the Charter of 1814, declared that it was advisable to return to the number of deputies fixed by that document. As this reduction could only be effected by the Chamber itself, it was advisable to hold new elections. "None of the articles of the Charter," continued this decree, "shall be altered. The Chamber of Deputies is dissolved."

The partisans of a reaction received this measure with intense dissatisfaction. They had been busily preparing fresh schemes of vengeance; and they had every reason to anticipate that, after a new election, they would find themselves in a minority, at all events in the Chamber of Deputies. The country at large, however, hailed the royal decree as a pledge of greater liberality; and out of two hundred and fifty-nine deputies not more than eighty were found to hold the extreme reactionary views which had prevailed in the former Chamber.

Soon after the opening of the new session, the Government brought forward an electoral law, of which the seventh article provided that "there shall be but one electoral body in each department, composed of all the electors of the department, whose deputies in the chamber it directly appoints. The law was drawn up by Lainé, Royer-Collard, a Royalist with Liberal tendencies, and Guizot; and its discussion in the Chamber of Deputies, especially in regard to direct election, gave rise to a warm debate. Benjamin Constant, and many other Liberals, approved of this extension of the Parliamentary franchise. In the House of Peers it was attacked by the ultra-Royalists, such as Châteaubriand, de la Bourdonnaye, de Bonald, and many others. In the end it passed the Lower Chamber by a vote of one hundred and eighteen to one hundred and six; whilst in the House of Peers, after the personal intervention of the King, it secured a vote of ninety-five against seventy-seven (January 30th).

The Government, early in the same year, also proposed two new laws, the first of which empowered the President of the Council of Ministers and the Minister of Police to arrest and detain any individual who was suspected of plotting against the King or his family, or against the safety of the State, whilst the second provided that no newspaper should be published without the authorisation of the King. The operation of both laws was limited to the 1st of January, 1818, and they were passed by considerable majorities, the opposition coming mainly from the reactionary party; Châteaubriand, in the Chamber of Peers, naturally finding a congenial theme in defence of the liberty of the press.

On the 11th of February, the Duke de Richelieu had the satisfaction of informing the Chambers that the Allies had consented to reduce the army of occupation, and the consequent charge on the national revenue, on the following 1st of August. This concession was the more welcome to France because she was at this time afflicted by a terrible famine, added to the other evils under which she laboured. The Government was compelled to buy corn abroad, whilst many of the large towns assigned funds for the purpose of reducing to the poor the price of the necessaries of life. The general scarcity naturally produced its effect in aggravating the political disturbances of the country, which were taken advantage of by the extreme reactionary party, or at least by the most unscrupulous of the officials, in order to gratify their rancour, or to curry favour with the Government. The most notable instance occurred at Lyons, where General Canuel, a bitter reactionist, had been constantly reporting to his superiors that the department of the Rhône was in danger from the disaffection of the multitude. In the month of June he declared that a plot was in existence to destroy the city. The warning was so far justified that a small rising actually took place, but it does not seem at any time to have possessed much significance. The fact, however, sufficed for the infliction of a sanguinary punishment. A sort of Bloody Assize was enacted in the department, during which twenty-eight persons were condemned to death and executed, whilst many others were visited with minor penalties. In the end the Government, suspecting that the sentences pronounced were too severe, sent Marshal Marmont to hold an inquiry on the spot; and the consequence was that General Canuel was removed from his command.

In the autumn new elections were held in seventeen departments, the result of which was to remove from the Chamber eleven more of the most bigoted reactionaries. Amongst the successful candidates elected in the capital were Laffitte, Casimir Périer, and B. Delessert, who constituted, with others, a group of independent Liberals, destined to become the virtual Liberal party in the French Chambers.

The unpopularity of the Restoration with the mass of the people was largely increased by the activity and influence of the clerical party, and especially by the zeal of the Congregation, a society composed chiefly of laymen, but directed by ecclesiastics, and which had sprung up at a time when the Roman Catholic religion was for the moment suppressed in France. The members of this society, to which Louis XVIII. and his brother belonged, received the name of lay Jesuits, *Jésuites de robe courte;* and their principles and practice are sufficiently indicated by saying that they were much the same as those of the Jesuits.

The session of 1817-8 was marked by the discussion of a very difficult question, namely, that of the reorganisation of the army. A law was introduced by the Government which proceeded on the principles of conscription by annual drawing of lots, of advancement by merit and seniority, and of the formation of a reserve by admitting those who had served under Napoleon. The conduct of the measure through the Chambers, as well as the practical work of reorganisation, was entrusted to Marshal Gouvion Saint-Cyr, who performed both tasks with great success.

In the summer of 1818 the army of occupation had been for three years on the soil of France. The Treaty of Paris provided that a hundred and thirty thousand men should occupy the northern and eastern frontiers for a period of five years, after which the Allies would consider the question of decreasing or wholly withdrawing their forces. At the close of the second year thirty thousand men had been withdrawn; and when the third year had elapsed, the Duke de Richelieu approached the Governments of the great Powers with the object of inducing them to anticipate the date stipulated in the treaty. Once more it was England and Russia who showed themselves the most considerate towards France, and the result of the negotiations was that the four Powers met at Aix-la-Chapelle, and agreed, on the 2nd of October, to withdraw their armies on the last day of November. Many of the extreme Royalists seemed to think that there was reason to fear a revolution as soon as the Allies should have left the country, and they began to intrigue for the purpose of prolonging the foreign occupation. The Count d'Artois went so far as to employ a certain M. de Vitrolles to write a

Memoir on the subject, in the hope of frightening the Allies into remaining; but Richelieu's sound common sense prevailed, and the evacuation was carried out on the appointed day. Nevertheless the great Powers signed a secret Convention amongst themselves, undertaking to renew the military Coalition in the event of another overthrow of the Government in France.

Meanwhile, the elections of 1818, which had taken place in October, resulted in a signal defeat of the Royalists and ministerialists, and in the increase of the party of independent Liberals by twenty fresh votes. Both the Royalists and their friends abroad took alarm at this significant expression of the popular antagonism to reactionary ideas. The plenipotentiaries of the Allied Powers exacted from the Duke de Richelieu a promise that he would take steps to counteract this feeling; and accordingly the Duke suggested the promulgation of a new electoral law, which was intended to limit the franchise. He had a somewhat serious disagreement on this point with his colleague M. Decazes, and the result was that both ministers, as well as all the other members of the Cabinet, sent in their resignations. The King charged the Duke to form another Ministry, and to exclude M. Decazes; but the task was found impossible by the conscientious statesman who, anxious to keep his word towards the foreign Powers, persisted in his attempt to limit the popular franchise, to increase the power of the wealthier classes, and to conciliate the extreme Royalists. In the end the King was obliged to accept the resignation of the Duke de Richelieu, and to give his support to M. Decazes.

Decazes, keeping the Ministry of the Interior for himself, appointed General Dessoles nominal President of the Council and Minister of Foreign Affairs, Saint-Cyr retaining the portfolio of War, and Baron Louis returning to the Ministry of Finance. The retirement of Richelieu, the "Liberator of the territory" as he was gratefully called, suggested a national testimonial to the ex-minister, who was known to be in the possession of very moderate means. A bill was brought forward in the Chambers to confer upon him an income for life out of the Crown lands. The extreme Royalists had the ill grace to raise a hostile debate on the subject of this dotation; so that, although the vote was passed by a majority of about four to three, the Duke declined to accept it, and assigned the income to the foundation of a charitable institution in his native town of Bordeaux.

The contest on the electoral franchise had only been deferred; it broke out again as soon as the question of the Duke de Richelieu's pension had been settled. On the 2nd of March, 1819, the Royalists in the House of Peers passed a resolution, by a majority of ninety-eight against fifty-five, by which it was agreed to request the King to present a project of law, causing " such modifications in the electoral colleges as might seem indispensable." At the same time the majority in the Peers rejected a financial bill sent up from the Lower House, and gave other signs of an aggressive tendency.

The King and his ministers were alarmed at these indications of a troublesome opposition; and they resorted at once to the strongest measure which it was in their power to adopt. On the 4th of March a royal decree nominated sixty new peers, of whom one-fourth had sat in the House during the Hundred Days. Public opinion had been greatly excited by the reactionary attempt of the Royalists, and more than a hundred thousand petitions poured in upon the Government, protesting against any alteration in the electoral law. The creation of the peers was justified by this forcible expression of opinion, and, coupled with the decisive rejection of the proposed change in the franchise by the Chamber of Deputies, sufficed to calm the mind of the nation.

In the same session of 1819 the law relating to the press was rendered more stringent, by the adoption of three measures brought forward by M. de Serre, Keeper of the Seals. The principal objects of these laws were to restrain violations of public morality, the establishment of trial by jury for press offences, and the adoption of a system by which newspapers were obliged to pay to the State a certain sum of money before they could be published. These laws, which were certainly not very remarkable for their want of liberality towards the press, were voted by large majorities; the chief modification being introduced into the text of the first, which was rendered applicable against outrages of "public morality and religion."

The annual renewal of the Chamber had up till now produced a regular increase in the numbers of the Liberal Opposition, which had in the first instance been called the Independent party, and corresponded to the modern Left and Extreme Left. The year 1819 was no exception to the rule, for the election of fifty-two new deputies resulted in the return of thirty Liberals (including General Foy), and raised the group to a total of about ninety. The Royalists were enraged by this result, and especially by the election of Grégoire, a former member of the Convention, at Grenoble, although they had themselves assisted in securing his success over the ministerial candidate, in order to provide an argument for their attacks on the electoral law. The King and his ministry were themselves frightened by the gradual strengthening of the Opposition, which threatened to become too powerful for them, and the foreign Powers began to make vigorous representations about the dangers by which France and Europe were likely to be menaced. The history of France was destined from this time forward to become a record of a long and hopeless struggle of monarchs and governments against the growing power of the people. That struggle gave indeed, to the rulers, not seldom a partial and intermittent success; but each success was followed, as a matter of course, by a more vigorous and definite reassertion of the national liberties.

Decazes, acting in consonance with the convictions of Louis XVIII., and of all the more influential councillors who surrounded the throne, now resolved upon that modification of the electoral law which he had declined to entertain twelve months ago; and a fresh ministerial crisis was the result. Gouvion Saint-Cyr, General Dessoles, and Baron Louis refused to unite in the unpopular scheme which Decazes contemplated, and they sent in their resignations. They were succeeded by de la Tour-Maubourg, Pasquier, and Roy; and the session of 1819–20 opened with a royal speech, in which the King spoke of "protecting the Chamber from the annual influence of parties by assuring to it a duration more in conformity with the interests of public order." The idea was simply to have a Chamber elected for a definite period; but the change was so manifestly contemplated as a counterpoise to the liberalism of the constituencies, and there was clearly so much reason to fear that more extreme measures would follow in due course, that the Chamber of Deputies and the country took alarm, and began to appeal to the Charter. Petitions from the provinces, as well as from the capital, commenced once more to besiege the Government, and the Opposition assumed greater force day after day. M. Decazes offered an uncompromising resistance, and went to the length of dissolving a "Society of Friends of the Press," which represented some of the most constant and yet moderate advocates of freedom in the country.

On the 13th of February, 1820, which happened to be the eve of the day on which the new electoral law was to be brought before the Chamber, the Duke de Berry was assassinated as he was leaving the opera. The assassin, Louvel, an old soldier, stoutly affirmed that he had no accomplices, and no political motives for the deed, except that he wished to save France from the rule of the Bourbons, by slaying the only prince who was able to perpetuate the race.[1] The ultra-Royalists affected to disbelieve this story, and even charged the President of the Council with being the instigator of Louvel's act, and with having made common cause with the Revolution. The Chamber voted an address of condolence to the King, and it was with difficulty that General Foy, who had already acquired considerable influence and note amongst his colleagues, persuaded them to speak of the death of the Duke de Berry as "regretted particularly by the friends of liberty, because they are persuaded that this frightful outrage will be taken advantage of to destroy the liberties which have already been granted, and the rights which the wisdom of the monarch has acknowledged and consecrated."

On the 15th, in addition to the bill for amending the electoral franchise, two exceptional laws were brought forward, one of which suspended the free publication of journals and periodicals for a term of five years, whilst the other renewed until the end of the next session the law passed in 1817, by

[1] On the following 29th of September, however, the Duchess was delivered of a son, the Duke de Bordeaux; so that Louvel's crime was committed in vain.

which the police or the President of the Ministry could arrest any suspected person.

The resentment of the Royalists was too deep, however, to be appeased by these measures. It passed all the limits of common sense, and M. Decazes was made the victim of numberless insults, even from those who had no excuse for their conduct—from newspapers like the *Débats* and the *Gazette de France*, and from men of refinement and learning like Châteaubriand. The King, it must be admitted, did his best to support his Minister, and even professed to believe that the extreme Royalists were aiming at himself through Decazes. He bade the latter endeavour to obtain a majority in the Chambers; but this was soon found to be impossible, and thereupon the Minister resigned. He was raised to the peerage, and sent as ambassador to London, whilst the Duke de Richelieu, at the earnest wish of the King, assumed the Presidency of the Council.

The new course upon which Louis XVIII. and Richelieu now entered, however reluctantly, was one of open antagonism to the Liberal feeling of the country, and of practical subserviency to the reactionary party. During the next ten years a continuous struggle was maintained between Louis XVIII., his successor Charles X., and the French nation, which was to end only in the second exile of the latter monarch, and in the second of the four revolutions which have made modern France what she now is. It was around the Charter in particular that a thirteen years' struggle was waged; and it began the moment the Duke de Richelieu assumed the reins of power. The two exceptional laws and the new electoral law were discussed with great warmth in both Chambers.

The new electoral law—not that of M. Decazes, which had been rejected by a majority of the deputies, but one which was proposed in its place by the Duke de Richelieu—provided for an electoral college in each department and in each arrondissement. The college of the arrondissement was to choose candidates equal in number to all the deputies of the department; and the college of the department—consisting of not less than a hundred or more than six hundred individuals—was to choose the deputies from the lists supplied by the arrondissements. The power was thus virtually thrown into the hands of the men of greatest weight and influence in the departments— that is to say, the landowners and the holders of office under Government.

The two press-laws had been passed before, and the electoral law was finally adopted on the 12th of June, but not until more than one riot had occurred outside the Palais Bourbon, in which the sittings of the representatives were held. In one of these popular outbreaks a student, named Lallemand, was shot by the police; and it was with the greatest difficulty that a conflict was avoided between the authorities and the populace.

The same year was signalised by yet more formidable troubles. Scarcely was the session at an end when the existence of a widespread military conspiracy, having for its object to expel the Bourbons, was made known to the Government on the eve of the projected revolution; and amongst those who were involved in it were Lafayette and other deputies. Many plots of greater or less importance were discovered during the next few years, and in a large number of instances their concocters were visited with the extreme penalty of the law.

The autumn elections of 1820 were regarded with especial anxiety because they were the first held under the new electoral law. Fifty-two of the former deputies had to be replaced, and a hundred and seventy-two new ones to be elected, in order to make up the total of four hundred and thirty decided upon for the whole country. As every one had expected, the choice was practically in the hands of the Royalists. Scarcely a single Liberal was returned, and the followers of Benjamin Constant, Foy, Royer-Collard, Manuel, and Camille Jourdan could muster barely seventy-five votes out of the whole Chamber. The King, apparently not a little against his will, chose from the ranks of the Royalists three new ministers, de Villèle, Lainé, and Corbière; and it was understood on all hands that a Ministry which meant to combat had come into power. The Revolution was once more attacked, in season and out of season; the Liberals were loaded with insults and objurgations; the tribune was made the battlefield of many a bitter struggle; the ministers themselves were not free from the attacks of the bigoted reactionary party. Words were soon translated into acts, and the electoral law was once more tinkered up by the abolition of a number of the most independent arrondissements.

At this particular juncture Liberalism was at its lowest ebb throughout Europe. At Naples the army had proclaimed a Constitution, in the month of July, 1820; and the King had abdicated in favour of his son. Similar acts had been accomplished in Spain and in Portugal; and the sovereigns of Austria, Prussia, and Russia met at the Congress of Laybach (December 17th, 1820) for the purpose of consulting on the best mode of protecting the thrones of Europe against the encroachments of popular freedom. It was resolved that an Austrian army should enter Naples and suppress the new Government; and the plenipotentiaries of France and England concurred in the scheme. The accomplishment of this unjust and cruel work was readily undertaken by the Austrian mercenaries. The effect of this unjustifiable intervention in Italy was to discourage the French Liberals, and to inspire the extreme Royalists with the confidence that, in case of need, they would be able to summon the allied armies back across the frontier, in order to protect them against their enemies. But, on the other hand, the activity of the Piedmontese patriots emboldened the party of progress to renewed struggles.

The session of 1821 ended amidst recriminations and debates on the law on donations and pensions. The Chambers consented to grant an indemnity, to be cancelled at the pleasure of the King, to those persons who had lost their pensions by the cession of territory in 1814. The majority took advantage of this grant to renew the insults which it periodically heaped on all Frenchmen who had been in any manner identified with the fortunes of the Empire.

The death of Napoleon Bonaparte, at St. Helena, on the 5th of May, 1821, closed for many Frenchmen a distinct chapter in their lives and their history. Those men who had clung to the hope that, by some means or other, the events of 1814 would be repeated, were now compelled to abandon the prospect, whilst to the Royalists, as to Europe at large, even the death of the solitary prisoner brought a sense of relief from a never-forgotten danger. Few people doubted that the imperial epoch was definitely at an end for France; and fewer still could have imagined that a second Napoleon was to sway the destinies of the nation more than thirty years after the death of the first.

The session of 1822 was notable chiefly for a Coalition between the extreme Royalists and the advanced Liberals of the Chamber of Deputies, which resulted in giving the direction of affairs into the hands of the former. The Duke de Richelieu once more retired; MM. de Villèle, Corbière, de Peyronnet, and the Viscount de Montmorency assumed portfolios; the last-named being one of the principal leaders of the Congregation, and adding, therefore, a strong religious element to the policy of the new Ministry. This year was also distinguished by a series of press prosecutions, one of the most remarkable of which was that of Paul Louis Courier, the author of a pamphlet headed *A Simple Discourse*. At the close of the same year the poet Béranger was prosecuted for outrages on public morals, and incitement to disobedience of the laws; and he suffered three months' imprisonment on this score.

The bargain, according to which the advanced Liberals had enabled the extreme Royalists to climb to power, contained a stipulation that the demand for prolonging the censorship on books, newspapers, and pamphlets should be withdrawn. This undertaking was duly observed; but in the letter rather than in the spirit. Early in the year 1822 the Government introduced a new law for offences committed through the press. A desperate parliamentary struggle was carried on in connection with this measure, and a similar one which had been previously brought forward by M. de Serre. Royer-Collard, General Foy, Casimir Périer, Manuel, and Benjamin Constant led the Opposition, with the utmost ability and persistence, during a long debate of seventeen days on the proposal of M. de Serre. It is true that they only mustered ninety-three votes in the division, against a majority of two hundred and thirty-four; but forty members of the Left abstained from voting, on the ground that the bill violated the Charter, and was, therefore, unconstitutional. The bill of the Government, intended to fulfil the same purpose as the prolongation of the censorship, was carried shortly afterwards by an equally crushing majority.

During these struggles in the Chambers, the country continued to be agitated by plots and conspiracies— amongst others by associations in sympathy with the Italian *Carbonari*, which went by the name of *Ventes*, and amongst the members of which were several deputies, such as Lafayette, Voyer-d'Argenson, and Manuel, and many Liberals as worthy of mention. Death or imprisonment was the lot of not a few of the conspirators; but the plots did not cease for all that. The military conspiracies attempted at Saumur, Belfort, and La Rochelle were amongst the most formidable of those which marked this year.

It was about this time that the predominance of the Church in matters of State, and especially in respect of education, began to force itself upon the notice of the public in France, by certain significant and almost incredible occurrences. In the year 1821 the course of lectures given by Victor Cousin, at the Sorbonne, had been suspended, without any adequate reason being assigned. On the 5th of June, 1822, a royal decree re-established the office of Grand Master of the University, the Abbé Frayssinous being appointed to the post; and from that moment it was understood that the Congregation, or the Church through the Congregation, was supreme in all questions of education. At the close of the year Guizot's lectures on modern history were stopped, the Normal School was suppressed, and advantage was taken of a slight disturbance at the

Paris School of Medicine to close these classes also. In the following year (1823) Villemain encountered the same fate as Cousin and Guizot, in the suspension of his lectures on literature.

This year France was brought on the threshold of a new war, by the desire of the King and most of the ministers to suppress the revolution in Spain. The Allied Powers, who, as we have already mentioned, had taken upon themselves, at Laybach, the task of curbing the popular risings in Naples and Spain, and who had given Austria her commission to dragoon the former country, met in October, at Verona. The Congress was attended for France by the Viscount, afterwards Duke, de Montmorency, Châteaubriand, de la Ferronnays, and the Duke de Caraman. The representatives of Austria, Russia, Prussia, and France decided upon recalling their ministers from Madrid, where a Revolutionary Government was virtually installed; but the Duke of Wellington, on behalf of the English Cabinet, of which Canning was at that time Secretary for Foreign Affairs, protested against the contemplated intervention, and refused his signature to the protocol. In France the people and the Liberal Opposition were indignant at the menaces held out to the Spanish revolutionary party, and at the unworthy attitude which the country was made to assume through these negotiations; the Viscount de Montmorency having taken such a tone that France appeared to be the chief instigator of intervention, and a mere tool in the hands of the allied sovereigns. Twice did the

Duke of Wellington in person dissuade the King and M. de Villèle from undertaking the war, and on both occasions he received assurances that France would abandon the idea; but the feeling of the Chambers was too strong to be resisted.

On the 28th of January, 1823, the King opened the session by a speech, wherein he spoke as follows :— " The blindness with which the representations made at Madrid have been repelled leaves little hope of the preservation of peace. I have ordered the recall of my ambassador from Spain; one hundred thousand Frenchmen, commanded by a prince of my family—by him whom my heart rejoices to call my son—are ready to march, in the name of God and Saint Louis, in order to maintain the throne of Spain for a grandson of Henry IV., to preserve this fine kingdom from ruin, and to reconcile it with Europe."

This speech was received more than coldly by the country, whilst it was welcomed with an outburst of indignation from the advanced Liberals, and in a like spirit by the majority of Englishmen. The French Ambassador in London communicated the King's speech to the English Premier, as well as an invitation to England to interfere with France, and endeavour to obtain freedom of action for the Spanish King, but he received a refusal couched in very forcible words.

In the French Chamber a majority of more than two to one supported the Ministry; but the debates were passionate in the extreme. General Foy and Manuel especially distinguished themselves by their opposition to the projected war; and the latter raised a storm of rage by attempting to justify the Revolution. "Is it necessary to remind you," he said, "that it was because the Stuarts relied on foreigners that they were driven from their throne? Need I tell you that the moment when the danger of the royal family in France became most grave, was when France—Revolutionary France—felt the necessity of defending herself by an entirely novel force and energy?" The speaker was interrupted by a passionate outbreak from the Royalists, who demanded his expulsion from the Chamber. The debate was adjourned, and renewed on the following days. At the end of a week the expulsion was voted—the advanced and moderate Liberals quitting the hall, in place of expressing an opinion on what they deemed a violation of the Charter.

Manuel would not submit to the vote, except by compulsion; and returning on the following day at the head of all the members of the Opposition, he took his seat as usual. The President called upon him to retire, but he refused. A piquet of the National Guard was then introduced, amidst the protests of Lafayette, Casimir Périer, and others; and, awed by these protests, the sergeant and his men refused to obey the order of their officer to remove the deputy. The gendarmerie now appeared on the scene, and Manuel was finally dragged out of the Chamber, followed by the bulk of the Opposition. On the next day sixty-two deputies addressed a protest to the President, which the Right refused to hear, and thereupon the entire Left quitted the hall, and refused to return during the remainder of the session. The Right then voted a credit of a hundred million francs, for the prosecution of the war, as well as a further measure calling out the veterans.

The Duke d'Angoulême took the command of the army on the 15th of March, and on the 6th of the following month he crossed the Bidassoa. On the 24th of May he entered Madrid, amidst the cries of "Long live the absolute King! Down with the Constitution! Death to the Constitutionalists!" Here, and in every other Spanish town entered by the French, the Royalists showed their joy by massacring the Constitutionalists and sacking their houses.

The Revolutionary Cortes held the Spanish King Ferdinand VII. under restraint in Cadiz; and on the approach of the French they set him at liberty (October 1st). Leaving behind him a force of fifty-four thousand men for the protection of Ferdinand against his subjects, the Duke returned to Paris, after an inglorious campaign, which would have been almost bloodless, if it had not been for the Royalist Terror which rose up in the track of his army, and which exhausted its fury on the Constitutionalists.

M. de Villèle, pressed hard by the Opposition, and having only a weak Ministry to aid him, thought that the prestige of this military parade—the first, be it remembered, since 1815—offered a good opportunity for obtaining a majority in a new general election. He dissolved the Chamber on the 24th of December, with the intention of passing, if possible, during the next session, a law for septennial Chambers, without partial renewals of the members. His instinct was not deceived. The country had, for the time being, allowed its Liberal enthusiasm to evaporate; and in the new Legislative there were scarcely twenty members belonging to the Opposition.

The project for a septennial Chamber nevertheless encountered a strong resistance. It eventually passed the House of Peers by a hundred and seventeen votes to sixty-seven, and the Chamber of Deputies, after an opposition led off by Royer-Collard, by two hundred and ninety-two against eighty-seven. A bill on the conversion of annuities was rejected by the Peers, after being accepted by a comparatively small majority in the Chamber of Deputies, whilst another measure, on the subject of sacrilege, was withdrawn by the Ministry. During the same session, the Cabinet was remodelled by the dismissal of Châteaubriand, who, as Minister of Foreign Affairs, had never been able to agree with de Villèle, and who, moreover, had by no means distinguished himself by his statesmanship.

Louis XVIII. had been in failing health for some time past; and on the 16th of September, 1824, he died at the age of sixty-nine, being succeeded by his brother, the Count d'Artois, as Charles X.

CHAPTER II.

§ I.—AN EFFETE MONARCH.

(*From September* 16*th*, 1824, *to July* 30*th*, 1830.)

THE new King, who had, since the Restoration, been known as the leader of the extreme Royalists, began his reign with moderation. At the official reception of the peers and deputies he declared, "As a subject I promised to maintain the Charter and the institutions which we owe to the King of whom Heaven has just deprived us. To-day, when by virtue of my birth, power has been placed in my hands, I will employ it to the utmost in consolidating, for the happiness of my people, the great Act which I have promised to maintain."

Charles X. abolished, moreover, the strict law of censorship of the press, and accorded an amnesty to certain persons who had taken part in the conspiracies of 1822. But he retained the Villèle Ministry, which, however great its majority in the Chambers, was far from popular with the bulk of the population. And, in short, the year was hardly at an end before it had become evident that Charles X. was the same as the Count d'Artois had always shown himself, an obstinate believer in the creed that the Bourbons were Kings by divine right, and a partisan of the privileged classes rather than an impartial friend of the people. In his speech from the throne, at the opening of the session of 1824-5, he made no reference to the Charter; and the Ministry soon showed that the spirit of its past would be exaggerated, not modified, in its future.

The first shock given by the Government of Charles X. to the sense and judgment of the country was in again bringing forward in the Chambers the law of sacrilege, which had been rejected the previous year. This law defined the crimes and offences included under the title of sacrilege, and established a series of punishments and penalties, amongst which were penal servitude for life, capital punishment, and death with mutilation. This time the bishops, who had previously held themselves debarred from voting for the penalty of death, contrived to overcome their scruples, and the measure became law, after some strong opposition in the House of Peers. Another bill was also passed, granting the sum of one thousand millions of francs[1] to indemnify those *émigrés* who had been deprived of their property under the Revolution.

It is only fair to say that the law on sacrilege was never put in force; but the mere fact of its passing created the greatest indignation in the country. It had been demanded and pressed forward by the clergy, whose influence over the King and the Government grew greater and greater every year. The "clerical party," as it was called, urged their pretensions with ever-increasing persistency; and the solemn consecration

[1] More precisely, 987,819,962 francs 96 centimes.

at Rheims of the new monarch (May 30th)—Louis XVIII. had not undergone this ceremony—gave them an encouragement which they were not slow to turn to account. They outraged public opinion on many occasions by refusing the sacraments, masses, Christian burial, in the most capricious manner. During this year the Abbé Lamennais, then at the zenith of his orthodoxy, published a treatise in which he anathematised representative Government, and heaped reproaches upon almost every act and word of the authorities which did not acknowledge the entire supremacy of the Church.

From this time forward the Liberal sentiment in France recovered its tone; the press began to speak more boldly, and, as a consequence, the censorship became once more severe and irritating. Two newspapers, the *Constitutionnel* and the *Courrier Français*, were prosecuted for the freedom of their criticism on public affairs.

If the Government were under the impression that the anti-clerical manifestations on the occasion of the representation of *Tartuffe* and kindred plays, lending themselves to such demonstrations of discontent, were simply the tactics of the hired mouthpieces of the Liberal Opposition, they soon had reason to be undeceived. M. Casimir Périer, going to Grenoble on some family business, General Foy, passing through Bordeaux on his way to the Pyrenees, received perfect ovations, whilst Lafayette, landing at Havre from America, was almost borne in triumph on the shoulders of the people, notwithstanding the efforts of the police and soldiery to check these outbursts of enthusiasm.

Nor was Paris behindhand in her expressions of sympathy with the Liberal leaders, notably on the occasion of the death of General Foy (November 28th), who had returned from the Pyrenees to breathe his last in the capital. A universal consternation prevailed, and on the day of the funeral the coffin was lifted from the hearse and borne all the way to the cemetery by the young students of the schools of art and commerce and of the University, amidst the impressive silence of the multitude, who crowded the route, despite the inclemency of the season. The following day a subscription was opened for the general's family, which in less than a week amounted to four hundred thousand francs, every one, from the highest to the lowest, contributing, and amongst these the Duke d'Orléans. This act drew upon him the displeasure of the Court, but this elicited the noble answer that his contribution of ten thousand francs was the tribute of a personal friend, and not that of a prince of the blood.

The second demonstration, which assumed the proportions of a victory for the Opposition, took place on the occasion of the trial of the two newspapers already mentioned, and which trial had been adjourned from the 20th of August to the 19th of November. On the 3rd of December a verdict of acquittal was pronounced, coupled with a recommendation that these newspapers should be more careful for the future.

The news of the acquittal having spread quickly through every quarter of Paris, the tacit encouragement to the Liberal press was hailed by the public with prolonged shouts of joy, for they understood well enough that this favourable issue was tantamount to a check on the part of the magistrates on the encroachments of the clerical party. The Royalist press and the Court were aware of the meaning of this openly expressed pleasure, and without daring to give vent to its discontent, attributed the decision of the judges to a wish for popularity.

Scarcely had this excitement subsided before the news of the death of Alexander, the Emperor of Russia, reached France, and as the late monarch had always shown himself a well-wisher to the French nation, his decease was universally regretted.

Thus closed the year 1825, during which the science of history had made rapid progress in France by the publication of two important works, the *History of the Norman Conquest of England*, by Augustin Thierry, and the *History of the Italian Republics*, by Sismondi, a Swiss. If her literary gains had been great, she also sustained a severe loss in the death of Paul-Louis Courier, foully murdered by a rural constable, who, acquitted for want of proof, afterwards, shielded by the verdict, confessed his crime, without revealing the motive.

The Court receptions which take place on the first day of the new year are usually devoid of all interest in their monotonous pomp and antiquated ceremonies, but they were marked in 1826 by an incident which produced a great sensation. The High Court of Justice, instead of receiving the usual gracious response to their congratulations, were dismissed with the harsh reply, "Pass on, gentlemen;" and, though the following morning the *Moniteur* substituted for this rebuff the words, "I accept the good wishes and the homage of the Court," the typographical reparation did not efface the impression from the public mind that the King was nursing a grudge against these legal functionaries on account of their lenient verdict in the late press prosecutions.

A royal message had fixed the opening of Parliament for the 31st of January, 1826, previous to which two elections were to take place, one at Vervins, to replace General Foy, the other at Lisieux. At the latter town, M. de Neuville, the son-in-law of M. de Villèle, the President of the Council, was chosen; but the Liberal candidate polled a comparatively large minority. At Vervins, Sébastiani, a Liberal, was elected, by one hundred and seventeen out of a total of one hundred and ninety-four votes.

The parliamentary position of the President of the Council was becoming difficult. He had against him the Left, deficient in numbers, but eloquent and well organised, usually carrying with it the Left Centre, as well as the Right, which was his openly declared enemy, and had but one aim—his overthrow, whilst his own party, though numerous, was powerless and of no note. His main support was the confidence of the King, but the courtiers disliked him, and his colleagues directed unceasing attacks against him, which Charles X. listened to, but left unnoticed.

The most influential of the Court party was Jules de Polignac, the son of Marie Antoinette's friend, the Duchess de Polignac, and who had taken part in the conspiracy of Georges Cadoudal. After two years' imprisonment, and subsequent detention, he managed to escape in 1813, and rejoined the Count d'Artois, whose aide-de-camp he became. M. de Villèle sent him to England as ambassador, probably in order to put a stop to his intrigues, which had nothing less for their aim than to become Prime Minister: Whilst in this country de Polignac became particularly impressed with the organisation of the English aristocracy, and without giving himself the opportunity of studying its historical origin, its constitution, and its political influence in the State, he admired, above all, its enormous fortunes, founded on the law of primogeniture. He, therefore, thought that by introducing such a law into France, he would create a powerful and flourishing aristocracy. He managed to imbue the King with this idea; a task the more easy as Charles's leanings were entirely towards institutions of the *ancien régime;* and he prevailed upon the monarch to make an attempt at re-establishing this law in France.

In the programme for the forthcoming session of the Chamber of Deputies to be indicated in the speech from the throne, the King and his council intended to mention first of all a bill against the freedom of the press, loudly clamoured for by the clergy and the Royalists. M. de Villèle being opposed to it, the King gave way, but insisted upon announcing the project of a law intended to improve the position of the clergy, and another to prevent the division of landed property, and to re-establish primogeniture. Despite M. de Villèle's objections to these laws, he was compelled to submit to the King's wishes. Throughout his entire ministerial career, the Prime Minister had ever acted thus; in the war with Spain, he had offered to resign sooner than consent, and still he had consented; he was an adversary of the law on sacrilege, but had presented it to the Chamber. This conduct may have resulted from affection to the King, but this affection neither honoured its object, nor promoted the minister's own dignity.

At the opening of the session, after a few words of sympathy on the death of the Emperor of Russia, and some stereotyped observations with regard to foreign and home politics, the King referred to the bill that was to settle the indemnities of the planters of St. Domingo, after which he congratulated himself and France upon her financial prosperity, which enabled him to bring forward a project for ameliorating the condition of ministers of religion. The proposed bill to check the progressive subdivision of landed property, and thus to re-establish primogeniture, was also touched upon; this, and an allusion regarding the liberty of the press, in which Charles X. declared himself strong enough to suppress all attempts against public order which might degenerate into license, whilst at the same time he should take care that no liberty was infringed, terminated the discourse. The speech satisfied no one. The Royalists were dissatisfied with the decision respecting St. Domingo; and if they rejoiced at the proposed amelioration of the clergy, they objected, on the contrary, to the intended immunity which the last paragraph of the speech promised to the press. This paragraph, however, as well as the one referring to St. Domingo, agreed with the wishes of the Liberal Opposition, who found a subject of discontent in the proposed privileges of the clergy, and, above all, in the projected re-establishment of the law of primogeniture. Under these circumstances the elections for the *bureau*[1] of the Chamber proceeded peacefully, M. Ravez being named its president by the King.

The address of the House of Peers, adopted without discussion, was presented to the King on the 9th of February, and specially agreed with the monarch's views respecting the law of primogeniture; but in the Chamber of Deputies, of which the members were nearly all extreme Royalists, the debates were more stormy. The decision about St. Domingo and the proposed comparative immunity to the press were vehemently attacked, and the results of the discussion were conveyed to the King in terms plainly encouraging him to take

[1] The *bureau* of the Chamber of Deputies is composed of the president, the vice-presidents, and the secretaries.

rigorous measures against the Liberal newspapers. M. de Villèle found himself between two fires: not wishing to offend the Liberals, not daring to attack the clergy. In this emergency he had recourse to subterfuge, and pointed out to Charles X. that the Chamber was encroaching on his sovereign prerogative. The result was a rather reproving reply of the King to the address, in which he told the deputies that he felt himself powerful enough to watch over the public welfare without the interference of any one.

This reply was much praised by the Liberal newspapers, though the ministerial adherents insinuated that the King had merely blamed the form, but not the substance, of the paragraph of the address. The enemies of the press seeking for an opportunity of revenge were not long in finding one. M. de Sallaberry, an extreme Royalist, succeeded in unearthing, and reading in the Chamber of Deputies, several articles published by the *Journal du Commerce* in the course of the previous year, and demanded that the editor should be brought to the bar of the Chamber, and condemned to the maximum penalty for having insulted the Assembly. In spite of the vehement opposition of Royer-Collard and others, the paper was found guilty, but the fine was reduced to the minimum—one month's imprisonment for the editor, and a payment of ten francs. The Chamber instead of being avenged had given a publicity and consequent importance to articles which, otherwise, would have been forgotten, and a notoriety to the editor which largely compensated him for his small term of confinement and nominal fine.

On the same day (February 10th) on which the Chamber of Deputies received the royal reproof, the Ministry laid on the table of the House of Peers the bill for reviving the law of primogeniture. Instead, however, of making that law compulsory the Government proposed that any testator might be at liberty to leave his landed property to his eldest son, if he wished to do so. Previous to the discussion of this bill in the Chamber of Deputies the St. Domingo indemnity was being debated, and much valuable time was lost, because, after all, the bill was adopted as it had been presented. But the bill on primogeniture met with opposition from the very men whom it was intended to benefit, as the equal right of children, established by the Revolution, had become too deeply rooted in the habits of the new generation. Every one knew this law to be an attempt to revive the *ancien régime*, as well as to place a check upon the democratic tendencies. The Government itself did not conceal or deny this, for the King, in his last speech to the Chamber, had declared that the equal sharing of a patrimony was "essentially contrary to monarchical principles." It was, therefore, the most daring challenge which as yet had been thrown to the Liberals, and as such it was regarded by the whole of that party, who prepared to combat the law vigorously.

The Opposition press valiantly led the attack, hundreds of pamphlets discussed the matter from every point of view, and throughout the whole of France, in public as well as private assemblies, nothing else was spoken of. The very heart of the country seemed to be touched. On the 10th of March the report on the bill was laid before the House of Peers by M. de Malleville. In the discussion that followed on the 28th of the same month, M. de Broglie, one of its most strenuous adversaries, showed that the passing of this bill, however important, was of less consequence than the principle it upheld—namely, a manifestation against the actual state of society; that it was meant simply as an introduction of the thin end of the wedge, as a preliminary to a score of similar laws, which, if not suppressed in the germ, would make anew of France what for the last forty years she had so manfully struggled against. He finished by saying that the Liberal party was not looking at the consequences, but at the principle of the proposed law.

M. de Broglie had well defined the aim of the Government. The supporters of the measure had but one objection, that it did not go far enough. Their countenance was given on the condition that it should be a preliminary to a more sweeping law. In spite of this support and the tactics of the Government, the bill was virtually thrown out (April 8th). The news spread rapidly through the capital, and was received with enthusiasm. The Parisians manifested their joy by illuminations and peaceful gatherings in the streets. The Government committed the blunder of dispersing these groups by repeated charges of cavalry. Undeterred, the illuminations were renewed until the 11th of April. But on the 12th, which was the anniversary of the entry into Paris of the King, and which might thus be looked upon as a kind of monarchical feast, not a light was to be seen. The hint was too significant to be mistaken, and the Royalist newspapers vented their displeasure by satirising the citizens, whom they called "vendors of cloth and weighers of sugar," a slight which was remembered in the elections of the following year.

The popularity that accrued to the House of Peers for their courageous rejection of the bill on primogeniture was still further increased by their sympathetic conduct with regard to the insurrection of Greece. It openly censured those French officers who had sold their services to the Turks, in order to assist in the subjugation of a Christian nation; and it carried an amendment declaring that the transport of Greek prisoners, men, women, and children, by French vessels, which was then going on in the Levant and on the coasts of Barbary, was contrary to law.

The remainder of the session was occupied in discussions of the budget, during which M. de Villèle had to bear the brunt of attacks from all sides, and though he was apparently the victor, his position in reality was most precarious.

The agitation prevalent throughout the whole of France during the discussion on the primogeniture bill had on the settlement of this vexed question received fresh fuel by the encroachments of the clerical party. A jubilee prescribed by the Pope, entailing a series of religious processions and ceremonies, in which the judicial, military, and civil authorities took part, either because they were ordered to do so, or from servility, led to serious troubles in several provincial towns; but when the Parisians saw the King and the Court, the former dressed in violet, supposed to be the colour of the Church, play an important part in those pageants, the rumour spread that Charles X. had been named a bishop. This was scarcely calculated to improve his waning popularity, which had been ephemeral at best. No one cared to inform the monarch how of late he had alienated public opinion by his encouragement of the extreme Royalist and clerical parties. His religious zeal led him to commit blunders, in which the nation, unacquainted with the secrets of the Court, saw nothing but a wish to bring France entirely under the sway of the priests. The intrigues of the clerical party were eagerly opposed by the Liberal newspapers, and the last generally remained the victors, notwithstanding the continuous prosecutions directed against them. The magistrates began to get tired of these never-ending lawsuits. Seeing this, the clergy resolved upon an extreme measure—they clamoured for a new press law, which the ministry was not altogether unwilling to grant. Interpellated during the latter end of the season on the re-establishment of the censorship, it replied, that if it found the measure to be necessary, it would not hesitate to propose it.

Meanwhile from the beginning of this year, the eyes of civilised Europe had been turned to Greece, but especially to the little fortress of Missolonghi. After a most heroic resistance of many months, its defenders,. decimated by hunger and disease, were at last compelled to yield, and its fall produced an immense feeling of grief as well as of indignation throughout civilised Europe. When, a few weeks later, in consequence of the capitulation of the Acropolis of Athens, the situation became more precarious still, the Greek question assumed a new aspect, which, though slowly, was to insure the independence of the country. Shortly before the fall of Missolonghi (April 22nd), England and Russia had signed a protocol, having for its object mediation in favour of Greece. France joined these two great Powers some time later, and the example was followed by other States, so that a treaty purporting to put a stop to the war of extermination by Turkey was signed at London, on the 6th of July, 1827. But even before this, the Sultan Mahommed had found himself beset on all sides by difficulties. His greatest obstacle in introducing reforms in the interior of his dominions had been the arbitrary power which the Janissaries exercised for so long a time; and, therefore, he resolved upon their wholesale extermination (14-16 June, 1826). Though this sanguinary measure had much increased the personal authority of the Sultan, it did not give new strength to the tottering empire, and he had been compelled to sign (October 6th, 1826) a convention with Russia, whereby the navigation of the Black Sea was secured to the latter Power, and the Danubian principalities were recognised.

Troubles arose in Portugal after the death of King John VI. (10th of March, 1826). His eldest son, Dom Pedro, Emperor of Brazil, was appointed his successor, but the partisans of the second son, Dom Miguel—who was the favourite of the clerical party—rose, and when they were defeated, crossed into Spain. The Government of the latter country gave them arms, ammunition, and money, and assisted them in various ways; so that they continually made inroads on Portuguese territory: this led to a cessation of diplomatic relations between Spain and France, while Great Britain prepared for a military intervention. In vain had France and England protested, Spain continued to encourage the Portuguese clerical party.

The rumours of a new press law for France had aroused some curiosity as to the tenor of the inaugural address for the session of 1827. After the usual observations with regard to the relations with the foreign Powers and an allusion to the affairs of Greece, the King announced his intention (December 12th) of introducing a bill which should put a stop to the license of the press, and thus preserve it from the consequences of its own excesses. The royal speech was ill-received on all sides, and the Ministry did not hasten to bring forward the bill, as other troubles had meanwhile arisen.

On the day following the opening of the Chambers, the text of the speech of Canning, Secretary for Foreign Affairs, in the House of Commons became known; and the insinuation that, though France had done much to prevent the inroad of bands of Spanish absolutists into Portugal, she might have done more, as her troops were occupying Spain, caused some uneasiness. But the Earl of Liverpool, the English Premier, wrote to M. de Villèle, that he had implicit faith in the sincerity and loyalty of the French Government, informing him at the same time, that if Canning's words had embarrassed France for the moment, it was only to do her service in the future. Nevertheless the advocates of Spanish absolutism in the French Chambers took the opportunity of harassing M. de Villèle, notably Châteaubriand, whose opposition was inspired by personal, not by political, animosity against the Prime Minister.

When the new press law came to be read, it was not found to contain any clauses to check license, but it made a clean sweep of everything in the shape of printed matter, save that emanating from the clerical party and vendors of religious books. From all parts of the country petitions poured in, and the excitement increased to such an extent that the French Academy, usually holding aloof from all political opinions, took up the cause, and sent an address to the King, in which it pointed out the damage which such a law would cause to literature. Charles X. refused to receive it, and the three Academicians who had proposed it were dismissed from the places which they occupied under the Government—a proceeding that embittered public opinion still more.

At the same time a bill was introduced to increase

the postage on newspapers, which, notwithstanding a determined opposition, passed. The further discussion on the press law, modified by several successive amendments, was postponed until the 14th of February.

On the 13th of this same month the Cabinet presented to the Chamber of Deputies two bills respecting the jury laws. One of these had previously been sent to the Peers, who had entirely remodelled it. This should, in the ordinary course of things, have been laid before the Deputies, but the Government, which was not satisfied with it, proposed a project of its own, which was rejected, and the Peers' bill was adopted in preference.

The 14th, so impatiently expected, dawned at last, and the discussion on the press bill began. It continued until the 12th of March, when, in spite of the most eloquent protestations, and the most vehement opposition, it was adopted by two hundred and thirty-three votes against one hundred and thirty-four. Seven days afterwards it was brought before the Chamber of Peers, which after a most careful inquiry and hearing of technical evidence, demolished its clauses one by one, until the King, by a royal ordinance, saw fit to withdraw it altogether on the 17th of April.

This being the first time that the ministers had, however reluctantly, acted in accordance with the will of the nation, the event caused an explosion of joy throughout the whole of France, mingled with congratulatory addresses to the Chamber of Peers, which the authorities were sensible enough not to suppress. In reality the Government was already taking measures of avenging themselves upon the Peers, whom they held guilty of Liberalism and hunting after popularity. For this popularity was the very thing the ministry lacked, having destroyed it by their frequent and unwarrantable interference with the liberty of the subject, and by their continual attempts to revive the institutions of a past, directly antagonistic to the spirit of the present. One of the most flagrant instances of this violation occurred at the funeral of the Duke de la Rochefoucauld-Liancourt (March 3rd), and which exercised a most baneful influence on the future of the Restoration.

Another event which had a graver and more immediate tendency to arouse discontent was the royal decree suddenly disbanding the National Guard (April 30th), the very day after that body had enthusiastically welcomed the King in its midst. This unprovoked slight caused great irritation, in which even the Royalist newspapers sided to some extent with the population. Some of the National Guards wanted to sell their uniforms and to send the proceeds to the insurrectionary Greeks, but they were dissuaded from doing this. Consequently they kept their clothes as well as their arms, which they had occasion to use three years later for the final overthrow of the Bourbon dynasty. Nor was the impression produced by this act confined to France. In England and on the Continent, where the supplement of the official newspaper, the *Moniteur*, containing the decree arrived without being preceded by the least explanation, it was believed that an insurrectionary movement had suddenly burst out in Paris. Another incident, consequent upon the election of a professor at the Collége de France, in which the Government acted against the wishes of the students, prolonged the public excitement, and though the Liberal deputies did their best to calm the effervescence of a section of the community, ever ready for revolt, one of the former, Benjamin Constant, gave the students the advice to reserve their energy for the future. He with many others already foresaw the troubles looming in the distance. The session of 1827 closed as usual with the debates on, and the passing of, the budget, which this year assumed a particular importance, the Opposition taking advantage of the general discussion to speak on every question of home and foreign policy. M. de Villèle was attacked on all sides, and could scarcely defend the tactics of his administration, as the financial condition of the State, hitherto satisfactory, was on the wane.

A few days after the closing of the session, General Lafayette, so enthusiastically received on his return from America, was elected deputy for the arrondissement of Meaux. M. de Villèle, who considered this election as a proof of public ill-feeling against himself, made it a pretext for taking a measure, legal in itself, but reserved only for extraordinary circumstances; he induced the King to promulgate a decree re-establishing the censorship for newspapers and periodical publications (June 24th).

Side by side with this long series of blunders the

Government committed one act, which redounds to its honour. It united with England and Russia in signifying to the Porte that unless she consented to accept within one month the mediation of the three Cabinets, these latter would oppose, by force if necessary, the prolongation of hostilities against Greece.

This same year saw the death of Canning, then English Premier, and that of Manuel, the great French orator, who had lived for the last five years in seclusion, but whose funeral was accompanied by demonstrations boding no good to the Government, and which began to find itself seriously hampered, as it was no longer unreservedly supported by the Chambers. The House of Peers was decidedly hostile to it, whilst in the Chamber of Deputies it had to struggle with serious opposition from two sides, the majority which it had commanded for so long a period gradually dwindling down to unimportant numbers. In this emergency there were two courses open to it—the resignation of the Ministry, or the dissolution of the Chambers. It was almost certain that the latter course would be adopted.

While these alternatives were being debated in the Councils of the Government, and nothing was decided, save a new creation of peers, in order to give the Royalists a majority, the electoral campaign began with a deluge of publications and an increased activity of the newspapers. The Ministry, apprehensive of too long a delay, intended to convoke the Legislative as soon as possible, so that the newspapers might not abuse their liberty, as, according to the law of 1822, the censorship was suspended during the preparations for a general election.

The King, who proposed to make a journey in the month of September to visit the camp near St. Omer, wished to be informed before starting what the Ministry had decided; and at the end of August the dissolution of the Chambers was resolved upon.

In addition to this journey of the King, the various members of the royal family visited the provinces, a measure counselled by M. de Villèle as likely to improve the waning popularity of the Court. The result was a disappointment; and though the King was welcomed everywhere with acclamations, the enthusiasm of the population proceeded from their love of sightseeing rather than from their attachment to the royal traveller. This reception was to be ascribed to the rumours that the King intended to abolish the Charter, to renew the absolute monarchy, and to return to Paris at the head of all the troops assembled in the camp. Nothing of the kind happened. Charles X. might have fostered such a plan, but he did not execute it, and at his arrival in the capital, after a long conference with his ministers, the dissolution of the Chambers, a consequent general election, a creation of seventy-six new peers, and the temporary suspension of the censorship were proclaimed in the last days of October. Among the newly-chosen peers there were five archbishops, one Marshal of France, Soult, and forty deputies chosen from the clerical party. The opening of the Chambers was fixed for the 5th of February, 1828.

The Liberal Opposition, recruited by the majority of the members of the Right, who aimed above all at the fall of M. de Villèle, entered with vigour upon the electoral struggle, during which the news of the battle of Navarino (October 20, 1827), which led to the independence of Greece, arrived.

On the other hand the Government did all in its power, by means of the administrative coërcion of its functionaries, to turn the scales in its favour; but these tactics were not successful, and many of the candidates of the Liberal party were elected, whilst the capital chose all her deputies from the ranks of the Opposition. The Parisian population, as usual, received the defeat of the Government with illuminations, fireworks, and demonstrations of joy. In the quarters of Saint-Denis and Saint-Martin, some windows were smashed, and the soldiers had to interfere. The same disturbances were repeated some days afterwards, when several barricades were erected, causing an affray between the military and the citizens, in which there were many wounded and killed. An inquiry which followed plainly proved that the fault lay chiefly with the military, who had provoked the citizens. This, however, did not influence the elections, which resulted in a majority against M. de Villèle. The Ministry could not withstand this defeat. On the 6th of December the King accepted its resignation, but it was difficult to find a satisfactory combination to succeed it, and the remainder of the month was passed in negotiations more varied than efficacious.

The battle of Navarino, already mentioned, was not the only point on which France found herself in conflict with Mahommedan barbarism. In consequence of the Algerians having captured a vessel belonging to the States of the Church, but sailing under the French flag, the Government demanded satisfaction for this insult. The Dey of Algiers not only refused this, but insulted the Consul-General charged with this mission, and the French blockaded the port of Algiers. This measure being found insufficient, as no man-of-war ventured out of the harbour, and as Algiers possessed no merchant fleet, it was decided to attack the town. Though this decision met with approval, its execution was postponed, M. de Villèle being occupied with weightier concerns, and the blockade being maintained in the meanwhile.

The year 1827 proved auspicious for the arts of peace. Several literary works of great importance appeared, notably Guizot's *History of the Revolution in England;* Victor Cousin's *History of Philosophy;* and Victor Hugo's drama of *Cromwell*, a work not intended for the stage, but accompanied by a preface, which became as it were the manifesto and programme of the romantic school, as distinguished from the classical. Industry was making vast progress, and an exhibition of its various branches received the approval of foreigners as well as of Frenchmen.

In view of a new Ministry to be chosen, Charles X.

consulted M. de Villèle, who dissuaded him from calling the Prince de Polignac to the direction of affairs, but counselled the King, however, to select his Cabinet from among the Royalists. The advice was well meant and monarchical, but scarcely rational, as the Opposition was powerful enough to claim a seat for some of its members in the Ministry. Nevertheless, the counsel was followed, and the new Ministry was composed of members chosen from among the various shades of Royalist opinion. M. de Martignac was its virtual chief, though not bearing the official title of president, which had been abolished for the time being (January 5th, 1828).

The Martignac Ministry was coldly received by the press; the Royalists did not deem its opinions sufficiently advanced; the Opposition, notwithstanding the attempts made by it to reconcile public opinion by various acts of supposed liberality, boldly stated that it was merely composed of new and second-rate men, brought together to act as their predecessors had done. Nor did the speech from the throne give satisfaction; the Liberals expected the enunciation of a new programme; the Royalists hoped that though the Ministry had changed the system would remain the same. The latter were less mistaken than the former, but both were equally dissatisfied. On the verification of the credentials of the deputies, some tactics of the former administration were brought to light, which, strongly condemned by the chief and other members of the new Ministry, compelled

MM. de Chabrol and de Frayssinous, who belonged to the late as well as to the present Government, to tender their resignation, which was accepted. Royer-Collard was elected President of the Chamber of Deputies; M. de Villèle and two of his colleagues were named peers, each with a pension of twelve thousand francs.

The result of the fresh elections, which had to be held because several constituencies had chosen the same candidate, and because the Committee of Inquiry annulled several elections, was that thirty-five out of the forty-five newly elected deputies were Liberals. It was on this occasion that the electors, instead of accepting the candidates named by the newspapers, held, for the first time, preparatory meetings, with which the Government did not interfere, though it prohibited public places being used for the purpose. In addition to the electoral and jury bills being passed, the attention of the Chamber of Deputies was drawn to the opening of letters by officials of the Post Office (May 3rd), an abuse which was instituted by the *ancien régime*, and re-established under the Restoration for the purpose of violating the secrets of correspondence. Notwithstanding the denial of the Ministry that such proceedings had taken place, it was proved that they had existed, and that only about three months ago M. de Martignac had obtained from the King the suppression of this iniquitous and disgraceful service. On the 14th of April, a new press bill was laid before the Chamber of Deputies, which, after many days' discussion, was finally carried three months later. During this interval, its most rigorous clause, relating to the amount of pecuniary guarantees which the newspapers had to pay to the State before they received permission to appear, had been considerably modified. An indictment was brought against the late Ministry, and referred to a select Committee, but the Chambers, after having voted the budget, broke up (21st July) without discussing it.

Previous to this, a Committee of Inquiry, which had been appointed to discover if there were any Jesuit colleges in France, had reported that there existed three small seminaries directed by some members of that brotherhood. At the same time it stated that the presence of those priests was in no way contrary to law. This conclusion, adopted by a majority of one, aroused vehement clamours from the Liberal party. Numerous petitions were sent to the Chamber to suppress this monastic order in France; but the King refused to do this, and based his decision on the statement of the Committee. He nevertheless signed a decree, somewhat circumscribing the sphere of action of these priests, and which, though sufficiently lenient towards them, caused them to raise the cry that they were persecuted. The pulpits rang with accusations of impiety against the whole of the Ministry, which would not enter upon an open struggle with the religious element. It asked for the interference of the Pope, who counselled to the priests confidence in the King and submission to the throne. They were obliged to yield; many elected to leave France, but those who remained ceased not to clamour for what they called "liberty of instruction," which meant simply liberty for themselves when they were no longer the masters. About the middle of August a French expedition was despatched to the Morea, with the mutual consent of Russia and England, who confided to France the task of forcing Turkey to evacuate Greece, a task which was faithfully and honourably accomplished by the end of October.

While on a journey through the east of France the King had the satisfaction of finding the feelings of his subjects more favourably disposed towards him; unfortunately on his return to Paris the struggle between the clericals and Liberals did not cease, but grew more vehement than ever. This induced the Ministry, when the prospects of the session of 1829 came to be discussed, to open negotiations with the Liberal party in order to secure a stauncher support, of which it stood in need. The Liberals were well disposed to enter the Government, rightly deeming this a beginning of sound parliamentary practice. General Sebastiani and Casimir Périer were already pointed out as probable ministers, while other deputies had been sounded as to their willingness to assume important offices in the public administration. Such was the state of affairs at the opening of the Chambers.

During the progress of these negotiations, M. Cauchois-Lemaire, a Liberal writer, published a pamphlet, *A Letter to the Duke of Orleans*, advising this prince to take under the constitutional monarchy a kind of moral royalty, and to constitute himself the chief of the Opposition, as some of the English princes had done. This letter produced a great sensation, but was generally disapproved. The author was prosecuted for provoking a change of dynasty, with unusual severity arrested before his trial, and afterwards condemned to fifteen months' imprisonment and a fine of two thousand francs, while the publishers also underwent three months' imprisonment. This blunder of the Government already designated the Duke of Orleans as the possible founder of a new dynasty.

With the exception of the King's unsuccessful attempt to introduce the Prince de Polignac into the Ministry, nothing of importance signalised the opening of the session for this year. Despite this Prince's formal declaration of attachment to the Charter, public opinion had not sufficient confidence in his protestations to entrust him with the management of part of the laws.

On the 9th of February, in accordance with the promise in the speech from the throne, M. de Martignac laid on the table of the Chamber of Deputies two bills purporting to change the administration of the departments and communes.

Until now every official had been appointed by royal authority, ministers, prefects, sub-prefects, and mayors, as well as general, municipal and arrondissement councillors. It was still the imperial organisation in its integrity. This was now to be changed, and every one had to be elected. Unfortunately the electors were chosen amongst those inhabitants who paid the most taxes, and their number was very limited. It was certainly an improvement upon the existing system, but for fear of being reproached with favouring the spread of democracy the Ministry had not gone far enough; and if the bills had passed they would simply have created certain privileged minorities. Nevertheless, the Right, indignant at the project, stigmatised it as a concession to the revolutionary spirit, while the Liberals thought it insufficient. As the Ministry found it impossible to conciliate both parties, the bills were withdrawn after much discussion. This incident led to the rupture of negotiations between the Ministry and the Left, nor could any good have come of it; for even if the King should have admitted to his councils the leaders of the Opposition, they would not have stayed. Various circumstances showed that the monarch was already resolved to entrust by a legal *coup d'état* the Prince de Polignac with the leadership of affairs. As if prophetically cognisant of this intention, General Lamarque, a Liberal deputy who was destined to obtain great fame as an orator in the Chamber, spoke of the danger of taking extreme measures, and pointed to what had happened in England when the Constitution had been violated there. Thus, in addition to the *Letter to the Duke of Orleans*, at the commencement of the session, forebodings and advice were not wanting. Unfortunately, as usual, they were not listened to. The Royalist press openly called for a conflict between the two parties, by inviting the Liberals to begin the contest, unless they wished to be attacked themselves. Under such threatening auspices the session of 1829 terminated on the 31st of July, the budget having been voted amidst the usual skirmishes extending for nearly two months.

On the 9th of August that which had been foreseen came to pass. The official newspaper, the *Moniteur*, contained a list of the members of the new Cabinet, in which the Prince de Polignac, the leader of the extreme Royalists, was entrusted with the portfolio of Foreign Affairs. This was an undoubted declaration of war against public opinion, and it was accepted as such. It caused an outburst of indignation from one end of France to another. The truce, entered upon with the advent of the Martignac Ministry, was broken, nothing remained but war. How and when the war was to be waged was not determined; whether the enemy fired the first shot or not, the nation was resolved not to retreat.

The Polignac Cabinet had no intentions of commencing hostilities. If anything, it was rather bent upon defence than aggression. All that the monarch wanted was to see his favourite in the Ministry; he would willingly have kept M. de Martignac, if such had been possible, or any other minister who would have consented to stay. Some of the members of the new Government had even been chosen without their knowledge, and after much deliberation. Two of them were in the provinces, and learned their nominations from the pages of the *Moniteur*, whereupon one proceeded leisurely to Paris, whilst the other hastened to the capital to refuse the proffered portfolio, notwithstanding the insistence of the King.

No President of the Council was appointed, though the public persisted in calling the new Cabinet by the name of the Polignac Ministry, not only because they considered that Prince its virtual head, but because his name appeared the most expressive signification of the policy for which the administration had been formed. Every intention of violence or *coup d'état* was repudiated by the executive, as the King and his favourite still believed it possible to carry on the government within constitutional and legal forms. It was the force of the political current that afterwards carried them away.

The hostility to the Polignac Cabinet was not confined to the Liberal press. Those newspapers which professed the sincerest attachment for the Bourbons were as bitter in their denunciations of the new ministers as the Opposition, the only flagrant exception to this universal discontent being the ultra-Royalist journal, the *Drapeau Blanc*, which by a cunningly executed manœuvre now appealed to the lower classes, for whom, as a rule, it professed the greatest contempt, against the middle classes, whom it designated as being the enemies of the aristocracy as well as of the people. To these lower classes it promised everything—work, bread, a provision for the future. Twenty years before 1848 the *Drapeau Blanc* constituted itself the champion of socialism.

Resignations of Government officials now poured in from all sides, whilst General Lafayette travelling through the provinces, received many ovations, because his well-known Liberal politics made him the incarnation of the Opposition to the Ministry, and because the people saw in him the personification of the first Revolution. But the reception of the Duke d'Angoulême in Normandy was very different, and when the prefect at Cherbourg wanted to organise a public subscription for a ball in honour of the Duke, no subscribers could be found.

The forebodings of a *coup d'état* caused associations to be formed having for their object the legal refusal of paying taxes. The conflicting verdicts of the various tribunals called upon to decide the legality of these acts testified but too plainly that in some quarters even the magistrates sided with the party of resistance. The *Journal des Débats*, a newspaper noted for its consistent upholding of the Bourbon interest, was indicted for publishing an article against the new Ministry, but the court after three hours' deliberation pronounced an acquittal. The *Courrier Français*, another newspaper prosecuted for an art criticism containing an expression which was considered by the clerical party as insulting to Christianity, was also acquitted. All this tended to show that the magistrates were determined to put a stop to priestly influence. Several modifications in the new

Ministry brought about a still greater degree of unpopularity, and this notwithstanding the attempts of Polignac to introduce various commercial improvements, which, as he thought, would lead to great prosperity. He had watched the commercial energy of England without staying to consider that it emanated from public and not from official initiative. He deemed it best to encourage a taste for material prosperity among the people, to substitute bodily welfare for political liberty, for he knew that when the mind is enthralled by physical comfort the task of governing becomes all the easier. Whatever might have been the results of his policy, he had not the time to put his plans into operation, and it is doubtful whether they would have succeeded, as public opinion was strongly opposed to him.

In spite of these interior disturbances, the year 1829 was fruitful in literary and scientific productions, while as regards foreign policy the Government had resolved to take more stringent measures against Algiers, a town which could not be reduced by the ordinary measures of civilised warfare.

The new year's receptions of the political and learned bodies of the State by the King were anxiously looked forward to. It had not been forgotten that Charles X. on a previous occasion had allowed the rancour of personal feeling to penetrate the courtesy of his usual deportment when the High Court of Justice had pronounced a verdict antagonistic to the royal idea on politics and religion. These expectations were not disappointed. This year, instead of contenting himself with remaining silent, the King presumed to give advice to the first president of the Court of Justice, whilst, at her private reception, the Duchess d'Angoulême, seeing the members of that same Court approach, merely motioned them to pass on. Contrary to public opinion, which expected that the Ministry would endeavour to govern without the aid of the Chambers, the latter were convoked for the 2nd of March, by a royal decree, published in the *Moniteur* of the 6th of January. This did not solve, but merely changed the aspect of the question, and led to the Liberal newspapers discussing what the Government would do in the event of the Legislative proving hostile and refusing to vote the budget. The Royalist papers took up the controversy, and defied the Chamber to refuse that vote, adding that it would then become a question of an appeal to arms, and that the King would be found to have a sufficient supply of them. This challenge was eagerly taken up by the Liberal press, notably by an entirely new paper, the *National*, edited by MM. Thiers, Mignet, and Armand Carrel. It was the pen of Thiers which first propounded the doctrine, "the King reigns, but does not govern." Every one was preparing for a conflict, and some members of the Liberal party already speculated on the as yet novel idea of substituting another member of the royal family for the present monarch, as had happened in England in 1688. The opinions of the *National* made a great many converts, whilst another newspaper, the *Tribune of the Departments*, still more advanced in its ideas, was said to be the organ of the Republicans, at that time few in number, but very energetic.

Polignac had laid down for himself a programme by which he could steer clear of all political complications and discussions. He meant to propose to the Chambers a great many projects, tending to develop an immense industrial energy, requiring vast capital, and by these means to avoid the measures more immediately connected with constitutional liberty. He still thought that he could reckon upon a majority of two hundred votes. In addition to this majority he hoped to revive the royal prestige by a vigorous expedition then preparing against the pirates of Algiers. Three elections which took place before the opening of the Legislative, and in which two out of the three chosen candidates professed Royalist opinions, strengthened the impression of the Prince of being able to weather the political storm.

Unfortunately the obstacle to this policy of tergiversation came from a quarter whence it was least expected. Whilst the minister strained every nerve to avoid topics of an irritating nature in the speech from the throne, the King insisted upon displaying his authority.

The coolness with which the King was received at the opening of the Chambers (March 2nd) was still further increased by his open declaration that in the event of opposition to his will and government he would know how to deal with it. It was throwing down the gauntlet there and then. Nor was the Opposition slow to take it up. In spite of the warnings contained in the reply to the royal speech, drawn up by a deputy of undoubted Royalist tendencies, the King decided upon an immediate prorogation of the Chambers, and even wished to refuse to receive this answer. But though this refusal was overruled by his Ministers, who wanted to give the conflict an appearance of having been begun under provocation, Charles X., nevertheless, insisted upon adjourning the Chambers on the 19th of March until the 3rd of September. This was tantamount to an official declaration of war. In the face of the hostilities aroused by these despotic proceedings, the Prime Minister continued to cherish the most erroneous illusions. These illusions were fostered by the official reports of various prefects, intended to remain secret, but which were published afterwards, and which represented France as solely interested in questions of material prosperity, and altogether heedless of politics; and that at the very time when politics occupied all minds. Deceived by these assurances, and also by his own calculations, which induced him to believe that he would have a majority of at least forty votes, Polignac persuaded the King to dissolve the Chambers (16th of May), to fix the new elections on the 23rd of June and the 3rd of July, and to convoke the Chambers thus elected for the 3rd of August.

In spite of Royalist intrigues, the elections of

the 23rd of June—from which, for reasons to be explained shortly, twenty departments had been excluded—resulted in the nomination of a hundred and forty-one Opposition candidates against fifty-seven Royalist or Ministerial ones. The Ministry tendered its resignation, which the King refused to accept, and the Council occupied itself with prospective measures, in case the elections of the 3rd of July should be equally unfavourable. At the same time it was proposed to change the electoral and press laws by royal decree; but this measure was adjourned until later. The second series of elections was as disastrous to the Government as the first. Nothing remained now but the elections for the twenty departments, which had been postponed, lest their well-known Liberal opinions and the consequent election of the Opposition candidates might have influenced others in following their example. What had been foreseen happened; the Royalists were again defeated. Out of four hundred and twenty-eight deputies, two hundred and seventy belonged to the Opposition, and one hundred and forty-five were Ministerialists; the remaining thirteen being of doubtful opinions. Up till then, though acting arbitrarily and ill-advised, the King had not transgressed his constitutional rights. But now he should have submitted to the will of the nation, conveyed to him in unmistakable terms, and sacrificed the Ministry to popular opinion. Instead of doing this, he began to have recourse to illegal proceedings.

Whilst these elections were going on some events

took place, which showed but too plainly that popular discontent was on the increase, and that it needed but a favourable opportunity to break out into rebellion. On the occasion of an entertainment given to the King and Queen of Naples, on their passage through Paris, several conflicts took place between the military and the citizens, the latter ending by setting fire to a heap of chairs round a bronze statue of Apollo, in the gardens of the Duke of Orleans. Even the successful termination of the expedition to Algiers (July 5th) failed to kindle the enthusiasm with which military triumphs were ordinarily received, a failure chiefly caused by the arrogance of the Royalist newspapers, and by the fear that a force which had subjugated a foreign foe might be turned against the people. These suspicions were not altogether unfounded, for it was known that General de Bourmont, the chief of that expedition, and appointed to this post in the face of public opinion, had, before his departure, expressed the hope that, in the event of a *coup d'état* being decided upon, the King would await his return with the victorious army. He was under the impression that the taking of Algiers would end the war in Africa, while, on the contrary, it was but the beginning of the strife, for each particular tribe which had fought for the Dey was resolved to continue the contest. The popularity of Charles X. seemed now irretrievably lost. On his return from the church of Notre-Dame, where a *Te Deum* had been celebrated in honour of the taking of Algiers, the crowd amidst which he had to pass received him in profound silence—a sad blow to one who loved popularity, but would not forego one iota of his own pretensions in order to endeavour to deserve it.

Even before the result of the elections was known, the King and his Ministers had determined upon a *coup d'état* rather than dismiss a Ministry which was distasteful to the nation. Charles X. pretended that the fourteenth article of the Charter gave him the power to cut any political knot by a royal ordinance. This power had been more than once invoked by Louis XVIII., but the Opposition had always contested its application, because, though the text might lend itself to it, the spirit of the Charter was against it. This fourteenth article conferred upon the King the power of issuing "the decrees and ordinances necessary for the execution of the laws and the surety of the State;" but it could not mean that he was justified in adopting the same prerogative for the violation of these laws. Divers attempts at solving the difficulty were discussed by the Ministry, and it was decided at last that by royal decrees the new Chambers should be dissolved; that no newspaper or periodical should appear without the permission of the authorities, which permission had to be renewed every three months; that the electoral law should be abrogated and replaced by a system closely resembling that of 1814, whilst the electoral colleges were summoned to assemble on the 6th and 13th of September, the Chambers (for a last sitting presumably) for the 28th, and lastly, that a number of councillors of State, dismissed under the Martignac Ministry, should be reinstated in their functions. Those of the Ministers who were opposed to these extreme measures consented, nevertheless, to sign the decrees, either from a feeling of affection for the King, or else from fear of being accused of deserting a sinking ship. They had no thought for France, which, by their acts, they exposed to the horrors of civil war; they deemed themselves the servants of royalty, not of the nation.

Foolhardy in his dependence upon the military forces, undeterred by the ominous warnings of so experienced a man as M. Sauvo, the chief editor of the *Moniteur*, Polignac published the royal decrees in that newspaper on the 26th of July. The capital was awestricken when it found the walls placarded with them, though they had been expected for several days. The 26th of July fell on a Monday, when thousands of artisans abstained from work, but the tranquillity of Paris was not disturbed. The press was the first to give the signal of resistance. At a meeting of the journalists of the Liberal newspapers, at the offices of the *National*, a protest was drawn up which has become historical, and which fully pointed out the illegality of the King's decrees. Contrary to the then prevalent customs of not signing articles in the papers, this protest was subscribed in full by forty of the principal editors and contributors to the organs of the Opposition, a boldness which caused the Government to give orders for their being arrested, and which orders were only prevented from being executed by the rapid march of events. Some of the printers of these Liberal papers became frightened, and refused to publish them any longer, whereupon their editors summoned them before the tribunals, and they were condemned to continue and print these papers, as the royal decrees had not yet been legally promulgated. Nor were the doings of the police, who had orders to dismantle the presses, more successful. The workmen whom they brought refused to obey, intimidated by the threats of the journalists, who qualified the proposed actions as illegal. In one instance, the Commissary of Police, at his wits' end, was compelled to have recourse to the assistance of the smith usually employed to chain the galley-slaves together. This was the only active resistance on the 26th. The capital was roused, anxious, on the alert, but not sufficiently excited to resort to violent measures. The military authorities took no precautions, the prefect of police, Mangin, held himself answerable for the public tranquillity, and the King, lulled to rest by this delusive security, started at seven in the morning for Saint-Cloud, to hunt at Rambouillet, forgetting, in his hurry, to send to Marmont, Duke of Ragusa, an order to invest him with the command of the troops. The Duke had, however, openly expressed his disgust at being probably called upon to risk his life for acts of which he disapproved, and on behalf of people whom he despised.

With the exception of the crowd surrounding the

carriage of de Polignac and pelting it with stones—a disturbance with which even a post of soldiers, which was quite near, did not interfere—the day passed without more serious demonstrations.

On the following morning, the 27th of July, the symptoms became more grave. The streets were crowded with compositors and printers whom their masters had dismissed. Joined by bands of artisans who had voluntarily left their workshops, they formed themselves into groups, eagerly discussing the situation, and shouting, "Long live the Charter." The young students from the various schools and from the University, and the clerks from the principal warehouses, came to swell their number and increase the excitement by inflammatory speeches. The proclamation that Paris was declared in a state of siege added but fuel to the flame. Some shots were fired between four and five in the afternoon by detachments of the guard and of the gendarmerie in the vicinity of the Palais Royal. Nothing more was wanted; the people immediately attempted to throw up barricades, to pull down the insignia of the Bourbons, to uproot pavingstones for defensive and offensive purposes, and to smash the street lamps, so that the darkness might hamper the movements of the troops. All this was accomplished in a few hours. On the 28th the insurrection was in full swing, and spread through every quarter, the royal armouries were emptied, and the National Guards showed themselves in their uniforms at the barricades. The tricolour flapped gaily in the wind from the Hôtel de Ville, and it was also hoisted on the church of Notre Dame and on a hundred public buildings. While the sight of this flag was hailed with acclamations of joy, the alarm-bell rang from all steeples; and, as Marmont informed the King by a message on the following morning, "it was no longer a riot, but a revolution." In spite of this alarming news, the King and his Court remained at Saint-Cloud unshaken in their confidence. Polignac and his Ministers sat in permanence at the Tuileries, where the head-quarters of Marmont were, and closed their eyes to their critical position. The troops of the line meanwhile fraternised with the people, and abandoned to them their barracks, arms, and ammunition. Shortly after Marmont had sent his message to the monarch, the firing was suspended by mutual consent, to await the result of the royal answer. All might have been settled in a manner comparatively peaceful even then, had not an unforeseen incident changed the situation.

Carried away by excitement, a detachment of soldiers stationed in the Place Vendôme left its post, to place itself at the disposal of the deputies assembled at the house of Laffitte, the banker of the Liberal party, Marmont, being informed of this, commanded one of the two battalions of Swiss charged with the defence of the Louvre to take the place of the troops of the Place Vendôme, and the other battalion to remain where it was. The captain of the latter told his men to assemble in the court-yard. As there were no longer any troops outside the Louvre, a youth made his way to the interior of the palace and boldly showed himself at the window. The soldiers, under the impression that the people had invaded the palace, fled hurriedly to the Tuileries, and communicated their terror to the troops who were stationed there. They also abandoned their post, and rushed to the gardens, where Marmont, with a great deal of trouble, rallied them, fell back with them upon the Bois de Boulogne, and marched to Saint-Cloud to announce that Paris was lost. Paris was indeed lost. The Revolution was virtually accomplished on the evening of the 29th, though the result proved less brilliant than the struggle to accomplish it had been heroic. This barren result was chiefly owing to the want of unanimity among certain deputies, and to the pusillanimity of some others. For the last three days they had assembled at various places, because many of them believed that they had not, and could not have, any legal right to meet before the 3rd of August, the day on which the Chambers had been convoked. Profuse as they were of words, they shrunk from action.

Meanwhile Lafayette, who had returned in great haste to Paris, took the command of the National Guards, and installed himself at the Hôtel de Ville. When it was found that all attempts at reconciliation between the deputies and the King were fruitless, a municipal Committee joined the General; but afraid of transgressing the constitutional forms, they did not dare to form a Provisional Government;

they wanted to preserve an appearance of legality in a situation which was absolutely illegal.

Until now the name of no one had been pronounced as that of a probable successor to Charles X., for the deposition of the King had not even been hinted at, and nothing had been determined. The editors of the *National*, probably apprehensive that an arrangement might be concluded, which would have again destroyed all liberal reforms, took the first step in attracting the public mind to a new Government. On the 30th of July they distributed throughout the capital a placard setting forth the impossibility of Charles X. returning to Paris, the difficulties of the re-establishment of a Republic, and ending with the recommendation that the nation should offer to the Duke of Orleans the crown of France. This suggestion met with general approval. But no one knew where the Duke was to be found, whether he was in the country, and even if he would accept the offer. M. Thiers and the celebrated painter, Ary Scheffer, who had given drawing lessons to the Duke's daughters, went to Neuilly and were received by the Duchess and her sister-in-law, Princess Adelaide. The first showed herself surprised and dissatisfied; the second declared that her family was at the disposal of France, and offered to inform her brother of the request.

On the return of the two delegates to the Palais Bourbon, where the deputies were assembled, a Committee of five members was sent to the House of

Peers, to propose the nomination of the Duke of Orleans as Lieutenant-General of the Kingdom. At the same time arrived a messenger from Charles X. revoking the decrees of the 25th; but the unanimous answer of the deputies, uninfluenced by the somewhat wavering attitude of the Peers, was that the revocation came too late. A message was sent to the Duke of Orleans to inform him of the resolution arrived at, and Charles X. had ceased to reign.

When the Duke received the news that the crown of France had been offered to him, he went to Paris to consult Laffitte, who informed of this arrival the Committee deputed by the Chamber to offer the Prince the Lieutenant-Generalship. The Duke still hesitated to accept the proffered post but was prevailed upon by the deputies, who told him that his refusal would inevitably entail the establishment of a Republic. This determined him, and a short proclamation was published, acquainting the Chambers and the nation with his decision, and ending with these memorable words—" Henceforth the Charter shall be a reality." Shortly afterwards an interview with Lafayette took place at the Hôtel de Ville, when the General frankly declared that he could have wished France to have become a Republic; but that, seeing the impossibility of permanently introducing it, he was prepared to support faithfully a monarchy surrounded by so many Republican institutions. The Duke and the General subsequently appeared together on the balcony of the

Hôtel de Ville, and the former was virtually accepted as the chief of the new dynasty.

However much Lafayette has been blamed for not introducing a Republican government in 1830, it should not be overlooked that he well knew the dangers attendant upon such a step, that he was perfectly aware of the small number of Republicans then existing in France, and of the slight hold their opinions had upon the masses. He accepted what he thought to be the best Government for his country, and if he sacrificed his ideal Republic he at least endeavoured to do that which was practicable.

The deposed King was still at Saint-Cloud, deserted by many of the soldiers and by several of his courtiers, who went to seek their fortune elsewhere. Charles X. decided upon removing to the royal château of Rambouillet, about twenty-five miles from Paris, with his body-guards, his Swiss troops, and other soldiers, whose fidelity was, however, doubtful. The new Government resolved to terrify him, and allowed a body of six or seven thousand armed men, without any order or fixed plan, either on foot or in different vehicles, to start for the castle where the aged monarch was. The Chamber had already sent three delegates to watch officially over the safety of the ex-King, and officiously to induce him to leave France as quickly as possible. When the delegates arrived (3rd August) Charles X. and the Duke d'Angoulême had already signed their abdication in favour of the King's grandson, the Duke de Bordeaux, and had appointed the

Duke of Orleans regent, with the title of Lieutenant-General.

It was finally resolved that the King and his family should embark at Cherbourg. During the journey, which lasted a fortnight, the inhabitants of the villages and towns which they traversed received them without uttering any exclamations, but when they arrived at their place of embarkation they found the populace very excited and the town itself everywhere decorated with the tricolour. The harbour of Cherbourg was, at that time, separated from the city by a large circular railing, and whilst the old King, his relatives, and suite, went on board two American vessels, the *Great Britain* and the *Charles Caroll*, which were the property of some members of the Bonaparte family, a great number of people crowded against the other side of the railings, animated by feelings of indignation or compassion. Before Charles X. left he recommended the pensioners of the civil list to the generosity of the conquerors, whilst his body-guards, which had already handed to him their standards, and accompanied him thus far, took their leave. "Then it was necessary to depart.[1] Standing on deck, the old King bade farewell to France. And, taken in tow by a steamer, the *Great Britain* unfurled her sails, whilst the guards ascended in silence the Cherbourg coast. Some spectators who had lingered on the shore followed with their eyes the track of this vessel on the waves, when they saw her suddenly

[1] Louis Blanc, *Histoire de Dix Ans*, bk. i., ch. 10.

turn round, and quickly retake the direction of the harbour. Was this in consequence of some violent order given by Charles X. to the crew? This might have been dreaded; but everything had been carefully foreseen. A brig, commanded by Capain Thibault, had received orders to accompany the *Great Britain*, and to sink her in case Charles X. should attempt to act as a master. This relentless foresight was not justified by subsequent events. The ship only returned to fetch some provisions, which had been forgotten amidst the disaster which overwhelmed the descendant of several generations of Kings. When everything was ready for departure, the order was given to start. The Bourbons set sail towards England, taking perhaps the same road on the ocean that formerly the vessel which bore the conquered Stuarts had taken. There was no tempest in the sky; the wind swelled the sails, and the ship disappeared on the sea."

Thus finished the Restoration, a result produced by the innate obstinacy of the Bourbons as well as by the natural course of events, and which brought about a Revolution really confined to Paris, but with which the whole of France sympathised. The sole conflict that took place in favour of the fallen dynasty was at Nantes, but it was of no importance. The Bourbons, who had returned to France amidst enthusiasm, departed amidst indifference.

Book VII.

THE REIGN OF LOUIS PHILIPPE.

CHAPTER I.

§ I.—THE BEGINNING OF THE ORLEANS DYNASTY.

(*From the 3rd of August,* 1830, *to the 28th of July,* 1836.)

THE first act of the Lieutenant-General, King of France in all but the name, was to convoke the Chambers for the 3rd of August, the date originally fixed by Charles X., but which had been indefinitely postponed by the decree of the 25th of July, dissolving the Legislative. In accordance with this initiative appeal of the Republican Government, the session opened on the day appointed, and after a short address of the Lieutenant-General, at once proceeded to the verification of the deputies elected. Several of the elections were invalidated because the secrecy of the ballot had been tampered with. On the 7th, the Chamber of Deputies discussed the modifications to be introduced into the Charter, which was no longer granted to the nation by the King, but imposed by the former on the monarch, as the first and principal condition of sovereignty. Article 14 was worded in such a way as to be no more susceptible of sophistical or ambiguous interpretations. The prescribed age for candidates was reduced, the septennial Legislature changed into an integral renewal of the Chamber every five years, and Roman Catholicism was abolished as the religion of the State, though it was officially stated that it was the creed professed by the majority of Frenchmen; the censorship ceased to exist; the jury was reinstated for all offences of the press laws; the tricolour was adopted as the national flag; the organisation of the peerage, the liberty of instruction, and various other questions were postponed till further discussion.

To the Charter was prefaced a declaration, stating that the throne was vacant *de facto et de jure*, and that it was necessary to provide for its being filled. The amended text of the new Charter followed this preamble. Then came the request to the Duke of Orleans to take the oath to the Charter and the institutions which it defined; and after his acceptance and oath before both Chambers assembled, to assume the title of King of the French.

The Chamber of Deputies adopted these measures by two hundred and nineteen against thirty-three votes, notwithstanding the protest of several Royalists against the proclamation of deposition and transfer of the crown. They abstained from voting, and gave up their seats afterwards.

In the House of Peers the only dissentient voice was Châteaubriand's, who vindicated the rights of the young Henry V., though he rendered homage to the energy and legality of the resistance of the Parisians, while condemning the councillors of the King, who had provoked this resistance. The great author announced at the same time his retirement from political life.

The deposition of the elder branch being thus officially accomplished, Louis Philippe accepted the title of King of the French, and proceeded to the composition of his first Cabinet (11th August), while on the same day the Royal Guards were disbanded. General Lafayette was invested with the temporary command of all the National Guards, which were rapidly re-organised. They were intended to form the basis of a military system which would considerably decrease the cost of a standing army.

Every revolution, however slight, tends more or less to suspend work and industry, and this last one was no exception to the almost general rule. Bands of destitute artisans, clamouring for work and assistance, were perambulating the streets of Paris, and the Government hastened to lay before the Chambers a bill authorising it to raise a credit of five million francs to provide for these pressing wants. Many masters and manufacturers, notably the master-printers, created, as it were, new enterprises, in order to provide employment. But notwithstanding all that the Government and private energy could do, some disturbances, which led to no grave consequences, were caused by this enforced idleness.

Four of the late Ministers of Charles X. having been arrested on various parts of French territory, public opinion demanded their prosecution, and almost their death. Both Chambers decided that they should be prosecuted; and they were confined to Vincennes during the drawing up of the indictment. Meanwhile, a deputy, Victor de Tracy, presented a bill for the abolition of capital punishment. He, as well as others, feared that the desire for vengeance might be the cause of sanguinary reprisals, the more to be regretted, as the Revolution had shed no blood, save in battle. The King, whose inclinations were all for mercy, and whose dislike for inflicting death made him even abandon the chase, was in favour of this proposed bill, and so were several of the Ministers, but the public considered it a means to shield Polignac and his accomplices from the punishment that might overtake them. Nevertheless, the bill might possibly have passed, but for the objections of the magistrates and military authorities against the sudden adoption of a measure which entailed an entire modification of penal legislation. In this emergency it was referred to a select Committee to report upon.

On the 18th of August the Chamber of Deputies discharged, as it were, a debt of gratitude, by voting a bill for granting pensions to the widows and orphans of those who had perished during the combats of the three days of July. Various other measures were introduced to satisfy public opinion with regard to election practices, especially one which obliged a candidate to seek again the suffrages of his constituency in case of his accepting an office under Government, as is done in England. The church of Sainte-Geneviève was reconstituted as a Pantheon for the sepulture of eminent men.

On the 29th of August, the King, accompanied by Lafayette, reviewed the National Guards in the Champ de Mars. The enthusiastic reception which he received left no doubt about the satisfaction felt on all sides, nor was Louis Philippe less prompt in testifying his delight at these marks of public affection.

This general joy was shortly to be marred by the report that the Duke de Bourbon had committed suicide. The partisans of the elder branch insinuated that the new King had incited the Duke's mistress, the Baroness de Feuchères, to murder the old nobleman, because Louis Philippe feared that his son, the Duke d'Aumâle, the probable heir of the Duke de Bourbon, might be disinherited. The news of this death, received the morning after the review held in the Champ de Mars, excited public opinion, and was eagerly taken advantage of by the King's political antagonists. Howsoever disagreeable these innuendoes might have been to Louis Philippe and his family personally, they contributed in no way to embarrass his Government, in the position in which it found itself with regard to the other European Powers, who might have objected to the expulsion of a royal dynasty, which they had helped to restore in 1815. That they did not do so was simply because the allied sovereigns had aimed in 1815 less at the reinstatement of the Bourbons than at the irrevocable exclusion of Napoleon and his family. If France, in resorting to a Revolution, did not at the same time put into action Imperial ideas of conquest, the European Powers did not feel called upon to declare war against her out of mere inclination for monarchs by divine right.

Besides, the condition of affairs had changed. Apart from his inherent love of peace, which was carried even to extremes, Louis Philippe was scarcely the man to disturb European peace in order to undertake a crusade for the sake of seeing the tricolour wave on the Rhine, the Pyrenees, or the Alps. As long as France was left the sole arbiter of her own destinies, she had no wish to kindle strife elsewhere. That is what Louis Philippe notified to the foreign Cabinets on the morrow of his accession; and the anxiety aroused by the three days of July subsided. England was the first to recognise the new Government. All the other States, save three—the Emperor of Russia, the King of Spain, and the Duke of Modena—followed England's example. With remarkable good sense, Louis Philippe took little or no notice of the slight, which induced the three sovereigns to reconsider the matter, and offer voluntarily what they had at first refused.

Truth to tell, the extreme peaceful disposition of the new King was hardly in accordance with the feelings of the majority of the French nation. There was dormant within her a sentiment of aggression, and under the cloak of resentment against the Bourbons, she was thirsting to revenge the defeats sustained in 1814, and the treaties which were the consequence of it. The glorious battles of the Revolution and the Empire found at every fireside poets, who, not content with describing them in the most glowing colours, opposed to them as contrasts the humiliations of the Bourbons, brought back in the wake of the foreigner. To sweep away the latter from the territory that had once belonged by right of conquest to France, and to avenge Waterloo, was the cherished dream of those who had fought under Napoleon; and if these veterans were too old they wished to bequeath that duty to their sons and brothers, younger, though not more energetic than they were. The Restoration understood this craving, and had endeavoured by diplomatic combinations to regain for France the left bank of the Rhine, of which public opinion regretted the loss, not perhaps from love of aggrandisement, but because its possession by Prussia was an indubitable proof of military humiliation. It is doubtful, therefore, whether its peaceful transfer to France by its present possessors would have satisfied those who had not yet forgotten the conquests made by the Republic and the Empire, who were content to forget the misery and desolation caused by the Revolution, the despotism and the exorbitant requisitions of the Empire, to remember nothing but its brilliant deeds and warlike struggles. Until recently the enthusiasm evoked by the grand Republican epoch had depended chiefly upon the verbal transmission of its eye-witnesses, but when M. Thiers' dramatic narrative of the *History of the French Revolution* appeared,[1] the admiration knew no bounds, and there was created a

[1] M. Thiers' *History of the French Revolution, from 1789 to the 18th of Brumaire*, was published in parts from the years 1823 until 1827.

kind of revolutionary legend growing more intense day by day, and which is lasting still. Various influences had combined to place the just wars of the Revolution and the iniquitous struggles of the Empire on the same line. Napoleon was regarded as the founder of French grandeur, as the victim of monarchs, as the apostle of liberty; and if his son had appeared at the opportune moment in July, 1830, it is probable that an irresistible impulse on the part of the nation would have proclaimed him Emperor.

From these undefined sentiments, scarcely understood, and owing more to impulse than to deliberate analysis, there arose a current of bellicose passion taking various shapes, but all tending to embroil France into war with her neighbours for the sake of propagating a crusade of universal Republicanism. This would at any time have been embarrassing to the new King and his Government, but peculiar circumstances combined just now to invest this tendency with a more serious aspect. England, but especially France, was filled with the most eminent advocates of Spanish Liberalism, whom the sanguinary despotism of Ferdinand VII. had driven from their country. The late French Government, which had restored Ferdinand to the Spanish throne, had been overthrown, and he had refused to acknowledge the new monarchy. No better opportunity could be desired to induce the French Republicans to make common cause with their Spanish brethren. An invasion was planned, arms bought, subscriptions raised, and two different bands entered

Spain, which were driven back. The Spanish King hastened to acknowledge Louis Philippe, and the latter was obliged to check all further attempts of the Spanish Liberals and their friends, to which hitherto he had shut his eyes. The refugees complained, and the French Republicans, who shared their opinions, blamed the Government; but they forgot or overlooked the fact that such offences against international law could be tolerated no longer the moment the two kingdoms had resumed their official relations.

On the 2nd of September, the Chamber of Deputies passed a bill which allowed all political exiles to re-enter France, with the exception of the Bonaparte family. This was a measure of security rendered necessary to public peace, though Louis Philippe himself was far from being hostile to the members of that dynasty. This official act of justice was followed by a popular demonstration in honour of those who, under the Restoration, had vindicated the cause of liberty at the cost of their lives. On the 22nd of September, the anniversary of the death of the well-known four sergeants of La Rochelle, a public meeting took place at Paris, on the Place de Grève, and a petition was signed requesting the abolition of capital punishment for political offences—a generous action, the more so, as the four Ministers of Charles X., who had given orders to shed the blood of the Paris population, and whose death was clamoured for, were then in prison. In consequence of this popular ebullition of feeling, it was officially decided that the scaffold would never more be erected on the Place de Grève, and this law has been faithfully adhered to.

It is with the human mind after the strong emotions of a revolution as with the ocean after a violent storm; it does not resume its calm all at once, but remains for some time agitated by the ground-swell of conflicting currents. Now that the Government was once more firmly established, there were not wanting various elements of dissension, which, under the Restoration, had been united, but became now again subdivided into Republicans, Bonapartists, and a new faction, the Legitimists. Added to these, a novel kind of opposition showed itself under the name of Socialism, including the disciples of Saint-Simon and Fourier. These latter were mostly bent upon accomplishing their reforms in a peaceful spirit; the political form of Government was almost indifferent to them, provided they were left free to meet without being disturbed, and to ventilate their opinions in the furthering of their cherished ideal of a community founded upon the system of every one employing his natural or acquired aptitudes for the benefit of his fellow-creatures. Foolishly enough the Government saw fit to interfere with these and similar meetings; and as a consequence the clubs disappeared, but they were replaced by secret societies. Before their dissolution, these societies had time, however, to organise a battalion which was sent to take part in the emancipation of Belgium, in revolt against the Dutch.

Since 1815 Holland and Belgium had been united

under one dynasty, that of the House of Nassau. The union could never be and never was cordial. The two populations differed too much in every respect, in religion, mind, and manners. The hostility was ever latent, and, instigated by the success of the Revolution in France, it broke out openly in August, 1830. The Dutch troops entered Brussels, but public feeling was too much against them, and they had to retire; a month later the whole of Belgium was in rebellion.

Prussia as a co-signatory of the treaty of 1815, prepared to send troops into Belgium, for this revolt constituted a violation of that treaty and changed as it were the organisation of one of the European States. France was opposed to this plan, and declared that a French army would enter at the same time as the Prussians. This threat put a stop to all further hostilities, and the question was referred to a diplomatic conference in London, which pronounced the separation of the two countries, to the great chagrin of the French, who would willingly have annexed Belgium, in.spite of the opposition of the natives themselves, and the decision of the other Powers, unwilling to stand by and see France extend her territory. Though accused of sacrificing the interest of his country to the consolidation of his dynasty, the French King with sound good sense preferred not to go to war.

Louis Philippe's Ministry was not so united as could have been desired. His first Cabinet had been recruited from the various shades of the former Opposition.

Thus composed, the diversity had become antagonism, and the Ministers were divided amongst themselves, for some belonged to the "party of resistance," as the partisans of a Constitutional monarchy were called, others to the "party of progress," a name given to the more advanced Liberals. The King himself leaned towards the former, but in the presence of a people, still proud of the victory of its reconquered rights, Louis Philippe felt the necessity of conciliating the party of progress. The dissension among the Cabinet first showed itself on the occasion of the discussion on the bill for abolishing capital punishment. The King's personal feelings were in favour of the bill, and he conveyed to the Chamber his intention of deferring in all things to its wishes (October 9). There is little doubt that this sentiment was inspired by the desire to prevent the four former Ministers of Charles X. from being sentenced to capital punishment, which sentence, once pronounced, it would have been difficult not to execute. In spite of the petition signed on the Place de Grève three weeks ago, in spite of the evident desire of the Chamber and the King, the newspapers of the Opposition discussed the proposed bill most violently, and excited great irritation amongst the Paris population. This led to a riot, and crowds of people entered the Palais Royal. Driven from there, they went to Vincennes, shouting, "Down with Polignac. Death to the Ministers." The firm attitude of the governor of that fortress soon convinced them that any attempt upon the former Ministers would be resisted to the utmost; they returned to Paris, continued their demonstrations for one or two evenings, and then finally dispersed. M. Guizot, one of the Ministers and the leader of the "party of resistance," would have had these rioters severely punished, the other members of the Cabinet insisted upon moderation and conciliation. The counsels of the latter prevailed, and thereupon MM. Guizot, de Broglie, Louis, Molé, Casimir Périer, and Dupin resigned.

On the 8th of December died Benjamin Constant, president of the Council of State, and formerly one of the most eminent members of the Opposition. His funeral gave rise to some disturbances, which were soon suppressed.

Meanwhile, the indictment against the four ex-Ministers of Charles X. having been drawn up, the prisoners were brought before the bar of the Upper House on the 10th of December, and the proceedings were throughout conducted in a spirit of moderation, which was but once departed from on the side of the prosecution.

While the Peers were engaged upon their judicial duties, with an appearance of calmness at least, the building in which they held their sittings was surrounded by a threatening crowd with difficulty held back by the National Guards. During the trial Lafayette employed all his energy to prevent an outbreak of popular feeling; for many persons, with a strange inconsistency, now demanded what some weeks ago they had unanimously wished to abolish.

Nevertheless, capital punishment was not pronounced on the political culprits; they were condemned to imprisonment for life, and the sentence was commuted to one of transportation, though France had no place to which to send them.

Popular feeling demurred against this sentence, which was considered too lenient. Though the National Guards shared in the general opinion, a conflict had nearly occurred between them and the working population. The authorities appealed to the loyalty of the students of the various schools, who, joining the Guards, perambulated the capital, counselling peace and submission to the laws. Both those defenders of public order were the subject of a vote of thanks of the Assembly, which was officially rejected by the young men, because some deputies had blamed them for having expressed the hope, that order being once established, liberty should be granted. They were incensed that the freedom of expressing their opinions, for which they had shed their blood in the three days of July, should now be conceded to them conditionally.

The Chamber of Deputies became aware of the danger of concentrating in one person the whole command of the National Guards, because it gave to its possessor a power far greater than that of any other authority. It was probably satisfied of the integrity and single-mindedness of Lafayette, who at present held this post, but it could not insure the same qualities in his successor, and therefore a bill was introduced prohibiting any one person from holding the command of all the National Guards, or even of those of one department or arrondissement. The moment Lafayette learned this he tendered his resignation, which was reluctantly accepted by the King. The latter would have acted wisely if he had created another post for the great Republican General, who had sacrificed his opinions in placing Louis Philippe on' the throne, an event which he might have easily prevented. Some persons even averred that the new monarch was but too glad to rid himself of an auxiliary who might have become embarrassing. At any rate, Lafayette, after he had given up his command, became, as it were, the chief of an Opposition, which, without aiming at the overthrow of the dynasty, desired rather to consolidate it, by bringing it back to a system more consistent with its origin; these attempts were, however, often dangerous to its safety.

Contrary to his expectations, but as might have been foreseen, Marshal de Bourmont had discovered that the taking of Algiers and the subjugation of the surrounding districts meant two different things. He nevertheless organised some effectual expeditions against the Arabs; but after the July days he was replaced in his command by General Clausel, who continued the energetic measures of his predecessor, but without any great results, owing to the recall of various troops and the stubborn resistance of the enemy.

The Conference of London had signed, on the 3rd of February, the final protocol which separated

Greece from Turkey, and constituted it an independent State. Prince Leopold of Saxe-Coburg was offered the vacant throne, but he refused; and the Powers were reduced to find another prince willing to accept the honour. France had played an important part in the emancipation of Greece from Turkish rule, and whatever may be thought at the present day of the inefficient rule of this kingdom, it is certain that the French Government does not deserve to be blamed for this. The diplomatists of Europe, instead of completing the work begun, deemed it fit to curtail Greece's independence by withholding from her the territory to which she was entitled, and which would have made of her a kingdom, not only capable of resisting the encroachments of her neighbours, but sufficiently strong to form a community which could have dispensed with foreign aid.

The French Revolution had kindled throughout Europe an impulse towards more liberal institutions, of which nearly every country availed herself to attempt to abolish the tyrannic encroachments of her rulers. Many nations failed in their attempts, but some of the minor States of Germany succeeded in obtaining a Constitution, whilst popular demonstrations in Savoy and Milan were promptly suppressed. In Poland the Revolution assumed serious proportions; the Grand Duke Constantin, brother of the Czar, was compelled to withdraw his troops from the latter country; and a Provisional Government was formed under the dictatorship of Chlopicki, an old general of Napoleon. A number of Republicans in France demanded that the Government should aid the Polish insurgents, but political reasons prevented this, and Poland was left to herself, destined to perish.

The Revolution of Belgium having terminated by the declaration of her independence and her erection into a monarchy, there remained nothing but to choose a King from among the foreign princes available for such an exalted position. Three candidates were proposed, the Archduke Charles of Austria, the Duke de Nemours, and the Duke of Leuchtenberg, a son of Prince Eugène de Beauharnais.

Louis Philippe was not only opposed to the annexation of Belgium to France, but had intimated that he would not accept the crown of this kingdom for any of his sons. The election of the Duke of Leuchtenberg was also objected to by the Powers. The new kingdom paid no regard to these objections, and in the Belgian National Congress the Duke de Nemours received ninety-seven out of a hundred and ninety-two votes, the Duke de Leuchtenberg seventy-four, and the Archduke Charles the remaining twenty-one.

Thanking the Belgian deputation, which had been sent to announce this election, for the great honour done to his son, Louis Philippe persisted nevertheless in his refusal (February 17th, 1831), basing it upon the disastrous consequences which had accrued to France by the attempts of Louis XIV. and Napoleon to impose princes of their dynasty on neighbouring countries. He, moreover, counselled the Belgians to select a monarch whose nomination should not give rise to a disturbance of the peace of Europe.

While France was thus trying to insure the peace of a neighbouring State, her own was broken once more by the intrigues of the Legitimist and clerical parties, who organised demonstrations on the anniversary of the death of Louis XVI. Emboldened by the indifference of the Parisians, which they accounted at least a negative success, these parties announced in their newspapers that a public demonstration would be held in the church of Saint-Roch (February 13th) to celebrate a service in commemoration of the death of the Duke de Berry, assassinated eleven years before.

This time the authorities interfered. The clericals transferred the ceremony to the church of Saint-Germain l'Auxerrois, but the mob, who saw in this manifestation a challenge of the priests to the Parisian population got excited, broke into the church, demolished everything, and, not content with this, sacked, on the following day, the palace of the Archbishop of Paris. To prevent a recurrence of these scenes, the authorities were obliged to take down the crosses outside the public places of worship, and also the emblems in which the lilies of the Bourbons were displayed. Even the King had these flowers effaced from his escutcheons, and from his carriages, as well as from the liveries of his servants.

The bad news from Poland provided the Parisians with another opportunity for tumultuous proceedings. They went in crowds to the Russian Embassy, and broke every window in the building (March 10th). The Ministers being harassed by dissensions, which compromised their authority with the Chambers, notwithstanding their honourable attempts to ameliorate the state of the existing laws, at last offered their resignation, leaving the King to form another Cabinet.

In spite of their difference of opinions, Louis Philippe entrusted Casimir Périer with the task of forming a new Ministry, which the latter undertook, on condition, however, of choosing for his colleagues only those who should agree with his views. On the 13th of March the new Cabinet was complete, and Casimir Périer, the President of the Council, took the portfolio of the Interior. He had all the firmness necessary for a good Minister; unfortunately, he disdained to be guided by the wishes of the majority, or even to listen to a minority; he could not brook opposition; his was the "party of resistance," which did not endeavour to convince its opponents, but sought rather to crush them, and, therefore, not seldom converted them into enemies. Popular demonstrations were to him a bugbear, and he looked upon them as so many threats to public order. In the course of his career, he never recovered from the terror inspired by the beginnings of the Revolution of July; consequently the first measure he proposed to the Chambers was a law against gatherings in the streets, and which authorised the military to fire after three summonses to disperse. The freedom of debate in public meetings inspired him with no less fear. "The principle of the Revolution," he said, "is not insurrection; it is resistance against the aggression of authority." How he would have resisted this aggression, unless by the same tactics as those employed in England, which he equally condemned, he never explained. His intentions were, no doubt, excellent, but he considered the Charter as perfect, and not open to progressive improvement.

At the end of the previous year France had, through the mouth of her then Prime Minister, Laffitte, expressly formulated the principle of non-intervention, provided the other Powers consented to adopt the same. But when the Austrians now declared that they would intervene by force of arms in the Italian Peninsula, France stood calmly by, and maintained the theory of peace at any price, provoking the exclamation of General Lafayette that such conduct was incompatible with the dignity of a great country.

This disinclination for war was carried too far perhaps; and the Legitimists began to attempt, without much success, to undermine the new dynasty by intrigues, which had proved so disastrously successful in 1793 in the Vendée. The King, on his journey through the east of France, was well received everywhere, and this apart from the fictitious enthusiasm always attaching more or less to the reception of a new monarch. There was a real and warm sympathy felt for the King, " sprung from the barricades;" and the rural populations, little accessible to the secondary causes which excite the Parisians, were not displeased with Louis Philippe for maintaining peace under any circumstances. Shortly before the King's journey the Chambers were dissolved and the new Legislative convoked for the 23rd of July; two hundred and twenty-two deputies of 1830 were re-elected.

The King himself opened the session for 1831, and in his speech from the throne intimated that he had offered to mediate in the affairs of Poland. Laffitte, the Prime Minister of the former Cabinet, but now a member of the Opposition, was named President of the Chamber, and two out of the four vice-presidents were of the same party. The debate on the King's speech was very stormy, the Government being reproached with having left Italy and Poland to their fate.

The Count de Montalembert, trusting to a clause in the Charter which admitted liberty of instruction, opened a school, which was closed by order of the Government. Being tried before the Chamber of Peers, a fine of a hundred francs was inflicted. The news of the fall of Warsaw caused also great agitation in Paris and in the Chambers.

On the 18th of October the hereditary right of the eldest sons of peers to a seat in the Upper Chamber was annulled by the Chamber of Deputies, and on the following day the Government created thirty-six new peers, the deputies having meanwhile passed a law proscribing the members of the elder Bourbon branch from entering French territory. On the 20th of the next month a terrible insurrection broke out at Lyons, caused by trade disputes. The troops and part of the National Guards were driven from the town, which remained at the mercy of the working men. When, however, the Duke of Orleans and the Minister of War arrived with an army, they found no difficulty in quelling the disturbances, without any bloodshed.

A scourge more terrible and difficult to subjugate than any of humanity's own making appeared in the beginning of the following year (1832). Travelling from the depths of Asia into Poland, the cholera, with one bound as it were, swooped down upon England. The towns on the French coast of the Channel were in hourly expectation of this dread visitant, the more terror-inspiring from his unknown nature. On the 26th of March, amidst the rejoicings of the mid-Lent day, the first victim fell in Paris. For a few hours the popular tumult concealed the horrible news. But the following morning the entrances of the hospitals were blocked by agonised sufferers. Whole quarters of the capital had been attacked. When a mysterious epidemic like this breaks out, the first cry of the ignorant is, " We are poisoned." Suspicion catches hold of the slightest imaginary motive, and suspicion meant death to the individual suspected. For one hundred and ninety-eight days the disease raged in the capital with almost unabated violence, carrying more than twenty thousand persons to the grave, and amongst them Casimir Périer. The mortality was greatest in Paris, though the sufferings of the provinces were also very severe.

Once more an insurrection was attempted in the Vendée, instigated by the presence of the Duchess de Berry. Four departments and several arrondissements having been placed in a state of siege, the disturbances were finally put a stop to by the arrest of Charles X.'s daughter-in-law on the 7th of November.

The funeral of General Lamarque (June 5th), who had been one of the most popular orators of the Opposition, was the cause of another disturbance. The Republicans hailed it as an opportunity for a counter-demonstration, vying in pomp with the official obsequies of Casimir Périer. The salvoes in honour of the defunct were mistaken for an attack on the population. In a short time the nearest barrack was invaded, and the few soldiers who were there handed over their arms and provided ammunition. A moment afterwards the struggle had begun.

With the quickness of lightning the insurrection spread, and in the evening, in spite of its having no settled plan or chief, it had made itself master of nearly all the left bank of the Seine and about half of the right. Martial law was proclaimed, several arrests were effected, newspapers and journalists were seized—notably Armand Carrel, the editor of the *National*, who was almost immediately set free, and soon the Republicans, too few in number, scarcely organised, were vanquished by arms; their heroic defeat added perhaps to the prestige of a cause, never without vehement partisans in France. On the 22nd of July, the Duke of Reichstadt, son of Napoleon I., died at Schönbrunn, in Austria, at the age of twenty-one.

Though the treaty signed in London in 1831 had proclaimed the independence of Belgium, the King of Holland refused to submit to this decision; and as he persisted in his refusal, and had sent troops into Belgium, the French army of the north, under Marshal Gérard, stationed on the Belgian frontiers, received orders to occupy that kingdom. Belgium felt herself slighted by this interference, which, though provided for by the treaty above mentioned, implied, as it were, her inability to fight her own battles; an implication felt the more bitterly as it was based on truth. Hence a series of misunderstandings and imaginary depreciations, which made the task of the Marshal one of great difficulty.

In the whole of Belgium the Dutch were masters only of the citadel of Antwerp. The war was thus, as it were, reduced to a siege, but the siege of a fortress which the greatest military authorities, including the Duke of Wellington, had proclaimed impregnable. Nevertheless the Dutch, under General Chassé, were forced to capitulate (December 23rd), having held out for nearly a month. The garrison was to be disarmed and conducted as far as the frontiers, where their arms should be restored to them, provided the King of Holland would consent to evacuate two forts still in his possession. This condition having been refused by the King, the garrison remained prisoners of war.

On the occasion of the arrest of the Duchess de Berry, the Government had promised that a bill to decide the fate of the prisoner should be proposed to the Chambers. The law proscribing the elder branch of the Bourbon family had provided no punishment in the event of their transgressing it, for the contingency was regarded as so problematical that no penalty had been deemed necessary. The present infraction, therefore, embarrassed all parties. The silence with regard to punishment could not mean merely expulsion from France. This would be tantamount to putting a premium upon the repeated attempts of the exiled family; and to tolerate, as it were, provocations to civil strife and its disastrous consequences. If a new law were passed it could not be applied to the Duchess, whose offence was anterior. If she were tried before the Royal Court of Poitiers and acquitted, it would be a virtual triumph for the adherents of Legitimacy. And on the other hand, she could hardly be executed even if a sentence of death were pronounced. These questions were debated by the newspapers of all parties with a bitterness, which, on the part of the Legitimists, did not even spare the King.

Public opinion was too vehement not to influence the Chambers. Various personal circumstances, affecting the health of the Duchess, who became a mother whilst in prison, tended to aggravate the embarrassing situation. At last the Government ordered her to be conducted to Palermo, as soon as she was able to bear the fatigues of the journey, and there she joined her second husband, the Count Lucchesi-Palli, whom she had married in secret, during her residence in Italy. Her accomplices were at the same time acquitted on the plea that the principal author of the conspiracy had been withdrawn from the jurisdiction of the court.

If the Legitimists were troublesome, the Republicans were more unmanageable still. In spite of its pacific intentions, the Government was forced to fine heavily and to imprison several journalists, who, by figuring as martyrs, added fresh fuel to the cause they so zealously had advocated.

No government could have taken the cause of France's welfare more to heart than that of Louis Philippe. Measures both liberal and well-intended were constantly brought forward, the principal work of this year's session, and which will remain an honourable monument of Louis Philippe's reign, being the law on primary education (June 18th). It imposed neither gratuitous nor obligatory instruction, two things still clamoured for by some isolated thinkers; it nevertheless insisted on each Commune having at least one school; no one was allowed to teach unless provided with a certificate of proficiency, the children of the poor had a right to eleemosynary tuition—in short, education received an impulse which could not be arrested even by subsequent laws intended to grant a supremacy to those schools managed by religious congregations. Whatever improvements were introduced afterwards owed their efficiency to the valuable basis of these primary measures. Nor were the material wants of France overlooked. Various projects were mooted for the defence of the capital, their execution being embarrassed and delayed by the opposition of the Republicans, who persisted in regarding them as being intended as a means of terrifying Paris rather than of protecting it.

Meanwhile, the French were but slow in establishing their sway in Algeria. Though the relations with the various tribes assumed more friendly aspects, the chief destined to wage the most formidable struggle against France was emerging from obscurity. That chief was Abd-el-Kader. After several skirmishes, General Desmichels committed the error of signing a treaty with him; and thus tacitly admitted and enhanced that warrior's importance by granting him several concessions regarded by the Arabs as so many tributes to their valorous resistance, and consequently as so many incentives for prolonging it.

Notwithstanding the rigorous crusade of the crowned heads of Europe against anything and everything savouring of liberalism and socialism, a new spirit of progress seemed, as it were, to animate the younger generation. In Italy the revolutionary ferment became almost chronic. Joseph Mazzini, aided by the Polish general Ramorino, of Savoy extraction, founded the society of Young Italy, destined to lay the foundation-stone of the idea whence was born Italian unity.

Unfortunately, and contrary to its promising beginnings, the Government of Louis Philippe felt tempted to imitate the measures of repression indulged in by other sovereigns, and began to deviate from the liberal path it had proposed to itself. In addition to the various attempts at gagging, or at least at circumscribing, the liberty of the press, the Government now introduced a bill (February 25th) which, whilst theoretically admitting the freedom of public associations for the purpose of political discussion, attacked it in practice by hampering it with the condition of preliminary authorisation. The Government overlooked, or rather disregarded, the fact that the formation of similar associations became impossible under such conditions, for the simple reason that the authorities could withhold their sanction if so disposed.

The debates on this bill were stormy and violent. The deputies opposed to it taunted some of the Ministers with having, under the last reign, belonged to secret societies; and argued that, therefore, they themselves could have been prosecuted by the former Government of Charles X. Nevertheless, the bill passed by a majority of a hundred and two votes, and was promulgated on the 10th of April.

The submission of the Lyons workmen, three years ago, had been but temporary. The struggle between capital and labour had again recommenced; the latter numerically the stronger, but the weaker in culture and financial resources, had .gained the upper hand for the moment. The workmen had started an association called the "Mutualists," which, after various negotiations with the masters, ordered a general strike, fortunately soon put an end to by the sensible intervention of the most influential of the Republicans. Nevertheless, six Mutualists were prosecuted for unlawfully assembling, and appeared on the 5th of April before the civil tribunal, which postponed judgment until the 9th. Added to this excitement the news arrived in Lyons of the violent debates in the Chambers on the law on associations, which set the whole of the town in a ferment. The Mutualists were bewailing the fate of their comrades on the point of being condemned; the members of the various other clubs awaited but the signal of their chiefs to begin an open struggle. When on the 9th the hearing of the case was resumed, a gun was fired in the midst of the speech for the defence, and a workman, killed by a soldier, was carried into court. Nothing more was wanting. A revolt broke out simultaneously in all parts of the town. For full five days it raged unabated; but on the 14th the town was in the hands of the troops, who had defeated the insurgents, discouraged by the absence of those leaders upon whose assistance they had reckoned.

The news of the Lyons insurrection caused great excitement in Paris. An expression of M. Thiers in the Chambers, misinterpreted by the Parisians, attributed the victory to the insurgents. The Paris malcontents judged the moment opportune to take up arms also; and a disturbance took place, which lasted for about four-and-twenty hours, though it had no more chance of success than that of Lyons, as its instigator, Captain Kersausie, had been arrested at its very commencement. Various other disturbances broke out in the provinces, and, for this reason, the Chamber of Peers was invested with the authority to judge all armed attempts against the State, committed by the members of prohibited associations. A decree of the 15th of April convoked this Court to judge the insurgents of Lyons and other localities. As an additional measure of precaution, the Government introduced a bill punishing those persons who secreted arms and ammunition, whilst, at the same time, it regulated their sale by manufacturers and dealers.

On the 20th of May died General Lafayette; and with him disappeared the last of the grand actors of the first Revolution. Twice he had witnessed the fall of the monarchy; the last time he might perhaps have re-established the Republic, if, to the honesty of a Washington, with whom he has so often been compared, he had added the American's fixity of purpose and energy of will.

Four days later the sessions terminated, and the following morning a royal decree dissolved the Chambers, convoking the electors for the 21st of June, and the new Legislative for the 29th of August.

For the first time since the fall of the Bourbon

dynasty, the Legitimist candidates presented themselves in large numbers. Where there was no candidate of their own party they voted from sheer hatred against Louis Philippe for the Republicans. Nevertheless, from their proneness to provoke revolutions, the latter lost many seats. This, as it were, created a *tiers parti*, or third party, of men of undecided opinions, not pledged to support either side, incapable in fact of doing so, and not having any distinct political aim beyond that of watching the march of events, and of being guided by them. The elections over, a royal decree convoked the Chambers for the 31st of July; and they were again prorogued till the 29th of December, after the address had been voted.

Meanwhile several changes in the Cabinet had taken place. Marshal Soult having resigned in consequence of some divergence of opinion between him and his colleagues about the administration of affairs in Algeria, his successor, Marshal Gérard, the new President of the Council and Minister of War, entered office with the distinct idea of bringing about an amnesty for all past political crimes and offences. But the King and the other Ministers showed themselves opposed to the measure, whereupon the Marshal resigned, and was succeeded on the 29th of October by M. de Rigny. The latter's tenure of office was short-lived, for, in a few days, in consequence of disagreements between the Ministers and the King, who frequently endeavoured to impose his personal opinions, the whole Cabinet, with the exception of two of its members, resigned.

To them succeeded a Cabinet chosen by the King from among the third party, and presided over by the Duke de Bassano. The Chambers were convoked about three weeks earlier than the time first decided upon, but, unfortunately, the new Cabinet, unable to agree upon certain measures of urgent policy, lived but three days, and is known in history by the name of the "Three days' Ministry." On the 13th of November the old Cabinet resumed its functions, under the presidency of Marshal Mortier, Duke de Treviso.

During the prorogation of the Chambers, the Court of Peers, invested with judiciary power, thought itself insulted by the newspaper the *National*. Its responsible editor was brought before its bar, and defended by one of his contributors, Armand Carrel, himself a prisoner for a similar dereliction; but notwithstanding his advocate's masterly speech the editor was condemned to a fine of ten thousand francs and two years' imprisonment. Shortly afterwards, though the King had been unwilling to accede to the request for an amnesty on the part of Marshal Gérard, the Ministry prevailed upon him to grant a pardon to a great number of political offenders (December 27th). But there was a considerable difference between a pardon and an amnesty.

Though not productive of any great military event, the occupation of Algeria during 1834 had brought about a more friendly state of feeling between the native tribes and the French; for the former had become alive to the advantages to be derived from a commerce with the military centres. These prospects of improving relations no doubt emboldened Marshal Soult—who was then still President of the Council—to meet the objections raised against the vote of credit for Algeria, by the firm statement that not only should the conquest of that country never be abandoned, as some deputies had proposed, but that the Government intended to inaugurate a system of colonisation, which, in the course of time, might bear the happiest results. Yet the demand that the Government should give up a hardly-earned conquest was not altogether unreasonable. The path to the permanent acquisition of Algeria must at all times have been beset with difficulties; and, apart from this, a counter-influence was springing up simultaneously with the extension of French influence, of which no one as yet could fathom the ultimate results. Abd-el-Kader, to whom, as we have already stated, were granted several concessions, while pretending to co-operate with the French, had utilised those marks of goodwill and consideration to enhance his power with the Arabs. Nevertheless, in furtherance of the project of ultimate occupation, a royal decree of the 22nd of July, 1834, appointed a Governor-General of Algeria, who should only be responsible to the Minister of War, and who was assisted by a civil intendant and a naval commander; a second decree regulated the administration of justice in that colony.

The year 1835 began inauspiciously. The King had always been desirous of making his influence predominate in the Ministry, and had attempted this several times during the past year; but the new Cabinet which was now in office, determined to show its power, which meant the subjugation, as it were, of Louis Philippe's personal pretensions.

The first opportunity that offered itself for a display of this emancipation was an interpellation about the frequent Ministerial crises. The former Cabinet had scarcely been reinstated before it was ready again for dissolution. Marshal Mortier had recognised his insufficiency, and the King, instead of simply appointing a new president, sought to reconstruct the whole administration. In furtherance of this project several former prime ministers were consulted; but the negotiations proved unsuccessful.

In the Chamber of Deputies (March 11th) the Marquis de Sade, who moved the interpellation, stated that an unfavourable impression had been produced in the country by the various Ministerial crises, because they implied anarchy in the very midst of the Government. He did not scruple to suggest that the fault lay entirely with the King, who was confounding the right which the Charter conferred upon him of selecting his Cabinet with that of an absolute monarch. The Ministry did not attempt to defend Louis Philippe, and on the next day the official newspaper, the *Moniteur*, published the nomination of the Duke de Broglie as Prime Minister, whilst all the former members of the Cabinet retained their portfolios. Almost at the outset of its career, the Ministry had to deal with a difficult question. The American Government had long since claimed an indemnity for the damage caused to her mercantile navy by the seizure or destruction of many of her ships, owing to the decrees of 1806 and 1807. This claim had been acknowledged by Napoleon I. in 1810, though he reduced it from seventy to eighteen millions of francs, a reduction which had not been accepted by the United States. Subsequent events left the matter pending until 1831, when it was revived. A new investigation took place which resulted in the fixing of an indemnity to the United States of twenty-five millions of francs, from which was to be deducted a million and a half which these States owed to France. In order to discharge this debt a vote of credit had been demanded in 1834, which the Chamber saw fit to reject.

Immediately after the Chambers met this year, the demand for the vote of credit was renewed, for a decision had become imperative. The rancour always more or less attending discussions on pecuniary compensation for injuries received many years ago, was in this instance embittered by a threatening message sent by the American President Jackson. The French Government had no other alternative but to recall its representative from the United States, and to offer the Ambassador of that country his passports. These incidents did but aggravate the polemics of the press on both sides, and awaken the susceptibility of public opinion. The sword was not actually drawn from the scabbard, but the hand was laid on the hilt.

These elements of discord found their echo in the debates, but the Ministry prevailed upon the majority to vote the credit of twenty-five million francs, and this was done on the 25th of April, on condition, however, that the payment was not to take place until the American Government should have furnished satisfactory explanations with regard to the violent expressions used by President Jackson. These were forthcoming, but there was left in France an impression that the Cabinet of Louis Philippe, from an inordinate love of peace, had been wanting in dignity.

By investing the Chamber of Peers with judicial authority in the various prosecutions for insurrection, the Government had imposed a heavy task on it. This deviation from the ordinary legal practices, though legalised by a recent law, gave that tribunal a somewhat specious character. In consequence of the revolt at Lyons, and of the last disturbances in Paris and the provinces, two thousand persons had been arrested and four thousand witnesses had to be heard. The accused who were finally tried by the Court were one hundred and sixty—of whom even forty-three were absent.

As is usual in all political prosecutions, the accused wanted to become accusers, if not judges, and to bring all existing institutions before the bar of public opinion, either through themselves or through the mouth of their defenders. How far they might have succeeded in their object if they had adopted a common line of defence is very problematical; but from a want of organisation or divergence, not of opinion, but of purpose, they failed. The whole trial was one scene of confusion. Some of the accused kept obstinately silent, others protested energetically; a few accepted the debates and answered the questions put to them; several objected to appear at all, and had to be dragged before the Tribunal, their garments torn, their faces covered with blood—a spectacle ill calculated to further the ends of justice; others again refused to dress themselves, and the authorities were compelled to leave them in their beds, as they could not be brought naked into court. It was simply another form of insurrection and resistance, but planned with as little foresight as those which had miscarried when attempted by arms.

Amidst these deplorable incidents a fresh trial was commenced, against several of the barristers and newspapers defending the Republicans, on account of the writing and publishing of a letter, severely reflecting on the Chamber of Peers. For full nine months, confusion, rancour, and agitation reigned supreme. No capital sentence was pronounced; the gravest punishment was transportation. From all this resulted a state of things pregnant with sinister forebodings of some great catastrophe. Some of the foreign and provincial newspapers mentioned even the report of a plot to assassinate the King. In the capital they referred to the very spot where it would take place, and the day it was fixed upon. The attempt was to be made either in the neighbourhood of the theatre of the Ambigu, or on the Boulevard du Temple, which the King would have to pass on his way to the review to be held on the anniversary of the Revolution of July. The police had received hints, which were insufficient, however, to lead to any discovery; the information simply pointing to an individual who could not be found.

Louis Philippe insisted upon holding the review, though fully aware of the rumours afloat. On the 28th of July, he left the Tuileries, accompanied by a numerous retinue. He had already passed the theatre of the Ambigu, and reached the Boulevard du Temple, opposite the Café Turc, when, stooping to receive a petition from one of the National Guards, he perceived, on resuming his position, a slight puff of smoke issuing from the top storey of a house. "This," he said to the Prince de Joinville, "is meant for me." Scarcely had the words left his lips, when a terrible detonation took place. When the smoke cleared up the King and his sons were found sitting imperturbably on their horses, whilst forty or more persons were lying dead or dying at their feet, and amongst them four or five officers of the King's suite and Marshal Mortier. After the first moment of stupor, the King resumed his route, amidst the deafening cheers of the multitude; whilst the National Guards and police invaded the house whence came the murderous discharge, and succeeded in tracing the assassin, who, terribly wounded, had descended by means of a rope, and dragged himself to the courtyard of an adjacent building.

That in an atmosphere of recrimination and hatred such an attempt would lead to mutual accusations was not surprising. The Government gave the example by implicating the Republicans, and arresting a great number of them, notably Armand Carrel. The Republicans retorted by accusing the Legitimists, who, in their turn, inculpated their accusers. In a short time it was proved, however, that this attempt at assassination had been the isolated act of one person, or at the most of a few individuals. The most officious of the Government organs persisted, nevertheless, in blaming the Republicans; and the funeral of the victims of this attempt was not expected to pass without some sort of violent demonstration. With the exception of an appeal to summary justice conveyed in the cry of "To the prisons," which started from the ranks of the National Guards, everything passed off quietly.

The King had issued a proclamation, which foreshadowed the adoption of rigorous measures, and it was not difficult to divine the institution at which these measures would strike first—namely, the press. As a natural consequence of the public ferment, these intentions were rather applauded than otherwise. The newspapers were blamed, justly or unjustly, for the depression of trade, and all those who had to live by commercial transactions imagined that they would resume their normal prosperity the moment the press was muzzled and the word Republican struck out of the dictionary.

In spite of the eloquent defence of Royer-Collard and others, the laws against the press, supported by the Duke de Broglie, the same who, twenty years before, had been the first to claim unrestrained freedom for the expressions of public opinion, were passed, and promulgated on the 9th of September. They remain historically infamous under the name of "the laws of September." The Government had obtained their passing, as it were, under false pretences. It knew that the crime committed on the 28th of July was not the work of a party, but it took advantage of the error to commit an iniquity. As we have already seen, the assassin, who was a Corsican, named Fieschi, was apprehended lying in the courtyard of a house adjacent to the one where the crime was committed. Transported to the hospital, the Hôtel Dieu, all the resources of medical science were employed to preserve the life of a man destined for the scaffold, who had tried all trades, save honest ones, and who had been an habitual criminal, living for some time in the most abject poverty. His crime was committed at the instigation of an old stoical Republican fanatic, named Morey, who kept obstinately silent before his judges, and carried his secret, if there was one, with him to the grave. Another accomplice was Pépin, a grocer of the Faubourg Saint-Antoine, who had provided the necessary funds. He showed some signs of weakness at his trial, but when the hour of death came, displayed a firmness scarcely expected. Of two other secondary accomplices, one was acquitted, and the other condemned to twenty years' imprisonment. Fieschi himself, actuated by the morbid curiosity of the public, who treated his every act as if he had been a man moved to his dastardly crime by the most exalted patriotism, posed as a hero, and continued to play this part throughout the trial, avowing his crime, however, no doubt thinking that his confession might save his life. But he and his two accomplices were executed on the 19th of February, 1836.

As if to counteract the sorrowful effects of the late events, the King had opened the session for 1836 on the preceding 29th of December, with a speech which breathed the utmost spirit of moderation and promised reforms, as well as the preservation of the nation's interests. These sentiments were endorsed by the President of the Chamber, but, unfortunately, were not destined to be realised. For the day before these words were uttered the Court of Peers had pronounced judgment on the many persons implicated in the late attempts at insurrection. The same Court was terminating the preliminary proceedings in the Fieschi trial, and darker prospects still were looming in the future.

On the 11th of January the Minister of Finances resigned in consequence of having imprudently introduced a bill analogous to that formerly projected by M. de Villèle for the conversion of Government annuities. This project was not altogether distasteful to a certain number of deputies, but they wanted more time for investigation than the Minister had been willing to allow. They now wished the entire Ministry to promise that it should revive the bill at some subsequent period, but rather than do this it elected to resign.

After various attempts to form a Ministry subservient to the King's influence, the *Moniteur* of the 22nd of February published the list of the new administration, which had to deal immediately with the same financial project that had caused the retirement of its predecessor. The new President, M. Thiers, promised, however, to lay, the following year, before the Chambers a bill dealing with the matter, unless unforeseen circumstances should prevent this. Being subsequently invited to explain its policy, the new Cabinet contented itself with generalising, without, however, laying down a fixed plan, probably intending to be guided by the course of events.

On the 25th of June there was another attempt to assassinate the King. At the moment when Louis Philippe, in his carriage, was bowing to the National Guards stationed at the Tuileries, a musket was fired, and the carriage became filled with smoke. The man who attempted the life of the King neither ran away nor offered any resistance. He frankly confessed his intention, and expressed his regret at not having succeeded, because he considered Louis Philippe as the arch-enemy of all Republican institutions, of which the would-be assassin, whose name was Louis Alibaud, was a fanatical partisan. He denied having any accomplice, and died on the 11th of July, proclaiming his unaltered devotion to the cause of the Republic. The opponents of the

Ministry took advantage of this event to censure the Cabinet. This was an act of injustice, for it had no more power to prevent this attempt than the late Ministry could have frustrated the previous one of Fieschi. Some time afterwards two young students were brought before the assizes of the Seine, accused of having written a letter, in which they expressed a wish to kill the King; but on confessing, however, that they had simply written it in order to gain some notoriety, the jury acquitted them.

Whilst the Republican party was being continually discredited by these insane attempts of fanatics, with whom it had not the slightest sympathy, it sustained an almost irreparable loss in the death of one of its most valued members. On the 22nd of July, Armand Carrel was mortally wounded in a duel with Emile de Girardin, the editor of the new ministerial organ, the *Presse*. After forty-eight hours of cruel suffering he expired. His death caused a deep sensation, for he was not only an eminent journalist, but a man of noble character, of unwavering loyalty to the cause he had adopted, and which he made respected even by its opponents, through his intelligent advocacy. A numerous concourse of distinguished men of various opinions attended his funeral.

Amidst these inauspicious events the anniversary of the Revolution of July drew near. It was impossible not to dwell upon the sad incident which had attended its last celebration. The Government received information of several projected attempts on the King's life.

Like the year before, no details were forthcoming to justify domiciliary search. But formerly the indications had also been of the vaguest kind, and had led to a most terrible reality. The only means to prevent a new crime was to dissuade Louis Philippe from holding the annual review. At first the King refused, because he would not shrink from the danger; and because he was fond of coming in contact with the National Guards, and had promised to inaugurate the triumphal arch de l'Etoile, only just completed. He gave way, however, to the entreaties of his Cabinet. The review was countermanded; and the triumphal arch was inaugurated by the Ministers, in the presence of an immense crowd. The Government, modifying the primitive idea which had led to its erection, consecrated it to the glory of the various armies of the Republic and the Empire, instead of to the victorious legions of Austerlitz, as was intended originally.

§ II.—THE END OF THE ORLEANS DYNASTY.

(*From the 28th of July* 1836, *to the 24th of February*, 1848.)

DURING the past five years of Louis Philippe's reign the relations of France with the foreign Powers had not been very cordial, save with England. When M. Thiers assumed office this friendly bond was in danger of being slackened, by the evident inclination of the Minister to exchange the intimacy with England for that of Germany and Russia. A marriage between the Duke of Orleans, the eldest son of Louis Philippe, and the Austrian Archduchess Theresa was planned, but the project was discountenanced by the Court of Vienna.

This rebuff to his matrimonial policy made M. Thiers turn anew to the English alliance. A combined action was conceived with the Cabinet of St. James's with regard to the affairs of Spain, to which Louis Philippe showed himself strongly opposed, and therefore M. Thiers tendered his resignation.

A new Ministry, with M. Molé as President, and which was almost the old one of the year 1832, save the Duke de Broglie and M. Thiers, entered upon office, and shelved the question of intervention in Spanish affairs; and this notwithstanding the pressure of public opinion, which was decidedly favourable to it, not because it loved Constitutionalism more, but because it loved Carlism, in its mind synonymous with absolutism, less.

It would have been well if the new Cabinet had adhered to the tactics of non-intervention with regard to Switzerland. Unfortunately it allowed itself to be induced by the Court of Vienna to demand from the Helvetian Republic the expulsion of those political refugees, who gave umbrage, not to France, but chiefly to Austria. The demand was couched in terms which could not but be offensive to the authorities, whilst, added to this, a French spy was caught on Swiss territory, charged with the secret mission of instigating the refugees, so that they might compromise themselves in such a manner as to give France an excuse for enforcing her demands. Neither M. Thiers nor his successor, M. Molé, had been let into the secret of these machinations; and when they were revealed they at first discredited them, until at last, unable to deny their existence, they were in a measure bound to attribute them to the refugees themselves. This suited the purpose of coercion equally well; and, as more pressing demands were addressed to the Swiss, they were obliged to promise satisfaction to France to avoid an unequal struggle.

In consequence of the death of the ex-King of France, Charles X., on the 6th of November, at Goritz, in Styria, his four late Ministers were liberated from their confinement, and Prince Polignac alone was expelled from French territory. Even before the aged ex-King of France was removed from this world another candidate for the throne arose. On the evening of the 31st of October, the Government received from Strasburg the fragment of a telegraphic message which stated that "this morning towards six o'clock Louis Napoleon, son of the Duchess de Saint-Leu, in concert with the colonel of artillery, Vaudrey, whom he had taken into his confidence, perambulated the streets of Strasburg with a party of . . ." This message had been conveyed by the old telegraph, and could not be farther deciphered on account of the gathering darkness. The Ministers immediately assembled at the Tuileries, where the remainder of the message was anxiously expected throughout the night.

The next morning an aide-de-camp of General Voirol, commander of Strasburg, arrived, and told the story of the attempt and failure of Napoleon I.'s nephew, Charles Louis Napoleon Bonaparte, the third and only surviving son of Louis Bonaparte, King of Holland, who had taken advantage of his residence in Switzerland to concoct with some of the officers of the Strasburg garrison a plot to overturn the monarchy of July. His plan was to tamper with the troops, to call the populace to arms, and march upon Paris, trusting to circumstances to fix upon the kind of government which was to result from this insurrection. Frustrated in his project by the presence of mind of the colonel and some officers of the 46th regiment of the line, the chief mover of the plot was arrested and brought to Paris, where he had a confidential interview with the prefect of police, which resulted in his being conveyed to a vessel lying at Lorient, in Brittany, and ready to start for America. No promise or engagement of any kind was demanded from him. He was treated with every consideration, and a sum of fifteen thousand francs was handed to him to provide for his most pressing necessities at landing. On the other hand, the chief mover of a military mutiny, which broke out at Vendôme on the same day as that of Strasburg, but who was only a non-commissioned officer, was brought before a council of war and condemned to death, which sentence was with difficulty commuted into one of transportion.

With the exception of the failure finally to subjugate Abd-el-Kader, and another attempt to assassinate Louis Philippe, when he went on the 27th of

December to open the sittings of the Chambers, the further political events of the year 1836 were without importance.

In the beginning of the year 1837 the assizes of the Lower Rhine acquitted the accomplices of Louis Napoleon in the Strasburg affair, as the prime mover of the plot had been withdrawn from legal jurisdiction. Instead of accepting the implied rebuke, the Government sought by an expedient to prevent the recurrence of such an acquittal. To effect this it presented to the Chambers a bill, by virtue of which soldiers and civilians engaged in the same conspiracy were to be judged by different tribunals; the civilians by civilians, the military men by court-martial. This was reversing the forms of jurisprudence hitherto applied. At the same time, a law was proposed, by which a part of the island of Bourbon was selected instead of Cayenne as a place for the deportation of political offenders, the latter colony having proved so fatal that transportation to it was tantamount to a sentence of death. Lastly, a third project revived some of the clauses of the penal code of the Empire, and proposed to punish all persons who should not reveal the knowledge of a projected attempt against the King's life. The opposition to this last law was very great, because if once passed it would virtually lead to a compulsory and legal system of spying.

The King had a large private fortune, yet he was sometimes heard to complain that there might come a time when his children should be in poverty.

Influenced by this hyperbolical dread he instigated his Ministry to propose to the Chamber of Deputies a measure to provide an allowance for the Duke of Orleans, and also one for the Duke de Nemours, which measure was thrown out, as well as the law granting separate tribunals to military men and civilians engaged in the same conspiracy. This involved the resignation of the Cabinet. After several weeks spent in fruitless combinations the members who represented energetically the party of resistance retired, and left M. Molé to construct another Cabinet, which was finally constituted on the 15th of April.

To judge from the opinions of its chief this administration was known to be one of conciliation; hence it was well received, for the country had got tired of the violent measures of repression and their concomitant outbursts of murderous frenzy. Though the Ministry did not revoke the laws on transportation and on the concealing of conspiracies of its predecessors, the Chamber did not discuss them, but voted (April 22nd) the bills for the allowance to the Duke of Orleans and for the jointure of the eldest daughter of the King, who had married Leopold, the new King of the Belgians, whilst the bill for an allowance for the Duke de Nemours was withdrawn. These pecuniary questions, however, left a feeling of discontent in the minds of many, which was fanned into greater flame by the Republicans, who made it a weapon to diminish the prestige of royalty. They had undoubtedly a right to do so, but it remained an open question whether those who were enamoured of a monarchy objected to pay the allowances asked for. A general amnesty for political offences promulgated on the 8th of May was received with great satisfaction.

On the 30th of the same month the Duke of Orleans married the Princess Helena of Mecklenburg-Schwerin. Though an alliance with the daughter of a more powerful monarch might have been desirable, and the Legitimists rejoiced that the royal prince had been unable to obtain a consort from one of the great sovereign houses, the graceful bearing and the unaffected manners of the young princess won many hearts, and even the Protestant religion which she professed was considered as a safeguard against clerical intrigues to which the Queen was suspected to be accessible. Another marriage took place the same year in the royal family. On the 17th of October the Duke Alexander of Wurtemberg married Princess Marie, a daughter of the King, and who was very popular in France on account of her artistic tastes. To these family joys was added the satisfaction of the successful expedition against Constantine, in which the Duke de Nemours had heroically played his part.

M. Molé, dissatisfied with the uncertain and small minority he could command in the Chambers, advised the King to decree their dissolution, which was done on the 30th of October, the electors being convoked for the 24th of the following month. Contrary to the Prime Minister's expectations, the new elections neither provided him with a more numerous majority nor consolidated his ministerial position.

This obliged him as it were to evade political discussions, and to confine himself to commercial measures. He had neither the tact nor the authority to carry through the bills he presented, so that the Chambers, taking advantage of this weakness, mutilated them to such a degree that little or nothing of their original scope remained. The various opposition parties combated this incapable and powerless administration each on its own account, and they combined to overthrow it. Public opinion, ever imbued with an innate sense of justice, saw in this Coalition something unfair. As long as the three opposition parties had fought each under its own flag for its own imaginary or real advantages, though they might differ from and harass each other, it was looked upon as consistent with parliamentary honesty; but when, in order to unite against a comparatively defenceless foe, they elected to forego their individuality, to subscribe to measures and opinions at complete variance with their hitherto professed creeds, the proceeding was regarded as unbecoming the legislators of a great country. This sentiment was re-echoed by the newspaper, the *Journal des Débats*, after the Coalition had gained the victory, when it wrote, "You may count upon our support, but never upon our esteem." Nevertheless the whole of this year was spent in preparing the Coalition campaign for 1839.

Meanwhile France was far from being tranquil.

Several prosecutions were instituted for conspiracy against the King's life. The Bonapartist attempt of Louis Napoleon at Strasburg was also not without its results. Under the ostensible form of a report, a former officer of the Sappers and Miners had published a virtual apology for this attempt at insurrection. He was condemned to five years' imprisonment, to pay a fine of ten thousand francs, and to perpetual police supervision; but his condemnation had nevertheless the effect of drawing again public attention to Louis Napoleon, who had returned from America to Switzerland. Ill advised, the French Government insisted upon his expulsion from the latter country, but as the Imperial Pretender had taken the precaution of becoming naturalised there, he refused to quit Swiss territory; a determination in which the authorities, in spite of themselves perhaps, were compelled to support him. Already French troops had been massed on the Swiss frontiers, and Switzerland in her turn was making preparations for having her rights respected, when Louis Napoleon, pretending to be magnanimous, declared that he would not be the cause of such a conflict, and went to England. The Government of Louis Philippe committed the blunder of allowing him to assume the important character of a political martyr, or rather of a victim to the name of his uncle.

While the dynasty of July was waging this ill-advised persecution against the Napoleonic pretender, a grandson, destined to perpetuate the royal line of Orleans, was born to Louis Philippe on the 24th of August. The child received the title of Count de Paris.

The small French garrison which had occupied Ancona, a small port on the Adriatic belonging to the Pope, since the year 1832, was recalled, and thus the Austrians, who were already masters of Lombardy and Venice, could enter the Papal States at any moment. Louis Philippe's Government felt itself also compelled to blockade various ports of Mexico and of the Argentine Republic, as it could receive no satisfaction for the maltreatment of several French residents by the inhabitants of these Republics, continually devastated by internecine wars.

On the 17th of December, the King opened the sessions of the Chamber for 1839, and as usual appealed to the feelings of concord and union of the deputies to consolidate the welfare of France. Never was an appeal addressed to men more determined not to yield. At the voting for the presidency of the Chambers, M. Dupin, the Government candidate, obtained but a majority of five over the candidate of the Coalition; and everything portended the victory of the latter. The sympathy which was felt privately for Louis Philippe, who had just lost his daughter, the young Princess Marie (January 2nd, 1839), did not prevent the Chambers from opposing each paragraph of the reply to the address from the throne. The most cruel classical epigrams were introduced into the debate, and though the Ministry succeeded in obtaining a victory, it was a victory more fatal than a defeat. The same day the Cabinet offered its resignation, having obtained from the King a decree dissolving the Chambers and convoking the electoral colleges (31st of January); but at the monarch's request it remained in office until the 8th of March. The adversaries of the Government had been again victorious, but like the robbers in the fable, when the booty had to be shared, the animosities and hatred which had slumbered when a victim was to be despoiled, now reappeared in full force; they could not agree among themselves, and were reduced to construct a provisional Cabinet, devoid of all political colour, and merely called into existence for the despatch of the most pressing business.

What peaceful measures were unable to effect an insurrection accomplished. On the 12th of May, an attempt at a revolt was made in Paris, which, though not dangerous in itself, opened the eyes to the expediency of the Government presenting a more united front to its dangerous and fanatical opponents. The ministerial complications suddenly ceased, the chiefs of the Coalition retired once more, and a new Ministry leaning to the side of the King's opinions was formed.

Almost at the outset of its career, the Cabinet found itself confronted by the Eastern Question, hostilities having broken out between the Sultan of Turkey and his hereditary vassal, the Pacha of Egypt, Mehemet Ali. France felt bound as it were to interfere—a credit of ten million francs for the amelioration and increase of the navy was asked for and granted by the Chambers.

Whilst the Eastern Question was obtruding its difficulties of settlement, public opinion clamoured more than ever for internal reforms, especially for the diminution of the monetary qualifications of the electors; reforms which, instead of being proposed by the Ministry, were continually shelved.

This policy of delay was the more unsound because the King, at the beginning of the sessions of this year, again requested an allowance for the Duke de Nemours in view of his projected marriage with the Princess Victoria of Saxe-Coburg, a provision for the Duchess in case of widowhood, and an additional sum to defray the incidental expenses, amounting in all to about a million and a half of francs. The request being rejected by the Chambers (February 20th), the King felt himself personally slighted; and, whilst attributing the refusal to his Cabinet, devised measures to construct a new one—M. Thiers, of all men the one whom the King liked least in such a position, being selected as its chief (1st March). For the third time the vexed question of the conversion of Government annuities was brought before the Chambers, and after a stormy discussion thrown out by the Peers.

A great surprise was in store this year for France. The English Government having consented to give up the remains of Napoleon, and the Chambers having voted a credit of a million francs to defray the expenses, a son of the King, the Prince de Joinville, started on the 7th of July for St. Helena, in order to bring them over.

Notwithstanding the refusal of a dowry for the Duke de Nemours, this Prince married on the 27th of April the Princess of Saxe-Coburg. On the 15th of July the sessions were closed. That same day England, Russia, Austria, and Prussia signed a treaty in London, by which they engaged themselves to compel the Pacha of Egypt to accept the proposals of the Sultan of Turkey. These proposals were the hereditary possession of Egypt by Mehemet Ali and his direct descendants, and the Pacha's occupation of Syria for his lifetime. The French Government demanded that Syria should also be considered an hereditary possession of the Pacha, and, suspecting that war in the East was going to break out, it called up a hundred and fifty thousand men, and collected its whole fleet at Toulon.

Emboldened no doubt by the revival of his name in France, Louis Napoleon attempted on the 6th of August, a landing at Boulogne, accompanied by about sixty individuals disguised as French officers. The whole affair savoured more of a burlesque procession than of a serious endeavour to overthrow a dynasty, though one soldier was wounded in this ridiculous attempt. Taken prisoner, the Prince was condemned to confinement for life in the castle of Ham. A few days after this condemnation, Louis Philippe was again shot at as he crossed the Place de la Concorde in a carriage with his family. The assassin, taken red-handed, was condemned to death about seven months later. Many people, alarmed at the prospect of a war with which

France was threatened at the moment, in consequence of the Eastern complications, saw in this attempt a demonstration of the Revolutionary party.

The difficulties about the Eastern Question becoming very grave, the King convoked the Chambers for the 28th of October to begin the sessions of 1841. When the speech from the throne was placed by the Ministers before Louis Philippe, he refused to subscribe to the somewhat threatening sentiments expressed in it in relation to the affairs of the East, which refusal compelled his Cabinet to resign.

M. Guizot having returned from England, where he had been Ambassador, a new Cabinet was formed under his auspices (29th October), of which the programme was warlike for the interior, but peaceful enough with regard to foreign nations. Public opinion was dissatisfied, and openly accused M. Guizot of having hampered at London the policy of M. Thiers. The accusation was unjust, and the Ambassador had faithfully executed the orders of the President of the Cabinet, though it was well known that they did not agree with his own views.

The opinion entertained by the public of the character of the new Ministry was confirmed by the speech from the throne, which expressed a hope that the peace of Europe would not be disturbed, whilst it announced at the same time a resolution to check anarchical passions by every means consistent with the existing laws. The Liberal press received this political programme with the greatest discontent.

France had become imbued with the idea that it was bound to defend the Pacha of Egypt, and she would willingly have drawn her Government into a war, but Louis Philippe and his Ministry were stoutly opposed to it. Hence the mutual recriminations in the Chambers, which were fortunately ended by a treaty signed later in London (10th of July, 1841), which at least for a time terminated all controversy on the subject. In the interval of these debates the remains of Napoleon had been brought back to France, and deposited on the 15th of December, 1840, amidst great pomp, in the chapel of the Invalides, preparatory to a vault being built for them. This task was not accomplished until ten years later. The recurrence of disturbances in Algeria during this year generally resulted in victories for the French.

In the beginning of the year 1841 the important discussions on the fortifications of Paris were renewed. The project was, notwithstanding its undeniable utility, received with every mark of disapproval by the various sections of the community. The Republicans, who were suspicious of the use the Government might make of them, rejected all attempts at fortifying the capital. The Legitimists seeing in the project an increase of strength for a town which originated every revolution and was the capital of centralisation, also opposed the scheme, whilst M. Molé and some of his former colleagues made the discussion an occasion of intrigue, to overthrow the Government and to facilitate their resumption of office. In spite of these tactics the bill passed and became law on the 3rd of April. After various minor bills had been adopted the sessions terminated on the 25th of June, 1841. Two days before their closing the Chambers sustained a great loss by the death of the principal Republican orator, Garnier-Pagès, who was replaced by Ledru-Rollin, destined to become as eloquent as his predecessor.

In July, August, and September of the same year (1841), disturbances broke out in several parts of the provinces caused by the collecting of the tax on doors, windows, and personal or real property. In the prosecution which followed, most of the offenders were acquitted. On the 20th of December a treaty was concluded between France, England, Russia, Prussia, and Austria, by which these nations granted each other the mutual right of searching their ships, in order to insure the better the abolition of the slave-trade.

The sessions of 1842, which began on the 27th of December, 1841, necessarily opened with the debate on the speech from the throne, in which the Government was somewhat severely handled not only by the Opposition, but also by its own party, for its share in the treaty with England relative to the right of search. Not that the slave-trade was defended, but according to the antagonists of the treaty, France had allowed herself to be placed by England in too humiliating a position by submitting to some of its clauses.

The discussion on the electoral reform came next in rotation. There were two bills proposed by private members, but both were rejected. On the 11th of

June the Chambers were dissolved, and the electors convoked for the 12th of July. The general elections resulted in a majority for the Conservative party. Nevertheless the various shades of Opposition when united were still capable of presenting a formidable front, which rendered the position of the Government sufficiently difficult.

Amidst all this political agitation the royal family was struck by a blow more cruel even than the loss of Princess Marie. On the 13th of July, 1842, the Duke of Orleans was going in a carriage from Paris to Neuilly when the horses bolted. He jumped out, but fell, and died from congestion of the brain a few hours afterwards. This death rendered necessary an immediate law to provide for the succession of the throne, as the Count de Paris, the son of the Duke, was at the time of his father's death only four years old. The Chambers were convoked for the 26th of July.

The King's bereavement had the effect of rallying round him all those who were not declared enemies of his dynasty. Nevertheless the laws on the regency were vehemently combated, the Charter not providing for such a contingency. The Duke de Nemours was appointed regent in case of Louis Philippe's death. The Chambers having been assembled for the purpose of voting this law, were prorogued immediately afterwards; the monarchy had meanwhile received a shock, more damaging than was at first believed.

The year 1843 and its sessions were almost bare of political events. The Ministry had already some time ago begun negotiations with Belgium to inaugurate a system of free trade, in all probability most advantageous to both countries. Intimidated by the great manufacturers of France, who could influence the elections and drive it from office, it broke off these negotiations. M. Guizot and his colleagues were behind their time; they were a Cabinet of resistance; and, as Lamartine pertinently remarked, a stone barrier would have served the purpose of checking all progress equally well. They ignored everything, corrupt practices at elections, fraudulent transactions in the matter of public contracts, as long as they were allowed to remain in their places, where they enacted the characters of scarecrows to every liberal and spirited measure.

The clerical party, who for a long time had worked in the dark, now appeared openly in the arena of political strife, and demanded freedom for secondary instruction, which meant liberty for themselves, and coercion and repression for all those who did not think as they did. All kinds of religious associations, brotherhoods, and similar societies flourished publicly, the police could not or would not suppress them, though they were forbidden by law. No one would have objected probably to liberty being granted to the clericals if the same tolerance had been extended to their adversaries also.

Notwithstanding their frequent and brilliant victories in Algeria, the French had not obtained there as yet a firm footing. Abd-el-Kader was for ever harassing them by instigating the various tribes to revolt. On the 16th of May, the Duke d'Aumale succeeded, however, in capturing several of the principal officers of the Arab chief, the latter himself escaping with difficulty. This surprise led to the complete submission of the tribes that had hitherto remained hostile.

The sessions of 1844 opened with an incident that gave rise to a most eloquent speech from M. Guizot, and an equally eloquent retort of M. Berryer. Several Legitimist deputies had been to London to pay their respects to the Count de Chambord, the son of the late Duke de Berry. The Prime Minister saw fit to rebuke this visit, and as a natural consequence recriminations followed between those who had made this voyage, and those who sought to defend it. Nevertheless a vote of censure was passed, couched in unparliamentary terms, which was not accepted by those deputies who were thus blamed. They resigned, and presented themselves to their constituencies for re-election in which they were successful. This rendered M. Guizot unpopular, and the feeling was increased by his obstinate adherence to the treaty with England relating to the right of search, of which we have already spoken, and which, according to the opponents of the Ministry, placed France in a humiliating position. Scarcely was the vote of censure passed on the Legitimist deputies when the news arrived that Admiral Dupetit-Thouars had taken possession of Otaheite in the name of France. One year before this event Queen Pomare had placed her dominions under the protectorate of the French by a treaty declared valid by England. Everything had gone smoothly until a Mr. Pritchard, combining the functions of ex-English consul, Protestant missionary, and physician to the Queen, had instigated her to throw off all allegiance to the French Government, and to disavow the treaty with France. Nevertheless the act of Admiral Thouars was illegal, and the Government hastened to disclaim having given any orders to occupy the island. In a short time, however, all controversy on the point ceased by the French arresting Pritchard, and sending him to England.

In Algeria also troubles were not at an end. After his late escape Abd-el-Kader endeavoured to instigate the Emperor of Morocco to measures of hostilities against the French, and by leading this monarch to believe that his dominions were being threatened by the proximity of a fort which the French had erected near his frontier. Yielding to popular pressure, the Emperor Muley-Abd-el-Rhaman despatched an expedition against General Lamoricière, which was, however, routed with the loss of two hundred men. Instead of regarding it as a declaration of hostilities, the French Government very sensibly treated this as a simple act of insubordination, sufficiently punished by its own failure. It was the more justified in this, as other nations were already on the alert for the results which might probably accrue from the near neighbourhood of the French to Morocco. For various reasons, but especially commercial ones, the British Government was watching with a certain interest the amicable or hostile relations that might be established between Algeria and Morocco. The French Government contented itself, therefore, with demanding compensation for the attack on the French troops, and insisted on the expulsion of Abd-el-Kader from Morocco, whilst, at the same time, it hastened to assure the Cabinet of St. James's that no territorial acquisition was contemplated. The English Government not only declared itself satisfied, but instructed its consul at Tangiers to support the demands for satisfaction advanced by the French, so as to avoid a war. The Emperor of Morocco, however, proving obstinate, and refusing to enter upon pacific negotiations, the Prince de Joinville partly destroyed Tangiers, Marshal Bugeaud defeated the Moroccan troops at Isly, Mogador was bombarded; and the Emperor was compelled to submit, and to expel Abd-el-Kader, who nevertheless found means to prolong his hostility.

Meanwhile the Pritchard affair, a version of which had arrived in England almost simultaneously with himself, was assuming an aspect calculated to lead to unpleasant relations between England and France. As may be imagined, the story supplied mainly from Pritchard's own evidence was not likely to be favourable to the French. Sir Robert Peel in the House of Commons expressed himself about it in terms which were offensive to France; and he even hinted at demanding satisfaction. The French session of the Chambers was about to close; but M. Guizot, being interpellated, refused all explanations, and argued that it was necessary to keep the pending negotiations secret. This unjustifiable behaviour led to a suspicion that the Cabinet was preparing some humiliating concession to England, and the nation consequently became irritated against the Ministry. M. Guizot treated the affair in a thoroughly business-like spirit, and offered Pritchard a pecuniary compensation, which was accepted; but the minister's haughty and disdainful behaviour towards the deputies, who had a right to demand explanations, left an unfavourable impression in the public mind.

At the opening of the sessions for 1845 (December 26th, 1844), notwithstanding the conciliatory tone of the speech from the throne, stormy discussions arose. In the House of Peers M. Molé accused the Cabinet of compromising the peace of Europe by its desire to preserve it at all cost. Animadversions on the Pritchard affair, on the treaty with Morocco, and on the right of search conceded to England, were not wanting. M. Guizot replied that other measures would be devised more in conformity with the wishes of the Chambers; and retaliated by accusing his opponents of wishing to compromise the friendly relations with England by their intrigues.

In the Chamber of Deputies M. Guizot met a more formidable adversary in M. Thiers, who supported a vote of censure on the Ministry, and was very bitter when finding fault and commenting upon the Pritchard affair; he blamed the indemnity paid to the latter, and this payment became one of the principal weapons against the Ministry in the hands of the Opposition. Though the vote of censure against the Government was rejected, the majority was so small that M. Guizot felt compelled to tender his resignation and that of his Cabinet. But the Conservatives taking the alarm begged him to remain; the King declined to accept his resignation, and M. Guizot sacrificed his dignity to his vanity. He asked for a grant of secret service money, which was equivalent to a vote of confidence, and obtained a majority of four-and-twenty (22nd of February).

Various other bills, relating to the organisation of savings-banks, the construction of new railways, and electoral reforms, were passed; but one of the chief incidents of the session was the interpellation of M. Thiers with regard to the illegal existence of several educational establishments directed by the Jesuits. The Government did not deny that the laws against them were still in force, but at the same time it expressed an opinion that it would be better to apply them according to circumstances. Nevertheless M. Thiers insisted upon the expulsion of the Jesuits, and was supported by a large majority. The Government found itself in a dilemma. It dared not disregard the will of the Chambers, and would not act against this religious brotherhood. In this emergency it bethought itself of applying to the Pope, and of inducing him to order the Jesuits to leave France. This expedient succeeded; but it was said by the Opposition that the laws of France were dependent for their execution on the pleasure of a foreign potentate.

In consequence of the objections against the right of search, a treaty modifying the former arrangement was signed with England on the 12th of May, which did not materially alter the measures for the abolition of the slave-trade, but left to each nation the duty of searching her own vessels. On the 21st of July the sessions for 1845 closed.

For some considerable time France had been agitated by the question of workmen's wages, and these disputes generally ended by the men striking. One of these strikes occurred in Paris and lasted three months. The Ministry interfered, arrested eighteen artisans for having combined to obtain a rise of wages, a combination forbidden in France by law, and condemned two among them—one to three, the other to two years' imprisonment. This measure had not the desired effect; the strike continued.

Nor was the Government more successful in their expeditions against Abd-el-Kader, who continued his resistance, often inflicting severe losses on the French. In one of these expeditions Colonel Pelissier was sent in pursuit of a very fierce Kabyle tribe which took refuge in some caves. As they repeatedly refused to surrender, he ordered lighted fascines to be placed at the mouth of these caves, which resulted in the death of six hundred Arabs, whilst two hundred more died after being taken out.

Though the whole of Europe was exercised by the cruelties perpetrated in Galicia at the instigation of Austria, M. Guizot declined to discuss them. The session for 1846 was closed on the 3rd of July, and a decree was published dissolving the Chambers, fixing the elections for the 3rd of August, and convoking the Legislative for the 19th of the same month. With the exception of various measures of home interest, the session had been productive of few political incidents, though M. Thiers made a brilliant speech in support of a proposition of M. de Rémusat to prevent Government officials from being elected members of the Chamber of Deputies, and which already foreboded as it were the great changes at hand to be accomplished in another year. The frequent attempts on the King's life testified to a feeling that Louis Philippe's dynasty did not meet with popular approbation, whilst the escape of Louis Napoleon from his prison at Ham (May 25th) rejoiced the partisans of the Bonapartist dynasty.

The attempts on the King's life were made use of by the Ministry and its adherents to arouse a sympathy with their cause, and to influence the general elections at hand. They succeeded; and the Ministerial candidates increased in number, whilst the ranks of the Opposition were thinned.

Nevertheless the words "electoral reform" were in everybody's mouth, and even on the lips of Conservatives. The electors hailed them with enthusiasm. The current was too strong to be withstood, and M. Guizot himself admitted that progress had become necessary, though he modified the admission by saying, that Conservative policy alone was capable of dealing safely with such reform.

A short session intended merely to verify the

elections was held, in which the Ministerial candidate was chosen as President of the Chamber by a majority of twenty-two votes against M. Odilon Barrot, the Opposition candidate for the office.

The political situation, sufficiently embarrassing at this period, was aggravated by a monetary crisis brought about by the failure of two successive harvests. The Government, appealed to for a reduction of the import duties, refused, alleging that there was nothing sufficiently alarming to warrant such a measure. When stern facts, however, belied the official statements, the Ministry was obliged to give way, and provisions from being scarce became abundant in the seaport towns, where they remained for want of means to transport them, as the inundations, which were especially severe in the south of France, suspended nearly all traffic. The municipalities did all they could, but by a little more timely interference of the Government many of the calamities resulting from this state of affairs might have been avoided. Spain and Algeria were also frequent causes of trouble to the French Government — the one by the constant discussions evoked by the matrimonial combinations with regard to the Infanta Isabella and her sister; the other by its periodical revolts under Abd-el-Kader, who at one time had three hundred French prisoners decapitated.

Under such mournful auspices dawned the year 1847, the combined monetary and food crises continued, and led to horrible outrages on the part of the famished populations in various parts of the country, which even the execution of five of their principal leaders failed to check. What was wanted most, instead of measures of punishment, was a sensible interference of the Government, which remained inert, harassed by the Opposition, but accomplishing nothing, and wasting its valuable time in discussions. The very adherents of the Government began to perceive that it lacked the energy needed at such a critical period. M. Guizot contented himself with a majority in the Chambers; beyond this he seemed to care for nothing save to continue his policy of resistance and hostility to every species of reform. No stone was left unturned to maintain the influence of numbers, and money that might have been better spent was wasted in evil practices, in screening frauds in the various departments of the administrations, and in trying to bribe newspapers to take up the cause of the Government.

To these home scandals were added the disastrous effects of M. Guizot's foreign policy. The marriage of the Duke de Montpensier, the fifth son of Louis Philippe, with the Infanta Louise Ferdinanda, sister of the Queen of Spain, which had taken place the year before (10th October, 1846), had produced a coolness between England and France, for which the Minister endeavoured to compensate by entering upon more cordial relations with Austria and other absolute Powers. He saw fit to interfere in the interior quarrels of the Helvetian Republic, an interference not only unjustifiable, but aggravated by his joining the retrograde party. Even in this his policy was too many-sided to be productive of either good or evil. He wanted to please Austria, who feared that the Swiss revolutionary movement might cause a similar movement in Italy; he did not wish for an open rupture with England. In this emergency he endeavoured to draw Great Britain into an alliance to which Russia and Prussia had already given their assent, and which aimed at crushing all attempts at emancipation from clerical and Austrian encroachments now being organised in Switzerland, and secretly fostered by the Liberal party in Italy, a country which, according to a saying of the Austrian Minister, Metternich, was at that time "merely a geographical expression." In these endeavours M. Guizot was not successful, for Lord Palmerston, obliged to submit to Parliamentary and public opinion, advanced many objections to the proposed alliance. In Italy, the people counting upon the liberal inclinations of Pope Pius IX., manifested at his accession to the Papal see, were preparing for an open revolt against foreign oppression, whilst England protested against the Austrian occupation of Ferrara. M. Guizot only sent a diplomatic note to Vienna, and this defiance of public opinion lost him the little popularity that he still possessed. The political horizon grew darker each day, cheered by no ray of light save that of the surrender of Abd-el-Kader (November 25th, 1847).

At the beginning of 1848 the situation of constitutional royalty was already seriously compromised The Opposition, finding it impossible to obtain the slightest concession of reform from a majority servile to M. Guizot and his Cabinet, had recourse to a series of political banquets in various parts of the country, where it ventilated its opinions. This proceeding should not have been objected to, as M. Guizot had himself given the example when, in 1846, he harangued the electors of Lisieux at a similar gathering. The first banquet held by the Opposition had taken place on the 9th of July, 1847; and nearly thirteen hundred people, among whom were eighty-six deputies, were present. It was a great success, and the provinces followed the lead. These banquets, as was at first intended, were merely political demonstrations to impress upon the Ministers the necessity of Parliamentary and electoral reform, but they became in a short time the instruments for expressing entire dissent from the Government, and for devising means for its overthrow.

Amidst these political agitations the sessions of 1848 opened. The King's speech, as a rule commonplace, replete with stereotyped phrases, was this time expected with great anxiety. The continuation of the political gatherings hostile to his dynasty could not pass unchallenged. Nor was public expectation disappointed. To the factions embarrassing his Government and dynasty he opposed the Charter, which he promised to preserve intact, in spite of "the blind and hostile passions" which endeavoured to overthrow it. These words "blind and hostile passions" did not only rebuke the various parties outside the Legislative Assembly, but struck at many of its members, who had initiated and organised the banquets, in order to bring before the nation questions which the Parliamentary majority, obtained by the Government at the sacrifice of everything consistent with honour, refused even to discuss. This majority was the only body that remained unaffected or pretended to remain unaffected by the gathering storm. With the most sublime indifference it elected the Ministerial candidate to the presidency of the Chambers, and took care to exclude every member of the Opposition from the Committee charged with composing the answer to the speech from the throne. Before this answer was being discussed, some facts came to light reflecting upon the honesty of the private secretary of the Prime Minister, who was accused of having been bribed by an individual who had solicited a place under Government. M. Guizot reluctantly confessed that such malpractices existed, and attempted to justify them by quoting precedents; the majority absolved him from all dishonest intentions.

The debate on the address, commenced on the 17th of January, 1848, provoked as usual a review of the home and foreign policy of the Government, in which the Opposition was not sparing of its censure, M. Thiers going even as far as to avow his sympathy with every revolution tending to bring about the amelioration of a state of affairs such as was then existing. M. Guizot, nevertheless, continued his system of resistance, and endeavoured to put down the political banquets about to be held. The Opposition, to show its complete defiance of the Ministry, organised a banquet for the 22nd of

February; but after long and fruitless negotiations, the Liberal deputies decided that it should not take place, lest it might lead to an insurrection. Unfortunately that decision came too late to be generally known. A number of students and artisans who were to take part in it having arrived at the place of meeting, M. Odilon Barrot's house, and not finding that deputy at home, went to the Chamber, their numbers swollen by an enormous crowd. On the Place de la Concorde they met with a company of the municipal guard, who barred their passage. They were, however, allowed to proceed, but on their return they encountered some squadrons of cavalry, between whom and the population a struggle ensued, in which several persons were wounded. In the evening Paris was quiet, but the following morning (February 23rd) the troops occupied various strategic positions. The National Guards were called out, and endeavoured to mediate between the military and the population, whilst making it a condition that the Ministry should resign or grant the required concessions. M. Guizot retired, and to M. Molé was entrusted the task of forming a new Ministry. Though the newly-appointed Minister was not an ardent Liberal, this change proved a temporary relief, and in the evening the town was illuminated; but many of the barricades remained, guarded by armed citizens, who threatened to proceed to the Chambers the next morning to demand the abdication of Louis Philippe.

This vapouring of some excited citizens would probably have led to nothing if an incident which occurred the next day (24th February) had not rendered all reconciliation impossible. In the evening the troops came into collision with the National Guards and the people by whom they were accompanied. A stray shot was followed by a murderous discharge on the part of the regulars; in a moment the streets were littered with wounded, and the Revolution was virtually declared. It was no longer the abdication but the deposition of Louis Philippe which was demanded.

M. Molé having been unable to form a Cabinet, M. Thiers was sent for, and, as a first condition, he insisted upon complete electoral and Parliamentary reform. The King refused to grant this; but, in the meanwhile, the troops had been ordered to suspend all hostilities, and M. Thiers issued a proclamation to the effect of his having been charged with the formation of a new administration, composed of several of the leading members of the Opposition. It was too late; the insurgent committee made a counter-proclamation, in which it stated that as Louis Philippe had ordered the people to be murdered like Charles X. had done, he had better go and rejoin the ex-monarch. The King, who had gone into the court-yard of the Tuileries to review some of the troops and National Guards, was met with a universal cry for reform, and had to retreat precipitately. Towards two o'clock in the afternoon it was conclusively shown that the last chance to save the dynasty was abdication. Louis Philippe signed this in favour of the Count de Paris, and appointed as regent the Duchess of Orleans, who was left alone in the Tuileries, while the King and his family made their way to the Place de la Concorde, where some carriages awaited them. From thence they started for Saint-Cloud, and in a few days they continued their route to Havre and embarked for England. The attempt to proclaim the Duchess of Orleans regent was equally unsuccessful. She was obliged to quit France, and to rejoin the royal family. And thus ended the Orleans dynasty. In the meanwhile a Provisional Government was appointed, at the head of which were MM. Arago, Lamartine, Ledru-Rollin, and some other well-known Liberals.

Book VIII.

THE SECOND REPUBLIC.

CHAPTER I.

§ I.—A FRESH ATTEMPT AT A REPUBLIC.

(*From the 25th of February*, 1848, *to the 2nd of December*, 1852.)

THE members of the Provisional Government were, as far as circumstances would allow, carefully selected by the deputies and the crowd which was present at the last sitting of the Chamber. This crowd did not exactly represent the opinion of the whole of the nation, but might safely be taken as a sample of the opinion of the capital, which, in France, is in all cases of a violent overthrow or of a sudden establishment of a dynasty the supreme arbiter, and which is virtually, if not nominally, listened to by the remainder of the country. If proof had been wanted that those elected were for the moment regarded as being the fittest to whom to entrust the helm of the State, it would have been forthcoming in the following curious coincidence. When the Revolution was merely a question of hours the newspapers the *National* and the *Reforme* assembled within their offices the leading members of the Opposition, and proceeded to draw up a list, if not of a Government, at least of a temporary Committee of Direction. With one or two exceptions the personages thus chosen were the same as those selected in the Chamber of Deputies.

The Provisional Government thus constituted proceeded to the Hôtel de Ville, and issued there a proclamation, setting forth the names of its members, and announcing at the same time that until further ratification by the nation a Republic had been decided upon; it also thanked the National Guards for their zealous co-operation in the crisis just passed. The exigencies of the moment necessitated prompt and complete action, consequently, contrary to custom, the executive and legislative powers were concentrated into the same hands. The Chamber of Deputies was dissolved, the Chamber of Peers prohibited to assemble, and various other measures were devised and executed to ensure the unhampered action of the preliminary administration. This once accomplished, the Government proceeded to discuss the legality of definitely proclaiming the establishment of a Republic, or to wait until the nation had been appealed to. Meanwhile the tricolour, supplemented by a red rosette, was selected as the national standard in preference to the red flag which the most vehement of the Republicans wanted to adopt. The National Guard, dissolved by a royal decree, was reorganised, and another question which had agitated the public mind for some time, namely, that of providing employment by Government interference for those who were willing to labour, but could not find work, was provisionally settled. The Government did promise to provide work for all artisans, but this was afterwards explained to mean that it would do its utmost to find them something to do. In the meanwhile so-called "national workshops" were opened, in which workmen without any means of subsistence received very small wages for very little work done. A natural result of every insurrection, howsoever mild in its character, is to disturb the framework of society, and the one of 1848 was no exception to this rule. Several noblemen's seats and public establishments were pillaged and destroyed, and the authorities were compelled to take severe measures and hand over the plunderers to public justice. Capital punishment for political offences was, however, abolished.

Contrary to expectations, a great propensity was manifested among those whose political opinions were not supposed to tend that way to declare their adherence to the Republic. Functionaries, hitherto staunchly monarchical, Marshals who had offered to fight for the fallen dynasty, bishops, clericals, and ultramontane newspapers, nay, several Legitimists, all of a sudden conceived a sincere attachment to the Revolution of February, which they were pleased to term a "warning given by Providence."

Among the many offers of service thus received there was one which the Provisional Government would have willingly spared. It came from Louis Napoleon, a nephew of the Emperor Napoleon I., and though ostensibly couched in the most Republican terms, it scarcely concealed the motives of a pretender. With an admirable foresight which must ever do it credit, these motives were fathomed by the Government, and the nephew of Napoleon was invited to return to England, whence he came.

No protest of any kind having been made against the establishment of the Republic, the Government felt itself justified in proclaiming it, and this was officially done on the 27th of February, amidst spontaneous acclamations of enthusiasm and approval.

In order that its intentions might not be mistaken by the foreign Powers, the Government hastened to assure them of their pacific intentions, pointing out that the treaties of 1815, though considered not altogether just, would be respected in so far as they related to territorial stipulations. At the same time the new Republic promised her support to those nations who might wish to regain their independence, or to defend themselves when threatened by monarchical aggression. It became also necessary to attend to matters of home interest, especially those connected with the finances, which were in a most deplorable state, not so much as a result of the late crisis, but rather as the very cause of it. Repudiation and bankruptcy, which were eagerly counselled by some, were wisely rejected, for it was the aim of the Government to do nothing that might be considered dishonourable, but to trust to the reviving confidence and to the adoption of sound financial measures to overcome the pecuniary embarrassment of the State. Nevertheless the members of the Provisional Government were not so united as could have been desired. Dissensions had sprung up, fomented by the various clubs, which took advantage of the right of public meeting, and propagated doctrines too Utopian to be ever realised. The result was a conspiracy to expel the more moderate members of the Government, and to replace them by men holding extreme Republican and Communist opinions. This plot (April 16th), discovered in time, was not only frustrated, but turned to the advantage of the Republic. The elections for a National Assembly, to be chosen by universal suffrage, were fixed for the 23rd of April, and the Assembly thus elected convoked for the 4th of May.

It was natural that the Government should desire the election of those candidates who had given proof of their attachment to Republican institutions. Nevertheless, with commendable good sense the Minister of the Interior discouraged all attempts to interfere with the voting, in order to show that the electoral system inaugurated by the Republic was fully practicable, notwithstanding the assertions to the contrary by many. The result was a success, for, with the exception of a few preliminary disturbances, the elections went off peacefully, and the majority of the newly-chosen deputies were sincere and honest Republicans. During the last days of the existence of the Provisional Government numerous decrees were promulgated, amongst which was one relating to the abolition of slavery in the French colonies, another for finishing the Louvre in Paris, a third for recasting the copper coin, and several others. In granting every citizen of twenty-one years the right to vote, the Provisional Government conceived the laudable ambition of also educating him to use this privilege for the benefit of the country. With this intention it prepared a plan by which education should be free, gratuitous, and obligatory, and which would have been beneficial to every one; but unfortunately, when afterwards the law passed, the clerical party took advantage of it, and frustrated its good intentions.

On the 4th of May the Second Constituent Assembly began its sittings in a temporary building erected in the court-yard of the Palais Bourbon, for the apartment hitherto devoted to the purpose was found too small to contain nine hundred deputies. After the preliminary ceremonies, the Provisional Government remitted its powers into the hands of the representatives of the French people, amidst the enthusiastic shouts of "Long live the Republic!" An enormous crowd had gathered outside the building, clamouring to see the representatives, who showed themselves in a body, and were eagerly welcomed. A vote of thanks to the Provisional Government having passed, the Assembly proceeded, after various proposals and debates, to elect its Executive Committee, consisting of five members. This committee was to appoint nine Ministers with portfolios, and a tenth who should preside over the Legislative. Neither of these ten could be a deputy; all and each of them were personally responsible to the Assembly.

It was not long before dissensions began to show themselves in the Assembly. Several of its members had been elected because they professed themselves Republicans, but they were not Republicans at all, and merely awaited an opportunity to embarrass and hamper the Legislative. Such an opportunity is never long wanting in France. It presented itself on the 15th of May in connection with a demonstration in favour of Poland held by the most democratic partisans of the Republic, who insisted that France should assist the former country, and avenge the cruelties inflicted upon her by Prussia and Austria. The Assembly was invaded, its members driven forth, and another Revolution might have been the result, but for the energy displayed by the National Guards, who dispersed the rebels and arrested the ringleaders, who were temporarily confined in Vincennes.

Though all the extreme democrats were not equally guilty, this attempt proved a cruel blow to the Republic, of which its adversaries, notably the Legitimists and Orleanists, were not slow to take advantage by insinuating that a Republic which was not able to take take care of itself was no Government at all. In consequence of several resignations and the simultaneous elections of some deputies by different constituencies, the department of the Seine was called upon to appoint eleven new members for the Constituent Assembly. Among the candidates was the Prince de Joinville, son of Louis Philippe. At the general election no Royalist had dared to come forward, but now they grew more bold. The Executive Committee deemed it prudent not to tolerate what it considered a first step to the presidency of the Republic, and consequently to the re-establishment of the monarchy. Hence it proposed to apply to the Bourbons of the younger branch the law which the latter had passed in 1832 against the elder branch. In spite of the protestations of the Duke d'Aumale and the Prince de Joinville, based upon the services they had rendered to France in the campaigns of Algeria, which country, as they truly said, they had left in deference to the national will, the bill expelling them was voted by a large majority. It would have been well if a similar prohibitive measure had been adopted with regard to the members of the Bonaparte family, but though there was actually such a law in existence, the sons of Jérôme, Lucien Bonaparte, and of Murat were sitting in the Assembly. It was difficult therefore to refuse the same privilege to their cousin, Louis Bonaparte, when he was elected for the department of the Seine. In order, perhaps, not to let this election assume too great an importance, the majority, after some discussion, voted the admission of Louis Bonaparte, though it might have been fully aware of the danger of permitting to sit as a deputy a man who had already twice attempted to overturn a former Government, and who under the veil of being a Republican was planning his own ambitious schemes. At this juncture the President of the Assembly received two letters of the new deputy—the one regretting that his name should be the cause of any disturbance; the other sending in his formal resignation, and stating that, when France should be more calm, he would re-enter it as a private citizen.

This was, as it were, the prologue to the play which Louis Napoleon Bonaparte meant to act, and in which he sustained the principal part for nearly twenty years.

Great hopes had been built upon the new Assembly, which it was thought would be able to cure all evils and realise all dreams. After a sitting of six weeks, matters instead of improving were growing worse, though not from the fault of the majority, but from the intrigues of those who had entered it under false pretences in order to overthrow, or, if that were impossible, to harass the Republic. Unfortunately a great many of these formed part of a Committee charged with the discussion and investigation of a problem as grave and momentous as any that had ever come before a Legislative Assembly. We have already mentioned the scarcity of work that prevailed for so long a time in France, and the proposed action of the Provisional Government to endeavour and provide employment. As a trial, the Government had created national workshops, to which resorted in a short time a hundred and ten thousand men, of whom many were not artisans, in the proper sense of the word, but who all were in sore want. It was proposed to have recourse to a somewhat cruel, but necessary weeding, and to send those men who did not habitually reside in Paris back to their own departments, but even then there would remain at least seventy-five thousand unprovided for. How to employ them usefully the Government was at a loss to conceive. They were a strong drain upon the finances of the country; and to turn them adrift homeless and penniless in the streets of Paris was more perilous still; it was provoking an insurrection which in addition to money might also cost blood. These considerations of humanity and prudence had no weight with the men who were bent upon the destruction of a Republic scarcely established. They stigmatised the national workshops as the haunts of idlers and miscreants, ever ready to sweep down upon Paris to pillage and devastate it. No doubt there were evil-minded men amongst so large a number of the working orders, but the majority were well disposed, and regretted their inability to procure other employment than that which was but almsgiving in disguise. The Executive Committee, baffled in its attempt to obtain more legitimate employment for these large masses, was at last compelled to adopt severe measures. It decreed that all unmarried workmen from eighteen to five-and-twenty employed in these workshops should enter the army, and that the others should be sent to that part of the department of Loir-et-Cher called the Sologne. In case of refusal on either side, the national workshops were to be closed immediately. The measure was not very considerate in more ways than one. To the honest workman, a military life in time of peace is laborious idleness, and as there was no prospect of war, there was not the remotest chance of improving his position by displaying his valour. On the other hand, removal to the provinces was tantamount to transportation for many of the men who had their families in Paris. Added to this came the knowledge that the Sologne was a hotbed of certain marshy fevers, which might destroy health, if not cause death. Under these circumstances the workmen drew up a petition praying for a delay in closing the national workshops. This was rejected, the petitioners assembled in crowds, and a fratricidal struggle took place, lasting for three days (23rd, 24th, 25th of June), in which more than seventeen hundred persons were wounded and twelve hundred killed. Among the latter were two deputies, the Archbishop of Paris, who was murdered while climbing over a barricade, and five generals, one of whom was General Bréa, who was assassinated whilst endeavouring to persuade the insurgents to lay down their arms.[1]

While this conflict was raging the report leading to the dissolution of the national workshops was quietly read, and the Executive Committee was urged upon even by the Republicans to abdicate, but it refused. When, however, a vote of the Assembly concentrated the whole of the Executive in the hands of General Cavaignac, and proclaimed martial law, the Committee sent in its resignation, declaring that it would not retire before an insurrection, a sedition, and a public danger, but that the moment the Assembly had pronounced it neces-

---

[1] In *Les Crimes du Deux Décembre*, by M. Schoelcher, ch. iv. § 2, pp. 214—216, there is in a note a letter of M. Nadaud, in which he attributes the assassination of that general to Bonapartist agents.

sary, it felt bound to obey, and to re-enter the ranks of the deputies, in order to devote itself with them to the salvation of the Republic.

When the worst agitation of this struggle of Republicans against their brethren had subsided, General Cavaignac remitted his temporary powers in the hands of the Assembly, which, after passing a vote of thanks, named him chief of the Executive, and President of the Council of Ministers, with the right of appointing and dismissing his colleagues. There was no man living so deserving of this trust as Cavaignac. From the 28th of June to the 20th of September, the time his Government lasted, his behaviour throughout was marked by a noble sentiment of justice and clemency. To him were due the numerous acquittals, and far more numerous lenient sentences on those who had taken part in the insurrection. In the choice of his ministers, he ever deferred to the voice of the Assembly, without nullifying his individual opinions. The worst measure passed during his rule—namely, a law for restricting the liberty of the press—was due not to himself, but to the inspirations of his advisers and the Assembly, who while suppressing immediately the ultra-Republican organs, left the field open to the furious and undisguised attacks of the Legitimists and Orleanists. Cavaignac was a sincere Republican. To the intrigues of those men who were hostile to the Republic he would have opposed all the honest means in his power; but, unfortunately, his tenure of office proved too short. Some elections having taken place on the 26th of September,

Louis Napoleon was elected as deputy for the department of the Yonne, and this time he accepted the honour. Meanwhile for the last six or seven weeks the National Assembly had been occupied with the debates on a new Constitution, destined to give stability to the Republic. The principal question it gave rise to was the nomination of a President of the Republic. Though inspired by different motives, Royalists and Republicans were much in favour of such an appointment. Only a small number of the members of the Assembly feared the peril that might accrue to France from investing one man with responsibilities and power closely resembling those of a Constitutional King. Among that small number was M. Jules Grévy, now (1878) the President of the Chamber of Deputies, who with a prophetic foreboding painted the evils of placing this power into the hands of an unscrupulous individual. To prevent these evil results, he proposed an amendment, which, notwithstanding its sensible provisions, was thrown out by a majority of four hundred and eighty-five, so that it was decided that a President of the Republic should be chosen. After much discussion as to whether the President should be elected by the Assembly or by universal suffrage, the latter mode was adopted. From that moment that election became the chief pre-occupation of the whole of France. The day on which it was to take place was fixed for the 10th of December, when by an overwhelming majority, Louis Bonaparte was elected President of the Republic, over the heads of such men as Cavaignac and Lamartine, not to speak of Ledru-Rollin and Raspail, fanatics perhaps, but honest men, not adventurers seeking nothing but the gratification of hereditary ambition. What led the people to elect Louis Bonaparte was the magic of his name, for he was no well-known personage, or even a hero, unless his ventures at Strasburg and at Boulogne gave him a right to be so called.

On Thursday, the 20th December, the Constituent Assembly proclaimed Louis Napoleon President of the Republic, and he retained that office from that day until the second Sunday in May, 1852. The new President having been invited to take the oath of fidelity to the Republic and to the Constitution, entered the hall, quietly ascended the tribune, and after having been sworn, made a short speech, in which he declared his intentions of fulfilling his duty as a man of honour; he then read the names of the Ministry, which he had already selected, and went up to General Cavaignac, to whom he offered his hand. The honest soldier reluctantly accepted it, and returned the pressure coldly.

When Louis Napoleon assumed office, the home affairs of France were, if not prosperous, at least tranquil; her relations with the other Powers were amicable, in spite of the various attempts that had been made to interfere in the affairs of Italy, which had been always politely but firmly declined by that country, whilst, when Cavaignac retired, negotiations were pending for a mediation between Austria and Sardinia. From the outset of his presidential career, and notwithstanding his assertions to the contrary, Louis Napoleon's aim was to overthrow the Republic. This, however, required time, and above all the dissolution of the Assembly, from which he had received his power. A bill was proposed, not by the Government, but by a private member, for dissolving the Assembly and for holding a general election, and this bill passed on the 14th of February, 1849. During the debates on this proposal the building where the Assembly met was surrounded by a strong cordon of troops, to guard it against a supposed formidable insurrection of the Mobile Guards, of whom, however, not a trace could be seen.

The prince-President owed a debt to the clerical party for having furthered his election. Without daring openly to acknowledge these obligations, he withdrew the laws on primary instruction, which were unfavourable to the priests; and he interfered in the affairs of Rome, ostensibly for the purpose of continuing the mediation inaugurated under the Government of Cavaignac, but in reality to re-establish the temporal power of the Pope. Some deputies protested, but without much result. On the 26th of May, the sessions were closed, the general elections having taken place on the 8th of the same month. The various intrigues employed by the reactionary party to intimidate the people with overdrawn pictures of socialism and communism resulted in a minority for the Republicans; but the Government abstained from influencing the elections, fearful lest they might unite all the clericals, Legitimists, and

Orleanists against it. The victory was shared between the extreme democrats and the reactionary party. In a short time after the new Assembly met there could no longer be a doubt whither matters were tending. In consequence of the news that the French and the Romans were confronting each other beneath the walls of Rome, Ledru-Rollin demanded the indictment of the President and his ministers, and threatened to have recourse to arms (12th June). On the following morning Paris was placed in a state of siege, several newspapers were suspended, thirty-two deputies were ordered to be arrested, the right of public meeting was abolished, and other severe measures were taken. "It is a dictatorship," exclaims M. Jules Grévy, who had foreseen all this. His cry was met by the ministerial answer, "The highest law is to save a nation." This answer henceforth served to cover many iniquities. Delivered from the Opposition, the President proceeded to please the clericals. Without having given the least cause for aggression, Rome was treated as an enemy, and the Pope brought back under the protection of French troops, who remained until the month of September, 1870. In a short time Louis Napoleon appointed another Ministry, as the first, though pliable enough, was not sufficiently servile for him, and still respected parliamentary traditions. A special message to the Assembly explained the apparent reasons for this dismissal (31st October). M. Rouher, whom in the course of the Empire we shall meet again, and who entered the Assembly as a

Socialist deputy, formed part of this new Ministry, which inaugurated the personal Government of Louis Bonaparte.

The first indication of the growing ascendency of the clerical party was the passing of two bills, virtually placing primary instruction in the hands of the priests. In vain some of the most eloquent and powerful of the deputies opposed the project; they wasted their energy to no purpose. In the meanwhile, the Republicans were persecuted with unabated vigour. If perchance some deputies of the Opposition were elected, their constituencies were threatened with all kinds of ignominy. A moral Reign of Terror commenced. Universal suffrage was mutilated by a bill of the 31st of May, which required of every elector a previous domicile of two years. Each crime brings almost always its own punishment, and in passing this law the Assembly prepared for itself a snare, for if the working population could have voted two years later, the *coup d'état* of the 2nd of December might have become impossible. Meanwhile the President made a journey through various parts of France, and absolutely disclaimed all intentions of any attempt against the Republic, with which he was already credited by public opinion. Nevertheless both he and a majority of the Assembly were working for the destruction of the existing form of Government, but this once attained, their common action would cease. The majority wanted the re-establishment of a Legitimist or Constitutional Monarchy, the President the re-establishment of the

Empire of Napoleon. To effect this, the army, ever susceptible to the influence of that name, was being tampered with. The generals known to be hostile to the President's plans were gradually removed to different distant centres; and new batches of superior officers were created in Algeria, who replaced and counteracted the influence of the former. Those generals whom it was found impossible to remove were chiefly members of the Legislative.

Thus the struggle went on, hidden as yet, but frequently breaking out in violent debates in the Assembly. The majority would not or could not determine upon a combined plan of action beyond the overthrow of the Republic. After that each party was determined to work for its own benefit. In vain were the warnings of several deputies, who saw what was looming in the future; notably that of M. Thiers, who foretold in the beginning of January, 1851, the advent of the Empire. "I do not know when it will come, but of this I am sure, that sooner or later we shall hear that the Empire is made," he said. In consequence of the dismissal of General Changarnier from the combined commands of the National Guards and the garrison of Paris, the Assembly passed a vote of want of confidence in the Ministry. The Cabinet was obliged to retire, and the President of the Republic, unable to compose a new one, either from the minority or the majority, created an administration formed of men devoid of the least political significance (24th January), but fit and able to perform their duties as ministers. This was against the wishes of the Assembly; and when, a few days afterwards, the Minister of Finances asked for an increase of the civil list for Louis Napoleon, it was refused, unless the latter would consent to form a Ministry reflecting the opinions of the majority of the Assembly. The President would not grant this concession; he had already determined to place himself in open antagonism to the Assembly, for on various public occasions he had uttered sentiments which left no doubt on this point. Amidst these dissensions the time gradually drew near for Louis Napoleon to remit his powers into the hands of those from whom he had received them, as the Constitution did not allow any one to be elected twice in succession President of the Republic. The extreme Democratic party announced its intention of putting forward as their candidate the representative Nadaud, who though honest and intelligent, was a mason, and, therefore, offended the prejudices of many of the tradespeople, who imagined him to be the personification of Socialism. Meanwhile the army was continually being tampered with and it was no longer doubtful that all the intrigues of the Executive concealed but imperfectly hostile projects to the Republic. The Assembly, though it perceived the danger, was reluctant to use its right of preventing it; the officials responsible for the security of the Legislative neglected their duties, and many were still unwilling to believe that the President would resort to violent measures.

The Assembly became discredited in public opinion;

the poorer classes owed it a grudge for having deprived them of their votes; the Republicans were against it on account of its openly expressed monarchical tendencies; whilst the Royalists, on the other hand, were dissatisfied because it prolonged the antagonism between itself and the President of the Republic. The industry and commerce of the country suffered through all these dissensions; and every one felt that a crisis was at hand, and wished for a quick solution of the difficulty. The partisans of Napoleon were masters of the situation, because they swayed the public administration in a country which had been for a long time accustomed to regard the Executive as the supreme voice of her ruler.

Louis Napoleon, the instigator and inspirer of the projected *coup d'état*, had entrusted its execution to other hands than his own. The moment for striking the fatal blow had been several times deferred. At last the 2nd of December was fixed upon, as it was the anniversary of the battle of Austerlitz. If the President did not believe in the favourable omen himself, he knew that this day could not fail to bring some advantageous recollections to the minds of the French nation. The night before the principal conspirators assembled at the Elysée, the residence of the President, to decide upon their final measures. To one accomplice, Persigny, was entrusted the task of taking possession of the building where the Assembly met; a second, de Morny, was to seize upon the Government offices and the telegraphs, whilst many others were told off to perform similar dishonourable actions.

The projected conspiracy was carried out silently and successfully. Thirty thousand troops were stationed in different parts of Paris, ready to crush the least attempt of resistance, or, in case of failure, to protect the flight of the conspirators. The first inkling of the *coup d'état* and its favourable issue was conveyed to the Parisians by a proclamation placarded on the walls of the capital, stating that the National Assembly was dissolved, universal suffrage re-established, and the French convoked to their electoral meetings, from the 14th to the 21st of December, whilst the capital and some of the adjacent departments were proclaimed in a state of siege. At the first news of the events of the past night, meetings were held at the houses of several members of the Opposition, but before the end of the day, these deputies were nearly all arrested. Thus left to herself, without representatives, without newspapers, without guidance, Paris was at first undecided. Some few unimportant attempts at resistance were made, but failed, and a new Ministry was appointed. In the meanwhile large crowds had assembled on the Boulevards; squadrons of cavalry perambulated the town, without meeting with overt resistance; only cries of "Long live the Republic!" were heard. The military, irritated by those manifestations, charged the people, and killed and wounded a great number, amongst whom were many inoffensive individuals. Nevertheless the whole of the 3rd and part of the 4th of this month passed in comparative tranquillity, a phenomenon so unexpected that the accomplices of the President, not being able to explain this calm, got frightened themselves. They, therefore, resolved to strike a terrible blow, and gave orders to the military to disperse the crowd by force of arms. This command was executed without any legal warning, so that, even according to official mendacious documents, nearly four hundred persons were killed by the fire of the cannons and of the soldiers.[1] This frightful massacre struck terror into the hearts of the Parisians, and the victory, if such a name may be given to such an action, remained with Louis Bonaparte. During the next few days the arrests became so numerous that the prisons were found too small, whilst in the provinces any resistance which might have been attempted was frustrated by want of organisation.

According to the programme laid down in the proclamation of the 3rd of December the nation was called upon, on the 20th and the 21st of the same month, to vote for the question whether Louis Napoleon should remain President of the Republic for ten years, and draw up a new Constitution. A majority of more than six millions sanctioned his usurpation, which was applauded by the leaders of the clerical party. In consequence of this all opposition was crushed, and thousands of his antagonists were transported or

[1] Details of this barbarous massacre, as given by English eye-witnesses, are to be found in the *Times* of the 6th and 13th of December, 1851.

exiled, and amongst the latter were eighty-two former representatives.

On the 14th of January, 1852, the new Constitution was promulgated, by which the President became omnipotent, the deputies were deprived of their right of interpellation, and of initiating or proposing amendments to the laws, whilst the Senate was no longer independent. One of the first acts of the new Executive was to confiscate part of the private property of the Orleans family, and to order a compulsory sale of the remainder, whilst, at the same time, it passed a decree compelling all officials to take the oath of fidelity to Louis Napoleon. Many subsequent decrees subverted everything which had hitherto been considered constitutional. The new Assembly, which met on the 29th of March, received the name of Legislative Body; but several of the Republican members elected refused to take their seats. For the Republican insignia were substituted on the standards of the different regiments the former Imperial eagle, and the initials of the prince-President. His effigy had already replaced the emblem of the Republic on its coins. In the month of September of the same year Louis Napoleon made a triumphal journey through the provinces, during which he was received everywhere with the most obsequious and official adulation. Many of the Government functionaries even went so far as to say that the nation desired the Empire, a statement which was ratified by the President, who proclaimed at Bordeaux that the re-establishment of the Empire meant peace. His utterances in the provinces had already prepared the way for the tacit admission that the Empire had become necessary, and on the morning after his return to Paris the *Moniteur* announced that the manifest demonstrations in favour of its re-establishment imposed on the prince-President the duty of consulting the Senate. The result might have been foreseen.' The nation was again called upon to decide on the next 4th of November whether the President should be Emperor, and whether the imperial dignity should be hereditary in his family, and this was replied to in the affirmative by a majority of nearly eight million votes (November 21st). A few days later (December 2nd), the President ascended the throne, and took the title of Napoleon III.

Book II.

THE SECOND EMPIRE.

CHAPTER I.

§ I.—THE REVIVAL OF IMPERIALISM.

(*From the 2nd of December, 1852, to the 1st of January, 1859.*)

IF proof were wanted that Napoleon III. was anxious to benefit himself first of all, it would be found in the promulgation of a series of decrees (11th December to 18th December) which regulated a civil list for himself and his relatives. A Court in many respects similar to that of the First Empire was formed, and several of the imperial dignities of Napoleon I. were revived. When a nation strongly imbued with the sentiments of liberty is to be trodden under foot by an autocrat, there are but two ways in which such subjugation can be accomplished: the despot must appeal either to her love of conquest and military glory, or else plunge her into a state of moral corruption. As long as Napoleon III. was not master of the situation, he was compelled to have recourse to the first means; but now such expressions of hostility to foreign countries might produce fatal consequences; therefore the new Emperor hastened to mitigate his former declarations by pacific assurances calculated to tranquillise public opinion in the interior as well as in the exterior. The first care of a founder of a dynasty must be to insure its duration by providing an heir-natural or adoptive. Various matrimonial negotiations with princely and sovereign houses having proved unsuccessful, a marriage was arranged between the Emperor and a Spanish lady of noble birth, Eugenie de Montijo, Countess of Teba. The news of the marriage, which took place on the 29th of January, 1853, caused great surprise, and was not altogether satisfactory to the nation, who expected that the Emperor should have concluded a more illustrious alliance. The example of the prodigious luxury set by the Court was imitated by all classes, and led to speculations on the stock-exchange and in other doubtful commercial enterprises to an extent which aroused the anxiety of many earnest well-wishers to the country. Nevertheless great public works were undertaken, which caused a large deficit in the budget; but in spite of this semblance of prosperity dissatisfaction prevailed, and though it dared not openly show itself, it led to conspiracies against the lives of the Emperor and Empress, which fortunately were discovered before they were carried out.

A sectarian quarrel between the Greek and Latin Catholics at Jerusalem furnished the Czar Nicholas with a pretext for attempting to overthrow the "Sick Man," as he called Turkey. England, having been consulted by the Russian Emperor with a view to co-operation in this projected crusade, refused. Undeterred by this, the Czar sent Prince Mentschikoff to Constantinople with demands which, if conceded, would virtually have made Turkey a province of Russia. About six weeks after these demands had been refused the Russian troops crossed the Pruth and entered Moldavia (July 2nd, 1853), whilst already on the 13th of June the English and French fleets had anchored in Besika Bay, ready to pass the Dardanelles, and to protect Constantinople, for the treaty of 1841 had placed Turkey under the guarantee of the five great European Powers, who later on held a conference at Vienna (September 7th–January 16th, 1854), but without result. On the 30th of November Russia began hostilities by destroying the Turkish fleet at Sinope, and at the end of January of the following year war between England, France, and Russia was determined on, but not declared. These warlike rumours caused great agitation in the French capital, and the newspapers being virtually debarred from giving accurate information, the opening of the Chambers was anxiously looked forward to, it being expected that the Emperor would refer to the prospect of war, whilst an additional motive for uneasiness existed in the failure of the crops. The Emperor tranquillised the public mind by announcing that large purchases of grain were already on their way to France, but he declared that war was imminent. In order, however, to attenuate this statement, he added that England and Germany were at one with France to repress Russia's ambition, to maintain Turkey's integrity, and to watch over the rights of the Christians of the East. A loan of two hundred and fifty million francs was voted, and so great was the enthusiasm of the nation that in ten days the public subscriptions amounted to nearly double that sum. On the 27th and 28th of March war was officially declared against Russia both by England and France; ten days later an increase of the military contingent for 1855 was voted by the Assembly, which was dismissed shortly afterwards. In the beginning of May an Anglo-French fleet entered the Baltic, and on the 14th of August bombarded the fortress of Bomarsund, which surrendered on the following morning.

Whilst the plan of attack was being discussed between the commanders of the united French and English armies, General Espinasse was despatched with two divisions to drive the Russians from the Dobrudscha—a fruitless expedition which cost the French above five thousand men. The allied generals received orders to land in the Crimea and to take the strongly fortified town of Sebastopol—an arduous task, as there were no efficient maps of the territory to be invaded, and the numerical strength of the Russian army was unknown, while a complete ignorance prevailed as to the resources of Sebastopol. This ignorance entailed extensive surveys, and the mouth of the Alma, near the ancient town of Eupatoria, was fixed upon as a landing-point. At the approach of the allied armies Prince Mentschikoff, the Commander-in-Chief of the Russian army, retired, not deeming it prudent to risk

an engagement under the fire of the two fleets.
The Allies continued their march towards the south
along the sea-shore, in order to have the advantage of
the support of their fleets, in case of a sudden attack.
The Russian commander awaited them with an army
of forty-six thousand men on the heights overlooking
the left bank of the Alma, securely entrenched by fortifications which Nature herself had rendered almost
impregnable. The Allies attacked him, and after a brilliant battle which lasted three hours and a half, the
Russians were utterly routed, and made a precipitate
retreat upon Sebastopol (September 20th), where they
took up a position to the east of the fortress, whilst the
allied fleet prepared to blockade it. When the Allies, who
continued their march, came within sight of that fortress,
it was found to be almost impossible to attack it from the
north side, and a series of flank marches was determined
upon in order to reach the small ports of Balaklava
and Kamiesch, the possession of which would enable
the besiegers to keep open their communications, and to
receive ammunitions and provisions. On the 17th of
October the Anglo-French troops began the trenchworks for a siege, the long duration of which was
scarcely then contemplated. Balaklava was occupied
on the 26th of September, and on the 25th of the
following month the Russians made a sortie from
Sebastopol, and took some redoubts from the Turks,
but when they attacked the English they were compelled to retire with heavy loss. During this battle
occurred the celebrated "Charge of the Light Brigade,"

in which only a hundred and ninety-eight men returned out of the six hundred and seventy British horsemen who rode down the "valley of Death." These reverses brought about in Russia a fanatical excitement against the invaders, fanned into flame by the fulminations of the priests. From all parts of the country troops and volunteers flocked to the Crimea, cheered by the presence of the Emperors's two sons. On the 5th of November, before daybreak, under cover of a thick mist, forty thousand Russians swooped down on the lines of the British, attacked eight thousand of them near the old fort of Inkermann, and intended to force them to advance in the teeth of their artillery, or to drive them into the sea. The English kept the Russians at bay for six hours, and when at last a reinforcement of six thousand French troops came up the onset of the enemy was stopped, and the troops of the Czar were driven back after a most sanguinary struggle, with a loss of fifteen thousand killed, wounded, and prisoners. Simultaneously with this onslaught, five thousand Russians attacked the trench-works of the French, to the left of the main army, and were also defeated. After this Gortschakoff, who had succeeded Mentschikoff in command, refrained from active operations, during the whole of a most severe and rigorous winter, when the Allies suffered privations of which the record has become historical. It was hoped at one time that the sudden death of the Emperor Nicholas I. (March 2nd, 1855) would have put an end to all hostilities; but his successor and son

Alexander II. signalised his accession by a most bellicose manifesto. The investment of Sebastopol was continued for eleven months, and after many sanguinary encounters and repeated bombardments, a grand assault was made on the 8th of September upon the Malakhoff tower and the Redans, the most important fortifications to the south of the town. The French succeeded in capturing and retaining the Malakhoff, the division under General MacMahon being the first to enter. The attacks of the English on the Great Redan, and of the French upon the Little Redan, were not so successful, for the Allies were compelled to retire after a desperate struggle with great loss of life. In the night the Russians abandoned the southern and principal part of the town and fortifications, destroyed everything they could not carry with them, sunk or burnt the remainder of their fleet, and occupied the northern forts. The Allies thereupon entered the town (September 9th), obliged the enemy to capitulate, and virtually put an end to a war which throughout had generally been conducted on both sides with every sentiment of humanity and honour, consistent with the stern necessities of modern warfare. This successful issue tightened the cordial bonds already existing between England and France. While the war was raging the Emperor and Empress paid a visit to the Queen of England, which visit was returned in the month of August, 1855, by Queen Victoria and Prince Albert.

The Legislative Body of 1855 passed all the laws presented to it; amongst others one which granted to the Government, the monopoly of finding substitutes for those who declined to enter the army, and another which created a fund for rewarding those soldiers who, after the expiration of their time of service, re-engaged themselves. New imposts were also voted, as well as another loan of one hundred and twenty-five million francs. Encouraged by the success of the English Exhibition of 1851, the French Government revived three years later a project for a universal exhibition already broached in 1848, and which was held with great success in 1855.

Under the new state of things, with all independent newspapers virtually suppressed, the French were uncertain whether the fall of Sebastopol meant the end of the war or the beginning of a new struggle. The Czar seemed disinclined to accept the conditions offered to him; but it was at last agreed that the final terms of peace should be discussed in a Congress, to be held at Paris, and to be opened in February, 1856, under the presidency of M. Walewski, Minister of Foreign Affairs. On the 26th of April peace was officially concluded between Russia and the allied Powers. About a month previously (March 16th) a son had been born to Napoleon III., and the Senate passed a bill appointing a regent, in the event of the Emperor's death.

Napoleon III. seemed now to have reached the zenith of his prosperity. From all sides foreign princes came to visit him, and Paris became the pleasure-ground of the universe. To render her fit for such an object she was transformed into a town of palaces; the working classes and the small tradesmen were compelled to leave the quarters they had formerly inhabited, and had to remove to the suburbs; rents rose, and inordinate speculations of all kinds, suspended for a moment during the war, increased in spite of the warnings of many eminent men, and even of the Emperor himself. Added to this came the failure of the crops of the year before, which increased the cost of living, already weighing too heavily on the least affluent classes, whilst in the provinces inundations devastated several departments. The dissensions between the clergy of liberal and ultramontane opinions about the doctrine of the Immaculate Conception, then promulgated, did not tend to foster the growth of religion among the people.

The session of the Legislative Body for 1857 was not marked by anything of importance, and though there was an increasing deficit in the budget, it was scarcely discussed. By the terms of the Constitution the general elections were to take place during this year; great administrative pressure was brought to bear upon them, and, as a natural consequence, the candidates of the Government obtained nearly everywhere large majorities.

As the *coup d'état* had driven from France all those men whose pens might have been employed in the vindication of justice and liberty, the tranquillity of public life remained undisturbed, save by the din of the imperial fêtes and the open display of a gallant and licentious court. The last vestige of the liberty of the press had been destroyed by imperial decrees, and this suppression soon resulted in lowering the intellectual standard of the nation; for, unable to discuss serious subjects, the few eminent authors remaining treated frivolous topics. Amidst this illusive silence an event occurred, which for a few days filled the whole of Europe with evil forebodings. At the New Year's receptions of 1858 the Emperor expressed his satisfaction at the continuation of the amicable relations between France and foreign nations, as well as at the undisturbed tranquillity of the Empire. A fortnight after (January 14th), an attempt was made on the lives of Napoleon III. and the Empress, on their way to the opera, by the throwing of explosive bomb-shells whilst their carriage was passing. It was at first believed that the plot was due to a conspiracy of French Republicans, but it was found afterwards that its prime movers were some Italians, of whom Orsini was the head, and who considered the Emperor to be the chief obstacle to the independence of Italy. As a consequence attention was drawn to the various refugees in England, Switzerland, and elsewhere, and a diplomatic note was sent by the French Cabinet to the English Government, demanding that vigorous measures should be taken to prevent in future similar attempts, and that the laws affecting political exiles should be altered. The House of Commons refused to sanction such an alteration, and the Prime Minister, Lord Palmerston, resigned. The Legislative Body at the opening of the sessions was called upon to sanction severe measures of repression. These accorded but too well with the task Napoleon had set himself of ruling France despotically, for, though ostensibly the result of Orsini's attempt, they in reality struck at the Republicans. At the end of January the Senate voted a Senatus Consultus, by which the Empress was appointed regent. The police having been reorganised, the Minister of the Interior, Billault, and the Prefect of Police, Piétri, resigned; the latter was replaced by General Espinasse, who had many guiltless persons arrested, and revived a system of terrorism, in no way inferior to that of the Restoration.

§ II.—PROGRESS OF THE SECOND EMPIRE.

(*From the 1st of January*, 1859, *to the 15th of February*, 1865.)

ON the evening of the 1st of January, 1859, the news spread through Paris that the Austrian Ambassador had been more than coolly treated at the official reception held that day; and after a lapse of three days the very words uttered by the Emperor were published, which foreshadowed a rupture in the diplomatic relations between Austria and France. The official newspaper, the *Moniteur*, tried a short time afterwards to combat the evil influence of these rumours by stating that no change had taken place in the political situation, but this statement received almost a virtual denial by the sudden journey of Prince Napoleon, a cousin of the Emperor, who went to Turin to marry Princess Clotilde, a daughter of Victor Emmanuel, King of Sardinia; for, as a result of this alliance, the French Emperor would probably support the latter in the now expected war against Austria. In opening the sessions on the 7th of February, Napoleon III. announced that the political situation with regard to Italy was calculated to cause some uneasiness, though he added "there was as yet no sufficient motive to lead to war, and he thought it was likely that peace should not be disturbed." These Imperial words failed to inspire the least confidence. "Rumours vague and absurd," as the organs of the Government chose to term them, continued to be propagated; but on the 5th of March these rumours were confirmed by the official notice that the Emperor had promised assistance to the King of Sardinia in case of any aggressions of Austria. In truth the situation of the latter country with regard to France and Italy had for some time caused uneasiness to the various Governments of Europe.

Already in the Conference held at Paris, after the Crimean war, the Sardinian Prime Minister, Cavour, had complained of the encroachments of Austria in Italy; for, by her military preparations in the minor principalities she was a source of constant anxiety to Piedmont, and could, by a sudden attack, establish her dominion throughout the whole Peninsula. When the Treaty of Paris had been supplemented and improved upon by the new Conferences, which were held two years later, Austria had shown such ill-will during the whole of these negotiations, that the French Emperor was thoroughly dissatisfied; a dissatisfaction of which Cavour was not slow to take advantage, as he himself had already broken off all diplomatic relations with the Aulic empire for more than a year. No one doubted that a war against Austria had really been decided upon, notwithstanding official denials, and the attempts of England at mediation; for it was well known that even before the late Conferences had terminated the Sardinian minister had been consulted by Napoleon III. about the creation of a new Italian kingdom, comprising Piedmont, Lombardy, Venice, the Duchies of Parma, Tuscany, Lucca, Modena, Piacenza, and Guastalla, and part of the States of the Church, whilst France, as a compensation for her assistance, was to receive Nice and Savoy. One alternative remained, namely, the holding of another Congress, and everybody expected that it should have assembled, when on the 19th of April, Austria issued an ultimatum giving the Cabinet of Turin three days to reduce her army to a peace-footing, and to disband her volunteers, who had converged from all parts of Italy. The Sardinian Government having refused, General Giulay received orders to commence hostilities on the day indicated. The French Government had meanwhile obtained the sanction of the Chamber to raise to a hundred and forty thousand men the contingent of 1859, and to contract a loan of five hundred million francs. It was officially announced by the President of the Assembly, de Morny, that no other Governments would participate in the conflict except those whose interests were concerned in it, and on the 3rd of May the Minister of Foreign Affairs stated that war was declared between France and Austria. In a proclamation of the French Emperor himself it was distinctly declared that no aggrandisement of territory was contemplated, that he was only actuated by a love for humanity and liberty, and that there was no intention to dethrone the Pope, but merely to free him from the pressure brought to bear upon him by the Austrians. Though no one believed in the disinterestedness of Napoleon III., though this war was regarded by many as a means used to divert public attention, and others pretended that he was only moved by the threats of the Italian secret societies, it was nevertheless popular in France.

On the 29th of April the Austrian commander crossed the Tessino, and entered Piedmont, which he could have overrun, but he did not even attempt it; and, later on, he echelonned his army, consisting of a hundred and fifty thousand troops from Pavia and Piacenza to Novra and Vercelli. On the 10th of May the French Emperor departed, amidst the enthusiastic acclamations of the assembled multitude, to take the command of the army, which had already entered Italy, taken up its position under the walls of Alessandria, and was everywhere received with the warmest manifestations of joy. On the arrival of the Emperor, Victor Emmanuel placed himself under his orders, and Napoleon took the chief command of the combined armies. Nothing of any importance took place before the 20th, when the Austrians made a sudden sortie on the Piedmontese vanguard, posted before Montebello, and drove them back on the French, who, taken unawares, wavered for a few moments, but soon rallied, repulsed the enemy, and compelled him to retreat (May 20th).

The Austrian commander thought that the Allied troops would cross the Po at certain points, and had taken his measures accordingly, but they passed the river farther down to the north-west. On the 30th the Sardinian army crossed the Sessia, and carried the bridge and village of Palestro, whilst an attempt of the Austrians on the following day to retake these points was vigorously repulsed (May 30th and 31st). On the 2nd and 3rd of the next month General MacMahon crossed the Tessino and defeated the Austrians at Turbigo. It was necessary for strategical reasons to gain possession of the bridge of Magenta, and on the 4th of June an outpost-skirmish to that effect assumed the proportions of a great battle, in which the position of the French army was endangered for many hours. It was only saved through the dash of the troops under MacMahon, who forced their way through the Austrians at the point of the bayonet, whilst Napoleon III. narrowly escaped being made a prisoner. Victors and vanquished passed the night on the battle-field, but the following morning the Austrians abandoned their positions—thus acknowledging their defeat—and left the way open to Milan to the French and Sardinians, who made a triumphal entry into that town on the 7th of June.

The Austrians on retreating to Lodi had fortified

the village of Malegnano, but Marshal Baraguay d'Hilliers dislodged them from this position and drove them behind the Mincio (July 8th). At that juncture the Austrian Emperor Francis Joseph assumed himself the command of his army, because Giulay had failed in all his operations. He took up his position on a ground perfectly well known to him, and recrossed the Mincio to attack the Allies, who boldly went to meet him. The generals of both armies were ignorant of the marches and counter-marches of the hostile troops; and therefore, instead of confronting each other in a body, isolated engagements took place on a line of great extent, of which the principal strategic points were the tower of Solferino and the village of San Martino. On this vast line three hundred thousand troops were hurled against each other during fifteen hours on the 24th of June, and the victory remained with the Allies, though a terrible storm arrested their further progress, and favoured the retreat of the Austrians to Verona.

The successes of the French and Sardinian armies led to several important events in Central Italy. The news of the landing of the French at Genoa on the 29th of April had been the signal for a rising in Tuscany, which compelled the Grand Duke to abdicate, while the dictatorship of that Duchy which was offered to Victor Emmanuel was accepted by him only temporarily. The Duke of Modena and the Duchess of Parma followed the example of their brother of Tuscany, and these States, as well as the Legations, ranged themselves under the banner of the King of Sardinia. Meanwhile Austria was threatened in Venice, where she was much hated; the French and Sardinian fleets had entered the Adriatic, expecting to meet with the vessels of the enemy near the island of Lossini, but they had already left it, whilst in Venice itself everything was prepared for a rising. In consequence of an autograph letter of Napoleon III. to Francis Joseph, inviting him to a personal interview, a cessation of hostilities was arranged, to the great dissatisfaction of the French, but more so of the Italians, who found themselves baffled in the task of completely freeing their country, so that a coolness arose between Victor Emmanuel and the French Emperor. The interview between the two Emperors took place in the village of Villafranca (July 11th), without any other person being present; and therefore, until this day, the details of the meeting have remained a secret. But its result became known officially: this was the formation of an Italian confederacy under the honorary presidency of the Pope; Austria ceding the whole of Lombardy, save Peschiera and Mantua, to France, to be handed by her to Italy, whilst Venice was to form part of the confederacy, though remaining an Austrian possession; the duchies were restored to their former princes, who promised to grant a general amnesty; the Pope should be asked to introduce certain reforms in his States; and all persons compromised in the recent revolt against Austria were to be amnestied. Within four-and-twenty hours of the meeting of the two Emperors, the treaty and counter-treaty, afterwards confirmed at Zurich (November 10th) were signed, and thus the judgment and will of both these monarchs decided the fate, the political future and the fortunes of two nations. Never were the stipulations of a diplomatic document more disregarded, for the rulers of the Duchies did not even attempt to return to their States, the Legations never returned under the Papal sway, and the Italian confederacy remained a dead letter.

The peace concluded at Zurich satisfied no one, but was forced on Napoleon by events which only reached their completion at the battles of Sadowa and Sedan. From this moment the imperial throne received a shock, of which the effects were perhaps imperceptible at first, but which made the Emperor conscious that his hold upon the French nation was dependent on a career of uninterrupted military victories, and that one serious defeat might overthrow him and his dynasty. This consciousness of his unstable tenure, no doubt, actuated him to grant a general amnesty for all political offences on the 15th of August; but this proffered Imperial favour was disdainfully refused by many of the most eminent exiles.

On the 20th of September the Pope delivered in a secret consistory an allocution, in which, after vehement lamentations on recent events, he declared the acts of his revolted subjects null and void, and threatened with excommunication all those who had participated in them. Many of the French bishops took up the text, and maintained that the spiritual power of the Pope would decrease with the loss of his temporal power. This led to bitter polemics; and though Napoleon III. was opposed to the maintenance of the temporal power of the Pope, he found himself compelled to consent to a prolonged military occupation of Rome, to support that which he actually condemned. At the beginning of the year 1860 (23rd of January) an important treaty of commerce was concluded between England and France, which at first was opposed by a part of the French nation, on account of the reduction of duties on English goods. Meanwhile the attacks of the clerical party in France against the Emperor's policy on the Roman question continued, and led him to abandon his idea of a confederacy for Italy, a land which aspired to nothing but Unity.

In opening the sessions (2nd March, 1860), the Emperor of the French admitted the necessity of constituting the north of Italy one great kingdom, and claimed as a compensation for furthering this project the French slopes of the Alps, not as a matter of aggrandisement, but as one of protection for the frontiers. The population of the Italian Duchies and of the Legations were invited to give their vote on this question, and unanimously demanded to be annexed to Sardinia. A similar vote was taken, with the same successful result, for the annexation of Savoy and Nice to France (April 15th–24th, 1860), in spite of the protest of some eminent

Italian Liberals, and the less openly expressed dissatisfaction of the European monarchs, who looked askance at this increase of territory, which seemed an attempt at the reconstruction of the old Napoleonic Empire. Italy thought herself absolved from all gratitude towards France, as she considered that the latter's services had been paid for, whilst the prolonged occupation of Rome by French troops added to her irritation. Pius IX., to resist the probable encroachments of the newly constituted Kingdom of Italy, ordered the formation of an army of twenty thousand men, of which the command and organisation were offered and accepted by the French general Lamoricière, with the permission of his own Government. The Italian Prime Minister, Cavour, pretended that a great part of the new Papal army was composed of foreign mercenaries, and constituted an infringement of the law of nations. He demanded that this army should be disbanded, and on the refusal of Pius IX., Italian troops entered Papal territory. Contrary to the Pope's expectation, France, instead of supporting him, merely recalled her Ambassador from Turin, whilst the Italian army defeated the Pontifical troops at Castel-Fidardo (September 18th), and compelled Lamoricière to shut up himself in Ancona, which capitulated some time afterwards, so that there would have been an end to all Papal government, but for the French Emperor increasing the garrison of Rome. About the same time, General Garibaldi, at the head of a troop of volunteers, made himself master of Naples, and contributed to the union and independence of Italy, which led to Victor Emmanuel being declared King of the whole of the Peninsula, except Rome and Venice (February 21st, 1861).

Syria, which had been restored to Turkey in 1841 by Mehemet Ali, Pacha of Egypt, was the constant scene of sanguinary quarrels between the Mussulman and Christian populations. Abd-el-Kader, who had been liberated by Napoleon, then President, had lately taken up his residence at Damascus. He came to the aid of the Maronite Christians, and saved a great number from the murderous violence of the Druses, a warlike people dwelling among the mountains of Lebanon. The news of the atrocities committed by the latter filled the whole of Europe with indignation. On the proposal of the French Emperor, an army of twelve thousand men was sent to Syria (August 3rd, 1860). When they arrived they found that peace had been restored, but, nevertheless, remained in the country six months longer to see that the arrangements concluded were carried out. The Syrian expedition and the war in Italy had for some time diverted public attention from the labours of the Legislative Body, which, as usual, implicitly obeyed the will of Napoleon III. The home and foreign policy, the Roman question, and the finances were often violently attacked and criticised by various deputies, without producing the least result, for the Imperial system was at that time at the height of its fictitious prosperity. Everything the Emperor undertook had succeeded; France was at peace in the interior and the exterior, and, nevertheless, a sentiment of uneasiness prevailed.

The treaty concluded in 1858 with China stipulated that the Powers who signed it should have the right of establishing a permanent embassy at Pekin. In June, 1859, an English fleet, presenting itself at the mouth of the Pei-ho, to conduct the ambassadors to Pekin, had found the passage barred, and the attempt to force it proved fruitless. After many negotiations, the English and French Governments insisted on avenging the insult done to their flags. An Anglo-French army of thirty-three thousand troops defeated the Chinese on several occasions, marched towards Pekin, and burnt the Emperor's summer palace. Finally a convention was signed, by which China was compelled to make an apology, and to pay immediately a large indemnity (October 24th, 1860). The session for the year 1861 was opened on the 4th of February, and the Senate had been convoked a few days before in order to grant the Legislative Body the right of discussing publicly an address to the Emperor on all matters regarding home and foreign policy.

Another expedition, which was at first undertaken in combination with England and Spain, but afterwards continued alone by France, was directed against the Republic of Mexico. Its purport was to demand satisfaction for many gross outrages on foreigners, as well as for the refusal of the payment of arrears due to bondholders. The Mexican Congress dissolved, and conferred full powers on the President, Benito Juarez.

The French troops advanced in the interior, and the Mexican President quitted the capital, whilst General Forey, who had arrived with two thousand five hundred soldiers, was appointed to the command of the expedition. The Mexican Congress protested in vain against this invasion (October 27th, 1862).

In the meanwhile, at the opening of the French sessions of 1862 (January 27th), and after several financial laws had been adopted, the discussion on the address to the speech from the throne revived in the Senate the religious question in connection with the Italian situation, whilst in the Legislative Body the same discussion furnished the occasion of a debate on the expedition of Mexico, which was violently attacked by some of the Liberal members, both on financial and political grounds. A few days afterwards unfavourable news arrived from Mexico, and the project of establishing a Mexican monarchy for the Archduke Maximilian of Austria, was mooted by France, and received with much favour by the Legislative Body, but was disapproved of by the British and Spanish Governments. After the passing of several measures, including the budget for 1863, both the Legislative and the Senate were prorogued.

The sessions of the year 1863 was opened with a speech from the Emperor, in which he confined himself to enumerate all the benefits which his Government had conferred upon France. The Legislative Body was approaching the term of its dissolution, the deputies were pre-occupied with their re-elections, and the

Senate did not care to disturb public opinion. All the debates were more or less shortened, whilst the discussion on the address in both Chambers, though it did not last long, betrayed the uneasiness felt at the continuation of the war with Mexico. In the Legislative Body the debates on the address furnished an opportunity to define the attitude of the country and the Government towards Poland, which had again risen in insurrection against Russia, because the latter State could not be prevailed upon to execute her stipulations and the treaties of 1815 with regard to this unfortunate nation. In fact, since the Polish Revolution of 1831 the Russian Government seemed to have abandoned all idea of conciliating Poland, and only thought of completely crushing it. Unable to suffer any longer, the Poles rose in 1862, and for more than a year successfully opposed the power of Russia, but the strength of numbers prevailed at last, and order was reinstated only by massacres and deportation to Siberia, whilst the intervention of the European Powers proved fruitless.

Notwithstanding all the pressure brought to bear by the prefects and other functionaries, the new elections in France resulted in a great moral success for the Opposition, though the numerical victory remained with the Government, a victory partly obtained by the promises even of the official candidates to induce the Emperor to grant liberal reforms. The spirit of liberty was stirring everywhere, and the capital herself declared almost openly against the Empire, by electing all the Opposition candidates. In consequence of this a new Ministry was formed, of which M. Billault was appointed the head; but at his death, which happened shortly after his nomination, M. Rouher was named in his place.

During this year (1863) the situation in Mexico had not made much progress. The French had taken Puebla (May 18th), and occupied the capital (June 10th). General Forey had appointed a junta of thirty-five notables, charged to elect a triumvirate, which, in its turn, had to convoke an Assembly of two hundred and fifteen members to determine the form of Government. This Assembly decided, on the 7th of July, that Mexico should become an Empire, and offered the crown to the Archduke Maximilian of Austria, who accepted it about a year later (10th April, 1864).

The opening of the sessions for 1864, which was fixed for the 5th of November, was looked forward to with some anxiety. People were eager to hear the explanations of the Government on the affairs of Poland, and to observe the attitude of the new Legislative. Napoleon, in his speech, cast the blame of the failure of the negotiations in favour of Poland on the European Powers, while, in reality, it was the distrust of the Imperial system which caused it. He also brought forward his favourite project of a Congress of Sovereigns, proclaimed that the treaties of 1815 had ceased to exist, and that such a Congress alone could solve the questions now pending. The crowned heads of Europe had already been invited, and the secondary powers gave their adhesion unreservedly; but others, Russia, Austria, and Prussia, stipulated for a specification of the points to be debated; England refused point blank, and all idea of a Congress was abandoned.

The verification of the powers in the Legislative Body lasted for nearly a month, with the result of exposing the prevailing electoral corruption, and the unseating of six members. In the Senate the debate on the address gave rise to an interesting discussion on Poland, during which one of the members eloquently pleaded her cause, and was supported by a cousin of the Emperor, Prince Napoleon. It was virtually admitted that though Poland was to be pitied, it was impossible to assist her. In the Legislative the debate on the address lasted for more than four weeks, and provoked a vigorous criticism of the Opposition on the home and foreign policy of the Government, but notably on the expedition to Mexico, which burdened the budget with a deficit of over nine hundred million francs, and compelled it to issue a loan of three hundred millions. In fact, nearly all the Liberals were opposed to the continuation of the interference in Mexican affairs, and expressed freely their opinions that it would be better for France to end it. But the Emperor, who had induced Maximilian to accept the proffered crown, before he started for his distant states, concluded with the Mexican monarch a treaty, by virtue of which the French army should be gradually reduced, whilst Mexico was to repay to France her expenses.

On the 28th of May the sessions were closed, and, though no virtual changes had been effected in the Constitution, a remarkable change began to be perceptible in the tactics of the Government towards the Chamber and the country. An energetic Opposition manifested itself, without as yet showing any tangible results, but paving the way for the evolution of ideas which gradually influenced public opinion. The Government felt but too well that if not in the presence of an irreconcilable enmity, it was already face to face with a vigorous antagonism. Finding it impossible to battle against the stream, it pretended that the Emperor was the promoter of a new system of liberalism. Though devoid of direct interest to France, the public mind was exercised by the war between Denmark, Prussia, and Austria, which annulled the treaty signed in London in 1852, regulating the succession to the throne of Denmark, and at which France had been one of the co-signatories. This same year the Emperor concluded with the King of Italy a Convention (September, 15th), by virtue of which France undertook to withdraw her troops from Rome, on the condition of Italy engaging herself not to invade the Pontifical territory, and to defend it against all attacks. This measure provoked the threats of the clerical party, against which the Government felt itself powerless to act.

§ III.—THE DOWNWARD COURSE OF IMPERIALISM.

(*From the* 15*th of February*, 1865, *to the* 4*th of September*, 1870.)

Though the Emperor by some recent acts had somewhat slackened the rigour of the Imperial system, he was resolved not to be coerced. If any illusions had been entertained to the contrary, they were fated to be dispelled by the speech from the throne, at the opening of the sessions (February 15th). After the usual self-gratulations of Napoleon III. with regard to his foreign policy, he concluded in the following words:— "While constituting ourselves the ardent promoters of useful reforms, let us maintain with firmness the basis of the Constitution, let us oppose ourselves to the exaggerated tendencies of those who provoke changes for the sole object of sapping what we have founded. Utopianism is to welfare what illusion is to truth; progress does not mean the realisation of a more or less ingenious theory." In spite of these warnings the discussions on the address were very animated, and reflected principally on the absence of all necessary liberties. The Emperor felt himself attacked by the extreme Liberals, and also by the partisans of a monarchy whose inclinations were not quite so absolute as his own. One of his chamberlains, in replying in the Chamber to these attacks, committed the blunder of speaking of "the man of genius" who had dragged France from an abyss on the 2nd of December. Then, for the first time for many years, was heard in public the right word to stigmatise the *coup d'état*. "The 2nd of December," cried M. Ernest Picard, one of the leaders of the Opposition, "the 2nd of December was a crime." To describe the tumult which followed would be impossible, and though these words were suppressed in the official report of the sitting, they had been uttered. On the 29th of April the Emperor quitted Paris for Algeria, and appointed the Empress Regent in his absence. Whilst he was in that colony, Prince Napoleon went to Ajaccio, in Corsica, to take part, on the 15th of May, in the unveiling of a monument in memory of Napoleon I. and his four brothers. As a natural consequence he was called upon to make a speech, in which he developed many democratic tendencies, and consequently offended his cousin. This occasioned some embarrassment in official circles, and the *Moniteur* made not even mention of the discourse, but published a letter of the Emperor rebuking the Prince.

At the opening of the sessions of 1866 (January 22nd) everything appeared calm: Napoleon III. had returned from Algeria, France was at peace with all foreign nations, the occupation of Rome was about to cease, and the French troops in Mexico were to be recalled; the difficulties that had arisen between Prussia and Austria with regard to Schleswig-Holstein seemed to be removed, at least temporarily. Nevertheless a vague feeling of uneasiness prevailed, which was not even allayed by the protestations contained in the speech from the throne that France should preserve a strict neutrality in the event of a war breaking out between the two German Powers. In the discussions on the address to the throne several members of the Opposition, notably M. Thiers, expressed themselves in forcible terms about the necessity of the Government taking the initiative of more liberal reforms.

The first note of alarm was, however, sounded by the Emperor himself, who, in a speech delivered at Auxerre (6th May) invoked the memory of his uncle, and declared his detestation of the treaties of 1815, which Europe persisted in considering as the basis of her present political system. As the state of affairs was very critical, this allusion was interpreted as foreboding the intention of the Emperor to consent, if not to contribute actively, to the remodelling of the map of Europe, for public opinion began now to occupy itself with the crisis impending between Prussia and Austria. The Emperor had renewed the proposal of his favourite project—a Congress of the European Powers—which was unsuccessful, mainly through the difficulties raised by Austria. Under these circumstances Napoleon III. felt himself called upon to lay down his programme in the form of a letter to his Minister for Foreign Affairs (June 11th). This letter professed to trace the conduct which the representative of France should have adopted, in case the proposed Congress had taken place. "You should have declared in my name that I disclaim all idea of territorial aggrandisement, as long as the balance of power in Europe is not disturbed; there would have been no thought of extending our frontiers, unless the map of Europe were modified to the exclusive advantage of one great Power, and unless the neighbouring provinces demanded, by freely expressed votes, their annexation to France." After attributing the conflict between Austria and Prussia to the vaguely defined geographical position of the latter Power, the wish of Germany for a political reconstruction more consistent with her general wants, and the necessity of Italy to assure her national independence, the letter continued: "I could have desired for the secondary States of the German Confederation a more intimate union, a more powerful organisation, a more important part to play; for Prussia more homogeneity and power in the north, for Austria the maintenance of her great position in Germany. I could have wished that, as an equitable compensation, Austria would give up Venice to Italy; for if, together with Prussia, and without regard for the treaty of 1852, it has waged against Denmark a war in the name of German nationality, it appears to me just that she should recognise in Italy the same principle by completing the independence of the Peninsula." The letter finished by stating that "if peace were disturbed, the Emperor had received from the Powers the assurance that, whatever might be the results of the war, none of the questions concerning France should be decided without her consent."

A few days after the publication of this letter war was declared between Prussia and Italy on the one hand and Austria on the other, and after a series of victories, of which the one at Sadowa (July 3rd) was the crowning success, peace was finally concluded with Prussia at Prague (August 23rd), and with Italy at Vienna (October 3rd). Venetia, which had been ceded to France by Austria, was finally annexed to Italy, which also came in possession of the four Italian fortresses,

Peschiera, Mantua, Verona, and Legnago, whilst in Germany a North Confederation had been formed, and Hanover, Hesse-Cassel, Hesse-Homburg, part of Hesse-Darmstadt, Nassau, and Frankfort had been annexed to Prussia.

In the meanwhile the Senate had voted a law by which the Legislative Body was prohibited from discussing or proposing any changes in the Constitution of 1852. The result of the Austro-Prussian war had changed the political condition of France, though the Government stated, in a circular addressed to her diplomatic agents abroad, "that the new distribution of European forces had nothing to alarm France." The French troops finally evacuated Rome (9th to 11th of December), whilst the official newspaper mentioned that in the spring of 1867 the army from Mexico should return to France.

The Constitution of 1852 had remained nearly unchanged during ten years, but an imperial decree suppressed on the 19th of January, 1867, the right which had been granted to the Legislative seven years before, of discussing the address to the throne, and substituted in its stead interpellations, which had to be authorised or could be adjourned by the majority. In opening the sessions (February 14th) the Emperor announced the withdrawal of the troops from Mexico, and the proposal of a law to increase the army, whilst a few days later in the Legislative Body some of the deputies interpellated the Government on a recent violation of correspondence. Another interpellation took place (25th and 26th of February) about the legality of the decree suppressing the address to the throne, but it led to no results; whilst M. Thiers, about a fortnight afterwards, interpellated the Government on their policy with regard to foreign nations—an interpellation which led to a discussion lasting four days, and in which the Opposition told the Government some bitter truths, though the Chamber voted by a large majority its satisfaction with the acts of the Ministry.

Negotiations had been in progress between the King of Holland and the Emperor about the annexation to France of the Grand Duchy of Luxemburg, but the great Powers interfered; and a Conference was held in London, in which it was decided (May 11th) that the King should remain Grand Duke, but demolish the fortifications of the town of Luxemburg, whilst the Prussian garrison was to evacuate that fortress.

In the discussion on the budget—a discussion which was still allowed—some financial arrangements of the Government were severely and deservedly criticised; the Legislative also passed a law to ameliorate the position of teachers in public schools, in spite of a strong opposition from the clerical party. On the 1st of April was opened in Paris the Universal Exhibition of Fine Arts and Industry, to which almost all nations had contributed, and which was visited by large numbers of strangers, amongst whom were nearly a hundred sovereigns and princes. The Emperor of Russia, Alexander II., who was one of these, was fired at by a Pole, just as he was returning with

Napoleon III. from a review. The news that the Emperor Maximilian had been shot, at Queretaro, in Mexico, on the 19th of June, produced a general consternation, and put a stop to the official *fêtes* given by the Court.

The Senate and the Legislative Body had been convoked for the 18th of November, and this was rather earlier than usual. The tone of the Emperor's speech was very peaceful and conciliatory. He stated that "the changes which had happened on the other side of the Rhine should be accepted, and that as long as the interests and dignity of France were not menaced the modifications which took place because various nations desired them did not concern her." And yet public opinion remained in a state of uncertainty, and commerce languished. Interpellations about the probability of the King of Italy seizing Rome took place in the Senate and in the Legislative Body, and during the discussions in the latter house one of the Ministers, M. Rouher, solemnly declared in the name of the French Government that it would never allow Italy to become master of Rome, neither of the capital nor of any part of the Roman territory, a declaration which later events have stultified. After much discussion, two new laws, the first regulating the raising of fresh levies for the army, the second instituting a new kind of National Guard, were passed on the 14th of January, 1868. The last law was not put into execution by the Government, owing to the death of its chief promoter, the Minister for War, Marshal Niel, which took place, however, more than a year and a half later, whilst the first law was received by the nation with great disfavour, and gave rise to severe disturbances in some of the large towns, in which the military had to be called out.

The Second Empire wished to slacken a little the bonds which had tied down the press until now. It therefore proposed a bill by which newspapers were allowed to appear without the authorisation of Government, did away with "official warnings," and transmitted to the tribunals the power which the administration had possessed of suspending or suppressing a newspaper, but it still maintained the pecuniary guarantees and penalties, as well as the prohibition of discussing the acts of Government officials. This bill was approved of by the Legislative Chamber as well as by the Senate, though in the latter body it met with some violent opposition. The very next day after it had become law several new Liberal newspapers appeared in the capital and in the provinces. A law was also passed regulating the holding of public meetings, which in reality gave the authorities the power of forbidding them whenever they should think fit so to do, and allowed a commissary of police, who had always to be present, the right of dissolving the meeting if he deemed it necessary. The Legislative Body spent an entire month (29th June till 29th July), in discussing the budget. Several members of the Opposition criticised the yearly increasing deficit, the continual augmentation of the expenses for the army, and the intricate and unintelligible manipulation of the finances of the State.

The sessions were closed on the 28th and 30th of July, but already rumours were bruited about that a dissolution of the Chambers was imminent, so that the deputies who presented themselves for re-election were obliged to profess more or less Liberal tendencies in their addresses to the electors. During this year several newspapers were prosecuted and condemned, as well as a few members of political societies. But a great sensation was produced by a prosecution undertaken against the newspapers which had proposed to open a subscription for erecting a monument in honour of Charles. Baudin, a representative who had been killed by the troops on the 2nd of December, 1852. Some of the most eminent barristers of the Liberal party, and amongst them M. Gambetta, defended these papers, and attacked the manner in which the Second Empire had been established. Their speeches, reproduced in all the newspapers, recalled to the mind of the nation the history of the *coup d'état* of the 2nd of December, a crime which, according to some of the partisans of the Imperial dynasty, had been absolved by the votes of the whole of France, but which was stigmatised by one of the barristers engaged in this lawsuit "as the most criminal deed which history shall ever remember, and which, as every act is followed by its consequences, shall, therefore, not remain unpunished." The accused editors were, of course, condemned to imprisonment and fines, as well as all the newspapers which had admitted in their columns the lists of subscribers to the proposed monument.

The term of the present Legislative expired on the 1st of June, 1869, and as the new elections were to take place in the second quarter of the year, they pre-occupied the nation to the exclusion of all other topics. Even the speech from the throne at the opening of the sessions (18th January, 1869), bore traces of this general pre-occupation. It alluded to the arduous task of the Government to erect on a soil so frequently shaken by revolutions an administration sufficiently impressed with the wants of its time to adopt the benefits of liberty, and sufficiently strong not to fear its excesses. After which the Emperor expatiated upon the prosperous condition of the army, and the perfect organisation of the arsenals and storehouses, which would the better enable France to proclaim her desire for peace, as no one could or would attribute it to weakness or want of preparation. Speaking of the revolution in Spain, which led to the deposition of Queen Isabella, the Emperor congratulated himself that it had caused no rupture of the cordial relations between that country and France, that, in fact, she was at peace with all the world. Referring again to the coming elections, Napoleon hinted that the time for more liberal reforms was at hand, a prospect which did not seem any longer to terrify the majority of the Legislative. There was even amongst the Government supporters a certain group of deputies who wanted more than the Emperor had promised. The complete liberty of the press was asked for; the Opposition did not hesitate to attack some of the personal favourites of the Emperor; in fine, a new era of liberty seemed to be approaching. The maintenance of peace, and the reduction of the army, on both economical and moral grounds, were eagerly discussed, and met by the Government in a spirit which, if it had been sincere, would have argued well for the future. Since then it has become doubtful whether there was not a deeper motive underlying this apparently conciliatory system. Notwithstanding this the elections were eagerly contested by the Opposition. The struggle was passionate on both sides, and the Government brought to bear all its pressure on the constituencies. The elections resulted in an almost open condemnation of the system hitherto pursued by the Imperial Government, and nearly all the large centres chose Opposition candidates, of whom some declared themselves absolutely irreconcilable to the Empire, notably MM. Gambetta and Rochefort, above all the latter, who by his revolutionary publications had become the idol of the Parisian population.

The growing opposition to the Empire was manifested in more ways than one; and every now and then the large towns were the scenes of unarmed demonstrations, which the Government saw fit to suppress by charges of cavalry and attacks of the police. It somehow was bruited about that these demonstrations were organised by the Government itself, in order to serve as a pretext for not disbanding part of the standing army, a measure which public opinion claimed as affecting the welfare of the nation. The partial divulging of the origin of these demonstrations led to the arrests of the editors and printers of several newspapers, who after being confined for some time were released without the least investigation having taken place.

The Legislative was convoked for an extraordinary session on the 28th of June, in order to proceed to the verification of the powers of the newly-elected deputies, which would take up too much time at the beginning of the ordinary session. The Liberal candidates brought again to light the manœuvres by which the Government had supported its own partisans. A large number of the majority reiterated also their demands for a more liberal Constitutional and Parliamentary system; they claimed for the Legislative the right of regulating the organic conditions of its labours and its communications with the Government. This was more than the Government in its most liberal moments had intended to grant. Still it could not openly reject these demands, and to grant them would have been against the terms of the Constitution, which reserved to the Emperor the initiative of Constitutional modifications. In this emergency the Legislative was prorogued and the Senate called together for the 2nd of August, to discuss the various reforms destined to establish the Government on new bases. On the 18th of July the Emperor announced his intention of granting these reforms. This would naturally lead to such a change in the Imperial system that the Cabinet felt itself bound to tender its resignation. Many Ministers, however, remained with the new administration, and by a Senatus-Consultus of the 8th of September several liberal measures were adopted, which already foreshadowed the advent of a Parliamentary system. The decree of the 13th of July proroguing the Legislative had not fixed a day for its re-assembling, and according to Parliamentary usage, this should take place within six months of the date of the last session. It was stated at first that this time should be reckoned from the day of prorogation, and measures had already been taken effectually to protest against such an intended delay; but the Ministry wisely convoked the deputies for the 29th of November. Meanwhile some supplementary elections had taken place, in which the most turbulent of the Republican party endeavoured to elect no other candidates but those who would refuse to take the oath to the Empire. Four ultra-Republicans were elected, amongst whom was M. Rochefort, the Government having given him a safe conduct to re-enter France.

At the opening of the sessions (29th of November) the Emperor once more referred to the difficulty of establishing in France "a regular and peaceful use of liberty," and ended by expressing his confidence in the maintenance of public order, provided the deputies would lend him their assistance in preserving liberty. After various interpellations, the verification of the powers of the deputies, interrupted by the sudden prorogation of the 13th of July, was proceeded with, and ended on the 27th of December, on which day the whole of the Ministry resigned. The following morning the official newspaper published a letter in which the Emperor requested M. Emile Ollivier, formerly one of the leaders of the Opposition, but who for some time had endeavoured to bring about a fusion between the Liberal and Imperial policies, to point out to him the persons most capable of forming with him a homogeneous Cabinet, faithfully reflecting the majority in the Legislative, and which was called upon to aid in the task of setting in motion a regular constitutional system. In order to understand the import of this event, it should not be forgotten that hitherto all liberal initiatives had been immediately followed by acts more or less neutralising such intentions. This tergiversation had produced a disastrous effect in more ways than one. The partisans of autocratic rule warned the Emperor that he was going too far, whilst the adherents of the Parliamentary system maintained that Napoleon did not go far enough, though they were, nevertheless, disposed to support him, as the military power was in his hand, and he could thus frustrate the violent attempts of all utopists and ultra-Republicans. These moderate reformers did not perceive that the Empire, born from the *coup d'état* of the 2nd of December, could not exist, if it would seriously practise liberty. Under these disquieting auspices the year 1870 began; no Cabinet had as yet been appointed.

On the 2nd of January the new administration was formed with M. Emile Ollivier as Prime Minister. Six days had elapsed in negotiations, for in taking the reins of power the new Premier was obliged to cooperate with politicians who up till now had been comparative strangers to him. As we have already seen, he in reality belonged to the Republican party, to which until lately he was attached by hereditary as well as personal bonds. The virtual desertion of his old allies rendered his position a false one. It was felt on both sides that he could not entirely be depended upon; and, therefore, he inspired but a mediocre confidence. Two of his principal colleagues, MM. Buffet and Daru, the former Minister of Finances, the latter Minister for Foreign Affairs, were known to be staunch defenders of the Parliamentary system, to which they had clung throughout.

The first care of the new Cabinet was to dismiss M. Hausmann, Prefect of the Seine, who had embellished Paris at so great a cost, and to appoint in his stead M. Chevreau, a gentleman who was more in harmony with the Liberal party. Suddenly the joy caused by the triumph of the Liberal policy was marred by an untoward incident. In consequence of a violent political controversy, the editor of an ultra-Republican paper sent two of his friends to Prince Pierre Bonaparte, a cousin of the Emperor, to arrange for an armed encounter. After a very short discussion, the Prince shot one of these gentlemen, M. Victor Noir, through the heart (January 10th). This murder, for such it was, aroused in the highest degree the indignation of the Republicans. The Prince was arrested, but by the terms of the Senatus-Consultus of 1852, which regulated the position of the members of the Bonaparte family, it was decreed that they could only be tried by a jury of members of all the counsels-general drawn by lot from the whole of France. The funeral of the murdered man would inevitably have led to a revolt without the intervention of a brother of the victim, and of several members of the extreme Liberal party, amongst whom was M. Rochefort, who was indicted for having written an article in which he was said to have instigated the people to rise in rebellion. He was condemned to six months' imprisonment, and a fine of three thousand francs, without forfeiture, however, of his civil rights. His arrest led to a disturbance, the pillaging of an armourer's shop, and to the erection of several barricades, which were left without defence and quietly demolished by the police. Nevertheless the nation was full of hopes that her expectations were about to be realised. The coalition which had always combated the Empire was dissolved, and the adherents of Parliamentary rule turned upon their former allies, the Republicans. A great Liberal current, fostered by the Government itself, had set in, and the people were hoping that the Emperor would grant liberty without a revolution. As is usual with such attempts at reform, the nation began to ask too much, not taking count of the Empire's past, and of her traditions, until some of the Bonapartist organs implored the Ministers to slacken their headlong career of innonovation. The partisans of autocracy were getting frightened. The Ministry proceeded, nevertheless, and was encouraged by public opinion.

In authorising M. Emile Ollivier to initiate a liberal Empire, Napoleon did not intend to proceed as far as his Ministry. He now thought it necessary to oppose a bar to the rising tide. On the 21st of March there appeared in the official newspaper one of those letters which he affected so much, and which invited the President of the Council to submit to him a plan for a Senatus-Consultus "intended to check the immoderate desire for change which possesses certain minds, and which disturbs public opinion by creating an unstable state of affairs." The new plan "should lay down once for all the fundamental dispositions, the necessary consequences of the appeal to the people of 1852, divide the legislative powers between the two Chambers, and restore to the nation the constituent power, which she had delegated to others." The Cabinet, or rather M. Rouher in its name, took seven days to draw up this Constitutional programme, which was placed on the table of the Senate on the 28th of March. It was nothing more or less than the skeleton of the Constitution of 1852, stripped of all its excrescences, and reduced to forty-five clauses. Clause 13 read: "The Emperor is responsible to the French people, to whom he has always the right to appeal," while clause 44 declared "that the Constitution could not be modified save by the people, and on the proposal of the Emperor." The first left always open the road to another 2nd of December; the second effectually prevented any or every constitutional reform displeasing to Napoleon III.; both clauses and many others were completely opposed to the spirit of Parliamentary Government. The agitation provoked by the presentation of this Senatus-Consultus was increased when it was proposed to have it ratified by an appeal to the people; as the Constitution of 1852 had been modified eight times already, without any of these changes ever having been sanctioned by the nation. It could therefore not be necessary now, and the objections which many deputies raised against it were perfectly rational. Nevertheless on the 5th of April the bill to have the change in the Constitution ratified by the people passed; the Senate had, meanwhile, commenced a debate on the new Constitution (April 19th), and voted the whole of the forty-five clauses of which it was composed on the following day. Three days later an imperial decree convoked for the 8th of May all the electors to sanction the following formula: "The people approves the liberal reforms introduced in the Constitution since 1860 by the Emperor with the concurrence of the principal bodies of the State, and ratifies the Senatus-Consultus of the 20th of April," whilst the Legislative was prorogued until after the nation had voted. The secret of this renewed appeal was contained in the last words of the Emperor's manifesto which accompanied it, which was, in fact, an attempt to establish the succession of the

Napoleonic dynasty on a more secure basis than hitherto.

The struggle between the partisans and the enemies of the Empire grew more violent than at the general elections of the year before; for, though the ostensible issue was simply the ratification of the Constitution, the real question was the continuance of the Empire. Many electors who detested the imperial rule, nevertheless gave it their votes, for fear of worse to follow, in case of its overthrow. This dread was cunningly kept up by the machinations of the Government, and to this was owing the great majority of nearly six million votes which it obtained. The large towns had almost all declared against the new Constitution, but the provinces and the rural populations had approved of it, so that the Emperor was justified in saying that a numerical majority of the nation had once more granted him leave to do with France what he liked. The Legislative re-opened after the appeal to the nation had been decided, and discussed several laws; amongst others it rejected the petition of the Orleans family to be allowed to return to France, and passed a bill to reduce the yearly levy by ten thousand men.

It had just begun its debates on the budget when a newspaper, the *Journal des Débats*, spread the report that the German Prince Leopold of Hohenzollern-Sigmaringen, a relative of the King of Prussia, had accepted the crown of Spain, offered to him by General Prim. The Government being interpellated on the subject, the Duke de Gramont, Minister of Foreign Affairs, confirmed the report, but stated at the same time that the Spanish people had not as yet pronounced their opinion, and that the French Ministry ignored the details of a negotiation which had been concealed from it. "But," continued he, "we do not believe that the respect for the rights of a neighbouring nation obliges us to allow a foreign State, which places one of her princes on the throne of Charles the Fifth, to upset to our detriment the actual balance of power in Europe, and to endanger the interests and honour of France. We are convinced that this eventuality shall not be realised. To prevent it we reckon on the wisdom of the German nation and on the friendship of the Spanish people; but if it were otherwise, strong in the belief of your support and that of the nation, we shall know how to do our duty without hesitation and without weakness."

The debate was adjourned, and for several days the Ministry refused to give further explanations, on the pretext that negotiations were pending. On the 12th of July the news that Prince Hohenzollern had refused the proffered crown arrived in Paris, and on the same day Napoleon III. informed two of the foreign ambassadors that the difficulty had been overcome, and that all prospects of war were at an end. The Bonapartists were far from satisfied with this solution of the question, and stated on the authority of the War Minister, Marshal Lebœuf, "that everything was ready for war, that the Prussians were not prepared, that it was necessary to put an end to the insolent pretensions of such an aggrandising Power, and that the campaign would not last six weeks," whilst they regarded with contempt those who differed from them in opinion. On the 15th of July an official statement was read in the Senate and Legislative, which set forth "the certainty that the nation approved the policy of the Government, and supported it; that in the negotiations which were just terminated care had been taken not to wound the susceptibilities or the independence of Spain; that the Cabinet of Berlin and the King of Prussia had declared not to have been aware of the arrangements between the Spanish Government and Prince Hohenzollern; and that the King had only interfered as the head of the family, and not in his capacity as a sovereign." The French Government further stated, "We cannot consider this reply satisfactory, we cannot admit this subtle distinction between the head of the family and the sovereign, and we have insisted that the King of Prussia should advise, and if need be, compel Prince Leopold to abandon his candidature. Whilst we were interchanging notes with Prussia, the news of the renunciation of the Prince came from a quarter whence we did not expect it, and was communicated to us on the 12th of July by the Spanish Ambassador. The King of Prussia having wished to remain aloof from this question, we requested him to connect himself with it, and to declare that if by one of those changes which are always possible in a country emerging from a revolution, the crown was anew offered by Spain to Prince Leopold, he would not again sanction his acceptance, so that the question might be considered as finally solved. . . . The King consented to approve the renunciation of Prince Leopold, but refused to bind himself not to sanction again in future the renewal of this candidature. . . . Although this refusal appears to us scarcely justifiable, our desire to preserve to Europe the blessings of peace was such that we did not break off our negotiations, and that in spite of our legitimate impatience, and fearing that discussions might hamper them, we asked you to defer our explanations. Therefore we were greatly surprised when yesterday we learnt that the King of Prussia had sent an aide-de-camp to our ambassador to inform him that he would no longer receive him, and in order to invest this refusal with a non-ambiguous character, his Government communicated this officially to the Cabinets of Europe. We heard at the same time that Baron Werther, the Prussian Ambassador in Paris, had received orders to take leave of absence, and that armaments were going on in Prussia. Under these circumstances to attempt more for the sake of conciliation would have been inconsistent with our dignity, as well as an imprudence. We have neglected nothing to avoid the war; we shall prepare ourselves to carry on the one offered to us, whilst leaving to every one his own share of the responsibility." This statement was received amidst the applause of nearly the whole of the Assembly, and the Government proposed immediately a loan of fifty million francs for the Ministry of War, in order to be ready for every contingency, which was granted at the same time, notwithstanding the refusal to vote of the members of the Opposition. One of these members, M. Thiers, made a speech, in which he observed that as the candidature of Prince Hohenzollern had been withdrawn, there was no occasion to shed torrents of blood about a mere question of etiquette; that he was ready to vote all the means necessary to the Government when war should be finally declared, but that he insisted upon the communication of the dispatches upon which this declaration of war was based, and that he declined the responsibility of a war which had so few grounds of justification. This speech was delivered amidst continual interruptions, loud hootings, and insults, which the President of the Chamber had the greatest difficulty to repress. M. Emile Ollivier, the Keeper of the Seals, stated in reply that the Ministry was fully alive to its duty, that it also believed that useless wars were criminal, and that if it decided upon this strife provoked by Prussia, it was because none was ever felt to be more necessary. He went on to say that none of the members of the Ministry had sought the opportunity of making war, that the Government had not discussed the fitness or unfitness of the hour for attacking Prussia, that it did not wish to attack at all either Germany or Prussia, but that it had received an insult which it could not bear, and a menace which, if allowed to be executed, would reduce

France to the lowest rank of nations. Finally, he refused to communicate to the Chamber the dispatches asked for, on the ground that they were confidential, and that it was contrary to diplomatic usages. The Opposition insisted, but without result, and the Minister repeated that France had been driven to this war, because she had done all that was humanly and honourably possible to avoid it. These words were received with much applause; and then the Minister of War presented two bills, the one calling out the Garde Mobile, the other asking for volunteers during the war. After which M. Ollivier resumed his speech, and accused the Opposition of having excited public opinion by averring that the battle of Sadowa had lowered France in the eyes of Europe. In spite of the many interruptions and the violent animadversions of the majority, M. Thiers in his reply to the Minister maintained that it was unlikely that Prussia should ever again support the candidature of Prince Hohenzollern, and that France had been lowered, not by the members of the Liberal party, but by the originators of the war in Mexico, who now accused these members of trying to embroil their native country, when, on the contrary, they wished to prevent the shedding of blood.

On the next day, the 16th of July, a great number of senators, headed by the president, M. Rouher, went to the Tuileries to compliment the Emperor, and three days afterwards the French diplomatic agent at Berlin notified to the Prussian Government that

France considered herself at war with Prussia, and the Duke de Gramont communicated this official declaration to the Legislative on the following day. Every evening large crowds perambulated Paris, shouting, "To Berlin, to Berlin!" Republican songs were heard in all the theatres and open-air concerts, by permission of the authorities, whilst those who declared themselves partisans of peace were maltreated in the public streets. In the provinces the excitement was not so universal, though the declared opponents of the war or of the Empire were not seldom threatened, and one unfortunate gentleman, accused of shouting "down with the Emperor" was seized by the peasants, brutally treated, and finally burnt alive. The Imperialist newspapers insulted all those who opposed this warlike impulse, and M. Thiers in particular became the object of the most violent attacks. The Legislative was occupied three days (20th to 22nd of July) in voting the budget, and in passing divers laws—amongst others, one granting a credit of four million francs to assist the families of the recruits called out. The sessions were closed on the following day in spite of the members of the Opposition, who protested against being dismissed when the country was at war.

Napoleon III. assumed the chief command of the army. By a decree of the 27th of July he conferred the regency on the Empress, and started on the following day for Metz, where his head-quarters were established. He did not pass through Paris, as he had done in 1859, but addressed a proclamation to the French nation, in which he reiterated that war had been provoked by Prussia, and that France did not wage war against Germany, but, on the contrary, wished that all the peoples of the great Germanic nationality should be unfettered in accomplishing their destinies. From the same town he also issued a manifesto to the troops, announcing that they were entering upon a long and arduous war, on a scene bristling with obstacles and fortresses, that he was certain that a French army would show once more what it could do when animated by a sentiment of duty, kept together by discipline, and urged by the love of country; that wherever it might wind its way beyond the frontiers it would find glorious traces of its fathers, and that it would show itself worthy of those immortal traditions.

France was without an ally. Though at the beginning of the Hohenzollern imbroglio the Foreign Powers had not left Prussia in ignorance of their sympathies with the French, the immoderate demands of the Imperial Cabinet after the renunciation of Prince Leopold had completely changed their dispositions. England was neutral; Italy was oscillating between France, who had given her Lombardy but who kept Rome, and Prussia, to whom she owed Venetia; Russia guaranteed Prussia against all attempts from the exterior; Austria was compelled to remain inactive lest she might lose her German provinces, already too inclined to sympathise with Prussia. A few days after the declaration of war the German Premier, Count von Bismarck, alienated the sympathy remaining for France in Europe by publishing the draft of a treaty which Napoleon III. had proposed to the King of Prussia after the war of 1866. In this treaty the Emperor recognised the union of North and South Germany, except Austria, in return for Prussia allowing him to take possession of Belgium, and assisting him in case of need with her troops. The French Ministry denied the existence of this document, which was proved to have been entirely written by the then French ambassador, M. Benedetti, who failed to give satisfactory explanations. The bitter feelings begotten by the exactions of Napoleon I. in Germany were rekindled by the attack of his nephew, and fanned into blaze by the aspirations of German unity, and by the belief that Napoleon III. was hostile to it. The existence of these feelings was not known at the Tuileries, and a similar ignorance prevailed with regard to the military organisation of Prussia, which could bring into the field almost a million of combatants, well disciplined, well armed, and hating the French invaders.

Already, during the first days of the mobilisation, the boasted organisation and discipline of the French troops were found to be imaginary. Everything was wanting or in disorder. No plan of the campaign was in existence, and the army scattered along the frontier waited for orders which did not come, and remained for some time inactive. In the war thus ventured upon, France had only at her immediate disposal two hundred and seventy thousand soldiers, which by a vigorous effort might be increased in a fortnight to three hundred and fifty thousand. These troops were composed of various corps, having no combined plan of action. There was no simple and rapid system of either mobilising or concentrating them. Only on one line of railways the regulations for the furtherance of military transport and service were sufficiently complete to be available, and these were not utilised, from ignorance of the fact in higher quarters. The result was that where provisions abounded there were no troops, and that troops were sent where there were no provisions. Such was the state of things at the opening of the campaign.

The military movements of the Prussians were not known. On the 15th of July, the King had ordered the army to be mobilised, and during the four following days the Grand Duke of Baden, the King of Bavaria, and the King of Wurtemberg did the same. Within a few days the North Germans had ready for action three hundred and eighty-three thousand footsoldiers and forty-eight thousand cavalry, without reckoning the garrisons of the different towns and fortresses, whilst South Germany was preparing to increase within a very short time these masses with a contingent of about two hundred thousand men. The Prussian army was composed of three *corps d'armée*. The first, of about sixty thousand, under General Steinmetz, with its right flanked by the neutral territory of Luxemburg, advanced by Treves and Sarrelouis;

the second, of a hundred and forty thousand, which was soon to be increased to a hundred and ninety-four thousand, commanded by Prince Frederick Charles was to march by Mayence and Mannheim towards the Saar, linking together the first and third corps; the third, of a hundred and fifty thousand troops, commanded by the Crown Prince, threatened Alsace, and protected the left bank of the Rhine against all surprises. The King of Prussia arrived on the 1st of August at Mayence, where he established his head-quarters. On the 2nd of August the first engagement, of little importance, took place, in order to drive out of Saarbruck a Prussian detachment, which hardly resisted. This trifling engagement was greatly magnified by the partisans of the Empire, and the French official newspaper announced that the French had taken the offensive, crossed the frontier, and invaded German territory.

Marshal MacMahon, recalled from Africa to take the command of the first French *corps d'armée*, arrived at Strasburg on the 24th of July. He found everything in disorder, and unable to obtain any information as to the movements of the enemy, he detached the division of General Douay on a reconnoitring expedition, which entered Weissenburg, a town in Alsace, protected by a strong line of fortresses. This division was attacked by superior forces, and after an heroic defence, the town was taken by storm by the Crown Prince, and the French General was killed (4th August).

On the next day Marshal MacMahon was ordered

by the Emperor to advance with the fifth and seventh corps towards the threatened point of French territory, and on the following day he took up his position on a ground chosen by himself between Wörth and Fröschwiller, in order to give his reinforcements time to come up. He was suddenly attacked by the army of the Crown Prince, superior in numbers, and defended himself during the whole day with great energy, but was obliged to succumb at last. The defeat became a complete rout, and the consequences would have been even more serious but for the vigorous stand made by the Algerian sharpshooters and two regiments of cuirassiers (6th August). On the same day the French under General Frossard sustained a severe reverse at Forbach, an almost impregnable position, which, though disputed inch by inch, was stormed and taken at last by the Prussians, at an enormous cost of life.

That very day a rumour spread in Paris that Marshal MacMahon had obtained a great victory, and had taken the Crown Prince and twenty-five thousand Prussian prisoners. Universal joy prevailed in the capital, nearly every house was decked with the tricolour, whilst crowds blocked the principal thoroughfares and sang the *Marseillaise;* but two hours later it was discovered that these tidings were false. In order to avoid such fictitious news, the Ministry promised to communicate henceforth and at once any news which it might receive from the army, and at one o'clock in the morning a telegraphic message was affixed to the doors of the Ministry of the Interior, which mentioned the retreat of General Frossard, though no details were given. On the next day the inhabitants of the capital were informed of the defeat of the army of MacMahon, the loss of Forbach, the retreat of the two armies, and the advance of the enemy. Mad with excitement Paris clamoured for arms. The Empress, who had returned from Saint-Cloud, issued a proclamation in which she entreated the people to be united, and stated that, faithful to her mission and duty, she would be the first to defend the standard of France, at any risk. The capital was declared in a state of siege, the Legislative and the Senate were convoked for the 14th of August, and the danger becoming more pressing, for the 9th. Proclamations addressed to the French and to the Parisians called upon the whole nation to rise as one man as they had done in 1792, and counselled the capital to remain calm.

On the 9th of August the Legislative meets, the building is surrounded by a dense crowd, which is kept in order by troops, who are received with the cry of "March to the frontiers." M. Ollivier attempts to prove that the military situation is not desperate, and solicits the confidence of the Assembly. M. Jules Favre, one of the members of the Opposition, proposes that guns should be distributed to all citizens capable of bearing arms, that the National Guards should be re-organised in conformity with the law of 1831, that a committee should be appointed composed of fifteen members of the Assembly to consider the best means of repelling the foreign invasion, and that the

Emperor should be no longer Commander-in-Chief. This last proposal causes a vehement outburst of conflicting feelings, and the President refuses to put it to the vote, as being unconstitutional. Finally, after a long debate, often interrupted, the Assembly decides that it will support a Cabinet capable of providing means for the defence of the country, and the Ministry considering this declaration tantamount to a vote of want of confidence, offers its resignation to the Empress, who accepts it, and entrusts the Count de Palikao with the formation of a new Cabinet.

It was evident to the whole nation that the Emperor and Marshal Lebœuf were incapable of fulfilling the duties entrusted to them—the one as Commander-in-Chief, the other as Major-General of the army. In the sitting of the 11th of August the Minister for War stated that Marshal Bazaine, who had gained his laurels in the Mexican campaign, had been appointed Commander-in-Chief. The Legislative voted the re-organisation and arming of the National Guards in all the departments, as well as a credit of fifteen million francs. It also adopted several financial measures proposed by the Ministry, but all this failed to satisfy the members of the Opposition, who distrusted the Government, and accused it of sacrificing the defence of France to the interests and preservation of the Imperial dynasty. Nevertheless, the Ministry actively urged the completion of the fortifications of Paris, victualled the capital, and appointed General Trochu its governor.

After the defeat of Fröschwiller Marshal MacMahon moved with the remainder of his army to the camp of Châlons, rallying on his march the division of General de Failly. When he reached the camp, part of the Canrobert division, as well as the reinforcements sent by the Minister for War, and the Garde Mobile of the department of the Seine, had already arrived. General Frossard's division and all the other army corps were concentrated at Metz, under the command of Marshal Bazaine. The Emperor, who had remained in the latter fortress until the 14th of August, resolved to rejoin MacMahon at Châlons. Whilst he was proceeding on his journey, Marshal Bazaine fought the battles of Borny (14th of August), Gravelotte (16th of August), and Saint-Privat (18th of August). In the first two he obtained the victory, but did not profit by them to pierce the enemy's line.

The troops in the camp of Châlons formed a total of about a hundred and forty-five thousand men. It was the proposal of Marshal MacMahon to retreat slowly with this army on Paris, in order to give the capital time to complete its preparations, and in the event of investment to secure for it an army which might come to its aid. On the 16th of August Napoleon III. arrived at the camp with his son and his cousin Jérôme. In a council of war held on the same evening, and at which Marshal MacMahon, Prince Napoleon, General Trochu, and several other generals were present, the plan of retreating on Paris was adopted, and the Marshal was appointed commander of the army of Châlons, and General Trochu Governor of Paris, and chief of the contingent destined to defend the capital. The next day General Trochu communicated these tidings to the Regent and Council of Ministers, but he met with a strong opposition, and the Empress declared that the return of her husband to the capital after so many reverses would be the signal for the outbreak of a Revolution. Almost at the same time the news arrived of Bazaine having obtained a signal and decisive victory, and the retreat on Paris was then considered unnecessary. The Minister of War, Count de Palikao, proposed that the army of Châlons should move towards the north, take the Prussians in the rear, relieve Metz, and join the army of Bazaine. This plan was not impracticable, but hazardous, for the Prussians under the Crown Prince were already moving on Paris. The council of war adopted this project, which was opposed at first by the Emperor and Marshal MacMahon, but finally both assented. In the morning of the 21st the army of Châlons, after having set on fire everything it could lay hands on, left its quarters, which the Prussians occupied the same day. On his arrival at Rheims (22nd August) Mac-Mahon received two despatches from Bazaine informing him of the latter's defeat at Saint-Privat, and of his intention to operate in the direction of Montmédy. The following day MacMahon's troops moved towards that place and arrived on the 26th at Vouziers in the Ardennes. The Crown Prince of Prussia, who had been at first ignorant of the movements of the Marshal, soon guessed their purport. He relinquished his contemplated march on Paris, ordered the army of the Meuse, under the Prince of Saxony, to effect a junction with his own, and hastened in pursuit of the French.

Marshal MacMahon's forebodings were now realised. He was cut off from Paris, and, in the event of his persisting to reach Montmédy, exposed to the danger of being surrounded. Being without tidings of Bazaine, who was shut up in Metz, he sent a message to tell him that on the 29th he would endeavour to fall back upon Mezières, and from there farther down westward unless he learned that the army of Metz had commenced its retreat. The Minister for War continued to urge on the Marshal to hasten to the relief of Bazaine; MacMahon obeyed, and resumed his forward march on the 28th. The next day some isolated engagements took place, and on the 30th the army crossed the Meuse, when a division under General de Failly was surprised at Beaumont and routed. During the whole of the night of the 30th and the following day, the retreat on Mezières might have been practicable, had not the Emperor ordered the army to concentrate round Sedan. On the evening of the same day the Prussians crossed the Meuse on bridges which the French had neglected to destroy, and cut off the route from Sedan to Mezières. The following morning the French were completely surrounded, and the only retreat open to them was Belgian territory. At dawn (September 1st) the battle began in the village of Bazeilles, when almost immediately

Marshal Mac-Mahon was wounded and had to be carried off the field, having transmitted his command to General Ducrot, who a little later handed it to General de Wimpfen, appointed Commander-in-Chief in the event of any accident happening to the Marshal. Pressed on all sides by superior forces, mown down by the artillery which poured shells upon them from the heights commanding their positions, the French were gradually driven back in the hollow at the bottom of which lies Sedan. About two o'clock Wimpfen offered to the Emperor to place himself in the midst of the troops and endeavour to cut a passage through the Prussians, but he refused, and told the General to ask for an armistice. The latter declining, Napoleon ordered the white flag to be hoisted, and the firing to cease along the whole line—an order which General Ducrot refused to sign, as well as General Wimpfen, who there and then resigned his command, a resignation which the Emperor did not accept. Napoleon III. wrote thereupon to the King of Prussia, that having been unable to die in the midst of his troops, there remained nothing for him but to give up his sword and to capitulate. The capitulation was accepted on the following conditions: "The French army to be prisoners of war; the officers to keep their swords and personal property; all other arms to be given up to the Germans." If on the next morning at nine o'clock these terms were not accepted, the bombardment would recommence. General Wimpfen obtained as a favour that the officers should return home upon signing an engagement not to combat any more during this war. The following morning (2nd September) at nine o'clock, Napoleon III. proceeded to the village of Donchery, where he met Count von Bismarck, who accompanied him to the Château of Bellevue, the head-quarters of the King of Prussia. On the 3rd of September, the Emperor was conducted to the castle of Wilhelmshöhe, near Cassel, the former residence of his uncle Jérôme, when King of Westphalia.

On the morning of the 3rd of September the Minister for War ascended the tribune of the Legislative, and after having referred to his promise of communicating to the Chambers all the tidings he should receive, stated that "serious events had just happened, and that he had received news which, though not official, might be true." He went on to say that Marshal Bazaine, after an engagement of about nine hours, had been obliged to fall back upon Metz, and had been unable to effect the proposed junction with the army of Marshal MacMahon. "On the other hand," he continued, "we have received information of a battle which was fought between Mezières and Sedan; a battle alternated by successes and reverses. We at first defeated part of the Prussian army, and drove it into the Meuse, but afterwards, somewhat overwhelmed by numbers, we were obliged to retreat either into Mezières or into Sedan, and even in small numbers on Belgian territory." He also informed the Chambers that Marshal MacMahon had been wounded and that the situation was critical.

In the evening the news of the disaster of Sedan arrived in Paris; large crowds went to the Louvre, the residence of General Trochu, and to the Legislative, and loudly demanded the deposition of the Emperor. Towards midnight an official proclamation was published, announcing the capitulation of Sedan, and the captivity of Napoleon III., whilst stating at the same time that the Government was taking the measures demanded by the critical aspect of affairs. At one o'clock at night a sitting was held by the Chamber, in which were proposed the deposition of the Emperor and his dynasty, the appointment of an Executive Committee to resist by all possible means the invasion, and to drive the enemy from French territory, and the maintenance of General Trochu as Governor of Paris. The discussion was adjourned till the next day (September 4th), when another proposal was submitted to the Assembly, conferring on the Count de Palikao the title of Lieutenant-General, and appointing an Executive Council selected by the Legislative. A third proposal, signed by M. Thiers and forty-seven deputies, to appoint an Executive Committee of National Defence, and to convoke a Constituent Assembly as soon as possible, was also laid before the Chamber. It was decided to refer these three proposals to a Committee, which should discuss them without delay, and the sitting was suspended until its report should be ready.

In the meanwhile several thousands of National Guards had gone unarmed to the building where the Assembly held its sittings, and which was surrounded by an enormous crowd of people, nearly all clamouring for the abdication of the Emperor. Troops and policemen were stationed everywhere, who only allowed the deputies to pass, as well as those persons who had tickets of admission; but they could not prevent many people from entering also. Whilst the Committee was deliberating, a large number of people had collected outside on the steps, and under the colonnade of the Hall of the Assembly, and they all loudly demanded the deposition of Napoleon III., a demand which was re-echoed by the great mass of individuals who filled the Place de la Concorde, the quays, and the Champs Elysées. The agitation of the assembled multitude increased, and finally they broke through the ranks of the soldiers and the police, and arrived before the building of the Legislative. The National Guards who were on duty fraternised with the people, and assisted them in climbing over the wall, whilst the regular troops looked on without interfering.

The crowd, which had invaded the Legislative, rushed through every passage, and penetrated into all the rooms, even into those in which the deputies were assembled in committee. The public tribunes became soon filled to suffocation, whilst M. Schneider, the president of the Assembly, did all that lay in his power to calm the excited multitude. The sitting was declared opened, and several leading members of the Opposition united their efforts to those of the president, and demanded in vain to allow the Assembly to deliberate. Many of those who had filled the tribunes descended to the seats of the deputies in the Hall, the doors were burst open, and fresh crowds arrived, who increased the tumult and loudly demanded a change of Government, as well as the proclamation of the Republic. At last M. Gambetta pronounced the deposition of the Imperial dynasty, amidst the vehement applause of the assembled multitude, who still insisted, however, upon the proclamation of the Republic. It was thereupon resolved to proclaim this new form of government at the Hôtel de Ville, and the leading members of the Liberal party went thither, followed by enormous masses of the people. They were soon joined by many other deputies, and the French Republic was then publicly declared. Acting upon the advice of some of her advisers, the Empress had already left for England.

The troops which were stationed in Paris offered no resistance to the people, and only a few National Guards kept sentry before the public buildings, which henceforth were considered as national property. A Government of National Defence was provisionally appointed, composed of the nine deputies of the department of the Seine, with General Trochu as its president.

"Thus fell the Empire;[1] not as the Restoration, vanquished after a prolonged and sanguinary battle; not as Louis Philippe, taking flight before the irritation of all, and having scarcely tried to hold his ground; but sinking beneath the responsibility of its treachery, and overwhelmed by its political and military

[1] F. Lock, *Histoire des Français*, vol. vi., ch. xxi., § 2.

faults. 1848 had been a revolution caused by contempt, 1870 was a revolution caused by disgust. The Empire lasted twenty years . . . a long period in the life of a human being, but a small one in the life of a nation. It had its foundation in the infatuation which rendered possible the crime whence it sprung; it owed its duration to the terror which its initiative crime inspired. In order to deter minds from thinking of liberty, it gave full scope to sensual appetites, for such is the policy of all despotisms. But on the very day when material pleasures no longer sufficed, and when it was compelled to utter the word 'Liberty,' it was lost. The ebb which was perceived from afar sapped the ground under its feet; it felt that the quicksand would do its work, and in order to save the dynasty, and without caring whether it was not going to ruin France, it had the folly to provoke the catastrophe by which, unfortunately, it was not overwhelmed alone."

THE END.

HISTORY OF THE RISE AND INFLUENCE OF THE SPIRIT

OF

RATIONALISM IN EUROPE.

By WILLIAM E. H. LECKY, M. A.

2 vols. small 8vo.   Cloth, $4.00; half calf, extra, $8.00.

Edinburgh Review.

"We closed these volumes with the conviction that Mr. Lecky is one of the most accomplished writers and one of the most ingenious thinkers of the time, and that his book deserves the highest commendation we can bestow upon it. We hope to see it take its place among the best literary productions of the age."

Athenæum.

"Mr. Lecky is the historian of the rise and progress of that resistance to the Christianity of clerical interpretation which has gone by the names of private judgment, rationalism, latitudinarianism, blasphemy, infidelity, or atheism, according to the speaker and his bias. Mr. Lecky is learned, sensible, and readable, and we wish his book a wide circulation. It comes at a time when it is wanted."

Pall Mall Gazette.

"Mr. Lecky has written an admirable book, now and then a little youthful in its eloquence, but, on the whole, full of learning and acute criticism on the modernization of the Christian theology. The history of the decline of credulity and of the growth of the demand for evidence in modern society, is exceedingly well given by Mr. Lecky."

Spectator.

"It is scarcely possible to overrate the value of Mr. Lecky's able and vigorous book, both to those who agree and to those who differ with its implied teaching, a book the style of which is as luminous and attractive as its learning is profound. No book more full of scholarly learning and popular interest, more graphic in thought, more lucid in exposition, more candid in temper, has been submitted to theologians for many years."

Daily News.

"The ability of the writer is unquestionable. He is gifted with a style of easy, natural eloquence. His manner of dealing with each separate topic which he brings under discussion is clear and masterly. On reading him it is impossible to avoid thinking of the late Mr. Henry Buckle. The differences between them are considerable, but there are marked features of likeness, and it is no discredit to the living writer to say that his readers might very often imagine themselves to be studying certain added chapters of the unfinished work of the great philosophic historian."

D. *APPLETON &* CO., *Publishers, New York.*

A HISTORY OF EUROPEAN MORALS,

FROM AUGUSTUS TO CHARLEMAGNE.

By WILLIAM E. H. LECKY, M. A.

2 vols., 12mo.   Cloth, $3.00; half calf, extra, $7.00.

Macmillan's Magazine.

"Mr. Lecky has treated the subject of European morals with great ability, and has written a book of great interest. He has brought to it wide and intelligent reading, much acuteness, and considerable powers of sympathy, and a characteristic boldness and sweep of generalization which often take the reader's mind by storm. The remarkable qualities which were conspicuous in Mr. Lecky's former book are present in this one."

The London Times.

"So vast is the field Mr. Lecky introduces us to, so varied and extensive the information he has collected in it, fetching it from far beyond the limits of his professed subject, that it is impossible in any moderate space to do more than indicate the line he follows. . . . The work is a valuable contribution to our higher English literature, as well as an admirable guide for those who may care to go in person to the distant fountains from which Mr. Lecky has drawn for them so freely."

Pall Mall Gazette.

"The present book, so far as its historical part is concerned, possesses, we think, all the merits of its predecessor in still greater maturity. It is obviously the fruit of a mind singularly full, ripe, judicious, and temperate; a mind stored with the results of an immense and well-digested reading, capable of retaining and surveying large masses of facts at once, and of placing its facts in due relation and subordination to one another. The book, in a word, is thoughtful, clear, accurate, and, above all, profoundly interesting and suggestive."

Albany Evening Times.

"It is a mine of information in a restricted but important province, and will long be quoted for its thoroughness in opening a study which, though touched by other writers, never before had such exhaustive consideration."

Detroit Free Press.

"In his methods, Mr. Lecky is a model of clearness and force. That his conclusions do not command universal acceptance is undoubtedly true, but they do command respect wherever honest thought and faithful labor, in search after truth, are appreciated."

Indianapolis Journal.

"The excellence of this work is already attested, and it has long ago been considered a standard. The controversial portion of the work is clear in its statements, and so masterly in its handling of the salient points that none but an exceedingly obtuse person could fail to catch the full force of the argument presented."

D. APPLETON & CO., Publishers, New York.

THE LEADERS

OF

PUBLIC OPINION IN IRELAND:

SWIFT, FLOOD, GRATTAN, O'CONNELL.

By WILLIAM E. H. LECKY, M. A.

1 vol., 12mo, ... Cloth, $1.75.

"A writer of Lecky's mind, with his rich imagination, his fine ability to appreciate imagination in others, and his disposition to be himself an orator upon the written page, could hardly have found a period in British history more harmonious with his literary style than that which witnessed the rise, the ripening, and the fall of the four men whose impress upon the development of the national spirit of Ireland was not limited by the local questions whose discussion constituted their fame. Especially has O'Connell found in Mr. Lecky a fond biographer, and a most conscientious and impartial judge. The volume is elegant and brilliant in style, and treats with equal ability and warmth the three other men whose names appear with that of O'Connell."—*New York Evening Post.*

"Mr. Lecky, while feeling strongly, writes with judicial calmness; a foreigner could not be more impartial. His paper upon Swift is charming merely as a literary study, but it is even more valuable for the light it throws upon the genuine patriotism of the unhappy dean. Mr. Lecky, indeed, has all the qualities of a biographer, and his sketches of Grattan and Flood are quite striking in their keen analogies. It is for O'Connell, however, that he has reserved his best work, and we especially commend this portion of the book."—*New York Christian Union.*

"To those who know anything of Mr. Lecky as a writer, it is not necessary to say that this volume is full of careful research, presented in correct, clear, and often beautiful language. The same finished, graceful style which distinguishes the historian of 'Rationalism' and of 'European Morals' gives its charm to this slighter work. Mr. Lecky discusses Irish opinion with all the enthusiasm of a Nationalist, not in the vulgar sense of that term, but as one animated by a deep and passionate love of country. At the same time, his work is altogether free from the prejudices of sect or party. His study of the past and present of Irish public life is both interesting and valuable."—*London Standard.*

"These sketches are very well done indeed. They are bright, vigorous, sympathetic, and laudatory, but always with discernment. The faults of his leaders are neither concealed nor defended."—*London Observer.*

"A very instructive little book, furnished with an important preface, which would be useful as a separate pamphlet, but which is far more useful as showing the necessity of examining present difficulties by the light of such historical researches as appear in Mr. Lecky's eloquent and impartial volume."—*London Examiner.*

D. APPLETON & CO., Publishers,

549 & 551 BROADWAY, NEW YORK.

A
HISTORY OF ENGLAND
IN THE
EIGHTEENTH CENTURY.

By *WILLIAM EDWARD HARTPOLE LECKY*,

Author of "History of the Rise and Influence of the Spirit of Rationalism in Europe," "History of European Morals, from Augustus to Charlemagne," etc.

2 vols., 12mo. Cloth, $5.00.

"No more important book has appeared of late years than this history, uniting as it does so engrossing a subject with so vital an object. . . . We say, again, that Mr. Lecky has made his mark upon our time by his careful and fascinating book, and we have reason to be glad that while he is still himself, and his pen has a sharp point and is held with a strong hand, his temper has gained gentleness with time, and his mind has not lost insight by laborious study. We congratulate the publishers upon what cannot fail to be a great success, and we wish them speed in their task for our sake and their own."—*New York Times.*

"On every ground which should render a history of eighteenth-century England precious to thinking men, Mr. Lecky's work may be commended. The materials accumulated in these volumes attest an industry more strenuous and comprehensive than that exhibited by Froude or by Macaulay, and, if its fruits are not set forth with the pictorial charm of the latter writer, they are invested with more authority. Mr. Lecky's style is lucid and effective, often spirited, sometimes eloquent. But it is his supreme merit that he leaves on the reader's mind a conviction that he not only possesses the acuteness which can discern the truth, but the unflinching purpose of truth-telling."—*New York Sun.*

"The author of these volumes has not trodden in the beaten path. His work is a record of the progress of art, of manners, of belief, and of political ideas. Judicial impartiality is a characteristic of his writings."—*The New York Churchman.*

"The work will enrich any library. The account of John Wesley in the second volume will be interesting to our Methodist readers; and if it is not in all details just, it is unexpectedly just in the general outlines of Wesley's work and character. The great influence of the Wesleyan movement is recognized, and especially the impetus it gave (against Wesley's wish) to nonconformity."—*New York Methodist.*

"Mr. Lecky belongs to the newer school of thinkers, who accept little which does not bring credentials that will bear the test of examination, and who do not hesitate to shock conventional ideas of authority. Not the least attraction of this history is the independence of thought in its author, the conscientious frankness of opinion, as well as the freshness of style which he brings to its discussions. Mr. Lecky adds to intelligence and fairness a remarkable reasoning capacity and a rare degree of literary skill; and his work is an invaluable addition to the higher literature of the day."—*Boston Gazette.*

D. APPLETON & CO., Publishers,
549 & 551 BROADWAY, NEW YORK.

D. APPLETON & CO.'S PUBLICATIONS.

Tactics for Non-Military Bodies:

Adapted for the Instruction of Political Associations, Police Forces, Fire Organizations, Masonic, Odd-Fellows', and other Civic Societies. By Major-General UPTON, U. S. A. 12mo. Cloth, $1.00; paper, 50 cents.

A New System of Infantry Tactics.

Double and Single Rank. Adapted to American Topography and Improved Fire-Arms. By Major-General UPTON, U. S. A. Revised edition. 1 vol. Bound in leather, with clasp, $2.00.

Artillery Tactics, U. S. A.

Assimilated to the Tactics of Infantry and Cavalry. 1 vol. Bound in leather, with clasp, $2.00.

HEADQUARTERS OF THE ARMY, WASHINGTON, *July* 17, 1873.

GENERAL ORDERS No. 6.

The following order, received from the War Department, is published for the information and guidance of the Army:

WAR DEPARTMENT, WASHINGTON CITY, *July* 17, 1873.

The revision of Upton's Infantry Tactics by the author, and the Tactics for Artillery and Cavalry [including the proceedings of the board—Major-General Schofield, President—instituted by General Orders No. 60, Headquarters of the Army, Adjutant-General's Office, series of 1869], assimilated to the Tactics for Infantry, pursuant to instructions from the General of the Army, by Lieutenant-Colonel Emory Upton, 1st Artillery, Instructor of Tactics, U. S. Military Academy: Captain Henry A. Du Pont, 5th Artillery, commanding Battery "F," 5th Artillery; Captain John E. Tourtellotte, 7th Cavalry, Colonel and Aide-de-Camp to the General; Captain Alfred E. Bates, 2d Cavalry, Assistant Instructor of Cavalry Tactics, U. S. Military Academy—having been approved by the President, are adopted for the instruction of the Army and Militia of the United States.

To insure uniformity, all exercises, evolutions, and ceremonies, not embraced in these Tactics are prohibited, and those therein prescribed will be strictly observed.

WM. W. BELKNAP, Secretary of War.

By command of General SHERMAN:

WILLIAM D. WHIPPLE, Assistant Adjutant-General.

The Armies of Asia and Europe:

Embracing Official Reports on the Armies of Japan, China, India, Persia, Italy, Russia, Austria, Germany, France, and England. By Major-General EMORY UPTON, U. S. A.

D. APPLETON & CO., 549 & 551 Broadway, New York.

FINANCE, CURRENCY, AND BANKING.

THE EXAMPLE OF FRANCE: Two Essays on the Payment of the Indemnity and the Management of the Currency since the German War, 1870-'74. By VICTOR BONNET. Translated from the *Revue des Deux Mondes* by George Walker. Paper cover, 50 cents.

PAPER-MONEY INFLATION IN FRANCE: How it Came, what it Brought, and how it Ended. A Paper read before several Senators and Members of the House of Representatives, of both Political Parties, at Washington, April 12, and before the Union League Club, at New York, April 13, 1876. By ANDREW D. WHITE, LL. D., President of Cornell University. Price, 50 cents.

NOMISMA; or, "Legal Tender." By HENRI CERNUSCHI, author of "Bi-Metallic Money." 1 vol., 12mo, cloth, $1.25.

The principal part of the information contained in this volume was given by the author, before a commission appointed by Congress, for the purpose of ascertaining whether it was feasible for the United States to introduce a Bi-Metallic Standard of Gold and Silver.
The author is an authority on finance in France, and his information is given in a clear and intelligible form, which cannot fail to be very convincing.

CURRENCY AND BANKING. By BONAMY PRICE, Professor of Political Economy in the University of Oxford. 1 vol., 12mo. Cloth, $1.50.

"His discussion on the subject of currency is very clear and satisfactory, as well as timely."—*New-Englander.*
"The idea that the government stamp on the coin gives to money its value, he disposes of in a sentence, yet it is a large part of the money argument."—*Hartford Courant.*
"The author puts forth his views as to the mode of resuming specie payments in this country without dogmatism and with common-sense."—*Evening Mail.*
"This is probably the best and most lucid work on the subject."—*Sunday Herald, Washington.*

MONEY AND THE MECHANISM OF EXCHANGE. By W. STANLEY JEVONS, Professor of Logic and Political Economy in the Owens College, Manchester. 1 vol., 12mo. Cloth, $1.75.

"Mr. Jevons's valuable book ought to be read by every statesman, legislator, and journalist, in the United States, who undertakes to discuss the monetary problems of the time."—*International Review.*
"Professor Jevons's work is of the greatest value, and no thinker who cares for his reputation will be willing to leave it unread."—*Hartford Post.*
"His work is properly written, and every page is replete with solid instruction of a kind that is just now lamentably needed by multitudes of our people who are victimized by the grossest fallacies."—*Popular Science Monthly.*

WEIGHTS, MEASURES, AND MONEY, OF ALL NATIONS. Compiled by F. W. CLARKE, Professor of Physics and Chemistry in the University of Cincinnati. 1 vol., 12mo. $1.50.

"We commend this carefully-prepared and convenient volume to all persons who wish to acquire information on the subject of which it treats."—*Boston Globe.*
"The work necessary to the production of this little volume has been judiciously planned and skillfully executed."—*Chicago Tribune.*

D. APPLETON & CO., Publishers, 549 & 551 Broadway, N. Y.

APPLETONS' PERIODICALS.

Appletons' Journal:
An Illustrated Monthly Miscellany of Popular Literature. Subscription, $3.00 per Annum; single copy, 25 cents.

The Art Journal:
An International Gallery of Engravings, by Distinguished Artists of Europe and America. With Illustrated Papers in the various branches of Art. Price, 75 cents per Number, $9.00 per Annum.

The Popular Science Monthly.
Conducted by E. L. & W. J. YOUMANS. Containing instructive and interesting articles and abstracts of articles, from the pens of the leading scientific men of different countries. Price, $5.00 per Annum; 50 cents per Number.

The Popular Science Monthly Supplement.
Containing the best articles from the European periodicals, so that the American reader may keep himself familiar with the thoughts of the great thinkers of the day. Price, $3.00 per Annum; single Numbers, 25 cents.

The North American Review.
Published Bi-Monthly. This old and valued periodical, under new and energetic management, has during the past year stepped into the front rank of literature, showing itself the equal, if not superior, of the great Reviews and Quarterlies of the Old World. Per Annum, $5.00; per Number, $1.00.

The New York Medical Journal,
Edited by JAMES B. HUNTER, M. D. Terms, $4.00 per Annum.

CLUB RATES.

APPLETONS' JOURNAL, POPULAR SCIENCE MONTHLY, POPULAR SCIENCE MONTHLY SUPPLEMENT, and NORTH AMERICAN REVIEW, will be sent to one address for $14.00.

D. APPLETON & CO., Publishers,
549 & 551 Broadway, New York.

D. APPLETON & CO.'S NEW PUBLICATIONS.

A Manual of the Anatomy of Invertebrated Animals.

By THOMAS H. HUXLEY, LL. D., F. R. S. 1 vol., 587 pages. Cloth, $2.75.

"All students of Comparative Anatomy have felt the want of such a manual as this, which supplements Professor Huxley's 'Manual of Vertebrated Animals,' published in 1871, and completes his undertaking to produce a treatise for students on this extensive and complex branch of anatomical inquiry. Professor Huxley's plan is somewhat similar to what is known as the zoölogical method, which groups animals in 'natural orders,' according to a taxonomic system, and in which the anatomical characters of the animals belonging to each of these orders are described and compared with each other. This is unquestionably the most suitable plan, as it prevents confusing the reader with a multitude of subordinate facts. The introduction and first and last chapters are specially interesting to the general reader, who is here furnished with the most compact account of the present aspect of the science of comparative anatomy in the English language."
—*Nature.*

The Ancient Life-History of the Earth.

A Comprehensive Outline of the Principles and Leading Facts of Palæontological Science. By H. ALLEYNE NICHOLSON, M. D., etc., Professor of Natural History in the University of St. Andrews. With numerous Illustrations. 1 vol., small 8vo, 408 pages. Cloth, $2.00.

Professor Nicholson gives us a compact and popularly-written introduction to a very important department of science. His opening remarks on the "Principles of Palæontology" sufficiently prepare those who may be totally unacquainted with the fundamental facts of geological science for a profitable perusal of the succeeding chapters. His work constitutes an able exposition and summary of the facts of palæontology, suitably arranged; and he has wisely availed himself, to the fullest extent, of woodcut illustrations in aid of his descriptions of the fossil forms.

The Physiology of Mind.

Being the First Part of a third edition, revised, enlarged, and in great part rewritten, of "The Physiology and Pathology of Mind." By HENRY MAUDSLEY, M. D. 1 vol., 12mo. Cloth. Price, $2.00.

"'The Physiology of Mind,' by Dr. Maudsley, is a very engaging volume to read, as it is a fresh and vigorous statement of the doctrines of a growing scientific school on a subject of transcendent moment, and, besides many new facts and important views brought out in the text, is enriched by an instructive display of notes and quotations from authoritative writers upon physiology and psychology; and by illustrative cases, which add materially to the interest of the book."
—*Popular Science Monthly.*

Physiological Æsthetics.

By GRANT ALLEN, B. A. 1 vol., 12mo. Cloth. Price, $1.50.

"Mr. Grant Allen has seized on a subject that is entirely ignored by physiological treatises, while those who have handled it from a psychological point of view have in general been ignorant of physiology. Mr. Grant Allen has read widely, and has read well, while he suggests several very interesting explanations of mental condition that have hitherto been involved in hopeless obscurity."—*The Lancet.*

Science and Literature in the Middle Ages.

By PAUL LACROIX. Illustrated with 13 Chromolithographs and 400 Wood-Engravings. 1 vol., 8vo. Cloth, $12; half calf, $15; levant morocco, $25.

It is unnecessary to recommend a new work by Paul Lacroix. The excellence of the volumes previously published has established the reputation of the author.

The first volume of this series illustrated Manners, Customs, and Dress, during the Middle Ages. The present volume is a continuation of the Study of Life during that period, with especial reference to Science, Literature, and Art. The illustrations, which adorn almost every page of the work, have been intrusted to the same skillful hands that illustrated the previous works by the same author.

D. APPLETON & CO., Publishers, 549 & 551 Broadway, N. Y.

UNIVERSITY OF TORONTO LIBRARY

Do not remove the card from this Pocket.

Acme Library Card Pocket
Under Pat. "Ref. Index File."
Made by LIBRARY BUREAU

www.ingramcontent.com/pod-product-compliance
Lightning Source LLC
Chambersburg PA
CBHW020836020526
44114CB00040B/799